Publisher's Note

The book descriptions we ask booksellers to display prominently warn that this is an historic book with numerous typos or missing text; it is not indexed or illustrated.

The book was created using optical character recognition software. The software is 99 percent accurate if the book is in good condition. However, we do understand that even one percent can be an annoying number of typos! And sometimes all or part of a page may be missing from our copy of the book. Or the paper may be so discolored from age that it is difficult to read. We apologize and gratefully acknowledge Google's assistance.

After we re-typeset and design a book, the page numbers change so the old index and table of contents no longer work. Therefore, we often remove them; otherwise, please ignore them.

We carefully proof read any book that will sell enough copies to pay the proof reader; unfortunately, most don't. So instead we try to let customers download a free copy of the original typo-free book. Simply enter the barcode number from the back cover of the paperback in the Free Book form at www.RareBooksClub.com. You may also qualify for a free trial membership in our book club to download up to four books for free. Simply enter the barcode number from the back cover onto the membership form on our home page. The book club entitles you to select from more than a million books at no additional charge. Simply enter the title or subject onto the search form to find the books.

If you have any questions, could you please be so kind as to consult our Frequently Asked Questions page at www. RareBooksClub.com/faqs.cfm? You are also welcome to contact us there.

General Books LLC™, Memphis, USA, 2012.

-¤c- -¤c- -¤c- -¤c- -¤c- -¤c- -¤c- -¤c-

THE LIFE AND PONTIFICATE OF LEO THE TENTH. IN FOUR VOLUMES.

—Tueri enim eorum memoriam, quorum merita multa in homines et praclara extiterunt, xquitatis et justitiae laudem habet.

Jo. Mich. Brutus, ad Tmgium. PREFACE. FOR almost three centuries the curiosity of mankind has been directed towards the age of Leo The Tenth. The history of that period has not, however, yet been attempted in a manner in any degree equal to the grandeur and variety of the subject. Nor is this difficult to be accounted for. Attractive as such an undertaking may at first appear, it will be found on a nearer inspection to be surrounded by many difficulties. The magnitude of such a task; the trouble of collecting the materials necessary to its proper execution; the long devotion of time and of labour which it must unavoidably require, and above a all, all, the apprehensions of not fulfilling the high expectations which have been formed of it, are some of those circumstances which have perhaps prevented the accomplishment of a work which has often been suggested, sometimes closely contemplated, but hitherto cautiously declined.

The same considerations, which have deterred others from engaging in so laborious and hazardous an attempt, would in all probability have produced a similar effect on myself, had I not been led by imperceptible degrees to a situation in which I could scarcely, with either propriety or credit, have declined the task. The history of the life of Lorenzo de' Medici, the father of Leo X. had opened the way to a variety of researches, not less connected with the events of the ensuing period, than with those of the times for which they were immediately intended; and even that work was considered by many, perhaps not unjustly, as only the vestibule to a more spacious building, which it would be incumbent on the author at some futureperiod to complete. Since that pub-

l.

several distinguished characters, both at home and abroad, have supplied me with many valuable communications and original documents, which without their countenance and favour, it would not have been in my power to have obtained. To have withheld these materials from the public, would have defeated the purpose for which they were communicated; and to have shrunk from the task under such circumstances, would have' given occasion for a construction almost as unfavourable to myself as the failure of success. These reflections have induced me, amidst the constant engagements of an active life, to persevere in an undertaking, which has occasionally called for exertions beyond what my time, my talents, or my health could always supply; and I now submit to the public the result of the labour of many years, in the best form in which, under all circumstances, it has been in my power to offer it to their acceptance.

Although I have entitled the following work The Life And Pontificate Of Leo X. yet I have not only thought it excusable, but even found it necessary, to enter into the general history of the times; without which it would have been impossi ble to give so full an idea of the character and conduct of this celebrated pontiff, as it was my wish to communicate. Nor can I regret the oppor a ¾ tunity tunity which has thus been afforded me, of examining more fully than has perhaps hitherto been done, a period productive of great and important events, and which exhibits almost every diversity of human character. Respecting the propriety of this union of "individual biography with general history, I am well aware, that doubts have been entertained by persons of considerable eminence in literature. That there are certain limits between the province of the historian, and that of the biographer, may readily be admitted; yet, as these branches of study are equally conversant with the individuals of our own species, it will unavoidably happen, that each of them will at times encroach upon the precincts of the other. In perusing the pages of Livy or of Tacitus, of Hume or of Gibbon, we find no parts which interest us more than the private and personal memorials of those great and illustrious men, who have acted a conspicuous part in the public events of the age; whilst, on the other hand, it would be impossible to form a correct idea of the character of an individual, without considering him in those relations, by which he stands connected with the general transactions of the times in which he lived, and which in truth have not only displayed, but in some measure formed his character. That these mutual concessions may admit of abuse, cannot be doubted; yet, if the great objects of pleasure and utility be obtained, that criticism would perhaps be too rigid, which would narrowly restrict so advantageous an interchange. In tracing the history of a people through any considerable portion of time, the attention is weakened, and the feelings are blunted, by the rapid succession of events and characters, in which we might have been more deeply interested, if our information respecting them had been more minute. The history of mankind may be compared to the surface of the earth, which is composed of wild woods and trackless desarts, interspersed, however, with cultivated spots, and peculiar appearances of nature. The traveller passes heedlessly over the undiversified prospect, and dwells only on such parts as for their beauty, sublimity, or singularity, he deems most worthy of his regard.

These observations, it is hoped, may serve as an apology for my having entered so much at large into the history of many transactions, which, although they were not influenced in any eminent degree by the personal interference of Leo X. greatly affected the fortunes of his early years. Of this this nature is the narrative of the irruption of Charles VIII. into Italy; an enterprise which, as Mr. Gibbon asserts, changed the face of Europe, and of which he at one time meditated a distinct and separate history. The siege of Pisa, as long and as eventful as the celebrated siege of Troy, is so closely connected with all the political events and negotiations of the time, and in particular, with the fate of the three brothers of the Medici, as unavoidably to obtrude itself upon our frequent notice. In adverting to the pontificate of Alexander VI. it is impossible to avoid being forcibly struck with the energy, or rather the atrocity of character by which that pontiff and his son Caesar Borgia were distinguished; and the singular transactions recorded of them, must occasionally give rise to doubts, which the labours of the most industrious and impartial inquirer will scarcely be adequate to remove. With the fortunes of the Medici, the effects of the memorable league of Cambray, which alone has been the subject of several volumes, are still more closely connected; whilst the conquest of Naples, and the expulsion of the royal family of Aragon by the united arms of Louis XII. and of Ferdinand of Spain, and the subsequent disagreement and contests of those monarchs, for the dominion nion of that kingdom, claim our attention, no less on account of their connexion with our principal subject, than by their intrinsic importance.

An opinion has of late been very generally advanced both in this country and abroad, that notwithstanding the improvement which took place in Italy, in the age of Leo X. a very moderate portion of it is to be attributed to the personal exertions, talents, and patronage of that pontiff; and that by giving to this period the ostentatious title of The Age Of Leo X. we deprive the other eminent patrons of literature who flourished during the same aera, of that praise to which they are justly entitled. I ought not very earnestly to oppose an opinion, which, if espoused by my readers, would relieve me from a great part of my responsibility. Yet, that Leo, during his short pontificate of less than nine years, exerted himself with considerable effect in the promotion of literature and the restoration of the fine arts, cannot be doubted; and as his services have never yet been sufficiently appreciated, or collected into one point of view, an attempt to supply what has hitherto been wanting in this respect, may be entitled at least to pardon. The effects produced by Leo on the character of the times, will, V1U will, however, be better estimated, when the transactions of his life shall have been more fully unfolded. I shall afterwards return to this important and essential part of my subject, and endeavour to ascertain the amount of the obligations due from posterity to Leo the tenth.

The earliest professed history of Leo X. is that of Paolo Giovio, better known by his Latin appellation of *Pavllus Jovius.* This author, the character of whose various productions is sufficiently known, had every opportunity of obtaining the most exact and authentic information on the subject of his history. His life of Leo X. written like the rest of his works, in Latin, is one of the most valuable of his productions, containing much authentic information, and being perhaps less tinctured than the generality of his labours, with that satirical spirit, which its author on many occasions evinced.

With this history of Leo X. by Jovius, and the Italian translation by Dominichi, printed at Florence in 1549, the learned world seems to have remained satisfied for upwards of two centuries. Many incidental anecdotes and brief memoirs of this distinguished pontiff, were in the mean time given to the public; but but the first serious intention of connecting the life of Leo X. with the history of the revival of learning, appears to have arisen in our own country, where the elegant and pathetic poet William Collins, about the middle of the last century, is said to have published proposals for such a history. "I "have heard him speak with great kindness," says Dr. Johnson, "of Leo X. and with keen resent"ment of his tasteless successor; but probably "not a page of the history was ever written." Much as we may regret the failure of this enterprise, those whom nature has endowed with the capacity of feeling the charm of the tender and impassioned productions of this author, will regret still more those calamities that prevented him from increasing the number of his poetical works, which have justly been characterized, as exhibiting '' a luxuriance "of imagination, a wild sublimity of fancy, and a "felicity of expression so extraordinary, that they "might be supposed to be suggested by some supe"rior power, rather than to be the effect of human "judgment or capacity." . i.'' .'

Among the friends of Collins, who seem to have shared his confidence and his studies, was Mr. Thomas Warton, by whom the design of giving a b history history of the restoration of Letters in Europe, was continued, or revived. In the excellent Essay of his brother Dr. Warton, on the life and writings of Pope, is the following passage. "Concerning the "particular encouragement given by Leo X. to "literature and the fine arts, I forbear to enlarge; "because a friend of mine is at present engaged in "writing the History Of The Age Of Leo The "Tenth. It is a noble period, and full of those "most important events, which have had the great"est influence on human affairs. Such as the dis"covery of the West Indies by the Spaniards, and st of a passage to the East by the Portuguese; the "invention of printing; the reformation of religion; "with many others; all of which will be insisted "upon at large, and their consequences displayed." As the Essay which contains this passage, was first published in 17 56, the same year in which Collins died, it is possible that this notice was intended to refer to his undertaking; but it is also certain, that on his death, the design was not abandoned by his surviving friends. In a conversation which I had the pleasure of enjoying with Dr. Warton, in the year 1797, the progress made in an undertaking which had been so long announced to the public, became an object of my inquiry. By him I was informed formed that it had been the intention of himself, his brother, and several of their literary friends, to give a history of the revival of letters, not only in Italy, but in all the principal countries of Europe; and that the history of English Poetry by Mr. Thomas Warton, was only a part of this great design. When

we advert to the various and excellent critical productions of these liberal and learned brothers, and consider that among the names of their coadjutors, would probably have been found those of West, of Walpole, of Mason, and of Gray, we cannot sufficiently lament the want of public encouragement, which was, in all probability, the chief cause that prevented this noble and extensive undertaking from being carried into complete execution.

In Italy the life and transactions of Leo X. have, within these few years, been the subject of a work of no inconsiderable merit. To the writings of the late much lamented and learned Monsignore Angelo Fabroni, *Provveditore,* or Principal, of the university of Pisa, I have before been indebted for many important facts in the Life of Lorenzo de' Medici; some of which I have examined with that freedom, which, to some authors, would have been a cause of offence, but which a liberal mind will always prefer to the b 2 vain vain homage of indiscriminate applause. The attempt which I then made to illustrate a period of history, which had been the peculiar object of his inquiry, had the good fortune to obtain his approbation. Under his auspices, the English Life of Lorenzo de' Medici was elegantly translated into Italian, by the Cavaliero Mecherini, and published at Pisa in the year 1799. I was afterwards honoured by the correspondence of Monsignore Fabroni, which was continued until the time of his death in the latter part of the year 1803; and in the course of which he transmitted to me his " Life of Leo X." written in Latin, and published at Pisa in the year 1797. In this work the learned author has not confined himself to the account given of Leo X. by Jovius, but has collected much original information respecting this pontiff, and the age in which he lived. By the aid of these resources he was enabled to throw additional light on his subject; whilst the valuable collection of documents published by him at the close of his work, not only confirm his narrative, but supply important materials for future historians. As the work was not, however,

intended by the author, so it must not be expected by the public, to contain a very full and extensive account of the progress made during the pontificate tificate of Leo X. in the departments of science, of literature, or of art; or of those very numerous and distinguished men, to whose writings and labours the reign of that pontiff is indebted for its principal lustre..i: . ,r ...

But besides these professed histories of Leo X. several works have appeared, which are chiefly confined to the elucidation of some particular parts of his life, or of those of the times in which he lived. Among these are the history of the League of Cambray, by some attributed to the pen of cardinal Polignac; the narrative of the battle of the Taro, between Charles VIII. and the allied army of Italy, by Benedetti; the lives of Alexander VI. and his son Caesar Borgia, by Gordon; the dialogue of Raffaello Brandolini, entitled Leo; and the commentary of Galeazzo Capella, on the efforts made for the restoration of Francesco Sforza to the duchy of Milan; with many other publications of a similar nature, of which it will appear that I have frequently availed myself, in the course of the following work.

The detached and particular histories to which I have before adverted, contain, however, but a small portion of that immense mass of information which remains remains to the present times, respecting the public and private character and conduct of Leo X. From the high dignity which he enjoyed, both as a secular and an ecclesiastical potentate, and from the active part which he took in all the transactions which affected the state of Europe, his life is intimately connected with the general history of the age; insomuch that there is not an author who has had occasion to treat on the events of this period, in whose work he does not occupy a conspicuous station.

To these, the recorders of the political, civil, and military events of the times, I might add a long train of literary historians, to whom I have been greatly indebted for that department of the following work, which is intended to illustrate the state of letters and of science; among these, must be distinguished the immortal work of Tiraboschi; the noblest specimen of that species of composition which any age or country has produced; and the accurate and comprehensive account of the writers of Italy, by Mazzuchelli, who in grasping at an object too extended for human talents, or human life, has executed in six volumes in folio, a comparatively small portion of his colossal attempt.

I shall

I shall not, on this occasion, weary the reader by enumerating the many other various and excellent authors, either in this department, or in that of the fine arts, in which the Italians abound beyond any other country, who have afforded their assistance in the following pages; but I must avail myself of this opportunity finally to observe, that I have made it an invariable rule, in the accounts which I have found it necessary to give of the writings and characters of men of literary eminence, to resort for information to their own works, as far as my opportunities would permit, and to found my opinions and draw my deductions from them, rather than from those of any subsequent writer. How far I have been enabled thus to derive my intelligence from its primitive channels, will sufficiently appear in the course of my work; in which it has been my practice to refer to the author from whom I have actually quoted; and who must be considered as answerable for the accuracy of the citation, when the original has not fallen in my way.

Such are the works relating to the life of Leo X. and the times in which he lived, which have already been published, and of which I have availed myself in the course of the ensuing narrative; but, besides sides these more ostensible sources of information, I have, during a series of years, been enabled to collect many original documents, which have served to throw considerable light on the times to which the following pages relate. Of these, one of the most important acquisitions consists of a series of letters and papers, copied from the originals in the archives of the

Palazzo Vecckio at Florence, and forming two volumes in folio, of about three hundred pages each. For this valuable collection I am indebted to the obliging and disinterested interference of a nobleman, who adds dignity to his station, not only by the firm and consistent tenor of his public conduct, but by his encouragement of those literary studies, in which he has himself made so distinguished a proficiency. The liberal views of Lord Holland were seconded by the kind assistance of Mr. Penrose, the late British resident at Florence, and were carried into complete effect by the generosity of the Grand Duke; who directed that access should be had at all times to the original state papers, and every possible facility given to these researches. The first part of this collection consists chiefly of letters, written by the great Lorenzo de' Medici, father of the pontiff, relating principally to the promotion of his son to the rank of of cardinal. From these letters, which have enabled me to place this event in its fullest light, I might have given much larger extracts, but as they elucidate only this single circumstance, it will perhaps be thought that I have been sufficiently copious in my authorities on this head. This collection also comprises a series of letters written by Balthazar Turini, commonly called Balthazar or Baldassare da Pescia, then at Rome, to Lorenzo de' Medici the nephew of the pontiff, who resided at Florence during the early part of the pontificate of Leo X. From these, none of which have heretofore been printed, it appears tlrat the writer was appointed assistant Datary, or Secretary, to transmit to Florence the fullest information on every event that took place at Rome, not only with respect to public transactions, but to the private concerns of every branch of the family of the Medici. In the execution of this office he seems to have acted under the immediate directions of the Cardinal Giulio de' Medici, afterwards Clement VII. who was intrusted by Leo X, with the superintendence of the government of the Florentine state, and to whose suggestions Lorenzo was expected implicitly to conform. These letters,

although they extend only from the month of March to the month of September, c in in the second year of the pontificate of Leo X. (1514) throw considerable light on the characters of the persons there mentioned, and suggest or illustrate many curious and important circumstances; but besides these, the most material subjects, this collection of papers is interspersed with other documents of considerable interest, not heretofore published, and which will be more particularly noticed in the course of the following work.

In adverting to the assistance which I have derived from the city of Florence, that cradle of the arts in modern times, I must'not omit to notice the favours conferred on me by the late venerable and learned Canonico Angelo Maria Bandini, late principal librarian of the Laurentian library there. Of a character so well known in the literary world, any commendation of mine would be superfluous; yet I cannot avoid remarking it as an extraordinary circumstance, that he maintained a high rank among the scholars of Italy during the long space of sixty years, and that the history of his life, with an account of his literary productions, was given in the great work of Mazzuchelli, the publication of which he survived nearly half a century. During this period he continued to enrich the republic of letters by many other other works; some of which, as they bear a particular reference to the history of the Medici, will be referred to in the following pages. To this eminent man, who retained his early and ardent love of literature to the close of his days, I am also indebted for the communication of several scarce and valuable documents, both printed and manuscript, as well as for various letters, indicating to me, with the utmost attention and minuteness, those sources of information which his long and intimate acquaintance with the subjects of the following volumes had enabled him to point out.

In the prosecution of this work, I was, however, well aware that the most important information for my purpose might be derived from the immense collections of the Vatican, and could not but regret, that from the calamitous state of public affairs, the distance of my own situation from these records, and other circumstances, there was little probability that I should be able to surmount the formidable obstacles that presented themselves to its attainment. From this state of despondency I was however fortunately relieved, by the unsolicited kindness of John Johnson Esquire, then on his travels through Italy, who with a liberality which demands c 2, my my warmest acknowledgments, obtained for me, by means of his acquaintance with the Abate Gaetario Marini, the learned Prefect-of the Archives of the Vatican, a considerable number of important documents, copied as well from the manuscripts in that collection, as from printed works of extreme rarity, which relate to the affairs of the Roman court in the time of Leo X. and which are, for the most part, to be found only in that collection. Among the former is the fragment of an unpublished life of Leo X. written in Latin, with considerable elegance, and brought down to the year 1516. The printed works consist principally of letters and orations of the ambassadors of foreign states to Leo X. and were probably only printed for the exclusive use of the Roman court. Besides these, I had also the pleasure of receiving an entire copy of the very scarce and curious tract of Jacopo Penni, containing the most particular account which now remains of the ceremonies and splendid exhibitions that took place in Rome on the elevation of Leo X. which, with many other pieces from the same authentic quarter, the reader will find in the Appendix to the ensuing volumes.

To the continued favour and friendly recommendations dations of the same gentleman during his progress through Italy, I am also indebted for my literary intercourse with the celebrated Abate Jacopo Morelli, librarian of S. Marco at Venice, well known to the learned world, as the author of many estimable works. From him I have received much useful information respecting the publications necessary for my purpose, accompanied by some scarce tracts, and by his own judicious and interesting remarks. I am sensible that in thus paying the tribute of gratitude to the most illustrious scholars of Italy, I may be suspected of endeavouring to support my own weak endeavours upon the established reputation of their names; but I have not been deterred by this consideration from discharging what I esteem to be an indispensable obligation to the living, and a sacred duty to the dead; being well convinced that the favours conferred upon me, can no more excuse the imperfections of my work, than those imperfections can detract from the high character, which the persons to whom I have referred have so justly and so universally obtained.

Respecting the private lives of Leo X. and his predecessors Alexander VI. and Julius II. considerable information is derived from the diaries of the successive successive officers of the Roman court, who were stiled Masters of the Ceremonies of the pope's chapel, and who seem to have considered it as part of their duty to keep a register of such transactions as occurred under their own eye, or came to their knowledge. The first of these officers whose labours appear to have been preserved, is Giovanni Burcardo Broccardo, or as he is more usually called, Burchard, a native of Strasbourg, and dean of the church of St. Thomas in that city. He afterwards transferred his residence to Rome, where he obtained several ecclesiastical preferments, and was appointed master of the ceremonies on the twentyfirst day of December 14 83, under the pontificate of Sixtus IV. A few months afterwards he commenced his journal, which during the life of Sixtus IV. was confined to a few slight and unimportant minutes. On the death of that pontiff he extended his plan, and has occasionally enriched it with anecdotes, and adverted to circumstances not strictly confined to the limits of his office. His diary is written in Latin, in a pedestrian and semi-barbarian style, but with an apparent accuracy and minuteness as to facts, which, notwithstanding the singular circumstances related by him, give it an air of veracity. Such part as adverts to the life of Alexander der VI. has been published almost entire. Large extracts from it have also been given by several authors who have been inclined to expatiate on the enormities of this pontiff, and particularly by Gordon, in his life of Alexander VI. and his son Caesar Borgia, printed at London in 1729. After the death of Alexander, Burchard was appointed by Julius II. bishop of Horta, in the possession of which dignity he died on the 16th day of May, 1506.

About two years before the death of Burchard, he had a colleague, or assistant in Paris de Grassis, who also succeeded him as master of the ceremonies. This officer has also kept a diary, which commences on the twelfth day of May, 1 504, and is continued throughout the rest of the pontificate of Julius II. and the whole of that of Leo X. It has never been printed entire, but some detached parts have been published; and it has also been consulted by several writers, who have given extracts from it in their works.

From the narrative of Paris de Grassis, it appears, that he was a native of Bologna, of a respectable family. His brother Achilles was, in the year 1511, raised by Julius II. to the dignity of the purple, pie, and was one of the most learned and respectable members of the college. Another brother, Agamemnon, (for the family names seem to have been sought for in Homer, rather than in the books of the Old and New Testament) was in the year 1510, ambassador from the city of Bologna to the Pope. The assiduities of Paris, as master of the ceremonies, could not conciliate the favour of that austere pontiff Julius II. but in the vacancy of the holy see, which occurred on the death of that pope, he obtained from the sacred college, as a reward for his services, the promise of the bishopric of Pesaro united with the abbey of Santa Croce. These dignities were afterwards confirmed to him by Leo X. who also nominated him a prelate of the palace, and appointed his nephew to be his coadjutor in the of. fice of master of the ceremonies. He survived that pontiff, and died at Rome on the tenth day of June, 1528.

The style of Paris de Grassis, like that of his predecessor, has little pretensions to elegance. It is,. however, rendered interesting by its simplicity, which gives to his narration a character of fidelity. In the exercise of his functions he seems to have been a more rigid disciplinarian than even Burchard himself, himself, and it is not unamusing to observe the importance which he frequently attaches to his office, and the severity with which he reproves those relaxations from the dignity of his high rank, in which Leo, on some occasions, indulged himself.

Among the objects of my earnest inquiry, was the unpublished part of the diary of Paris de Grassis, which yet exists in the library of the Vatican, and of which copies are also found in the National library at Paris. Of this diary, as well as of that of Burchard, some of the most interesting particulars have already been given to the public, in the work entitled, *Notices et Extraits des Manuscrits de la Bibliotheque du Roi,* which has been continued under the title of *Notices et Extraits des Manuscrits de la Bibliotheque Nationale;* but as the extracts thus made are not in general given in the original Latin, but are for the most part abridged, and translated into French, I have not derived from this work the advantages which I might otherwise have obtained. It happened, however, fortunately for my purpose, that in the summer of the year 1802, my particular friend and neighbour the Reverend Mr. Shepherd, well known as the author of *The Life of Poggio Braccioli-ni,* paid a visit to Paris. On this occasion I scrupled not to d request request his assistance in examining for me the different manuscripts of the diary of Paris de Grassis, and making such extracts from them, in the original, as he conceived would be most interesting. As no one can be better qualified for such a task, so no one could have entered upon it with greater alacrity. During his stay at Paris, a considerable portion of his time was passed in these researches, in which he met with every possible facility from the librarians; and on his re-

turn, he brought with him several curious 'extracts, which have enabled me to throw additional light on the history of Leo X. and particularly on the singular circumstances attending his death.

Nor have I, in the course of my inquiries, wholly omitted the opportunities which even this country affords, of collecting information from unpublished documents respecting the times in question. Among the Cottonian Manuscripts in the British Museum, are contained many original letters from the Roman court and the English ambassadors resident there, to Henry VIII. and his ministers, explanatory of the political transactions of the age. I had not an opportunity of examining these papers, until my work was considerably advanced, vanced; but by the kind assistance of my highly respected friend John Walker, Esq. of BedfordSquare, and by the obliging attention of Mr. Planta, principal librarian of the British Museum, I have been enabled to inform myself of such documents as were more particularly applicable to my purpose, some of which the reader will find, either given entire in the appendix, or referred to in the course of the work.

Although I have for several years endeavoured, at great expense, and with considerable success, to collect such printed works as appeared to be necessary for the present undertaking, yet I have not neglected to solicit the assistance, or to avail myself of the offers of several persons, on whose friendship and liberality I could rely, to furnish me with such publications as I had not had the good fortune elsewhere to obtain. To the very obliging liberality of Richard Heber, Esq. of Hodnet, whose library is particularly enriched by the early editions of the works of the modern writers of Latin poetry, I am indebted for the use of many of the scarce publications in that department, referred to in the following volumes, which have enabled me to discuss the subjects to which they relate, with greater confi d % dence dence than I could possibly have done through the secondary medium of other writers. His extensive collection of medals has also been freely

opened for the use of the engraver, in improving the ornamental part of the work. The very select library of my early literary associate, and long valued friend, William Clarke, Esq. of Everton, has also been of frequent use to me in the course of my researches, during which I have derived additional assistance from his extensive learning, and very particular acquaintance with the literary history of Italy. My acknowledgments are also due for the use of scarce books and manuscripts, or for other favours in the course of my work, to Dr. James Currie, late of Liverpool, but now of Bath, well known by his many valuable publications, both on scientific and literary subjects, and whom I am proud to record on this occasion, as my long esteemed and excellent friend; the Rev. Wm. Parr Greswell, author of *Memoirs of Italian Scholars who have zuriU ten Latin poetry;* Sir Isaac Heard, Knight, Garter principal King of Arms; Mr. Wm. Smyth, Fellow of Peter House, Cambridge; Henry Brown, Esq. of Liverpool; the Rev. Mr. Hinckes, of Cork; the Rev Mr. Crane, Vicar of Over, in Cheshire; the Rev. John Greswell, of the college, Manchester; and and to several other persons, who will, I hope, excuse a more particular acknowledgment, in the confidence that I am not insensible of their favours.

With respect to the execution of the following work, I cannot but be well aware, that many circumstances and characters will be found represented in a light somewhat different from that in which they have generally been viewed, and that I may probably be accused of having suffered myself to be induced by the force of prejudice, or the affectation of novelty, to remove what have hitherto been considered as the land-marks of history. To imputations of this kind, I feel the most perfect indifference. Truth alone has been my guide, and whenever she has steadily diffused her light, I have endeavoured to delineate the objects in their real form and colour. History is the record of the experience of mankind, in their most important concerns. If it be impossible for human sagacity to estimate the consequences of a falsehood in private life, it is equally impossible to estimate the consequences of a false, or partial representation of the events of former times. The conduct of the present is regulated by the experience of the past. The circumstances which have led the way to the prosperity or destruction struction of states, will lead the way to the prosperity or destruction of states in all future ages. If those in high authority be better informed than others, it is from this source that their information must be drawn; and to pollute it, is therefore to poison the only channel through which we can derive that knowledge, which, if it can be obtained pure and unadulterated, cannot fail in time to purify the intellect, expand the powers, and improve the condition of the human race.

As in speaking of the natural world, there are some persons who are disposed to attribute its creation to chance, so in speaking of the moral world, there are some who are inclined to refer the events and fluctuations in human affairs to accident, and are satisfied with accounting for them from the common course of things, or the spirit of the times. But as *chance* and *accident,* if they have any meaning whatever, can only mean the operation of causes not hitherto fully investigated, or distinctly understood, so *the spirit of the times* is only another phrase for causes and circumstances which have not hitherto been sufficiently explained. It is the province of the historian to trace and to discover these causes, and it is only in proportion as he accomplishes this object, that that his labours are of any utility. An assent to the former opinion may indeed gratify our indolence, but it is only from the latter method that we can expect to acquire true knowledge, or to be able to apply to future conduct the information derived from past events.

There is one peculiarity in the following work, which it is probable may be considered as a radical defect. I allude to the frequent introduction of quotations and passages from the poets of the times, occasionally interspersed through the narrative, or inserted in the notes. To some it may appear that the seriousness of history is thus impertinently broken in upon, whilst others may suppose, that not only its gravity, but its authenticity is impeached by these citations, and may be inclined to consider this work as one of those productions, in which truth and fiction are blended together, for the purpose, of amusing and misleading the reader. To such imputations I plead not guilty. That I have at times introduced quotations from the works of the poets, in proof of historical facts, I confess; nor, when they proceed from contemporary authority, do I perceive that their being in verse invalidates their credit. In this light, I have frequently cited the *Decennale Decennale* of Machiavelli, and the *Vergier (T honneur* of Andre de la Vigne, which are in fact little more than versified annals of the events of the times; but in general, I have not adduced such extracts as evidences of facts, but for a purpose wholly different. To those who are pleased in tracing the emotions and passions of the human mind in all ages, nothing can be more gratifying than to be informed of the mode of thinking of the public at large, at interesting periods, and in important situations. Whilst war and desolation stalk over a countrv, or whilst a nation is struggling for its liberties or its existence, the opinions of men of genius, ability, and learning, who have been agitated with all the hopes and fears to which such events have given rise, and have frequently acted a personal and important part in them, are the best and most instructive comment. By such means, we seem to become contemporaries with those whose history we peruse, and to acquire an intimate knowledge, not only of the facts themselves, but of the judgment formed upon such facts by those who were most deeply interested in them. Nor is it a slight advantage in a work which professes to treat on the literature of the times, that the public events, and the works of the eminent scholars and writers of that period, thus become a mutual tual comment, and serve on many occasions to explain and to illustrate each other.

The practice which I have heretofore adopted of designating the scholars of Italy by their national appellations, has given rise to some animadversions. In answer to which I beg to remark, that whoever-is conversant with history, must frequently have observed the difficulties which arise from the wanton alterations, in the names of both persons and places, by authors of different countries, and particularly by the French, who, without hesitation, accommodate every thing to the genius of their own language. Hence the names of all the eminent men of Greece, of Rome, or of Italy, are melted down, and appear again in such a form as would not in all probability have been recognised by their proper owners; Dionysius is *Denys,* Titus Livius *Tite Live,* Horatius *Horace,* Petrarca *Petrarque,* and Pico of Mirandola *Pic de Mirandole.* As the literature which this country derived from Italy was first obtained through the medium of the French, our early authors followed them in this respect, and thereby sanctioned those innovations which the nature of our own language did not require. It is still more to be regretted that we we are not uniform, even in our abuse. The name of *Horace* is familiar to the English reader, but if he were told of *the three Horaces,* he would probably be at a loss to discover the persons meant, the authors of our country having commonly given them the appellation of the *Horatii.* In the instance of such names as are familiar to our early literature, we adopt with the French the abbreviated appellation; but in latter times we usually employ proper national distinctions, and instead of *Arioste,* or *Metastase,* we write, without hesitation, *Ariosto,* or *Metastasio.* This inconsistency is more sensibly felt when the abbreviated appellation of one scholar is contrasted with the national distinction of another, as when a letter is addressed by *Petrarch* to *Coluccio Salutati,* or by *Politian* to *Ermolao Barbaro,* or *Baccio Ugolini.* For the sake of uniformity, it is surely desirable that every writer should conform as much as possible to some general rule, which can only be found by a reference of every proper name to the standard of its proper country. This method would not only avoid the incongruities before mentioned, but would be productive of positive advantages, as it would in general point out the nation of the person spoken of, without the necessity of further indication.

Thus, Thus, in mentioning one of the monarchs of France, who makes a conspicuous figure in the ensuing pages, I have not denominated him *Lodovico XII.* with the Italians, nor *Lewis XII* with the English, but *Louis XII.* the name which he himself recognised. And thus I have also restored to a celebrated Scottish general, in the service of the same monarch, his proper title of *d'Aubigny,* instead of that of *Obignit* usually given him by the historians of Italy.

I cannot deliver this work to the public without a most painful conviction, that notwithstanding my utmost endeavours, and the most sedulous attention which it has been in my power to bestow upon it, many defects will still be discoverable, not only from the omission of much important information, which may not have occurred to my inquiries, but from an erroneous or imperfect use of such as I may have had the good fortune to obtain. Yet I trust, that when the extent of the work, and the great variety of subjects which it comprehends are considered, the candid and judicious will make due allowance for those inaccuracies against which no vigilance can at all times effectually guard. With this publication, I finally relinquish all intention of prosecuting, e 2 with with a view to the public, my researches into the history and literature of Italy. That I have devoted to its completion a considerable portion of time and of labour will sufficiently appear from the perusal of the following pages, and it may therefore be presumed that I cannot be indifferent to its success. But whatever inducements I may have found in the hope of conciliating the indulgence, or the favour of the public, I must finally be permitted to avow, that motives of a different, and perhaps of a more laudable nature, have occasionally concurred to induce me to persevere in the present undertaking. Among

these, is an earnest desire to exhibit to the present times an illustrious period of society; to recall the public attention to those standards of excellence to which Europe has been indebted for no inconsiderable portion of her subsequent improvement; to unfold the ever active effect of moral causes on the acquirements and the happiness of a people; and to raise a barrier, as far as such efforts can avail, against that torrent of a corrupt and vitiated taste, which if not continually opposed, may once more overwhelm the cultivated nations of Europe in barbarism and degradation. To these great and desirable aims, I could wish to add others, yet more exalted and commendable; commendable; to demonstrate the fatal consequences of an ill directed ambition, and to deduce, from the unperverted pages of history, those maxims of true humanity, sound wisdom, and political fidelity, which have been too much neglected in all ages, but which are the only solid foundations of the repose, the dignity, and the happiness of mankind.

Allerton,

Slh March, 1805-

CHAP. I. 1475—1493. BlRTH of Giovanni de Medici afterwards Leo. X—Sovereigns of Christendom—Political state of Europe—Peculiarities of the papal Government—Temporal power of the popes— Union of the spiritual and temporal authority—Advantages of the papal Government—Destination of Giovanni de Medici to the church—His early preferments—His father endeavours to raise him to the rank of a Cardinal—Marriage of Francesco Cibo and Madalena de" Medici—Giovanni raised to the dignity of the purple—Letter from Politiano to the pope— Studies of Giovanni—Bernardo Dovizio da Bibbiena—Defects in the character of Giovanni accounted for—His father endeavours to shorten the term of his probation—Giulio de' Medici afterwards Clement VII.—Giovanni invested with the insignia of his rank—Quits Florence to reside at Rome— Eminent Cardinals then in the college—Zizim brother of the Sultan Bajazet delivered into the custody of the pope—Ermolao

Barbaro patriarch of Aquileja—Rumours of approaching calamities. GIOVANNI DE' MEDICI, afterwards supreme pontiff by Chap./the name of Leo The Tenth, was the second son of Lorenzo A. D. 1475. de' Medici, called the Magnificent, by his wife Clarice, the Birth of Gio. daughter of Giacopo Orsino. He was born at Florence, on vamiide'Me. the eleventh day of December, 1475; and most probably ward5Le0x. received his baptismal name after his paternal great uncle, Giovanni, the second son of Cosmo de' Medici, who died in the year 1461; or from Giovanni Tornabuoni, the brother of Lucretia, mother of Lorenzo de' Medici, who was then living.

Vol. 1. A At CHAP. I.

At the time of the birth of Giovanni, the age of porA. D. 1475. tents was not yet past; and it has been recorded with all the gravity of history, that prior to that event, his mother dreamt that she was delivered of an enormous, but docile lion; which was supposed to be a certain prognostic, not only of the future eminence of her son, but also of the name which he was to assume on arriving at the papal dignity, fa,) Whether the dream gave rise to the appellation, or the appellation to the dream, may admit of doubt; but although nothing appears in his infancy to justify his being compared to a lion, in his early docility he seems at least to have realized the supposed prognostics of his mother.

The year in which Giovanni was born is distinguished in the annals of Italy as a year of peace and tranquillity, whilst almost all the rest of Europe was involved in the calamities of internal commotions or of foreign war. It was also solemnized as the year of Jubilee, which was thenceforwards celebrated once in twenty-live years.

SoTereigns of Europe at hat time.

At this period the pontifical chair was filled by Sixtus IV. who had not yet evinced that turbulent disposition which was afterwards so troublesome, not only to the family of the Medici and the city of Florence, but to all the states of Italy. The kingdom of Naples was governed by Ferdinand, the illegitimate son of Alfonso king of Naples, Aragon, and Sici-

ly; who had bequeathed the first of these kingdoms to his son, but was succeeded in the two latter by his brother John II. the father of another Ferdinand, who now enjoyed them, and by his marriage with Isabella, the *(a) Jorii, vita Leonis* x. *lib.* i. *Ammirato, Ritratto di Leone* x. *in Opvsc.* iii. 62.
the daughter of Henry IV. of Castile, united the king-Chap, L doms of Aragon and Castile under one dominion. The A D 1473 «tates of Milan were yet held by Galeazzo Maria, the son of the great Francesco Sforza. Frederick III. had long worn the Imperial crown. Louis XI. was king of France; Edward IV. of England; and the celebrated Mattia Corvino, had lately been elected by the free voice of his countrymen to the supreme dominion of Hungary.
The political system of Europe was as yet unformed. The despotic sovereign, governing a half-civilized people, had in general only two principal ends in view—the supporting his authority at home by the depression of his powerful nobles, and the extending his dominion abroad by the subjugation of his weaker neighbours. Devoted to these objects, which frequently required all their talents and all their resources, the potentates of Europe had beheld with the utmost indifference the destruction of the eastern empire and the abridgment of the christian territoiy, by a race of barbarians, who were most probably prevented only by their own dissensions, from establishing themselves in Italy and desolating the kingdoms of the west. It was in vain that Pius II. had called upon the European sovereigns to unite in the common cause. The ardour of the crusades was past. A jealousy of each other, or of their own subjects, was an insuperable obstacle to his entreaties; and the good pontiff was at length convinced that his eloquence would be better employed in prevailing on the Turkish Emperor to relinquish his creed and embrace Christianity, than in stimulating the princes of Europe to resist his arms.faj
A 2, The *(a) Pii. Ii. Epist. ad Illustrissimum Mahumetem Turcomm principem, inter ejus Ep. imp. per Anto-*

nium Zarothum. Mcdiulun. 1487 meat.
Chap. i. The establishment and long uninterrupted continuance of A. D. 14-5. ne PaPal government, may justly be considered as among Nature of the tne most extraordinary circumstances in the history of manpapalgoYem-kind. To the sincere catholic this indeed is the great evidence of the truth of the religion which he professes, the perpetual miracle, which proves a constant extension of the divine favour to that church, *against which the gates of hell shall not prevail;* but they who conceive that this phenomenon, like other events of the moral world, is to be accounted for from secondary causes and from the usual course of nature, will perhaps be inclined to attribute it to the ductility and habitual subservience of the human mind, which when awed by superstition and subdued by hereditary prejudices, can not only assent to the most incredible propositions, but can act in consequence of these convictions with as much energy and perseverance, as if they were the clearest deductions of reason or the most evident dictates of truth. Whilst the other sovereigns of Europe held their dominions by lineal succession, by choice of election, or by what politicians have denominated the right of conquest; the Roman pontiff claimed his power as the immediate vicegerent of God; and experience has shewn, that for a long course of ages his title was considered as the most secure of any in Europe. Nor has the papal government, in later times, received any great trouble from the turbulence of its subjects, who instead of feeling themselves degraded, were perhaps gratified in considering themselves as the peculiar people of a sovereign, whose power was not bounded by the limits of his own dominions, but was as extensive as Christianity itself.
Without entering upon a minute inquiry into the origin of the temporal authority of the Roman pontiffs, it may be sufficient temporal power of the popes. sufficient to observe, that even after they had emerged from Chap, L their pristine state of poverty and humility, they remained *A* D 1473. for many ages

in an acknowledged subordination to the Roman emperors, and to their delegates, the exarchates of Ravenna, to whom, when the seat of empire was transferred origin of the to Constantinople, the government of Italy was intrusted. As the power of the emperors declined, that of the popes increased; and in the contests of the middle ages, during which the Huns, the Vandals, the Imperialists, and the Franks, were successively masters of Italy, a common veneration among these ferocious conquerors for the father of the faithful, and the head of the christian church, not only secured his safety, but enlarged his authority/a,! From the time of the emperor Constantine, various grants, endowments, and donations of extensive territories, are said to have been conferred by different princes on the bishops of Rome; insomuch that there is scarcely any part of Italy to which they have not at some period asserted a claim. That many of these grants are supposititious, *(a)* The coining of money by the Roman pontiffs may be considered as a mark of sovereign and independent authority; but at what precise period they began to exercise this right, is not easily ascertained. Muratori, in his *Annali d' Italia, vol.* iv. *p.* 464, informs us, that the popes coined money, in gold, silver, and copper, from the time of Charlemagne, (about the year 800) and that the city of Rome had enjoyed that privilege *ab antiquo.* Other writers have assigned an earlier date, which opinion they have founded on a coin of Zacharia, who filled the pontifical chair from the year 740 to 751— P. *Dissertaz. del Conte Giacomo Acami deir origine ed antkhid dclla Zecca Pontificia, p.* 8, *Ed. Rom.* 1752. This subject has given rise to serious controversy, even among the firmest adherents to the church. Muratori and Fontanini have embraced different opinions, which they have endeavoured to support in several learned publications, in which the ancient rights of the emperors and the popes to various parts of Italy are particularly discussed. All collectors however agree in commencing their series from Adrian I. created pope in 782, from which time Acami has given a succession of thirty-four coins of different pontiffs, some of which, are however supposed, to have issued from the metropolitan sees of England, for the purpose of paying tribute to Rome.

Chap. i. supposititious, is generally acknowledged; (a) whilst the valiD. 1475. dity of others, which are admitted to have existed, frequently rests merely on the temporary right of some intruder, whose only title was his sword, and who, in many instances, gave to the pontiff what he could no longer retain for himself. Under the colour however of these donations, the popes possessed themselves of different parts of Italy, and among the rest, of the whole exarchate of Ravenna, extending along a considerable part of the Adriatic coast, to which they gave the name of Romania, or Romagna.(j The subsequent dissensions between the popes and the emperors, the frequent schisms which occurred in the church, the unwarlike nature of the papal government, and above all the impolitic transfer of the residence of the supreme pontiffs from. Rome to Avignon, in the fourteenth century, combined to weaken the (a) The donation of Constantine, is humourously, but boldly placed by Ariosto, with the trumpery which, being lost on earth, was found by Astolfo stored up in the moon, among the prayers of the wicked, the sighs of lovers, the crowns of forgotten sovereigns, and the verses written in praise of great men.

"Di varj fiori ad un gran monte passa;
"Ch'ebbe giA buono odorc, or puzza forte-,
"Questo era il dono, se pero dir lece,
"Che Costantino al buon Silvestro fece.
"

Orl. Fur. cant. 34. st. 80.

(b) The validity of these donations, and particularly those of Pepin, king of France, and of his son Charlemagne, is strongly insisted on by Ammirato, who attempts to shew, that the authority of the popes extended far beyond the limits of Italy; but as he appears not to have distinguished between their temporal and their ecclesiastical power, little reliance is to be placed on his opinion.

Ammir. Discorso come la Chiesa Romana sia cresciuta ne' bent temporali. Opnsc. v. ii. p. 67. Those readers who are inclined to examine more particularly into this subject may consult the *Fasciculus rerum Expetendarum Sf Fugiendarum, tom. i. p. 124.* the authority which the popes had in the course of so many Chap. i. ages acquired; and in particular the cities of Romagna, A D li7 throwing off their dependence on the papal see, either formed for themselves peculiar and independent governments, or became subject to some successful adventurer, who acquired his superiority by force of arms. No longer able to maintain an actual authority, the Roman pontiffs endeavoured to reserve at least a paramount or confirmatory right; and as the sanction of the pope was not a matter of indifference to these subordinate sovereigns, he delegated to them his power on easy conditions, by investing them with the title of vicars of the church. It was thus the family of Este obtained the dominion of Ferrara, which they had extended, in fact, to an independent principality. Thus the cities of Rimini and Cesena were held by the family of Malatesta; Faenza and Imola by the Manfredi; and many other cities of Italy became subject to petty sovereigns, who governed with despotic authority, and by their dissensions frequently rendered that fertile, but unhappy country, the theatre of contest, of ra-. pine, and of blood.

From this period the temporal authority of the popes was chiefly confined to the district intitled the patrimony of St. Peter, with some detached parts of Umbria, and the *Marca d' Ancona.* The claims of the church were not however suffered to remain dormant, whenever an opportunity of inforcing them occurred, and the recovery of its ancient possessions (a) *Guicciardini, Historia. d' Italia, lib. iv.* The passage here referred to, in which the historian has traced with great ability the rise and vicissitudes of the temporal authority of the popes, is omitted in the.general editions of his worts, and even in that of Torrenfino, *Tlor. fa.* but may be found in those of Stoer, 6'36, 1645. *Genera.*

Chap. i. possessions had long. been considered as a duty indispen. D. H75. saDly incumbent on the supreme pontiff. But although for this purpose he scrupled not to avail himself of the arms, the alliances, and the treasures of the church, yet, when the enterprize proved successful, it generally happened that the conquered territory only exchanged its former lord for some near kinsman of the reigning pontiff, who during the life of his benefactor, endeavoured to secure and extend his authority by all the means in his power.

The Roman pontiffs have always possessed an advantage over the other sovereigns of Europe from the singular union of ecclesiastical and temporal power in the same per

UnioB of the temporal a" son, which' long experience had taught them to use with the thority. same dexterity, with which the heroes of antiquity availed themselves by turns of the shield and the spear. When schemes of ambition and aggrandizement were to be pursued, the pope, as a temporal prince, could enter into alliances, raise supplies, and furnish his contingent of troops, so as effectually to carry on an offensive war; but no sooner was he endangered by defeat, and alarmed for the safety of his own dominions, than he resorted for shelter to his pontifical robes, and loudly called upon all Christendom to defend from violation the head of the holy church. That these characters were successively assumed with great address and advantage, *fa*) Bayle, in his dictionary, *Art. Leonx.* note p. has some observations, rather more fanciful than solid, on this union of spiritual and temporal authority in the same person: which he concludes by relating the story of a German bishop, who was also a count and baron of the empire, and who having attempted to justify to a peasant the extraordinary pomp which he assumed, by adverting to his temporal dignity, *yes,* replied the rustic, *but when my lord the count and baron is sent to hell, where Kill then be my lord the bishop f* venuuent.

tage, will sufficiently appear from the following pages; and CHAP-I: although some difficulties might occasionally arise in the ex-A. D. 1475,. ercise of them, yet, notwithstanding the complaint of one of the ablest apologists of the Roman pontiffs, foj the world has, upon the whole, been sufficiently indulgent to their situation; nor has even the shedding of Christian blood been thought an invincible objection to the conferring on a deceased pontiff the honour of adoration, and placing him in the highest order of sainthood conferred by the church, fb)

It is not however to be deniedT that the papal govern-some«i«nment, although founded on so singular a basis, and exercised pGowith despotic authority, has been attended with some advantages peculiar to itself, and beneficial to its subjects. Whilst the choice of the sovereign, by the decision of a peculiar body of electors, on the one hand preserves the people from those dissensions which frequently arise from the disputed rights of hereditary claimants; on the other hand, it prevents those tumultuous debates which too frequently result from the violence of a popular election. By this system the dangers of a minority in the governor are avoided, and the sovereign assumes the command at a time of life, when it may be presumed that passion is subdued by reason, and experience matured into wisdom. The qualifications by which the pope is supposed to have merited the supreme

B authority, (a) " Ollre a do, esi difficile 1' cmpier con gli altri principi insieme le parti di Padre "nello spirituale, e di competitore spesso ncl temporale, che talora son ripresi dalla fama "come troppo interessati, o poco caritativi i pontefici, perchei hanno b difeai b ricuperati "quei sudditi alla cui protezione gli obliga il patto scambievol e tra'l signore e'l vassallo." Pallaviani, Istoria del Cone, di Trenlo. c. i. p. 47. Ed. Rom. 1665. (b) San Leone Ix.

Chap. i. authority, are such as would be most likely to direct him iri A. D. 1475. the best mode of exercising it. Humility, chastity, temperance, vigilance, arid learning, are among the chief of these requisites; arid although some of them have confessedly been too often

dispensed with, yet few individuals have ascended' thd pontifical throne without possessing more than a common share of intellectual endowments. Hence the Roman pontiffs have frequently displayed examples highly worthy of imitation, and have signalized themselves, in an eminent degree, as patrons of science, of letters, and of art. Cultivating, as ecclesiastics, those studies which were prohibited or discouraged among the laity, they may in general be considered as superior to the age in which they have lived; and among the predecessors of Leo X. the philosopher may contemplate with approbation the eloquence and courage of Leo I. who preserved the city of Rome from the ravages of the barbarian Attila; the beneficence, candour, and pastoral attention of Gregory I. unjustly charged with being the adversary of liberal studies; the various acquirements of Silvester II. so extraordinary in the eyes of his contemporaries as to cause him to be considered as a sorcerer; the industry, acuteness,. (and learning of Innocent III. of Gregory IX. of Innocent IV. and of Pius II. and the munificence and love of literature so strikingly displayed in the character of Nicholas V.

Notwithstanding the extensive influence acquired by the Cboks of the Roman see, that circumstance had not, for a long course of Giovanni de' time, induced the princes of Europe to attempt to vest the Medici tothe pontifical authority in any individual of their own family.

Whether this forbearance was occasioned by an idea that the long course of humiliation by which alone this dig church.

nity could be obtained, was too degrading to a person of mA:p-xroyal birth, or by a contempt for every profession but that A. D. 1475. of arms may be a subject of doubt; but from whatever cause it arose, it appears to have been, in the fifteenth century, completely removed; almost every sovereign in Italy, and perhaps in Europe, striving with the utmost ardour to procure for their nearest relations a seat in the sacred college, as a necessary step to the pontifical chair.

What the European princes endeavoured to accomplish in the persons of their own kindred, the popular governments attempted in those of.their most illustrious citizens; and the favours bestowed by Paul II. upon his countrymen the Venetians, may reasonably be supposed to have operated upon the sagacious and provident mind of Lorenzo de' Medici, to induce him to attempt the establishment of the chief ecclesiastical dignity in one of his own family. Nor is it improbable, that whilst he was actuated by this motive, he was impelled by another of no less efficacy. By the resentment of the papal see he had lost a much-loved brother; and although he had himself escaped with his life from the dagger of the assassin, yet he had experienced, from the same cause, a series of calamities, from which he was only extricated by one of the most daring expedients recorded in history. To prevent, as far as possible, the recurrence of a circumstance which had nearly destroyed the authority of his family, and to establish his children in such situations as might render them a mutual support and security to each other, in the high departments for which they were intended, were doubtless some of the motives which occasioned the destination of Giovanni de' Medici to the church, and produced those important effects upon the religion, the politics, and the taste of Europe, which are so conspicuous in the pontificate of Leo X. B 2, That

Chap. i. That it was the intention of Lorenzo, from the birth of a. D. H82. his son, to raise him eventually to the high dignity which He receives the he afterwards acquired, cannot be doubted; and the authority uTpinted which he possessed in the affairs of Italy, enabled him to«nabbot of Fon-gage in this undertaking with the fairest prospects of success.

Soon after he had attained the seventh year of his age, Giovanni de' Medici had received the tonsura, and was declared capable of ecclesiastical preferment. At this early period his father had applied to Louis XI. to confer upon him some church living. In the reply of the

French king, which bears date the seventeenth day of February, *1482,,* he thus expresses himself:—" I understand from your letter of "the thirtieth of January, the intentions you have formed "respecting your son, which, if I had known them before "the death of the cardinal of Rohan, I should have endea"voured to have accomplished; but I have no objection, on "the next vacancy of a benefice, to do for him whatever "lies in my power.'Y10 Accordingly, Giovanni was, in the following year, appointed by the king, abbot of Fonte-dolce; and this was speedily followed by the investiture of the rich And of Pa»ig-monastery of Passignano, bestowed upon him by Sixtus IV.

who, towards the close of his days, seemed desirous of obliterating from the minds of the Medici the remembrance of his former hostility. The particulars of this singular instance of ecclessiastical promotion, and of the additional honours bestowed upon Giovanni de' Medici, are given by Lorenzo himself, in his *Micortli,* with great simplicity. "On the nine"teenth day of May, 1483," says he, "we received intelli1483. it gence, that the king of France had, of his own motion, "presented to my son Giovanni, the abbey of Fonte-dolce.

"On *(a) Fabronii, vita Lour. Med. in adnot.* 298. *et v. App. No. I* s On'the thirty-first, we heard from Rome, that the pope CHAP-1 "had confirmed the grant, and had rendered him capable of A. D. i4S3. "holding a benefice, he being now *seven* years of age. On the "first day of June, Giovanni accompanied me from *Poggio fa)* ." to Florence, where he was confirmed by the bishop of "*Arezzofb), and* received the tonsura; and from thence"forth was called *Messire Giovanni.* The before mentioned "circumstances took place in the chapel of our family. "The next morning he returned to Poggio. On the eighth "day of June, Jacopino, a courier, arrived with advices "from the king of France, that he had conferred upon "Messire Giovanni the archbishoprick of Aix, in Provence; "on which account a messenger was dispatched, on the "same evening, to

Rome, with letters from the king to the "pope and the cardinal di Macone. At the same time dis"patches were sent to count Girolamo, which were for"warded by Zenino the courier to Forli. On the eleventh, "Zenino returned from the count, with letters to the pope "and the cardinal *S. Giorgio,* which were sent to Rome "by the Milanese post. On the same day, after mass, all "the children of the family received confirmation,. ex"cepting Messire Giovanni. On the fifteenth, at the sixth hour of the night, an answer was received from Rome that "the pope had some difficulty in giving the archbishoprick "to Messire Giovanni, on account of his youth. This answer "was immediately dispatched to the king of France. On "the twentieth, we received news from Lionetto *that the "archbishop was not dead!* On the first day of March, 1484, 1484 "the abbot of Passignano died, and a message was dispatched

"to *(a) Poggio a Cajano,* a seat of Lorenzo de' Medici.
(bj Gentile d' Urbino. *v. Life of Lor. de' Med. vol.* i. *p.* 72. 4o. CHAP-*L* "to Giovanni Vespucci, the Florentine ambassador at A. D. us. "Rome, that he should endeavour to prevail on the pope "to give the abbey to Messire Giovanni. On the second, "he took possession of it under the authority of the state, "by virtue of the reservation granted to him by Sixtus IV. "and which was afterwards confirmed by Innocent VIII. "when my son Piero went to pay him obedience at Rome, "on his elevation to the pontificate.'YoJ It would not be difficult to declaim against the corruptions of the Roman see, and the absurdity of conferring ecclesiastical preferments upon a child; but, in the estimation of an impartial observer, it is a matter of little moment whether such preferment be bestowed upon an infant, who is unable, or an adult, who is unwilling, to perform the duties of his office, and who, in fact, at the time of his appointment, neither intends, nor is expected, ever to bestow upon them any share of his attention.
The death of Sixtus IV. which happened on the thirHi» father at-teenth day of August 1484, and the elevation to the

pontifi£Tto cate of Giambattista Cibo, by the name of Innocent VIII. openrank of cardi-ed to Lorenzo the prospect of speedy and more important advancement for his son. Of the numerous livings conferred on this young ecclesiastic, a particular account has been preserved; but the views of Lorenzo were directed towards still *(a)* The original is given in the Life of Lor. de' Medici, *Appendix, vol.* ii. *No.* £ri».
(b) It appears that Giovanni was at the same time a canon of the cathedral of Florence, of Fiesole, and of Arezzo; rector of Carmignano, of Giogoli, of S. Casciano, of S. Giovanni in Valdarno, of S. Piero at Casale, and of S. Marcellino at Cacchiano; prior of Monte Varchi; precentor of S. Antonio at Florence; proposto of Prato; abbot of Monte Cassino, of S. Giovanni of Passignano, of S. Maria of Morimondo, of S. Martino, of
Fonte-dolce, still higher preferment. In the month of November he dis-CItAP . patched his eldest son Piero to Rome, accompanied by his A. D. i484. uncle. Giovanni Tornabuoni, with directions to promote as much as possible the interests of his brother Giovanni,-hi the instructions of Lorenzo to his envoys at Rome, the same object was strongly insisted on; and such arguments were constantly suggested, as were most likely to induce the pope to nominate Giovanni de' Medici, on the first opportunity, a member of the sacred college.

In the mean time, Lorenzo thought it advisable to strengthen the friendly connexion which already subsisted Marriage of between himself and the pope, by an union between their S"0 families. Before his adopting an ecclesiastical life, Innocent dalena de'Mc had several children, *(a)* the eldest of whom, Francesco dlci' Cibd, was married in the year 1487, to Maddalena, one of the daughters of Lorenzo, a woman of great beauty and 1487 accomplishments, and who lived to share the honours enjoyed by her family in the elevation of her brother. Besides the inducements to this measure, which the pope probably found in the increasing influence and authority of Lorenzo de' Medici, the

near relationship which subsisted between

Maddalena

Fonte-dolce in France, of S. Lorenzo
of Coltibuono, of S. Salvadore at Va-
jan6, of S.

Bartolommeo at Anghiari, of S. Maria
at Monte Piano,, of S..Giuliano at
Tours, of S.

Giusto and S.-Clement at Volterra, of
S. Stefano of Bologna, of S. Michele in
Arezzo, of

Chiaravalle at Milan, of the diocese of
Pino in Pittavia, and of the Casa Dei
at Chiaramonte; and in 1510 he became
archbishop of Amain.—" Bone Deus,"
exclaims Fabroni,

4 quot in uno juvene cumulata sacerdo-
tia!" *Fabr. vita Leon.* x. *in adnot. p.* 245.
(a) Sanazzaro adverts to this circumstance in the following ironical lines.

M Innocuo priscos aeqvmm est debere
quirites:

"Progenie exhaustam restituit patriam."
Epigram. lib. i. *Ep.* 37. *Ed. Comino,*
1731.

CHAP- Maddalena and the family of the
Orsini, was a powerful A. D. U87. motive with him to conclude the match.
The event was such as the pope expected. The hostility between him and the
Orsini speedily subsided; and he found
on many subsequent occasions the high
importance of their attachment and their
services.faj

As the advancement of Giovanni de'
Medici to the dignity of the purple, was
the fortunate event which led the way to
his future elevation, and to the important consequences of that elevation to
the christian world, it may not be uninteresting to trace the steps by which he
acquired, so early in life, that high rank.
This we are enabled to do with great
accuracy, from the letters of Lorenzo
and his confidential correspondents, the
originals of which are preserved in the
archives of Florence, and which exhibit
such a degree of policy and assiduity
on the part of that great man, as could
scarcely fail of success.; 1488. From
these it appears, that early in the year
1488, the cJioranni de pope, who had
not before received any additional
members ptimed *mt* tne college had

formed the intention of making a prod-
inai. motion of cardinals, and had communicated his purpose to Lorenzo, to
whom he had also transmitted a list of
names for his remarks and approbation.
Such however was the inactivity of the
pontiff, that he delayed from time to
time the execution of his plan. From the
age and infirmities of the pope, Lorenzo was fearful that this measure might
be wholly frustrated; and as he had already formed the design of *(a) Muratori, Annali f Italia,* ix. *556.* of procuring the name of his son to be included
among those Ciiap. L of the new cardinals, he directed his envoy at Rome, A
D 1488

Giovanni Lanfredini, to lose no time
in prevailing upon the a.iEt.*s.* pope to
carry his intentions into effect. I observe," says he, in a letter which bears
date the sixteenth day of June, 14 88,fa,)

"what you mention respecting the
promotion of cardinals,

" to which I shall briefly reply, that
this event ought not *.v* to be delayed
longer than can possibly be avoided; for
"when his holiness has completed it, he
will be another 4' pope than he has hitherto been—because he is yet a head

".without limbs, surrounded by the
creatures of others;

M whereas he will then be surrounded by his own. You

"will therefore importune and exhort
him to adopt this de

M termination as soon as possible,
because there is danger in

"delay. As to the persons nominated,
I approve all

"those whose names are marked with
a point; they are the

"same as you before mentioned to
me. It seems better to

"lay before him many, that he may
have an opportunity

"of selection. He may also gratify me
if he thinks proper."

A few months afterwards, when a
promotion of cardinals was positively
determined on, Lorenzo became more:
strenuous in his exertions, and omitted
no solicitations or persuasions which
might obtain the favour, not only of the
pontiff himself, but of the cardinals,

whose concurrence was, it appears, indispensable.. In a letter to the pope,
which c bears *(a)* MSS. *Tlorent. v. App.
No. II. (b)* In the articles or concessions
signed by Innocent on his election, he
had solemnly promised not to raise any
person to the dignity of a cardinal who
had hot attained thirty years of age, that
such promotion should never be made
in secret, that he would not. create more
than one from his own family, that the
number should not in the whole exceed
twenty-four, and that he would not
name any new ones till the college
should be reduced-to that number. *Burcard. Diarium. ap. Notices Set* MSS. *du
Roi.* i. 7-5.

C:HAP- bears date the first day of October, 1488, he most earnestly A. D.
1488. intreats, that if he is ever to receive any benefit from his A.t. 13. holiness, it may be conceded to him on that
occasion, and requests his favour with
no less fervency than he would from
God the salvation of his soul *(a).* With
equal eagerness, and to this or a similar
effect, he addressed himself to all the
members of the sacred college, whose
interest he thought essential to his success. Where he could not obtain an absolute promise of support, he considered it as of great importance to have
prevented opposition. "You appear to
me," says he to Lanfredini, *(c)* "to have
done no little in removing the objections
of M j. you cannot induce mm to proceed further, I

"wish you to thank him for this; and
assure him, that "knowing his inclination, I shall owe to him the same "obligation for it, as I shall to others for their
positive "favours. At the same time, if it
were possible, I should "be highly gratified by his assistance." On this important occasion Lorenzo availed himself
greatly of the services of the Cardinal
Ascanio, brother of Lodovico Sforza,
and of Roderigo Borgia, then vice-chancellor of the holy see. "I reply," says he,
addressing himself to Lanfredini *(dj,* "in
a letter under my own hand to the vice-
chancellor "and Monsig. Ascanio. The
letter which they have "written me, and
the trouble which, as you inform me,
"Monsig. Ascanio takes every day on

my behalf, merit

"other (a) Fabr. in vita Leon. X. ad-mit. 245. et v. App. No. III. (b) Of these, his letter to Battista Zen, Cardinal of S. Maria in Portico, and nephew of Paul II. may serve as a sufficient specimen. *MSS. Florent. App. No. IV. (c) MSS. Flort-nt. App. No. V.*

(&) MSS. Florent. App. No. VI.

4i other returns than words. I well know, both from vour CHAP-1 "infor-mation and my own reflections, where my honour A. D. 14ss. V and my hopes would have remained, had they not been a.£t.is, 4 brought to life by him, and by those whom his relation"ship, friend-ship, and connexions, have obtained for me. "The difficulty of this business, and his constant diligence "and attention, render the benefits he has conferred on us so "important, that they oblige not only me and M. Giovanni, "but all those who belong to us; for I consider this favour "in no other light than if I were raised from death to life." He expresses himself respecting the vice-chancellor with equal gratitude, desiring Lanfredi-ni to assure him of the sense he enter-tains of his favours, which he cannot do himself, " because in effect he feels the obligation too strongly, "and is more de-sirous of repaying it, when in his power, "than he can possibly express."

At this critical juncture, when every hour was pregnant with expectation, the hopes of Lorenzo were cruelly, though unintentionally, disappointed by Lan-fredini, who, having a confidence of success, wished to be informed by Lorenzo in what manner he should an-nounce the great event. To this end he inclosed to Lorenzo the form of a public letter, which it might be proper to send, on such an occasion, for the inspection of the citizens at large. Lorenzo replies *fa),* " you "will have time enough to send for the form in which it "may be proper to announce the news. The method you "took had however nearly given rise to a great error; for, "as I read your inclosure before your letter, and there did "not appear either the word, *copy, or any* other indication c *2,* "to *(a) MSS. Florent. App. No. VII.*

Chap. i.-*11* to that effect, I thought

the information true, and was a. D. H88. "ver7 near making it public. It seems to me of little conseA. *£u* 13. "quence in what manner you communicate it. The business "is here so publicly spoken of, that it cannot be more so. *Kt* You can therefore send no intelligence that is not expected "by every one except myself; for, I know not how it is, I "have never been able to confide in the event."

This however seems to have been the last agony which Lorenzo had to sustain in this long conflict, for, on the ninth day of the same month, he received the consolatory intelligence, that his son was elevated to the dignity of a cardinal, under the title of S. Maria in Domenica. *(a)* His feelings on this occasion are best expressed in his own words, addressed to his envoy at Rome, *(b)* "Thanks be to God for the good "news which I re-ceived yesterday at the ninth hour, re-: "specting Messire Giovanni, and which appeared to me so "much the greater, as it was the less expected; it seeming "so far above my merits, and so difficult in itself, as to be "esteemed impossible. I have reason to hold in remem"brance all those who have assisted me in this busi-ness, "and shall leave a charge that they be not forgotten by "those who may succeed me; this being the greatest ho-nour "that ever our house experienced." "I know not whe"ther his holiness may be displeased with the demonstra"tions of joy and festivity which have taken place in Flo"rence on this occasion; but I never saw a more general or

"a more *(a)* This event was communi-cated to him in a letter from the cardinal ofAnjou, yet preserved in the Florentine Archives. *App. No. VIII.* It is also ad-verted to in the Latin verses of Philo-musus, who has there in a spirit of poet-ic prophecy foretold the future honours of his patron, which he also lived him-self to celebrate. *App. No. IX (b) Vide App. No. X.* 41 a more sincere exulta-tion. Many other expressions of it Chap. i. "would have occurred, but I did all in my power to prevent A D..1488. "them, although I could not wholly succeed. I mention a. *£x.* is. "this, because the el-evation of M. Giovanni was intended "to have remained for the present a se-

cret; but you have "made it so public in Rome, that we can scarcely incur "blame in following your example; nor have I been able "to decline the congrat-ulations of the city even to the "lowest ranks. If what I have done be improp-er, I can "only say that it was impossible for me to prevent it, and "that I great-ly wish for instructions how to conduct myself "in future, as to what kind of life and manners M. Giovanni "ought to observe, and what his dress and his at-tendants "ought to be; for I should be extremely sorry to begin to "repay this immense debt by doing any thing con-trary to 41 the intentions of his holi-ness. In the mean time M. Gio"vanni re-mains with me in the house, which from yester "day has been continually full of people. Advise me "therefore what is to be done with him. Inform me also, "when you next write, what signature or seal he ought to "use. In expediting the bull, you will, I am sure, use all "due diligence, and will transmit it as soon as possible for "the satisfaction of our friends. I send you herewith the "mea-sure of his heighth, but in my eyes he appears to have "grown and changed since yesterday. I trust in God you will receive due honour for your exertions, and that his "holiness will be pleased with what he has done. I wish "for your opinion whether I should send my son Piero, as I "intended; because it seems to me that a favour of this "magnitude calls for no less, than that I should pay a visit "to Rome myself."

Politiano, to whom the early educa-tion of Giovanni de'

Medici

Chap, *t* Medici had been intrusted, thought it also incumbent on a. D. 1488. himself, upon this occasion, to address to the pope a letter, A.iEt, 13. in which he has exhibited the character and early acquirements of his pupil in a very favourable light. Some allowance must however be made for the partiality of the tutor, and perhaps for the blandish-ments of the courtier; nor are we im-plicitly to believe, either that Louis XI. was the most pious of kings, or that Gio-vanni de' Medici, although from vari-ous circumstances his proficiency was beyond his years, had realized in him-self,

"That faultless monster which the world ne'er saw." *Jgnolo Politiano to the supreme Pontiff, Innocent VIII.(a)*

"Although the mediocrity of my for-tune, and the jn"significance of my sta-tion in life, might justly deter me Let-terfromPo-"from addressing myself to your holiness, the vicar of God, "and chief of the human race; yet, amidst the public ex"ultation of this city, and the peculiar satisfaction which I "myself experience, I cannot refrain from ex-pressing my "joy, and returning thanks to your holiness, for having adopted in-to the sacred college, Giovanni, the son of Lo"renzo de' Medici, and the de-served favourite of his coun"try; and for having thereby conferred on this flour-ishing "community, and on so noble a family, such high honour M and dignity. Allow me also to congratulate your *ho*11 ness, that by this exertion of your own discriminating 4' judgment, you have added to your other great dis-tinc"tions immortal honour. Not to mention Lorenzo him

"self, litiano to the pope.

(a) In the preceding-year Politiano had inscribed to-the pope his elegant trans-lation of HcroJian, in return for which Innocent had not only written to him, but had presented him with 200 pieces of gold. *Polit. Ep. lib.* viii. *ep.* 1, 2, 3, 4. Politiano had also addressed to the pope, soon after his elevation, a fine Sapphic ode. *Polit. op. Aid.* 1498.

"self, whose favour you have perpetual-ly secured by this CHAP i.

"instance of your regard, where shall we find a person A. D. Uss.

"more accomplished, in every re-spect, than our young car-a.iEt. is.

"dinal? I shall neither indulge my own feelings, nor

"flatter the choice of your holiness. What I shall say is

"known to, and testified by all. He has had the happiness

"to be so born and constituted by na-ture, so educated and

"directed as to his manners, so insti-tuted and taught as to

"his literary acquirements, that in his genius he is inferior

"to no one, neither is he surpassed by any of those of his

"own time of life in industry, by his preceptors in learn

"ing, or by mature age in gravity and seriousness of de

"portment. The native goodness of his disposition has

"been so industriously cultivated by his father, that he has

"never incurred censure by the slight-est levity or impro

"priety of speech. In his whole con-duct and deportment

"there is nothing that it is possible to blame. At his early

"period of life he has attained such a maturity, that the

"aged recognize in him the genius of the venerable Cosmo,

"whilst we, who are younger, ac-knowledge in him the

V very spirit of his father. His dispo-sition to religion and

"piety he may be said to have im-bibed with the milk that

"nourished him. From his cradle he has meditated on

"the sacred offices of the church, to which he was destined

"by his provident father, even before his birth; and the

"hopes entertained of him have been encouraged by many

"favourable presages. Such was the specimen which he

"had given, whilst yet a child, of his virtues and talents,

"that the reputation of them induced that most wise and

"most pious king, Louis XI. to judge him not unworthy of

"the high dignity of an archbishop. You have therefore the

"king as your precursor in the favours you have bestowed.

"He

"He began the web which your holi-ness has thought proper "to finish. It is not requisite that you should "number his years. He has attained his virtues be-fore his "time. Doubt not but he will fill the august purple. He "will not faint un-der the weight of the hat, nor be dazzled

"by the splendor that surrounds him. You will find in him "a person not un-qualified for such a senate, not unequal to "such a burthen. Already he appears in full majesty, and "seems to exceed his usual stature."

Whatever credit the foregoing letter may confer on the rhetorical talents of Politiano, it must be confessed that it is not calculated to increase our favourable opinion of his judgment; as in attempting with too much earnestness to convince the pope of the rectitude of his conduct, it betrays a suspicion that such conduct stands in need of justifi-cation. Lorenzo himself appears to have regarded this laboured production with no great approbation. In one of his let-ters toLanfredini he thus adverts to *it.fb)* "Messire Agnolo da Monte"Pulciano writes an epistle to his holiness, which is sent here"with, superscribed by Ser Piero, returning him thanks, *kc.* "It is pretty long—He would have been glad, had it been "received in time, to have had it read in the consistory, "and not merely to his holiness. I think we should proceed "cautiously in delivering it to the pope, to say nothing of "the rest. I submit it however, to your judgment." As no answer to this letter appears in the works of Politiano, it is not improbable that it was suppressed, in consequence of these cautionary and well founded re-marks.

It *(a) Pollt. Ep. lib.* viii, *Ep. 5.*
fbj MSS. *Florent. App. No. XI.*
(c) The public thanks of the government of Florence were also transmitted to the pope, CHAP. I.
a. D. 1488. A. iEt. 13.

It must however be acknowledged, that if Lorenzo de' CHAP-i.' Medici was indefatigable in obtaining for his son the honours A. D. 1489» and emolu-ments of ecclesiastical preferment, he displayed *A..jex..* an equal degree of as-siduity in rendering him worthy of them. The early docility and seriousness of Giovanni, the EduC8tion of

»'. Giovanni (lc proficiency which he had made in his studies, and the d IS-' Medici, tinctions with which he had been honoured, intitled him to rank as an associate in those meetings of men

of genius and learning which continually took place in the palace of the Medici. Among the professors of the Platonic philosophy the chief place was held by Marsilio Ficino; the authority of Aristotle was supported by his countryman and warm admirer, Joannes Argyropylus; in classical and polite literature Politiano had revived the age of Augustus; *fa)* whilst Giovanni Pico of Mirandula, united in himself the various kinds of knowledge which were allotted to others only in distinct portions. Conversant, as Giovanni de' Medici was, with these men, and residing under the eye of his father, to whom every production of literature and of art was submitted as to an infallible judge, it was impossible that the seeds of knowledge and of taste, if indeed they existed, should not be early developed in his mind. Hence it is probable that the business of education was to him, as indeed it ought to be to every young person, the highest amusement and gratification; and Vol. i. D 'that for the honour conferred on that city by the adoption of the cardinal de' Medici into the sacred college. The letter on this occasion was written by Bartolommeo Scala, then chancellor of the republic, and is given in the *Coilectio veterum aliquot monumentorum,* of Bandini.—*Arezzo, .*1752.
(a) " Nimirum ad optimum indolem optima accessit institutio, et fclicissimi ingenii tui solo, longe bellissimus obtigit cultor, politissimus ille *Politianus;* cujus opera non spinosis istis ac rixosis Uteris, sed veris illis, nec sine causi bonis appellatis, ac mansuetioribus, ut vocant, musis es initiatus, *ice."* Erasm. Ep. lib. ii. Ep. 1. ad. Leon. x. To the instances of confidence and friendship between Lorenzo de' Medici and Politiano, I shall add a letter from the latter, not before published. *App. No. XII.* CHAF-that he never experienced those restraints and severities A. D. 1489. which create a disgust to learning instead of promoting it. A. £t. 14. Amidst the extensive collections of pictures, sculptures, medals, and other specimens of ancient and modern art, acquired by the wealth and long continued attention of his ancestors, he first imbibed that

relish for productions of this nature, and that discriminating judgment of their merits, which rendered him, in his future life, no less the arbiter of the public taste in works of art, than he was of the public creed in matters of religion.

The youthful mind of Giovanni de' Medici was not however wholly left to the chance of promiscuous cultivation. Besides the assistance of Politiano, who had the chief direction of his studies, he is said to have received instructions in the Greek language from Demetrius Chalcondyles and Petrus j£gineta,fa) both of whom were Greeks by birth. His education was also promoted by Bernardo Michelozzi, who was one of the private secretaries of his father, and eminently skilled both in ancient and modern literature *fb)* but his principal director, in his riper studies, was Bernardo Dovizi, better known by the name of Bernardo da Bibbiena. This elegant scholar and indefatigable statesman, was born of a respectable family at Bibbiena, in the year J470, and was sent at the age of nine years to pursue his studies in Florence. His family connexions introduced him into the house of the Medici, and such was the assiduity with which he availed himself of the opportunities of instruction there afforded him, that at the age of seventeen, he had attained a great facility of Latin composition, *(a)* Mench. vita Polit. p. 98. *Lettres de Langiits. ap. Bayle, Diet. Art. Leo. x.* Many other persons are mentioned by different authors as having been his instructors, but perhaps without sufficient foundation.

(b) Paminii, in vita Leon. x.
Bernardo Do position, and was soon afterwards selected by Lorenzo as one Chap. i. of his private secretaries. When the honours of the church A D us9. were bestowed on Giovanni de' Medici, the principal care of A. £t. i±. his pecuniary concerns was intrusted to Bernardo; in the execution of which employment he rendered his patron such important services, and conducted himself with so much vigilance and integrity, that some have not hesitated to ascribe to him, in a considerable degree, the future eminence of his pupil. Notwith-

standing the serious occupations in which Bernardo was engaged, in his temper and manners he was affable, and even facetious, as appears by the representation given of him by Castiglione, in his *Libro del Cortegiano,* in which he is introduced as one of the interlocutors. Nor did he neglect his literary studies, of which he gave a sufficient proof in his celebrated comedy, *La Calandra,* which although not, as some have asserted, the earliest comedy which modern times have produced, deservedly obtained great reputation for its author, and merits, even at this day, no small share of approbation. The high rank which Bernardo obtained in the church, and the distinguished part which he acted in the political transactions of the times, will frequently present him to our notice. Of his character and talents different opinions have indeed been entertained, but his title to eminent merit must be admitted, whilst he claims it under the sanction of Ariosto. *(a)*

But whilst it may be presumed, that the subsequent *J % r* Defects in ttie honours and success of Giovanni de' Medici are to be attri-character of buted in a great degree to his early education, and to the ad-T" de vantages which he possessed under his paternal roof, it must be allowed, that those defects in his ecclesiastical character,

D 2, which *(a) Orland. Furioso. Cant. xxvi. st. 48.*

Chap. i. which were afterwards so apparent, were probably derived a. r. U8ft. from the same source. The associates of Lorenzo de' Medici A. iEt. 14. were much better acquainted with the writings of the poets, and the doctrines of the ancient philosophers, than with the dogmas of the Christian faith. Of the followers of Plato, Lorenzo was at this time considered as the chief. He had himself arranged and methodized a system of theology which inculcates opinions very different from those of the Romish church, and in a forcible manner points out the object of supreme adoration as one and indivisible. Hence, it is not unlikely, that the young cardinal was induced to regard with less reverence those doctrinal points of the established creed, the belief of which is considered as indispensable to the clerical character; and hence he might have acquired such ideas of the supreme being, and of the duties of his intelligent creatures, as in counteracting the spirit of bigotry, rendered him liable to the imputation of indifference in matters of religion. A rigid economy in his household was certainly not one of the first qualifications of Lorenzo, and the example of the father might perhaps counteract his precepts in the estimation of the son; whose liberality in future life, too often carried to profusion, reduced him to the necessity of adopting those measures for the supplying his exigencies, which gave rise to consequences of the utmost importance to the Christian world. From the splendid exhibitions which werefrequently displayed in the city of Florence, he probably derived that relish for similar entertainments which he is supposed to have carried, during his *(a) V. L'Altercazione, CapUolo.* This, together with other poems of Lorenzo de' Medici and several of his contemporaries, has been given to the public by Messrs. Nardini and Buonaiuti, in an elegant volume under the title of "Poesie Del Mac. Lorenzo De' *u* Medici, E Di Altri Suoi Amici E Contemporanei." *Londra,* 1801. 4fo.

his pontificate, to an indecorous, if not to a culpable excess; whilst the freedom and indecency of the songs with which the spectacles of Florence were accompanied, *(a)* of many of which Lorenzo was himself the author, could scarcely have failed to banish at intervals that gravity of carriage which the young cardinal was directed to support, and to sow those seeds of dissipation which afterwards met with a more suitable climate in the fervid atmosphere of Rome. The nomination of Giovanni de' Medici to the dignity of cardinal, was accompanied by a condition that he should B«ademy at not assume the insignia of his rank, or be received as a member Pi,sber of the college for the space of three years. This restriction was considered by Lorenzo as very unfavourable to his views. His remonstrances were however ineffectual; and as the pontiff had

expressed his wishes, that during this probationary interval, Giovanni should pursue the studies of theology and ecclesiastical jurisprudence, the young cardinal left Florence, and repaired to Pisa, where by the exertions of Lorenzo, the academy had lately been re-established with great splendour. At this place he had the advantage of receiving instructions from Filippo Decio and Bartolommeo Sozzini, the most celebrated professors of civil and pontifical law in Italy, *(b)* Whilst a resident in Florence,,he had frequently visited the monastery of Camaldoli, where he formed an intimacy with Pietro Delfinio, and Paullo Justiniano; the former of whom he regarded as his model and instructor, the latter as a second parent. The advantages which he received *(a)* The *Canti Carnascialeschi,* and *Canzone a hallo,* of which some account is given in the Life of Lorenzo de' Medici, i. 304. 307. 4fo. *ed. (b) Fabr. vita Leon, x, p.* 10..

CHAP. I.

Chap. i. received in his youth from this society were not forgotten in a. D. 1489. his riper years, when he conferred many favours on the A..fit. 14. monastery, acknowledging with great satisfaction, that "he "had not only spent much of his time, but had almost re"ceived his education there." *(a)*

His father en

Whilst Giovanni de' Medici, by a constant intercourse with men of rank, talents, and learning, was thus acquiring shorten his a fund of information, and a seriousness of deportment much probation. beyond his years, his father was indefatigable in his endeavours to prevail on the pope to shorten the period of his probation. Piero Alamanni, one of the Florentine envoys at Rome, in a letter which bears date the eighth day of Ja1490-nuary, A90,*(b)* thus addresses Lorenzo. "I made my ac"knowledgments to his holiness for the favours received "from him in the person of M. Giovanni, giving him to "understand how agreeable they were to all the citizens of "Florence, and how highly they esteemed the obligation. "I then ventured, in terms of the utmost re-

spect and civi"lity, to touch upon that part of the business, the accom"plishment of which is so earnestly desired, the public "assumption of M. Giovanni; alledging all the reasons "which you suggested to me, but at the same time assuring "him that the city of Florence, and you in particular, "would be perfectly satisfied with his determination. In "reply he spoke at considerable length; in the first place "observing, that the mode which he had prescribed was in "tended to answer the best purposes, as he had before ex "plained *(a)* " —— Adolescentiae suae tempore, non solum versatus, sed pene educatus fuerit." *Fabr. in vita Leon. x. p.* 10.

(b) Fabr. in vita Lour. Med. in adnot, p. 301.

"plained by means of Pier Filippo (Pandolfini). He then CHAP i. "entered on the commendation of M. Giovanni, and spoke A. D. 1490. "of him as if he had been his own son, observing, that he *A.m. 15.* "understood that he had conducted himself with great pro"priety at Pisa, and had obtained the superiority in some dis"putation, which seemed to give his holiness great pleasure. "At last he expressed himself thus: *Leave the fortunes of M.* "*Giovanni to me, for 1 consider him as my own son, and shall* "*perhaps make his promotion public when you least expect it; for* "*it is my intention to do much more for his interest than I shall* "*now express."* In order to promote this business, and to try the temper of the cardinals, Lorenzo dispatched to Rome his kinsman Rinaldo Orsini, archbishop of Florence, but he derived no advantage from this measure; and indeed from the letters of the good prelate on this subject, it appears, that he was but ill qualified for the intrigues of a court *(a).* The motives which induced Innocent to persevere in the terms which he had prescribed, are more fully disclosed in a letter from Pandolfini to Lorenzo, dated the nineteenth day of October, 1490 *fb);* from which it appears, that the pope could not admit Giovanni into the college of cardinals without either giving offence to others who had not been received, or receiving the whole, which he did not think proper to do; as he considered the state of suspence in which the college was kept, as favourable to his views and interests.

During the early years of Giovapni de' Medici, he had a GiuUo de' Me constant companion and fellow student in his cousin Giulio, cw"" the natural son of Giuliano de' Medici, who had been assassinated *(a) MSS. Florent. Jpp. No. XIII. (b) Fabr. vita Lour, in adnot. p. 302. ct. v. Aprp. No. XIV.* CHAP 1 nated in the horrid conspiracy of the Pazzifa,). The dispositiA. D. 1490. on of Giulio leading him when young to adopt a military life, A. &t. 15. ne na(been early enrolled among the knights of Jerusalem; and as this profession united the characters of the soldier and the priest, he was soon afterwards, at the solicitation of Lorenzo de' Medici, endowed by Ferdinand, king of Naples, with the rich and noble priory of Capua *b).* Grave in his deportment, steady in his family attachments, and vigilant in business, Giulio devoted himself in a particular manner to the fortunes of Giovanni, and became his chief attendant and adviser throughout all the vicissitudes of his early life. On the elevation of Giovanni to the pontificate, the services of Giulio, who was soon afterwards raised to the rank of cardinal, became yet more important; and he is, with great reason, supposed not only to have earned into execution, but to have suggested, many of the political measures adopted by Leo, and to have corrected the levity and prodigality of the pope by his own austerity, prudence, and regularity. It did not however appear, on the subsequent elevation of Giulio to the pontificate by the name of Clement VII. that he possessed in so eminent a degree those qualities for which the world had given him credit; and, perhaps, the genius and talents of Leo had contributed no. less towards establishing the reputation of Giulio, than the industry *(a) Ammirato (Opitsc. iii. 108.J* places the birth of Giulio one month, and Macchiavelli *(Stor. Fior.lib. v'm.)* several months, after the death of his father. It appears, however, from yet more authentic documents, that he was

born a year before that event, viz. in 1477; and was consequently two years younger than his cousin Giovanni de' Medici, *life of Lorenzo de' Medici, v.* i. 196-4ro. *ed.* Panvinius, the continuator of Platina, in his life of Clement VII. has followed, in this respect, the erroneous ac-. counts of the Italian historians. *(b) Ammirato Opusc. v.* iii. 102. MSS. *Florent. App. No. XV.* industry and vigilance of the latter had concurred in giving credit to the administration of Leo X. _ The long expected day at length arrived, which was to confirm to Giovanni de' Medici his high dignity, and to admit him among the princes of the" christian church. The ceremonial of the investiture was intrusted to Matteo Bosso, superior of the monastery at Fiesole, whose probity and learning had recommended him to the favour of Lorenzo de' Medici, and who has thus recorded the particulars of the investiture which took place on the ninth day of March, 1492. "On the evening of the preceding day, Giovanni "ascended the hill of Fiesole to the monastery, simply clad, "and with few companions. In the morning, being Sunday, "Giovanni Pico of Mirandula and Jacopo Salviati, who had "married Lucretia, one of the daughters of Lorenzo, arrived "at the monastery with a notary, and accompanied the young cardinal to the celebration of mass, where he took the holy sacrament with great devotion and humility. The superior then bestowed his benediction on the sacred vestments, and receiving the bull or brief of the pope, de"clared that the time therein limited for the reception of "the cardinal was expired; expressing at the same time his "most fervent vows for the honour of the church, and the "welfare of the cardinal, his father, and his country. He "then invested him with the *pallium,* or mantle, to which "he added the *biretum,* or cap usually worn by cardinals, and "the *galerus,* or hat, the distinctive emblem of their dignity, Vol. i. E "accompanying 11 CHAP. I. a. D. 14.90. a.iEt. 15. Giovanni Medici receives the insignia of his rank. 1492. *(a)* The original is given from the *Recvperationes Fesitlanee* of Matteo

Bosso—in App. to the Life of Lorenzo de' Medici, *vol.* ii. *No. 65.*
Chap. i. accompanying each with appropriate exhortations, that he A. D. 1492. " would use them to the glory of God and his own salva*A.&t.* 17. "tion; after which the friars of the monastery chaunted at "the altar the hymn, *Veni Creator."* The cardinal having thus received a portion of the apostolic powers, immediately tried their efficacy, by bestowing an indulgence on all those who had attended at the ceremony, and on all who should, on the anniversary of that day, visit the altar at Fiesole. The company then retired to a repast; after which, Piero de' Medici, the elder brother of the cardinal, arrived from the city, accompanied by a party of select friends, and mounted on a horse of extraordinary size and spirit, caparisoned with gold. In the mean time an immense multitude, as well on horseback as on foot, had proceeded from the gate of S. Gallo towards Fiesole; but having received directions to stop at the bridge on the Mugnone, they were there met by the cardinal, who was conducted by the prelates and chief magistrates of the city towards the palace of the Medici. On his arrival at the church of the *Annunciata,* he descended from his mule, and paid his devotions at the altar. In passing the church of the *Reparata,* he performed the same ceremony, and proceeded from thence to his paternal roof. The crowds of spectators, the acclamations, illuminations, and fire-works, are all introduced by the good abbot into his faithful picture; and the rejoicings on this event maybe supposed to be similar to those which celebrate, with equal delight, a royal marriage, a blood-stained victory, or a long-wished for peace.

On the twelfth day of March, 1492, the cardinal de' Medici quitted Florence, for the purpose of paying his respects to the pope, and establishing his future residence at

Rome. Quits Florence to reside at

Rome. He was accompanied to the distance of two miles Chap, t from the city by a great number of the principal inhabitants, A. D. 1492. and on the evening of the same day he arrived at his abbey A. *Jex. 17.* of Pasignano, where he took up his abode for the night. His retinue remained at the neighbouring town of Poggibonzo, nomc whence they proceeded the next morning, before the cardinal, to Siena. The inhabitants of that place being thus apprized of his approach, sent a deputation to attend him into the city, where, for several days, he experienced every possible mark of attention and respect; which he returned with a degree of urbanity and kindness that gained him the esteem and affection of all who saw him. From Siena he proceeded by easy stages towards Rome, having on his way been entertained by his relations of the Orsini family. At Viterbo he was met by his brother-inlaw Francesco Cibo, son to the pope, who with many attendants, had waited his approach, and accompanied him to Rome, where he arrived on the twenty-second day of March, in the midst of a most abundant shower of rain. Notwithstanding the inclemency of the weather, he was met by many persons of rank, who attended him to the monastery of *S. Maria in Popolo,* where he reposed the first night after his arrival. On the following morning, all the cardinals then in Rome came to visit him, and immediately led him to the pope, who received him in full consistory, and gave him the holy kiss; after which he was greeted with a similar mark of respect from each of the cardinals, and his attendants were permitted to kiss the feet of the pope. On his return to his residence, the rain still continued to pour down in copious torrents, and as the luxurious convenience of a modern chariot was then unknown, the

E 2 cardinal

Chap. i. cardinal and his numerous attendants, were almost overA. D. U92. whelmed in their peregrinations. In the performance of

A. j£t. 17. these ceremonies, we are assured by one of his countrymen, that he surpassed the expectations of the spectators; and that in his person and stature, no less than by the decorum of his behaviour, and the propriety of his language, he displayed the gravity of a man, and supported the dignity of a

prelate. Such are the authentic particulars of the first entry into Rome, of one who was destined to revive her ancient splendour. The dignity of history may perhaps reject the unimportant narrative of processions and ceremonials; but the character of an individual is often strongly marked by his conduct on such occasions; and the interest which that conduct generally excites, is a sufficient proof, that it is considered by the public as no improbable indication of his future life and fortunes.

Notwithstanding the numerous avocations which engaged the cardinal on his arrival at Rome, he did not fail to communicate to his father every particular which occurred/ In reply, Lorenzo transmitted to him that excellent and affectionate letter of paternal advice, which may with confidence be referred to as a proof of the great talents, and uncommon sagacity of its author; and which, as *(a) V. Appendix, No. XVI. (b)* One of these letters, preserved in the Florentine Archives, and not before printed, will be found in the Appendix, No. XVII. As this is probably the earliest production now extant of its illustrious author, and was written in an unpremeditated manner, on his first entrance into public life, it cannot be perused, unadorned as it is, without peculiar interest.

Cardinals of as having been written only a very short time before his CHAP-L death, has been, not inelegantly, compared to the last mu-A. D. 1492. sical accents of the dying *svran.fa)* a.Jft.17.

At the time when Giovanni de' Medici took his seat in the sacred college, it was filled by many men of acknowledged abilities, but of great diversity of character; several of whom afterwards acted an important part in the affairs tbe college" of Europe. The eldest member of the college was Roderigo Borgia, who had enjoyed upwards of thirty-five years the dignity of the purple, to which he had, for a long time past, added that of vice-chancellor of the holy see. He was descended from the Lenzuoli, a respectable family of the city of Valencia in Spain, but on the elevation to the pontificate of his maternal uncle, Alfonso

Borgia, by the name of Caljxtus III. he was called to Rome, where, changing his name of Lenzuoli to that of Borgia, he was first appointed archbishop of Valencia, and afterwards cardinal of S. Nicolo, being then only twenty-five years of age. The private life of Roderigo had been a perpetual disgrace to his ecclesiatical functions. In adhering to his vow of celibacy, he had alleviated its severity by an intercourse with a Roman lady of the name of Vanozza, who, by the beauty of her person, and the attractions of her manners, had long possessed the chief place in his affections. His attachment to her appears however to have been sincere and uniform, and although his connexion was necessarily disavowed, he reregarded her as a legitimate wife. By hcr hc had scveral children, to whose education and advancement he paid great *(a) Fabr. in vita Law. Med. App. p.* 312; and for this letter, *v. Life of Lor. de' Med.* ii. 146.

Chap. i. great attention. Notwithstanding the irregularity of his a. D. 14. 92. private life, his acquaintance with the civil law, and with a.Et. 17. the politics of the times, had procured him the honor of many important embassies, on one of which he had been deputed by the pope, to accommodate the differences that had arisen between the kings of Portugal and of Aragon, in respect of their claims on the crown of Castile. Roderigo was not, however, formed by nature for a mediator, and returning without having effected the object of his mission, he had nearly perished by shipwreck in the vicinity of Pisa, one of the vessels which accompanied him having been wholly lost in a violent storm, with one hundred and eighty persons on board, among whom were three bishops, and many other men of rank and learning. If the character of Roderigo, who afterwards became supreme pontiff by the name of Alexander VI. is to be taken on the implicit credit of contemporary historians, this calamity was not greatly alleviated by the escape of the cardinal; on the contrary, had he shared the same fate, his destruction would have been a sufficient compensation to the world for the loss of all the rest.

Another member of the college was Francesco Piccolomini, the nephew of Pius II. the celebrated iEneas Sylvius, He had also long enjoyed his dignity, having been created cardinal by his uncle in the year 1460, when only seventeen years of age. The purity of his life, the regularity of his conduct, and his zeal in discharging the duties of his station, formed a striking contrast to the profligacy and effrontery of Roderigo Borgia, and occasioned him to be chosen by his colleagues to heal those wounds which Roderigo had, in the course of his pontificate, inflicted on the christian christian world; but the short space of time in which he CHAP-i. administered the affairs of the church, under the name of A. D. 1493. Pius III. frustrated the hopes which had been formed on a.iEt. 17. his elevation. Among those who had been nominated by Sixtus IV. was Giuliano della Rovere, cardinal of *S. Pietro in Vincola.* The ambition and military spirit of this prelate seemed to have marked him out for a different employment; but in those days the crozier and the sword were not incompatible, and Giuliano made his way by the latter, rather than the former, to the supreme dignity which he afterwards enjoyed, by the name of Julius II. By the same nomination there still sat in the college, Raffaelle Riario, cardinal of *S. Giorgio,* who, under the directions of his great uncle Sixtus IV. had acted a principal part in the bloody conspiracy of the Pazzi. In assuming his seat among the fathers of the christian church, Giovanni de' Medici therefore, found himself associated with one who had assisted in the murder of his uncle, and attempted the life of his father; but the youth and inexperience of Riario, had alleviated the enormity of a crime perpetrated under the sanction of the supreme pontiff, and subsequent transactions had occurred between the families of the pope and of the Medici, which might have obliterated the remembrance of this event, had not the pallid countenance of the cardinal occasionally recalled it to mind, *(a)* Among those of royal or of noble birth, the principal rank, after the death of Giovanni

d'Aragona, son of Ferdinand king of Naples, was due to Ascanio, brother of Lodovico Sforza, who supported the dignity of his office with great splendor. The families *(a) V. Life of Lor. de' Med.* i. 189.

Chap. r. families of the Orsini and the Colonna, generally maiuA. D. 14. 92. tained a powerful interest in the consistory, and the noble a. *£t.* 17. family of the Caraffa, which has long ranked as one of the principal in the kingdom of Naples, had also a representative in the person of Oliviero Caraffa, who had been nominated by Paul II. and was one of the most respectable members in the college.

Among the cardinals who had been nominated by Innocent ziam, brother VIII. at the same time with Giovanni de' Medici, was Pierre of the suitan d'Aubusson, grand master of Rhodes, upon whom that honor had been conferred as a reward for bavnrg surrendered into custodyofthe tne custody of the pope, an illustrious Turkish fugitive, who had been compelled, by the rage of fraternal resentment, to seek for safety among those of a different nation and a different faith. On the death of Mahomet, in the year 1482, that ferocious conqueror left his extensive dominions to his two sons, Bajazet and Zizim. Bajazet was tempted to avail himself of the powerful plea of primogeniture, to the exclusion of his brother, who had endeavoured by personal merit, to compensate for the pretensions of seniority. The principal leaders of the Turkish troops were divided in their attachments to the two brothers, and perhaps that circumstance, rather than the courage or conduct of the duke of Calabria, delivered Italy from the devastation with which it was threatened by the Turks, when they had possessed themselves of the city of Otranto. After a struggle of some years and several bloody engagements, victory declared for the elder brother, and Zizim, to avoid the bowstring, threw himself into the hands of the grand master of Rhodes, whilst his wife and children sought a refuge in Egypt, under the protection of the Sultan. The r reception reception which he

met with was highly honourable both to CHAP-Ihimself and his protector; but the grand master, conceiving A. D. 1492. that his longer continuance at Rhodes might draw down a.J£t. 17. upon the island the whole power of the Turkish state, sent him to France, whence he was soon afterwards transferred to Rome, into which city he made his public entry on the thirteenth day of March, 1489. Considerations of policy, if not of humanity, induced Innocent to receive him with great kindness; and Francesco Cibo, with a long train of nobility, was deputed to attend him into the city. On his being admitted to an audience of the pope, in full consistory, he deranged the solemnity of the ceremony; for notwithstanding the instructions which he had received, to bend his knees, and kiss the feet of his holiness, he marched firmly up to him, and applied that mark of respect to his shoulder. A chamber in the apostolic palace was allotted for his residence, and a guard appointed, which, under the pretext of doing him honour, was directed to prevent his escape. *In* this situation an attempt was made to destroy the Turkish prince, by Cristoforo Castagno, a nobleman of the *Marca d' Ancona,* who having entered into stipulations for an immense reward, by the terms of which, among other advantages, he was to be invested with the government of the island of Negrpponte, repaired to Rome, for the purpose of executing his treacherous task. Some suspicions, however, arose; and it being discovered that he had recently returned. from Constantinople, he was apprehended by order of the pope, and confessed, upon the rack, his atrocious intentions. Those apprehensions which Bajazet could not extinguish whilst his brother was living, he endeavoured to alleviate by prevailing on the pope to retain him in secure custody, for which he repaid him by the bribery of Christian relicks, Vol. 1. F and CHAP-1 and the more substantial present of considerable sums of a. D. 1492. money; and Zizim accordingly remained a prisoner at a.iEt.17. Rome until the ensuing pontificate of Alexander *Yl.(a)*

Notwithstanding the tranquillity

which Italy had for

Rumours of. i l r' «.»'.

public caia-some time enjoyed, the rumours ol approaching calamities mities. were not unfrequent. Those alarms and denunciations which have generally preceded great public commotions, although they may not arise from any supernatural interposition, are not always to be wholly disregarded. On the approach of the storm, the cattle, by a native instinct, retire to shelter; and the human mind may experience a secret dread, resulting from a concurrence of circumstances, which although not amounting to demonstration, may afford strong conviction of approaching evils, to a person of a warm and enthusiastic temperament. Those impressions which he is ready to impart, the public is prepared to receive; and the very credulity of mankind is itself a proof of impending danger. Whilst the city (a) On this occasion the Turkish emperor transmitted to the pope *the head of the spear which pierced the side of Jesus Christ.* This relick, according to an ancient chronicle, had been preserved at Constantinople before the capture of that place by the Turks, where it had been concealed by a citizen, from whom it was purchased by the emperor for 70,000 ducats. Some doubts arose among the members of the college, as to the authenticity of this relick, it being contended by some, that the true spear was at Nuremberg, and by others, that it was preserved in the *Sainte Chapelle* at Paris; but Innocent disregarded their objections, and directed that the present should be received in a solemn procession, in which it was carried by the pope himself, o11 the day of Ascension, inclosed in a case of crystal. He was, however, so fatigued with the labour, and so oppressed by the tumults of the crowd, that he was unable to fmish the ceremony. *Burcard. Diar. ap. Notices des MSS. du Roi.* i. 94. The rage for collecting relicks, seems at this period to have been at its height. In the official letters of Bartolommeo Scala, as chancellor of the Florentine Republic,' we find one addressed to the grand Turk, requesting his interference with the inhabitants

of Ragusa, to induce them to deliver up *the left arm of St. John the Baptist,* which they had intercepted in its way to Florence. *Band. Monument. p.* 17 city of Florence trembled at the bold and terrific harangues CHAP-i. of Savonarola, who was at this time rising to the height of A. D. 1492. his fatal popularity, a stranger is said to have made his ap-a. A17pearance at Rome, who in the habit of a mendicant, and with the appearance of an ideot, ran through the streets, bearing a crucifix, and foretelling, in a strain of forcible eloquence, the disasters that were shortly to ensue; particularly to Florence, Venice, and Milan. With a precision, however, which a prudent prognosticator should always avoid, he ventured to fix the exact time when these disorders were to commence; and had the still greater folly to,-add, that an angelic shepherd would shortly appear, who would collect the scattered flock of true believers into the heavenly fold. But the prescribed period having elapsed, the predictions of the enthusiast were disregarded; and he had the good fortune to sink into his original obscurity, without having experienced that fate, which has generally attended alike the prophets and pseudo-prophets of all ages and all nations. *CHAP. II.* A. D. 1492.

STATE of literature in Rome—Pomponius Lietus—Calli MACHUS EXPERIENS PAOLO Cortese Serafino D'aquila

—*State of literature in other parts of Italy* — *Neapolitan academy* — *Giovanni Pont A No* — *His Latin poetry compared with that of Politiano*—*Giacopo Sanazzaro*—*His Arcadia*—*And other writings*—*Enmity between the Neapolitan and Florentine scholars*—*Cariteo*—*Other members of the Neapolitan academy*—*State of literature in Ferrara*— *The two* Strozzi—Boiardo—Ariosto—Francesco Cieco—Nicolo Lelio Cosmico—Guidubaldo Da Montefeltri *duke ofUrbino*—Francesco Gonzaga *marquis of Mantua*— Battista Mantuano—Lodovico Sforza *encourages men of talents*—Lionardo Da Vinci—*Eminent scholars at the court of Milan*—*The* Bentivogli *of Bologna*—Codrls Urceus— Petrus

Crinitus—Aldo Manuzio, *his acquaintance with Alberto Pio, lord of Carpi, and Pico of Mirandula*—*His motives for undertaking to print and publish the works of the ancients*—*Establishes his press at Venice, and founds an academy there*—*Progress and success of his undertaking.*

Although many causes concurred to render *the City,* as Chap. n. Rome was then emphatically called, the chief place in Italy, ture in Rome.

yet it was not at this time distinguished by the number or AA.Et!i7? proficiency of those scholars whom it produced or patronized. An attempt had been made in the pontificate of Paul II. to state of liteTM, establish an academy, or society for the research of antiquities, but the jealousy of that haughty and ignorant priest had defeated its object, and consigned the wretched scholars to the dungeon or the rack. Among those who had survived his barbarity was Julius Pomponius Laetus, who by his various CHAP-various writings and indefatigable labours, had at this early A. D. 1492. period been of no inconsiderable service to the cause of lia.iEt. 17. terature. To the testamentary kindness of Bartolommeo Platina, who had been his companion in his studies, and his fellow-sufferer in his misfortunes, and who died in the year 1481, Pomponius was indebted for a commodious and handsome residence in Rome, surrounded with pleasant gardens and plantations of laurel, where he yet lived at an advanced age, devoted to the society of his literary friends, (a) His associate Ca) Pomponius derived his origin from Calabria, and is supposed to have been of illegitimate birth; but his parentage, and even his real name, have escaped the researches of his admirers. The appellation of Julius Pomponius Laetus he doubtless assumed as an academical or scholastic distinction; but the name of Laetus was sometimes exchanged for that of *Fortunatus,* or *Inforlunatus,* as the circumstances of his situation seemed to require: and Vossius supposes that Julius Pomponius Sabinus is no other than the same person. *(de Histor. Latinis, lib.* iii. *p. 6lS.)* From the letters of Politiano, it appearsthat a frequent communication subsisted between these two eminent scholars, and that Pomponius was accustomed to furnish his learned friend with such curious monuments of antiquity as his researches supplied. We also learn from Crinitus, that Pomponius transmitted to Lorenzo de' Medici an antique marble, which exhibited the order of the months of the year, and of the Roman calendar; and the frequent commemoration of the family of the Medici, in the letters of Pomponius, manifests the good understanding that subsisted between them, which was probably increased by the arrival of the cardinal in Rome. The works of Pomponius are very numerous, and many of them have frequently been reprinted; but his most useful production is his description of the antiquities of RomeErasmus commends the unaffected elegance of his style. "Pomponius Laetus, elegantia "Romana contentus, nihil affectavit ultra." Bartolommeo Martiano *(diss. Voss.* ii. 242.J has justly appreciated the merits of this early scholar, whom he ranks with Tortelli and Blondo. "Scripsfere nullo pene discrimine, vera pariter et falsa, apta atque incpta; tamen 11 eos qui primi omnium hanc scribendi provinciam aggressi sunt, ob earn causam non in"dignos lauds existimavimus, quod ad plura utilioraque invenienda viam posteris osten"disse videinusj' To Pomponius we are also indebted for the earliest editions of several of the Roman.classics, and among others, *Terentius Varro, Ven. 474.Jb. Silius Italicus, Romce,* 1471, *fo. Quintus Curtius-, Roma, per Georgium Later, absque ami not a. Columella,* published with the *Rei Rusticce Scriptores, Bonon.* 1494, where he stiles himself Pomponius Fortunatus, in consequence of which lie is cited by the bibliographer,, *de ure,* as a distinct author. *Bibliogr. Instr. No.* 1527 associate Filippo Buonaccorsi, better known by his acade-Chap. H. mical name of *CaUimachus Experiens,* had quitted Italy under A. D. 1492. the impressions of terror, excited by the cruelty of Paul, and A,iEt. sought a refuge in Poland; where, under Casimir and John Albert, the suc-

cessive sovereigns of that country, he enjoyed caUimachusExfor several years some of the chief offices of the state. The distinguished favours bestowed on him by those princes could not fail of exciting the resentment of their subjects, who were jealous of the interference of a foreigner and a fugitive; but the virtue or the good fortune of CaUimachus were superior to the attacks of his adversaries, and he retained his eminent station, with undiminished honour, to the close of his days, *(a)*
Vol. 1. G But *(a)* This illustrious scholar was born at San Gemignano, of a noble family, in the year 1437. On associating himself with Pomponius in the Roman academy, he relinquished his family name, and adopted that of *CaUimachus,* which he probably thought expressed in Greek the same idea as Buonaccorsi in Italian. His addition of *Experiens* is conjectured by Zeno to have arisen from the vicissitudes which he met with in life; but this is to suppose, that he did not assume it till after those vicissitudes had taken place. It is more probable that he merely meant to infer, that all true knowledge must be founded on experience. His flight to Poland is thus adverted to by Cantalicio, a contemporary poet, and prelate or the church. It must be premised, that the name of Paul II. was Pietro Barbo.
"Callimachus, Barbos fugiens exurbe furores,
"Barbara quae fuerant regna, Latina fecit."
His history of the affairs of Hungary, which he wrote at the instance of the great Mattia
Corvino, is preferred by Jovius to any historical work which had appeared since the days of Tacitus. *Voss. de Hist. Lat. lib. m,p.* 619. He died at Cracow, in the year 1496.
His remains were deposited in a tomb of bronze, with the following inscription:
Philippus Callimachus Experiens, *natione Thuscns, vir doctissimus, utrius-*
gue fortunes exemplum imitandum, at que omnis virtutis cultor prcecipuus,
divi olim Cazimiri *et* Johannis Alberti, *Polonice regiim, secretarius*

accept issimus, Relict is ingenii, ac rerum a se gestarum, pluribus momimentis,
cum summo omnium bonorum marore, et regice domus, atque hujiu reipub. incommodo, anno salutis nostra, MCCCCXCVJ. caiendis Novembris, vita. deadens, hic sepultus est. t.
Paolo Cortese.
CHAP-". But although the misfortunes which had befallen this A. D. 1492. early institution, had considerably damped the spirit of A. £x. 17. improvement at Rome, yet the disaster was in some degree repaired by the talents of Paolo Cortese; who, at an early period of life, had signalized himself by his dialogue *De hominibus doctis,* which he had inscribed to Lorenzo de' Medici.fa The approbation which Politiano expressed of this youthful production, was such as that great scholar was seldom induced to bestow; not because he was jealous of the talents of others, but because he was sincere in his commendation of their works, and was enabled, by his own proficiency, to judge of their merits and defects. Some years afterwards, when Cortese was appointed one of the apostolic notaries, a new institution was formed by him, the members of which met under his own roof, and passed their time, without formal restrictions, either in the perusal of such works as his elegant library supplied, or in conversation on literary topics. Besides his treatise before mentioned, he was the author of many other works*(b)* but his premature death prevented the world from reaping the full fruits of his talents and his labours.
Among *(a)* The dedicatory epistle, is as honourable to the talents of the author as to the character of the patron. The work itself met with great applause; and the friends of Cortese advised him to publish it; notwithstanding which it remained in MS. till the year 1734-, when it was given to the public by Manni, from a copy found by Alex. Politi, at S. Gemignano.
(b) Among these are his treatise *De Cardinalatu,* and several theological works. *Tirab. Storia-de/la Itt. Ital. vol. i,par.* 1, *p.* 85. 232. In another depart-

ment of letters, he was however excelled by his brother Alessandro, who was one of the most elegant Latin poets of that period, as appears by his heroic poem, intitled *Laudes beUicec Matthice Conim Hungariee regis. Carm. illustr. Poet. Ital.* iii. 157-From this piece it appears, that Alessandro had followed the fortunes of this great prince, who was not excelled in his love of literature by any monarch of his time.

Among those who attended the literary meetings of CHAP-Ii. Cortese, was the poet Serafino d'Aquila. At a time when the A. D. 1492. Italian language was yet struggling to divest itself of its im-A-*W.* purities and defects, the works of Serafino were not without Sejfinod'Aiuisome share of merit. He was born at Aquila, in Abruzzo,. of a respectable family, and passed a part of his youthful years in the court of the count of Potenza, where he acquired a knowledge of music. Returning to his native place, he applied himself for three years to the study of the works of Dante and of Petrarca, after which he accompanied the cardinal Ascanio Sforza to Rome. During his whole life Serafino seems to have changed the place of his residence as often as the favours of the great held out to him a sufficient inducement. Hence we find him successively in the service, or at the courts, of the king of Naples, the duke of Urbino, the marquis of Mantua, the duke of Milan, and finally of Caesar Borgia. Nor must we wonder, that Serafino was sought for as a companion, to alleviate the anxiety, or banish the languor of greatness; for he superadded to his talent for poetical composition, that of singing extempore verses to the lute, and was one of the most celebrated *Improwisatori* of his time. This circumstance may sufficiently explain the reason of the superior degree of reputation which he obtained during his life time, to that which he has since enjoyed, *(a)*.

G 2-Such *(a)* The works of Serafino were often reprinted in the early part of the sixteenth century. The first edition is that of Rome, 1503; butthat of the Giunti, I51f, is the most beautiful and correct. Amidst the hasty effusions of Serafino, we sometimes meet with passages which prove him to have been a genuine poet; as in the opening of his Capitolo to Sleep:

"Placido sonno, che dal ciel in terra

"Tacito scendi a tranquillar la mente, *u* E de' sospir a mitigar la guerra!

". Berk *Chap,* it Such was the state of literature, and the talents of its a. D. 1492. chief professors, in the city of Rome, at the time when the A. *Jei.* 17. cardinal de' Medici took up his residence there; and it must State of meTM-be confessed that, notwithstanding the laudable exertions of pansofitaiy. tne few distinguished scholars before mentioned, that place had not hitherto brought forth those fruits which might have been expected from the munificence of Nicholas V. and the example of Pius II. Nor is it to be denied, that in almost every other city of Italy, the interests of letters and of science, were attended to with more assiduity than in the chief place in Christendom. At Naples an illustrious band of scholars had, under better auspices, instituted an academy, which had subsisted for many years in great credit. Of this the celebrated Pontano was at this time the chief director, whence it has usually been denominated *the academy of Pontano.*

"Ben fai tu spesso i miei desir contenti.

"Che in lieto sonno a me conduci quella,
"Che pasce il cor de si lunghi tormenti."

These lines seem to have been imitated by the celebrated Giovanni della Casa, in the sonnet beginning,

"O sonno, o della queta, umida, ombrosa,
. Notte, placido figlio."

And more evidently by Filicaja, the finest modern lyric poet of Italy, about the year 1700, in his terzine, *Al Sonno.*

"Cara morte de' sensi, oblio de' mali. "

Serafino died in 1500, in his thirty-fourth year. On his tomb, in S. Maria del Popolo, was inscribed the following hyperbolical eulogium, by his friend Bernardo Accolti:

"Qui giace Serafin: partirti o puoi;

"Sol d'aver visto il sasso chc Io serra "Assai sci debitor agli occhi tuoi."
tano. (a) It was, however, originally established, in the reign of Alfonso I, by Antonio Beccatelli, Bartolommeo Facio, Lorenzo Valla, and other eminent men, whom that great patron of letters had attracted to his court. The place of assembly was denominated the Portico, and being situated near the residence of Beccatelli, that distinguished scholar, and favourite of Alfonso, was its earliest and most constant visitor. *(b)* After the death of Beccatelli, his friend and disciple Pontano, was appointed chief of the academy, and under his direction' it rose to a considerable degree of respectability.

Chap. ii.
a. D. 1492.

A. *At.* 17: Neapolitan academy.

Few scholars, who have owed their eminence merely to their talents, have enjoyed a degree' of respect and dignity equal to Pontano. His writings, both in verse and prose, are extremely numerous; but, as they are wholly in the Latin language, he cannot be enumerated among those, who, at this Giovanni p0»period, laboured, with so much assiduity and success, in the improvement of their native tongue. The versatility of his talents, and the extent of his scientific acquirements, are chiefly *(a)* On entering the Neapolitan academy, Pontano changed his baptismal name of *Giovanni* for *Joviamu.* This custom is pleasantly ridiculed by Ariosto, in his sixth satire, inscribed to Pietro Bembo.

"II nome, che d' Apostolo ti denno,

M O d' alcun minor santo, i padri, quando Christiano d' acqua, non d' altro ti fenno, "In *Cosmico,* in *Pomponio,* vai mutando;

"Altri Pietro in *Pierio,* altri Giovanni
"In *Juno* c in *Jovian* va riconciando; '"

"Quasi che'l nome i buon giudicj inganni,
"E che quel meglio t'abbia a far Poeta '? Che non fara lo studio di mok' anni."
k *(b)* For some account of Beccatelli, *v. Life of Lor. de' Medici,* i. 51.
CHAP-n-chiefly evinced by his works in prose; *(a)* in which he appears A, D.

H92. successively as a grammarian, a politician, an historian, a A. *£x. 17.* satirist, a natural and a moral philosopher. These writings are now, however, in a great degree, consigned to oblivion; nor is it difficult to account for the neglect which they have experienced. His grammatical treatise *de Aspiratione,* in two books, instead of exhibiting a philosophical investigation of general rules, degenerates into an ill-arranged and tiresome catalogue of particular examples. Nor do we feel more inclined to indulge such a trial of our patience, on account of the instance which he alledges of the orator Messala,. who wrote a whole book on the letter *s.* In natural philosophy his writings chiefly relate to the science of astronomy, in which he appears to have made great proficiency; but they are at the same time disgraced by a frequent mixture of judicial astrology; and afford a convincing proof that, when an author builds on false grounds, and reasons on false principles, the greater his talents are, the greater will be his absurdities. His moral treatises are indeed the most valuable of his writings; but they are injured by the unbounded.' fertility of his imagination, and exhibit rather all that can be said on the subject, than all that ought to be said. From some scattered passages, it appears, however, that he had formed an idea of laying a more substantial basis for philosophical inquiries, than the world had theretofore known; and; had obtained, though in dim and distant prospect, a glimpse of that nobler edifice, which about a century afterwards, was displayed in all its proportions to the immortal Bacon, and in comparison *(a)* First collected and published tmder the directions of Pietro Summonte, by Andrea d'Asoli at Venice, *vol.* i, 1518. *Vols.* ii. *and* iii, 151pi *Svo.* afterwards published at *Basil,* 1538. comparison with which, the airy fabrics of the schoolmen, like. CHAP nthe magic castles of romance, have vanished into *smoke.(a)* A. D. 149c. a. iEt. 17V

Of the satirical talents of Pontano, if we take his *Asinus* as a specimen, no very favourable opinion can be entertained, *(b)* His poetry is, however, en-

titled to great approbation, and will always rank him, if not the first, in the His Latin P0 very first rank of modern Latin Poets. Under his control Wuh that of that language displays an ease, a facility, a grace, to which it had been for upwards of a thousand years a stranger; and in the series of Latin writers, his works may be placed next to those of the Augustan age, which they will not disgrace by their proximity. They display a great variety of elegiac, lyric, *(a)* " De spe ita quidem mibi persuadeo, brevi fore quod dixi, ut et philosophia cla"norem formam induat, cumque una sit et certa Veritas, minime futura sit tam varia et "lubrica, et qui eloquentiam sequuntur habeant unde fecilius hauriant, quod exornare ver"bis possint." *Pont. de Obedieniia. Tirab. Storia della Lett. ltd. vi.par.* i. *p.* 297.

(b) This is a kind of drama, in which a traveller, an innkeeper, and a courier are introduced, rejoicing in the restoration of peace, which the courier attributes to the exertions of Pontano. The blessings of peace are then chanted by a chorus of priests, after which Altilio, Pardo, and Cariteo, three of his most intimate friends, lament together the insanity of Pontano.; who has of late devoted all his time to the soothing, feeding, and decorating an *ass.* Pontano soon afterwards appears, accompanied by his gardener, with whom he holds a long and serious conversation, on the grafting of trees, and the improvement-of his garden. A boy then brings in his favourite *ass,* and Pontano determines to wash and comb him; but beginning at.the tail, is molested by a very natural circumstance. He then undertakes to perform that operation on the head; when in return for his kindness, the stupid animal seizes and bites him by the hand, and Pontano finds, too late, *that they uho attempt to wash the face of an ass, lose both their soap and their labour.* "Asino caput "qui lavant, eos ©peram cum sapone amittere." This piece has been said to refer to the.duke of Calabria,.who, as Pontano thought, did not sufficiently repay the services which he had performed, in effecting a peace with the pope, in the year I486; but if Pontano

was capable of this gross abuse of the son of his great patron and benefactor, whom he constantly celebrated with the most open flattery, he deserves as much censure for the malevoJence of his purpose, as for the imbecility of its execution.

Politiano.

CHAP-lyric, and epigrammatic productions; but bis *Hendecasyllabi* A. D. 1492. are preferred to the rest of his writings, *(a)* An eminent a. iEt. 17. critic has not indeed hesitated to give Pontano the preference in point of elegance, to Politiano himself./*J* Nor will a candid judge be inclined to oppose this opinion, as far as relates to ease and fluency of style; that of Pontano being uniformly graceful and unlaboured, whilst in that of Politiano, an attempt may at times be perceived to force the genius of the language to the expression of his own ideas. But if an inquiry were to be instituted into the respective merits of these great men, this circumstance alone would not be sufficient to decide the question. The subjects on which Pontano has treated, are mostly of a general nature: amatory verses, convivial invitations, or elegiac effusions. Even in his *Urania,* or poem on the stars, and his *Hortus Hesperidum,* or poem on the cultivation of the orange, he seldom treads at any great distance from the track of the ancients. His sentiments are therefore rather accommodated to the language, than the language to his sentiments. But with Politiano the case is reversed: with a more vigorous mind, and a wider range of thought, he disdained to be limited to prescriptive modes of expression, and in embodying his ideas, relied on his own genius. Hence, whilst Pontano is at sometimes an imitator of Virgil, and at others of Horace, Catullus, or Propertius, Politiano is himself an origiginal, and owns no subserviency to any of the great writers of antiquity; whom, however, he has shewn that he was capable *(a)* The poetical remains of Pontano were published in 2 vols. 12mo., the first by Aldo, in 1513, the second by Andrea d' Asola, the associate and successor of Aldo, in 1518. *(b)* " Politiano adhucpolitior." *BorricAius,*

depoetis, ap. Blount, Censuraauthorum.
502. CHAP. II. capable of imitating, had
he chosen it, with great exactness
Pontano may therefore be allowed to
take the precedence of A. D. ugz. Politiano, with respect to the grace and facility of his verse, A--Et*17* without de-
tracting from the intrinsic merits of that
sound scholar and very extraordinary
man/aj

Not less celebrated than the name of
Pontano, is that of his friend and countryman, Sanazzaro, who is equally distinguished by the excellence of his Latin
and Italian compositions. He was born
at Naples, in the year 1458, of a respectable family, which claimed consanguinity with San Nazzaro, one of the
saints of the Roman church.f Under the
instructions of Giuniano Majo, Sanazzaro chiefly acquired the knowledge of
the Greek and Latin languages, the latter of which he cultivated in an eminent
degree. On enVol. i. H tering *(a)* The
political and literary labours of Pontano,
and the chief circumstances of his public and private life, are commemorated
in a beautiful elegiac poem of his friend,
Sanazzaro. *Eleg. lib.* i. *El. 9. Ed. Comm.*
1731.

"Qui primus patrios potuit liquisse
penates." *(b)* By a singular coincidence,
Sanazzaro was born on the very day devoted to that saint, being the twenty-
eighth day of July. Of the opulence, the
rank, and the achievements of his ancestors, he has left in his writings many
memorials. From these it appears, that
his family was originally of Spain, and
that Niccolo, one of his ancestors, followed Carlo Durazzo in a high military
capacity, when he obtained possession
of the kingdom of Naples. His services
were repaid by the princely reward of
the castle of Mondragone, and an extensive territory in the province of Lu-
cania, which were enjoyed by Giacopo,
his son, the grandfather of the poet, till
he was deprived of them by his opposition to the dissolute conduct, and op-
pressive measures, of Joanna, the sister
and successor of Ladislaus, king of
Naples. From that period the possessions of his family were considered as
inferior to their rank; and, although they
still enjoyed an honourable independence, their reduced state, and lost honours, are a frequent subject of the poet's
complaint. *Arcadia, prosa* 7. *Crispo vita
di San. p.* 2. His nativity, on the feast of
San Nazzaro, is commemorated in the
»

Chap. n. tering into the Neapolitan
academy, he relinquished his apA: D.
1492. pellation of Giacopo, and adopted
the name of *Actius SynK.sx.yj. cerus,* by
which he is usually known. The friendship of Pontano, and his own merits,
recommended him at an early age to
the favour of Ferdinand, king of Naples,
and of his sons, Alfonso and Federigo,
to whom, throughout all their calamities, he maintained an unshaken attachment. For the amusement of these
princes he is said to have written several
dramatic pieces in the Neapolitan dialect, which highly delighted the populace; *(a)* but perhaps the earliest assign-
able date to any of his works, is the year
149, when the great events and changes
which occurred in the world, by the expulsion of the Moors from Grenada, and
the discovery of Hispaniola by Colum-
bus, attracted in a high degree the public
attention in. every part of Europe. It is
indeed a singular coincidence, that in
the same year in which the Spanish sovereigns freed their country from the op-
probrium of a foreign yoke, they should
themselves have commenced a similar
the following inscriptive lines, on ded-
icating a chapel to that saint, and in
many other parts of his works:
. " Divo Nazario.
"Natali quod, Dive, tuo, hicem editus
hausi;
"Quod tua nascenti lux mihi prima fuit;
"Actius hoc riguo parvum cum fonte sa-
cellum
"Dedico; tu nutu fac rata vota tuo;
"Ut quae Sextiles lux venerit ante calen-
das
"Quarta, sit hic generi bis celebranda
meo;
"Et quod solennes revocat tua festa per
aras;
"Et quod natalem contigit esse meam.
"

"*(a)* Nfi pur oggi & fatto antico in
Napoli, fra gli altri suoi componimenti,

uno, detto'1 dal volgo di essa Citta,
Gliomero, nome conveniente all' opera,
in cui si raccolgonb tutte "sentenze, e
voci goffe, del parlare antico Napolitano, con digressioni molto ridicole,
segni"non oscuri della fertility dell' ingegno di esso poeta." *Crispo, in vita
San. p. 9.* a similar invasion on the natural rights of others. The dis-CHAF-
ncovery of the new world gave rise to
iriany singular and A. D. 1492. extrav-
agant notions, which are striking proofs
of the crechi-a.jEt. 17. lity of the age.
(a) But the conquest of Grenada was
celebrated throughout all Christendom
(b) and with particular splendor at
Naples, the sovereigns of which were so
nearly allied, both by blood and marriage, to the reigning family of Spain.
On this occasion Sanazzaro produced a
dramatic poem, which was performed
before Alfonso, duke of Calabria, at
Naples, on the fourth day of March,
1492. *(c)* Nor was it only by the labours
of the peri that Sanazzaro obtained the
favour of his great patrons. The contests
which arose in Italy had called forth the
military talents of Alfonso, who after
having expelled the Turks from Otranto,
fought the battles of his country with
various success. In these expeditions he
was accompanied by Sanazzaro, who in
his Latin poems frequently adverts to
his warlike exploits, with the consciousness of one whose services have been
neither unknown nor unimportant.

Of the writings of Sanazzaro in his
native language, the His Arcadia, most
celebrated is his *Arcadia,* which, for the
purity of

H 2 style *(a) JilonaHeschi, Commen-
taru Historici, lib.* xvi. *Ed. Ven.* 1784-
Bembo, Istoria Veneta, lib. vi.
(b) An account of the rejoicings in London, on this occasion, may be found in
Hollingshead's chronicle. *(c)* The plan
of this piece is extremely simple. Mahomet first appears lamenting his defeat, and flying before the Christian
army; after which, *Faith* and *Joy* successively enter the stage, in appropriate
habiliments, and exult in his defeat, and
the representation terminates with a
masquerade and a dance. This *Farsa,* as
it appears to have been intitled by the

author, remained in MS. till the year 17-19, when it was published at Naples, and has since been usually annexed to the Italian writings of Sanazzaro. CHAF-11 style, and elegance of expression, is allowed to have exA D. 1492. celled all that Italy had before produced. This performance A. iEt. 17. is also a species of drama, in which the interlocutors express themselves in verse; but every dialogue is preceded by an introduction in a kind of poetical prose, the supposed dialect of Arcadian shepherds. If the applauses with which this piece was received, and the commendations bestowed upon it in the lifetime of the author, be considered as inadequate proofs of its merit, the numerous editions of it, which appeared in the course of the ensuing century, are a more unequivocal testimony of its excellence; and the latest historian of Italian literature acknowledges, that after the lapse of three centuries, the Arcadia is justly esteemed as one of the most elegant compositions in the Italian language.*(a)* It must however be confessed, that this piece is not now read without some effort against that involuntary languor, which works of great length, and little interest, never fail to occasion. This may perhaps be attributed to the alternate recurrence of prose and verse, a species of composition, which has never succeeded in any age, or in any country, and which even the genius of La Fontaine could not raise into celebrity *(b)* to the use of poetical prose, that hermaphrodite of literature, equally deprived of masculine/ vigour and of feminine grace; to the repetition of the *versi sdrucciolix* which terminate every line with a rapidity approaching to the ludicrous, and prevent that variety of pauses *(a) Ttrcb.* vii. *par.* 3. *p.* 74. About 60 editions of the Arcadia appeared before the year lf00. *(b) Let Amours de Psycie Sf de Cupidon* pauses which is essential to numerous composition. If to CHAP-n these causes we add the very inartificial, and almost uncon-A. n. 1492.. nected plan of the poem, and the total want of variety in *A-17* the sentiments and characters, we shall be at no loss to account for the present neglect of a work, which may how-

ever be esteemed as a production of uncommon merit at the time when it appeared, and as having contributed in an eminent degree to form and to refine the Italian tongue.

If, however, the Arcadia of Sanazzaro had never been written, his sonnets and lyric pieces would have secured to him the distinction of one of the chief poets that Italy has produced. It has indeed been supposed, that if the increasing celebrity of Pietro Bern bo, had not deprived Sanazzaro of the hope of being considered as the principal restorer of Italian literature, he would have pursued that object with still greater energy and success, *(a)* The rivalship of these two eminent men, whilst it rather cemented than relaxed the friendship that subsisted between them, eventually led them to pursue, by a kind of tacit consent, each a different path to fame; and whilst Bembo persevered in cultivating his native tongue, Sanazzaro turned all his powers to the improvement of his talents for Latin poetry, in which department his productions will unavoidably occur to our future notice.

When we advert to the great degree of attention paid to the cultivation of polite letters, both in Naples and in Florence, at this period, it may seem extraordinary that so little intercourse

And other,ings.

(a) Crispo. Vita di San. p. 24. *et not. 63.* Chap. n. intercourse subsisted between the scholars in those places. A. D.1492. In the *Epistolaoi* Politiano, we find indeed a letter from him a. *Jex.* 17. jto Pontano on the death of Ferdinand of Naples, written in Elii" the most respectful and flattering terms *(a)* but no answer tan and Fio-to this letter appears in the collection, and as it was custom-lan. ary for Politiano to insert the replies of his friends, we may be assured, that either none was returned, or that it was not calculated to do much honour to the person to whom it was addressed. It also appears, that Pontano had, on some iforrher occasion,-excused himself from the task of correspondence; to which, Politiano, with an unusual degree of condescension, replies, "you have my full consent, as long "as I know you honour

me with your esteem, not only, not to reply to my letters, but even not to read them." This indifference on the part of Pontano, who has, on no occasion introduced the name of Politiano in his works, may perhaps be taken as n6 equivocal indication of his disregard, whilst his intimacy with Scala and Marullus, the avowed enemies of Politiano, may serve to confirm the suspicion. But the works of Sanazzaro afford examples of more direct hostility. In the year 1489, Politiano published his *Miscellanea,* in which he conjectures, that Catullus, under the emblem of his sparrow, concealed an idea, too indecent to be 'more fully expressed.*)* Why this observation should excite the resentment of the Neapolitan scholars, who were by *(a) Pol. Ep. lib.* ii. *ep. 7. (b)* This he infers from the conclusion of an epigram of Martial;

"Da mi basia, sed Catulliana,
"Quae si tot fuerint quot ille dixit,
M Donabo tibi passerem Catulli."
Polit. Miscel. lib i. *cap. 6.* by no means remarkable for the moral purity of their com-CIA?-IJ; positions, it is not easy to discover; fici but among the A. D 1492. epigrams of Sanazzaro are some verses addressed *Ad Pulicia-A, £x.* 17 *num.,* (a term of reproach of which Scala had set the example) in which he with great severity alludes to this criticism, which he treats with the utmost ridicule and contempt. Not satisfied with this attack, he returns to, the charge; and, in another copy of verses, bestows on the object of his resentment the most unqualified abuse.fc In other parts of his works he inveighs against certain authors, who contaminate the precincts of Parnassus by their envy and their malignity; among whom it is highly probable that he meant to include the Florentine scholar. *(d)* As Politiano was, of all men living, the most unlikely to submit to these insults, without a reply, we may be allowed to conjecture, that these hostile pieces, at whatever time they were written, were not made public till after his death.

Another member of the academy, and distinguished literary ornament of Naples, was the poet Cariteo, whose

Cariteo. family-name has been lost in his poetical appellation. He is *(a)* Pontano had himself not only commented on the works of Catullus, as appears by an epigram of Sanazzaro, *Dc emendatione Catulli; ad Jovianum,* but had adopted and amplified the idea of Politiano in an epigram, which he intites *Cut donaturu sit suam columbam. Op. poet.* i. 232 *(b) Sana-Mr. Epig. lib. i. Ep.* 6"l.

"Ait nescio quis Pulicianus."

A piece much more remarkable for its indecency-than its wit, and infinitely more reprehensible than the passage to which it adverts.

(c) lb. Ep. 61. (d) Eleg. lib. i. *El.* 11. *In maledicos detractores.*

Chap. n. is said to have been a native of Barcelona, and it appears a. D. 1492. from his own writings, that he was connected by consana. iEt. 17. guinity with Massimo Corvino, bishop of Massa, who also held a place in the academy.*a)* Of his friendly intercourse with the first scholars and chief nobility of Naples, and even with the individuals of the reigning family there, his works afford innumerable instances, whilst in those of Sanazzaro and Pontano, he is frequently mentioned with particular affection and commendation, *(b)* His writings, which are wholly in the Italian tongue, aré characterized by a vigour of sentiment, and a genuine vein of poetry. Without rivalling the elegance of the Tuscan poets, they possess also a considerable *(a)* " E tu, Corvino mio, poi ch'io ti mostro,

"Che di sangue e d'amor son teco giunto,

"Parla di me con penna, e con inchiostro."

, Canteo, contra i malevoli, in fine. (b) Thus Sanazzaro:

"Quin et rite suos genio diariteus honores

"Prabeat, et festas concinet ante dapes." *Eleg. lib.* i.

And Pontano addresses *Ad Chariteum,* his Hendecasyllabi, in which he celebrates the iaths of Baia. Cariteo himself thus anticipates the applause of his friends:

"Parle di me il *Pontan,* quel bel

tesoro

"D'Apollo, e delle Aonide sorelle,

"Che con la lingua sparge un fiume d'oro. "Depinto io son nel opre eterne e belle

"Del mio bel *Sanazar,* vero *Syncero,*

"Ch' allora io giugnero fin a le stelle. " *Cariteo, contra i malevoli.*

He also attributes the name by which he is now known, to the favour of Sanazzaro:

"Quando di quel liquor Parthenopeo "*Syncero* mi pascea, dolce cantando, "Con le charite, ond'io fui Chariteo." *Cariteo, Pascha. Cant. 6. in fin.* considerable share of ease and harmony. Some of these CHAF-ITcompositions refer, in a very particular manner, to the charac-A. D. 1492. ters of the principal persons, and to the political events of Athe times.*(a)* The animosity of the Neapolitan scholars against those of Florence, is further evinced by the writings of Cariteo. In one of his *Canzoni* he insinuates, that the splendor of Dante and of Petrarca has eclipsed the fame of all their countrymen, an observation evidently intended to humiliate the present race of scholars, under a pretext of paying homage to the past *(b)* and in his *Risposta contra i malevoli,* to whomsoever he meant to apply that appellation, he has exceeded Sanazzaro himself in expressions of resentment and abuse.

The other members, who composed the literary institution of Naples, were arranged according to the different 0thCT memb«» districts of the city, or the realm, and the society also asso-poutan ciated to itself, as honorary members, the most eminent *Aemy*scholars in other parts of Europe. Among those who Vol. 1. 1 contributed *(a)* They were collected and published by his surviving friend, Pietro Summonte, at Naples, 1509, 4to. From this edition, a Canzone consecrated to the praise of the royal family of Naples, and of his literary friends, and containing some passages of great merit, is given in the Appendix. It is to be observed, however, that the predictions of the poet were speedily reversed, by the entire ruin of his great patrons, *v. Appendix, No. XVIII.* *(b)* " Se i due soli, di cui F Arno si gloria

"Onde *Beatrice* e *Laura* hor son divine,

"OflTuscan l'altre stelle Fiorentine,

"Non torran a *Sebeto* la sua gloria. M Vivan lc muse."

(c) It is to be regretted, that the Neapolitan historians have supplied us with little more than the names of those eminent men, who at this early period did so much honour to the literature of their country; and even these lists are not correct, as they contain the names of several

Chap, Il contributed at this time to its credit, was Andrea Matteo a. D. 1492. Acquaviva, duke of Atri, on whom all the academicians of a.iEt.17. Naples have bestowed the highest honours.fa Pontano dedicated to him his two books *De rebus Ccelestibus;* Piero Summonte inscribed to him all his works. He is celebrated in the poems of Sanazzaro, no less for his warlike exploits, than for his literary accomplishments.Alessandro de' Alessandri dedicated to him the first book of his *Geniales dies,* and Cariteo enumerates him among his particular friends.fc Of his writings there yet remain his commentaries, called by Paulo Giovio his *Encyclopaedia,* and according to the last mentioned author, four books of moral disquisitions, which, as he says, contain *Di bellissime Sottilezze;* but these are the same work, published under different titles, *(d)* He lived to an several persons who flourished at a later period. We are indeed informed by Apostolo Zeno, *(Dkser. Voss. cap. 7&,)* that Bernardo Cristoforo, a learned Neapolitan, had written the history of this early institution, in a work entitled *Academia Pontani, sree titce illustrhim virorum, qui cum Jo. Jotiano Pontano Neapoli jioruere;* but the manuscript has been irrecoverably lost. I cannot, however, pass over these illustrious names, without giving such particulars respecting them as have fallen in my way.

(a) " Principem virum," says Pontano, "et in mediis philosophantem beHi ardori"bus." *Pontan. de Magnanim. (b)* "*De Andrea Matthoto Aquivivo* "Cernis ut exsultet patriis Aquivivus in armis,

"Duraque spumanti frena relaxet

equo? "Quis mites illum Permessi haussisse liquores "Credat, et imbelles excoluisse lyras?" *San. Epig. lib.* ii. *Ep.* 2. *(c) Cariteo, Risposta contra i Malevoli. (d) Commentarii in translationem libeUi Plutarchi Chceroncei, de virtute morali. Neap. txOff. Ant.de Fritik.* 1526. This was printed at the author's own press, at Naples; It was afterwards republished by his son, Antonio Donate, and intitled *Ittustrium et cxqvisitissimarum* an advanced age, and distinguished himself, with various CIIAP-Irsuccess, in the wars which soon after this period, desolated A. D. 1492. his country. His example descended to his posterity; and a./Et.17. the dukes of Atri are celebrated as an uninterrupted series of great and learned men. His brother, Belisario Acquaviva, duke of Nardi, was also a member of the society; and, as appears by his writings, attained great proficiency in those studies, to which he had been incited by the example of his near and illustrious relative,*(a)* whom he also rivalled in his military talents, and towards whom he displayed an act of magnanimity, which confers lasting honour on his memory, *(b)*

These noblemen were of the district of Nido; *(c)* as was 12, also *exquisitissimarum disputationum libri quatuor, quibus omnes Divinee et humance sapient Ub, preesertim animi moderatrias, musicce, qtq. astrologice arcana, in Plutarchi Chceroncei de virtute morali prceceptionibus recondita, summo ingenii acumine retecta patefiunt, et Jiguris, suo quceque loco, Ulustrantur. Helionopoli. ap. Jo. Theodobaldum, 1609, 4to. (a)* The principal work of Belisario consists of his treatises *De Venatione, et de Aucupio; de re militari et singulari certamine; de instituendis principum liberis, Paraphrasis in Economies Aristotelis.* First printed at Naples, 1519, folio, afterwards at Basil, 1578, 8vo. Sanazzaro, in one of his Epigrams, *lib.* ii. 38. *De Lauro, ad Neritinorum ducem,* has celebrated his munificence in re-establishing, in his city of Nardo, the academy *Del Lauro.. (b)* On the descent of Charles VIII. into Naples, the duke of Atri, being suspected of having

favoured the cause.of the French, was deprived, by his sovereign, of the fee of Comersano, from which he derived his title of count, which was conferred on his brother Belisario; but no sooner had these commotions subsided, than Belisario voluntarily relinquished his new possessions in favour of his brother, to whom they were restored by the king; and Belisario was created count, and afterwards duke of Nardi.

Mazzuchetti, Scrittori f Italia i. 120. *(c)* The origin of these divisions of the city, of Naples, called by the inhabitants *Seggi,* is Rally explained by Giannone in his History of Naples, *lib.* xx. *cap.* 4. to which I must refer. CHAP-n-also Trojano Cavanilla, count of Troja and Montella, anoa. D. 1492. ther splendid ornament of the Neapolitan academy, to whom *ArM.17.* Sanazzaro has inscribed his poem, entitled *Salices(a)* and who, although not enumerated by the Italian historians among their authors, appears to have signalized himself by his researches into antiquity. From the same district was also Giovanni di Sangro, a Neapolitan patrician, to whom Sanazzaro, dying of unsuccessful love, commits the care of his poetical rites.*(c)* Of the department of Capua were Girolamo Carbone, known to the world by his poetical writings, and frequently *(a)* " Accipe flumineas properatum carmen ad undas,

"O mihi non dubia, *Cabaniti,* cognite fama;--..

"Sed longe varios rerum spectate per usus:

"Nam tibi me doctae sic devinxere sorores,

"Sic mea felici permulcent pectora cura,

"Ut vix ulla queam melioris tempora vitae

"Te sine, vix placidos per noctem carpere somnos." *Cb)* " Ipse suae referat *Cabanilius ardua Trojae*

"Mcenia, et antiquos, Appula regna, lares."

Sanaz. Eleg. lib. i. *el.* II.

(c) " Proh superi, tenues ibit Syncerus in auras?

"Nec poterit nigri vincere fata rogi?

"At tu, quandoquidem Nemesis jubet,

optime *Sangri,*

"(Nec fas est homiui vincere posse deam)

"Accipe concussae labulas atque arma carinae,

"Naufragiique mci collige rcliquias;

"Errantesque cie quocunque in littore manes;

"Taliaque in tumulo carmina caede meo:

-"Actius hic jaceo, spes mccum extincta quiescit;

"Solus de nostro funere restat amor." *Sanaz. Eleg. lib.* i. *el.* 10.

(d) Sonttti, Sestine, erf alt re poesie di Girolamo Carbone, Cavaliero Napolitano Napoli. 1506, *in fo.* quently mentioned with particular applause by Pontano, Chap, Ii. Sanazzaro, and Cariteo;fa and Tristano Carraccioli, who is A. D. 1492. commemorated by Sanazzaro in his Arcadia,*(b)* and a.iEt.17. who has left a brief memoir, in Latin, of his patron, with whom he appears to have lived on terms of great intimacy, *(d)..*

No one of the academicians was held in higher esteem for his judgment in matters of taste, than Francesco Poderico, or Puderico, of the district of Montagna. To him Pontano and Sanazzaro inscribed many of their works, and Pietro Summonte addressed to him, after the death of its author, the dialogue of Pontano, intitled *Aetius.* Although deprived of sight, the talents of Poderico rendered him the delight of all his literary friends.fie Such was the respect paid to his opinion by Sanazzaro, that in the composition of his celebrated poem *(a)* " At tu castaliis non inficiande chords

"Castalidos, Carbo, nunc cane regna tux." *Sanaz. El. lib.* i. *El.* 11.

Et v. Pontoon Hendec. p. 215. *De Sermone, p.* 231. *Eridan. p.* 105. also the beautiful elegy of Pontano, inviting him to a rustic supper. *Eridan.* i. 120, and the sonnet of Cariteo,

"Carbone, in cui scintillan bragie accese." *(b)*" Ma a guisa d'un bel sol, fra tutti radia ,'.. " Carracciol, ch'in sonar sampogne e cetere,

"Non trovarebbe il pari in tutta Arcadia."

But perhaps, some doubt may be entertained, whether this passage may not relate to Gian. Francesco Carraccioli, who lived at this period, and whose poems were printed at Naples, in 1506. *v. Quadrio* ii. 222. „ *(c)* Printed by Roberto de Sarno, at the end of his life of Pontano. *Napoli.* 17)1.

(d) Pontani, de Sermone, lib. iv. *p.* 231.

(e) Pontani, Hendec. lib. .p.206..

Chap, n. poem *De partu Virginis,* which he was twenty years in conv A. D. 1492. pleting, he is said to have consulted him upon every verse, a. *£x. 17.* and frequently to have expressed the same verse in ten different forms, before he could please the ear of this fastidious critic.*(a)* Among the *Tumuli* of Pontano, which his officious kindness frequently devoted to his living friends, is one inscribed to Poderico, from the title to which it appears, that he ranked among the nobility of Naples./

''...Of the district. of Porto were Pietro-Jacopo Gianuario, of whom, an Italian poem, in manuscript, has been preserved, and his son, Alfonso Gianuario, of Portanova.

The only member of the academy from the district of

Porta,

'' *(a)* In one of his poems, of which only a fragment remains, Sanazzaro solicits the favour of his friend.

"Tuque ades, o nostri merces non parva laboris,

"Quem Phoebus mihi, quem doctae, mea turba, puellae

"Conciliant; dumque ipse ratem de litore pello,

"Da vela insinuans, pelagoque excurre patenti

"Pars animae, Puderice, meae." *Sanaz. Op. Ed. Comino,* 91.

And in celebrating the day of his nativity, he has the following passage:

"Adde tuos, Puderice, sales; adde inclyta patris

"Eloquia; adde animo tot bona parta tuo. "

Sanaz. Eleg. lib. ii. *El.* 2.

Which, however, it must be observed, is addressed to Alberico, the son of Francesco, of whom Pontano relates the following anecdote: *De Sermone, lib.* iv. *p.* 231, " Garriebat "quispiam, nostra

in porticu, quem ferre Albericus Pudericus Francisci nostri filius, cum "non posset, nullo dato responso, manu sublata, monuit, nasum ut emungeret; quo esigno "mirificus inter astantes exortus est risus." *(b) Pontani, Tumul.* where he is called " ex nobilitate Neapolitana." *ft) Vita di Sanazzar. da Crespo. Ven.* 1752, *p.* 8, where it appears, that this poem was formerly in the possession of Matteo Egizio, an Italian lawyer.

Porta, if we except Sanazzaro, was Alessandro de' Alessan-CHAR dri, author of the *Geniales Dies,* a work which has been A-, K i4£W. esteemed, and frequently commented on, as one of the A-*m*-17. classical productions of the Latin tongue. He was born of a noble family of Naples, about the year 1461, and in the early part of his life, exercised with reputation, the profession of an advocate, at Naples and at Rome; but his intimacy with the learned men of his time, seduced him from his employment, and led him to the study of polite literature. Besides his principal work, he is said to have been the author of several dissertations on dreams, spectres, and on houses haunted by evil spirits, which are considered as proofs of childish credulity *(a)* but it may be doubted, whether these are any other than his chapters on those subjects in his *Geniales Dies.* Of that collection very different opinions have been entertained, and he has been accused of having stolen even the plan of his work from Aulus Gellius. But what is there peculiar in a plan, which consists only in dividing a certain number of unconnected observations into a certain number of books? In truth, his works prove him to have been a man of extensive reading, great industry, and a considerable share of critical ability, and he was perhaps as little tinctured with superstition, as most of the writers of the age in which he lived.f) i.,

Among those who resided beyond the districts, were Antonio Carbone, lord of Alise; Giovanni Elio, called also

Elio *(a) Tirab. Storia Mia Lett. Ital.* vii. *par* 2. *p.* 240.

(b) The *Geniales Dies* were first published at Naples, in 1522. In the first

chapter of the second book, is an interesting account of the manner in which Sanazzaro was accustomed to entertain his literary friends.

Chap. ii. El0 Marchese *(a)* Ciuniano Majo, the preceptor of Sanaz a. D. 1492. *zzrobj* and who has left a monument of his singular learning, in his treatise *Depriscorumproprietate verborum (c)* Luca Grasso; Giovanni Aniso, whose Latin poems are published under the name of Janus Anysius, and author of a tragedy entitled *Protogonos(d)* the poet Cariteo; Pietro Compare, frequently addressed by Pontano as his associate in the rites of Bacchus and of Venus *(e)* Pietro Summonte, himself an elegant writer, and to whose pious care we are indebted

"Musefilo et Majo, animc argute,

"Ciascune Quintiliano al secol nostro,

"Moderator de l'aspra gioventute." *Contra i malevoH. (c)* First printed at Naples, in 1475, and again in 1480; it was also printed at Treves, 1477 and 1480, and at Venice, 1482.

(d) Jani Anysii variapoemata et Satyra, Neap. 1531, *4to. Ejusdem Anysii Tragedia cuititulus,* Protoconos, *Neap.* 1536. 4fo. Caelio Calcagnini thus adverts to the writings of Aniso,

"Quis non Anysii dulcc carmen, et Musas

"Exosculetur? quae aded dulce dictarnnt 4' Carmen; cui invidere plurimi possint; "Quod aemulari aut alter, aut queat nemo."

Carm. ittustr. Poet. Ital. iii. 68.

(e) Pontan. Hcodec, p. 189, 213. *Epigr.* 233; some of which rival Catullus, both in elegance and indecency. That Piero was distinguished by his own writings, appears from the beautiful and affectionate lines of Sanazzaro, on his death. *Epigr. lib.* ii. 15.

He indebted for the preservation of the works of many of his-CHAP. n. learned friends *(a)* Tomaso Fusco *(b)* Rutilio Zenone *(c)* A. D. 1492. Vol. 1. K Girolamo a.t.i7

He is also enumerated by the poet among his particular friends, and celebrated for his wit and vivacity:. s.

"Nec minus et Musae repetens monimenta jocosae

"Compater, argutos ingerat ore sales."
Sanaz. Eleg. lib. i. *el.* 11.

Pontano dedicated to him a monument in his chapel at Naples, with the following, inscription.

"Petro Compatri, Viro Officiosissimo,
"Pontanus Posuit, Constantem Ob Amicitiam.

(a) For which he is celebrated in the following exquisite verses by Sanazzaro; .
,. "Excitat obstrictas tumulis Summontius umbras; "Impleat ut sanctae munus amicitiae:
"Utque prius vivos, sic et post fata sodales..
"Observat; tristes et sedet ante rogos:
"Nec tantum violas cineri, ac beneolentia ponit
"Serta, sed et lachrymis irrigat ossa piis.
"Parva loquor: cultis reparat monumenta libellis;
"Cum possint longam saxa timere diem.
"At tu, vivaci quae fulcis nomina Kama,
"Poscenti gratas, Musa, repende vices;
"Ut quoniam dulces optat sic vivere amicus, i
"Vivat, et in libris sit sacer ille meis."
Sanaz. Epigr. lib. ii. 9. To Summonte, Cariteo has also addressed the highly commendatory sonnets, beginning,
"Summontio, in dubbio sono ove nascesti." and

"Summontio mio, dal summo Aonio monte." *(I)* To.Tomaso Fusco, Sanazzaro. has addressed his Elegy on the Calends of December, *lib.* iii. *el.* 3..
(. *(c)* " Certent Socraticis Zenonis scripta libellis;
"Cujus apis vernos intulit ore favos."
Sanaz. Eleg. lib., i. 11. CHAP.n. Girolamo Angeriano, whose poems have been published A. D. 1492. with those of Marullus and Johannes Secundus;foJ Antonio *A. Ax. if.* Tebaldeo, an Italian. poet, of considerable eminence, who chiefly resided at Ferrara, and whose writings will occur to our future notice; Girolamo Borgia, a Latin *poetfbJ* and Massimo Corvino, bishop of Massa, who had in his youth distinguished himself by his poetical compositions.*(c)*

Of the Regnicoli were Gabriele Altilio, bishop of Polycastro, author of the celebrated Epithalamium on the marriage of Gian-Galeazzo Sforza with Isabellaof Aragon, and the frequent subject of the panegyric of his contemporaries *(.d)* Antonio

Galateo *(a) Poetce tres ekgantissimi; scilicet, Michael Marullus, Hieronymus Angerianus, et Joannes Secundus.* Paris, 1582. Many of his works are also inserted in the *Carmina illustr. Poet. Italorum,* the merits of which he has himself well appreciated in the following lines, intitled, *UbeUum ad Lectorem. ,*

"Doctrinam si forte cupis, si forte lepores "Pierios, Domini, ne lege scripta mei;
"Dum nimis igne calet, solum describit inertes
"Curas, et quanta est Celia, quantus amor." *Carm. illustr. Ital.* i. 298.
(b) A favourable specimen of his writings is given in the *Carm. illustr. Poet. Ital.* ii. 427. One of the Elegies of Pontano is addressed *Ad Hieronymum Borgium, poet am elegantissimum. Amores, p.* 129, frm which we learn, that the family of Borgia was originally of Spain, and that his ancestors, having visited Italy, on a warlike expedition, had there taken up their abode. *(c)* " Quique velut tenera surgit novus arbore ramus
"*Corvinus,* quavis aure probanda canat. "
San. Eleg. i. 11. *(A)* This Epithalamium is published in. the *Carm. illustr. Poet. Ital.* i. 129. And is also printed, with a few other pieces of the same author, at the close of the works of Sanazzaro, by Comino, *Patau.* 1731, *4io.* where numerous testimonies are collected of the merits of Altilius. Some of these pieces had, however, before been printed with the works of Sanazzaro, Daniel Cereti, and the brothers of the Amalthei, illustrated by the Galateo of Lecce, deservedly held in high estimation in his CHAP-n profession, as a physician, and whose attainments in natural A. D. 1492. and moral philosophy, were much beyond the level of the A. *17'* age in which he lived *(a)* and Giovanni Eliseo, of Anfratta, in Apulia, better known as a Latin poet, by the name of Elysius Calentius.ffy
The associated strangers, whose names

have been preserved to us, were Lodovico Montalto, of Syracuse;*(c)* Pietro Gravina, a canon of Naples, and a Latin poet of the

K 2, first the notes of Peter Vlamingii, *Amst.* 1728, in one vol. 8vo. which may be united with the variorum editions of the classics. The Epithalamium was translated into Italian by Giovanni Battista Garminati, a Venetian nobleman; and published by Comino, in the year 1730, after the death of the translator. *Quadrio* ii. 587.
(a) Galateo is said to have indicated the possibility of the navigation to the East by the Cape of Good Hope, in his treatise *De situ Elementorum,* published in 1501, but written tome years prior to that period. *Tirab.* vi. 1.166. In his moral writings, he combated, with sound reason, the prevailing notions of supernatural agency. *Tirab.* vi. 1. 296. He also illustrated the topography of his native country with accurate maps and descriptions. *Giovio,Iscritt.* 211. Galateo is not only celebrated in the works of the poets of the time, for his great acquirements and amiable qualities, but was himself also a poet of considerable merit.. *(b)* His works were printed at Rome, in 1503, under the title of *Opuscula Elysii CalentH, Poettt darissimi, fyc.* This volume is extremely rare; having, as it is supposed, been suppressed, although sanctioned by a privilege from the court of Rome, *v. de Bure,* 2892. This author has obtained a place among the Unfortunate sons of literature, whom Tollius has enumerated in his Appendix to Valerianus, *p.* 11. It appears, however, that his misfortunes were occasioned by his amorous propensities, which engrossed both his talents and his time. To this the following elegant lines of Angelo Colocci refer.
"Sumpserat *Elysius* calamum scripturus amoris. "Saevitiam, tenuem risk amor calamum:
"Pectus et arrepta transfixit arundine, dicens,
"Judice te, dic, quis fortior est calamus. "
Coloccii vita, a Ubaldino. Rom. 1673.
(e) His praises are warmly celebrated by

Sanazzaro. *Eleg. lib.* ii. *El.* 6.

CHAF"first celebrity; Marc-Antonio Flaminio, of Sicily, a dis-. A. D. 1492. tinguished scholar, but not to be mistaken for the celebrated A. *&t.* 17. Latm poet of the same name, a native of Serravalle; Egidio, afterwards cardinal of ViterbO;f# Bartolommeo Scala, of Florence; Basilio Zanchi, of Bergamo, distinguished by the elegance of his Latin compositions,/ and whose beautiful verses on the death of Sanazzaro were translated into Italian, by the great Torquato Tasso; Jacopo Sadoleti, afterwards secretary to Leo. X. and who, at a more advanced period of life, attained the dignity of the purple; Giovanni Cotta, of Verona, who followed the fortunes of the celebrated Venetian General, Bartolommeo d'Alviano, and whose Latin poems may aspire to rank with those of Navagero, Fracastoro, and Aniso, with whom he lived in habits of friendship;*(t)* Matteo Albino *(f)* Pietro Bembo; Antonio Michele, of Venice; Gidvan-Pietro Valeriano, of Bel luno; *(a)* The Epigrams of Gravina are preferred by Sanazzaro to those of all his contemporaries. His poems were printed at Naples, in 1532, 4to. A few of them are also inserted in the *Carm. iihutr. Poet. Ital.* v. 366. Among the Hendecasyllabi of Pontano is an invitation to Gravina, to partake with him the voluptuous retreat of Baja. *Pont. Op. p.* 20S. *(b)* A disciple of Mariano Genazzano, and said by Giovio to have far excelled his master in learning and eloquence. *Iscritt.* l6l. In his youth he cultivated Italian poetry, and his stanze, intitled *Caccia d'Amore,* evince considerable poetical talents. They have often undergone the press, particularly, with the works of Girolamo Benivieni, *Ven.* 1526. and with sundry poems of Benivieni.and Bojardo. *Ven.* 1537- *(c) life of Lorenzo de' Medici,* ii. 86, 88. *(d)* Published at Rome, 1540, 4to. and again at Basil, 1555, 8vo. *(e)* The poems of Cotta are printed in the scarce volume of the *Carmina* v. *illvstriwn Poetarum, scilicet, Petri £embi, And. Naugerii, Btdth. Castilioni, Joannis Cottce, et M. Ant Flaminu. Ven. Valgrisi,* 1548, 8»o. Some of them also appear in the *Carm.*

illustr. Poet. Ital. iii. 490, and in other collections-. *(f)* " Et qui Pieriis resonat non ultimus antris,

»' *Albinus,* referat principis acta sui." luno *(a)* Nicolas Grudius, of Rohan *(b)* Giacomo Latino, CHAP-n of Flanders; Giovanni Pardo, often celebrated in the writings A. D. 1492. of Sanazzaro and Pontano;*(c)* and Michaele Marullus of A-*17k* Constantinople, who excelled all his countrymen in the elegance of his Latin compositions.

Of this numerous catalogue it is but justice to observe, % that there is scarcely an individual who has not, by the labours of the sword or of the pen, entitled himself to the notice of the biographer, and the approbation of posterity. Nor would it be difficult to make considerable additions tu it, if the foregoing account were not amply sufficient to demonstrate *(a)* Author of the treatise *De Literatorum Infelicitate,* and a distinguished Latin poet, to whose works we shall have occasion to advert.

(b) Probably the father of the poet Joannes Secundus, and his two learned brothers, Nicolas and Hadrian Marius, whose works were published together at Leyden, by Vulcanius, *ap Eh.* l6l2. *(c)* A few scattered productions of Pardo appear in the works of Pontano, and Sanazzaro; which shew that he had imbibed the same elegance of Latin composition that distinguished the other members of the Neapolitan academy. Cariteo denominates him

"Pardo insigne, e chiaro, "Per gemino idioma al mondo altero." *Contra % malnoH. (&)* His works were published at Florence, 1497, under the title of *Hymni et Epigrammata Marulli, Mo.* The commendations bestowed upon him by the younger Beroaldo, are highly honourable both to the Greek and the Italian, whose countrymen were too often jealous of the reputation of the eastern fugitives. "Ille homo transmarinus "nostrates versu provocavit; atque in hoc stadio ita enituit, ut cum quolibet non Suae "modo aetatis vate, sed etiam antiquorum conferri possit. Epigrammata scripsit, quibus "humanos affectus, mores, actionesque, mirè complexus est » executus jucunda lepide, "gravia severe

mcesta flebiliter, taxanda mordaciter, grandia audacter, sententiosa sapi"enter; omniaque haec pari ingenio. Hymnos vero primus apud Romanos, et eo quidem spiritu conscripsit, ut ab ipsis Diis quos celebravit, quodam numine afflatus esse videatur." *Beroald. Ep. ad Herm. BentivoUum. in Op. Codri Urcei. p.* 285.

Chap. n. demonstrate the ardour and success with which polite letters a. D. 1492. were cultivated at Naples, under the princes of the house of *A.jex.* 17. Aragon./ltzJ

State of literature in Fer

Next to the cities of Naples and Florence, perhaps no place in Italy had fairer pretensions to literary eminence than Ferrara. During the whole of the fifteenth century thc family of Este, who had held the sovereignty of that place for many generations, had displayed an invariable attention to the cause of letters, and had rewarded their professors with a munificence that attracted them from all parts of Italy, and rendered Ferrara a flourishing theatre of science, and of arts. At the close of the century that city, with its dependent states of Modena and Reggio, were under the government of Ercole I. whom the favour of the populace had preferred to his nephew Nicolo d'Este, the son of their former sovereign, the celebrated Leonello. The succession to the sceptre of Ferrara, exhibits indeed a striking instance of the disregard which was then paid to the laws generally f *a)* To this enumeration of the Neapolitan poets, at the close of the fifteenth century, I must, however, be allowed to add the name of *FUlenio GaBo,* of Montesano; of whose writings a MS. copy, of this period, is in my possession. Paullo Giovio, who with a laudable curiosity, collected the portraits of many of the eminent men of his own, and preceding times, enumerates at the close of the first book of his *Elogii,* the names of several distinguished persons, of whom he had already obtained portraits, and whose characters he intended for his second book—" che essendo ancora in vita, godono l'eccelsa "gloria de'lor fecondi ingegni." Among these, he enumerates

Ptylandro Gallo, who may, perhaps, be presumed to be the same person who is above, and in his own writings called *Filknio.* With the exception or this doubtful reference, I find no account of this author in any of the records of Italian literature. That he lived towards the close of the fifteenth century, abundantly appears from his writings; which consist of Eclogues, Sonnets, Sestini, and other lyric compositions. His style approaches nearer to that of Sera» fino d'Aquila than any other author. In the Appendix to the present volume, may be found a specimen of his writings, none of which have before been printed, *v.App. No. XIX.* » generally established on that subject, and of the great attention bestowed on personal merit. By Ercole the University of Ferrara was maintained in high respectability; the library of his family was increased; a superb theatre was erected for the representation of dramatic performances, in which the first piece acted was the *Menachmus* of Plautus, which is said to have been translated into Italian for that purpose by the duke himself. When such was the character of the sovereign, we shall not be surprized at the number of learned men who frequented his court, and who dignified his reign by the acknowledged excellence of their productions. Not to dwell on the merits of Ottavio Cleofilo, Luca Riva, Lodovico Bigi, Tribraco Modonese, Lo dovico *(a* We learn from a Latin elegy of Battista Guarino, that the representation of this piece in the year 14-86, attracted the attention, and excited the wonder of all Italy. After describing the splendid preparations made for that purpose by the duke, he adverts to the great concourse of people which it attracted to Ferrara—

"Venit et ad magnos populosa Bononia ludSs, "Et cum finitimis Mantua principibus;

"Euganeis junctae properarunt collibus urbes,

"Quique bibunt lymphas, Arne vadose, tuas;

"Hinc plebs, hinc equites plauserunt, inde senatus,

"Hinc cum Virgineo nupta caterva choro."

Pandolfo Collenucio of Pesaro, who excelled not only as a professor of the civil law, but in other departments of literature, as appears from the correspondence between him and Politiano, *(Pol. Ep. lib.* vii. *Ep.* 32. 35.*J* produced two dramatic pieces for the theatre of Ferrara. The *Anfitrione,* printed at Venice, 1530, and *Joseph,* in 1564. Girolamo Berardo, of Ferrara, the Count Matteo Maria Boiardo, and Battista Guarino, also exerted their talents on this occasion, *v. Tirab. Storia della Let. Ital.* vi. 2. 187.

(b) A contemporary writer assures us, that poets were as plentiful in the city, as frogs in the territory, of Ferrara. „. Nam tot Ferraria vates, . "Quot ranas, tellus Ferrariensis, habet." *Bartol. Pag. Prignani. op. Tirab. Storia della Lett. Ital.* vi. 2. 218. dovico Cairo, and others, who cultivated Latin poetry with various success; the works of the two Strozzi, Tito Vespasiano, the father, and Ercole, the son, are alone sufficient to place Ferrara high in literary rank among the cities of Italy.

These distinguished Latin poets were of the illustrious ThetwoStroai. family of the same name at Florence, from whence Nanna Strozzi, the father of Tito, passed to Ferrara in the military service of Niccolo III. in which he acquired great honour.faj The rank, the talents, and the learning of Tito, rendered him a fit person to negociate the affairs of Ercole, duke of Ferrara, with foreign powers, and he was accordingly employed as his ambassador on several important missions. He also occasionally held some of the first offices in the state; in the execution of which, he appears to have incurred, at times, no small share of popular odium. In the midst, however, of the occupations and storms of his public life, he cultivated his talents for Latin poetry with unremitting attention, and has even endeavoured to render his compositions the vehicle of his justification to posterity. The writings of Tito are distinguished by their i" CHAP. II.

(a) Tit. Veip. Strdizac Epitaph, pro Nanne patre, in op. 145. *(b)* The scholars of the fifteenth century thought it as necessary to have an adversary, on

whom they might lavish their abuse, as a mistress, to whom they might address their amorous effusions. The satirical talents of Tito are directed against some person, whom he denominates Gorellus, and who, if we may credit the poet, "civilibus arm is

"Expulsus patria, jam quattuor exulat annos,

"Damnatiis Romae furti, se carcere fracto

"Eripuisse cruci fertur, Senamque profectus,

«1 Dum their simplicity, and purity of diction, rather than by their Chap. n. strength of sentiment, Or energy of style *.(a)* In some of A D 14yC! his pieces he has celebrated the antiquity of his family, and *k.sx.i.* the opulence and achievements of his ancestors; whilst in others he has taken occasion to acquaint posterity with some particulars of his own life and character. Ercole Strozzi stands yet higher in the annals of literature, than his father. Eminently skilled in the Greek and Latin languages, he had not neglected the cultivation of his own, in which he wrote with distinguished elegance. By his fellow-citizen, Celio Calcagnini, he is celebrated for his integrity, his magnanimity, and his filial piety; and for all those qualities which endear a man to his friends, and to his country. A short time before his death, Tito Strozzi had begun a Latin poem, in praise of Borso d'Este, of which he had completed ten books, and which he requested his son to finish and publish, with a correct edition of his other poems; but Ercole did not survive long enough, either to complete the task imposed upon him, by the publication of his father's writings, or to correct his own; having been assassinated in the year 1508, and in the prime of life, by a nobleman who had unsuccessfully paid his addresses to the lady whom Vol. i. L Ercole

"Dum cauti, atque manu prompti Lenonis, amicam

"Pollicitus maria ac montes, abduccre tentat,

"Turpiter amisit, truncatis naribus, aures."

He afterwards enters into a justification of his public conduct, *v. Serm. ad Bonav. Pis-tophilum. Op.* 142.

(a) We are informed by Tiraboschi, that many unpublished poems of this distinguished scholar remain in the ducal library at Modena " ed alcune assai piii eleganti di H quelle, che han vedute la luce." *Storia della Let. Ital.* vi. *par.* ii. *p.* 209.

(b) Calcagnini, *Oratio tn Funere Herculis Strozce, in fine Strozz. Op. p.* 148. Chap. ii. Ercole had married.*fa)* That task was therefore intrusted a. D. 1492. by Guido and Lorenzo, his surviving brothers, to the celeA. *J£x7.* brated printer, Aldo Manuzio, who in the year 1513, gave these poems to the public in an elegant and correct edition.

In enumerating the learned men, who at this time reBoiardo. sided in the state of Ferrara, it would be unpardonable to omit another accomplished scholar, and celebrated poet, who died in the year 1494, and who will not therefore occur again to our particular notice. The eminent Matteo Maria Boiardo, Count of Scandiano, was born in the territory of Ferrara, about the year 1430, and spent in that city the chief part of his life, honoured with the favour and friendship of Borso, and Ercole d'Este, and frequently intrusted by them, as governor of the subordinate cities in their dominion. Boiardo is principally known by his epic Romance, of *Orlando Innamorato,* of which the yet more celebrated poem of Ariosto, is not only an imitation, but a continuation. Of this work, he did not live to complete the third book, nor is it probable that any part of it had the advantage of his last corrections; yet it is justly regarded as exhibiting, upon the whole, a warmth of imagination, and a vivacity of colouring, which render it highly interesting; *(a)* In one of his elegies, *lib.* i. *p.* 69. he seems not to have been without apprehensions of his untimely fate; after indulging in the idea that his mistress would lament his death, he adds—

"Sed jam summa venit fatis urgentibus hora,
"Ah! nec amica mihi, nec mihi mater adest;

"Altera ut ore legat properae suspiria vitae,
"Altera uti condat lumina, et ossa tegat. "

(b) In particular, he held the chief command for several years at Reggio, where he interesting;/ nor is it perhaps without reason,, that the CHARn simplicity of the original has occasioned it to be preferred A. D. 1492.

to the same work, as altered or reformed by Francesco Berni, A *£t-17'* who has carried the marvellous to such an extreme as to deprive his narrative of all pretensions to even poetic probability, and by his manifest attempts to be always jocular, has too often destroyed the effects of his jocularity./

Less known, but not less valuable, than his epic poem, are the three books of sonnets, and lyric pieces, by Boiardo, collected and published after his death, under the Latin title of *Amores,fcJ* although wholly consisting of Italian

L *2,* poems.

died, on the twentieth day of February, 1494; as appears by a MS. chronicle of his contemporary, Bernardino de' Zambotti, cited by Mazzuchelli.—" A di 20, Febbraro "il Magnifico Conte Matteo Maria Bojardo, Signor di Scandiano, Capitano di Reggio, "e della Cittadella, mod in Reggio, il quale era valente uomo, e dotto in versi, in prosa, "e in rima; faceto, cauto, e sapientissimo; molto diletto al Duca nostro, e a tutta la casa "d'Este." Sec. *Scrittori d' ltd. v.. p.* 1438. *(a)* The *Orlando Innamorato* was first printed in Scandiano, *per Pettegrino Pasquali, ad istanza del Conte Camillo Boiardo,* son of the author, about the year 1495, and afterwards in Venice about the year 1500; which latter de Bure erroneously cites as the first edition, *Bib. Instr. No. 3377.* The labours of Boiardo had terminated at the ninth canto of the third book, from which period, it was continued by Niccolo degli Agostini; and of this joint production, numerous editions have been published. *(b)* Besides the *rifacciamento* of this poem by Berni, of which the best editions are those of Calvo, *Milan,* 1542, and the Giunti, *Venice,* 1545; the poem was corrected and al-

tered by Lodovico Dominichi, and published at Venice, by Girolamo Scotto, in 1545, and several times afterwards. *(c)* Printed at Reggio, *per Maestro Francesco Mazolo,* in 1499, and at Venice, per *Sessa,* in 1501, 4to. "Rarissime sono amendue queste edizioni," says Mazzuchelli. *.p.* 1443.—Besides this volume, Boiardo is the author of *Cinque Capitoli in terza rima sopra il Timore, la Gelosia, la Speranza,l'Amore, edilTrionfo delvano mondo;* which have been frequently printed, with other detached poems by Benivieni and the Cardinal Egidio da Viterbo, of which editions it may be sufficient to cite that of Venice, by *Nkolo tP Aristotele, detto Zoppino,* 1537 CHAP-n-poems. When it is considered, that the greater part of these A. D. 1492. pieccs were written at a time, when the Tuscan poetry was A.iEt. 17. i n its lowest state of debasement, we may justly be surprized at the choice of expression which they frequently display, and the purity of style by which they are almost invariably characterized. At the request of his great patron, Ercole, duke of Ferrara, Boiardo also composed his comedy of *Timone,* founded on one of the dialogues of Lucian./a Nor was Boiardo only one of the most eminent poets, he was also one of the most learned men of his age. From the Greek, he translated into his native tongue, the history of Herodotus, and the *Asinus* of Lucian,/ Of his Latin poetry, many specimens yet remain, and Tiraboschi has mentioned ten eclogues, in that language, inscribed to Ercole I. which are preserved in the ducal library of Modena, and which, as he assures us, are full of grace and elegance.frf/

At this time, the celebrated Ariosto, who was destined Ariosto. to build his immortal work upon the foundation laid by Boiardo, was only eighteen years of age; but even at this *(a)* First printed without note of date, or place, afterwards in Scandiano, 1500, Venice, 1504, &c. "Questa Commedia," says Mazzuchelli, "che £ in terza rima, divisa "in cinque atti, & degna di stima per quanto portava quel secolo; ed ha poi un pregio "distinto, ciod, d'essere considerata la piil antica delle Commedie Italiane, comeche il "Crescimbeni la ponga piuttosto nella specie delle Farse." *Scrittori d'Italia,* v. 1443.

(b) Frequently re-printed after the first edition of Venice, 1533. *(c)* Printed at Venice with the *Proverbj* of Antonio Cornazzano, by *Zoppino,* 1523, 8ro. Several other works of Boiardo are cited by the indefatigable Mazzuchelli, *ui sup. (d) Tirab. Storia della Letter. Ital.* vii. *far* i. 176.. *(e).* His father, Nicolb di Rinaldo Ariosto, was a nobleman of Ferrara. In a pass port this early period, he had exhibited that strong inclination Chap. H. to the cultivation of literature, and particularly of poetry, A. D. 1492. which distinguished him to the close of his days, and the A-*m-1 7*story of *Tkisbe,* as adapted by him to a dramatic form, was represented by himself, with his brothers and sisters, in his father's residence *.(a)* He was first destined to the study of the law; but after five years of irksome and unprofitable labour, he finally quitted that occupation, and applied himself to the cultivation of the Latin language, under the instructions of Gregory of Spoleto./ His predilection for theatrical compositions, which he had further displayed in his two comedies, intitled *La Cassaria,* and *I Suppositi,* both written in prose, whilst he was very young, *(c)* probably recommended him to the notice of Ercole I. whom he accompanied in the year 1491, to Milan, for the the purpose of port granted to him in the year 1471» by Lodovico Gonzaga, Marquis of Mantua, he is honoured with the title of Count, and denominated the friend of the Marquis. *Tirab. Storia della Let. Ital.* vii. *par.* iii. 100. Lodovico was born in the year 1474, at the Castle of Reggio, of which place his father was governor..,'. *(a) Pigna, i Romanzi. p.* 72. *(b)* " Ahi lasso, quando ebbi al Pegaseo melo "L'eti disposta, e che le fresche guancie "Non si vedeano ancor fiorir d'un pelo, "Mio padre mi caccio con spiedi e lancie "Non che con sproni, a volger testi e chiose, E m'occupi) cinque anni in quelle ciancie.'

(c) They were afterwards altered into *versi sdruccioli,* by Ariosto, and have been frequently printed, as well separately, as together with his other works. Chap, a cr enjoying the theatrical amusements, by which that place A.d. 1492. was distinguished. From this time he devoted himself a. iEt. 17. to the service of the family of Este, either in the court of the duke, or in that of the cardinal Ippolito, and will occur to our future notice, not only as a poet, but as engaged in the political transactions of the times. / t.

The city of Ferrara may indeed be considered as the Francesco Cie-cradle of modern epic poetry *(a)* for, besides the two celebrated authors before mentioned, that place might at this time have boasted of a third, whose writings not only obtained for him, during his life time, a great share of celebrity, but have afforded passages which have since been imitated by the immortal *Tasso. (bj* Of their author, Francesco Cieco, very few particulars are known. That he had enjoyed the favour of the Cardinal Ippolito, and was therefore, in all probabiHty, a native of Ferrara, may be inferred from the dedication of his epic poem, of *Mambriano,* published by his surviving relation, Eliseo Conosciuti, in the year 1509.*(c)* This piece, which extends to forty-five cantos, relates the adventures of a king of Asia, whose name *(a)* "In a period of near three thousand years," says Mr. Gibbon, adverting to the works of Ariosto and Tasso, in his Antiquities of the House of Brunswick, " five great "epic poets have arisen in the world; and it is a singular prerogative, that two of the "five should be claimed as their own, by a short age, and a petty state." *(b) Zeno, note al Fontanini,* i. 259. where he conjectures, that this work was written about the time of the descent of Charles VIII. to the conquest of Naples, in 1494-It is intitled *Libro d'arme e d'amore, cognominato Mambriano, di Francesco Cieco da Ferrara. Ferrarice, per Joannem Baciochum Mondeman,* 20 *Octobru,* 1509, 4fo.

(c) " Prego che sotto il suo auspizio, Mambriano del servitore suo venga im-

presso, e "per suo solito benignitade non neghi alla memoria d'esso Francescho quel favore, di che "vivendo lui, quelle tante volte gli fu liberalissimo." name forms the title of the work. That it long maintained Chap, n. its rank with the great contemporary productions of Italy, A. D. 1492. is sufficiently apparent; and the neglect which it has in A--iEt-*l?*later times experienced, is attributed by Zeno, to its not having had the good fortune, like the *Orlando Innamorato* of Boiardo, to meet with any one to continue its subject, or to reform its style...

Few persons enjoyed at this period a higher share of literary reputation, than Nicolo Lelio Cosmico, and few persons have so effectually lost that reputation in the estimation of posterity. He is not even enumerated by the diligent Crescimbeni as one of the poets of Italy; yet three editions of his works were printed in the fifteenth century, (ia and he is the frequent subject of applause among the most distinguished scholars of the *time.(bJ* He was a native of Nico15 *UUo* Padua, and spent some of his early years in the court of the marquis of Mantua; but the chief part of his life was passed in *(a)* Quadrio enumerates only two editions, *Ven.* 1478, and *Vicenza* 1481; but besides these, another edition of the fifteenth century, appears in the catalogue of the Pinelli library. *(b)* Sabellicus, inviting his poetical contemporaries to celebrate the nativity of the Virgin, addresses himself to Cosmico—

"Nec decantati todes remorentur amores
    "Te, mihi sed cultam, Cosmice, tende chelyn."

He is also enumerated by Platina, in his treatise *De honesta voluptate,* or art of Cookery, among his temperate friends. *Lib.* v. *Cap.* i. And Giacomo delle Pellinere, Professor in Medicine and Moral Philosophy at Padua, has apostrophized him in an epistle in terza rima, addressed to Pamfilo Sasso —

"Cosmico, dove sei, col soave archetto?"

Chap, Il m tie society 0f the scholars of Ferrara. His own composia. D. 1492. tions were principally Italian; but he also aspired to the A. iEt. 17. reputation of a Latin poet; and Giraldi, a judicious critic, whilst he censures the arrogant and satirical disposition of the author, acknowledges the merit of his writings. The freedom of his opinions, or of his conduct, incurred the notice of the Inquisition-; but the interference of Lodovico Gonzaga, not only protected him in this emergency, but has conferred an illustrious testimony on the character of a writer, who is now no longer estimated from his own works . *(a)*

The attention paid by the family of Este to the promotion of literature, was emulated by that of the Gonzaghi, marquisses of Mantua, and the Montefeltri, dukes of Urbino. The intercourse which subsisted between these families, and which was founded on an union of political interests, and confirmed by the ties of consanguinity, gave indeed a common character to their courts. Francesco Gonzaga, marquis of Mantua, married Isabella of Este, the daughter of Ercole I. duke of Ferrara; and Elizabetta, the sister of the marquis, became the wife of Guidubaldo da Montefeltri, duke of Urbino.

„JUlI, Federico, the father of Guidubaldo, had rendered his

Guidubaldo da o' »

Montefeltri, name illustrious throughout Italy, not only as a distinguished patron of learning, but by his military and political talents. In the rugged situation in which the city of Urbino is placed, he *(a)* In recommending Cosmico to the favour of his relation, Antonio da Bolza, Lotlovico denominates him " Uomo virtuoso, ed existimato per tutta Italia." *Tirab, Storia delta Let. Ital.* vi. *par.* ii. *p.* 225.

he had erected a palace, which was esteemed one of the Chap. n. finest structures in Italy, and had furnished it in the most A D 149o sumptuous manner, with vases of silver, rich draperies of A. *ft.* 17. gold and silk, and other rare and splendid articles. To these he had added an extensive collection of statues, and busts, in bronze and marble, and of the most excellent pictures of the times; but the pride of his palace, and the envy of

his contemporary princes, was the superb and copious selection of books, in the Greek, Latin, and other languages, with which he had adorned his library, and which he enriched with ornaments of silver, and of gold.*(a)* If, however, the father was an admirer and a protector of literature, the son united to these characters that of a practical and accurate scholar. With the Latin language, we are told, he was as conversant as others are with their native tongue, and so intimate was his knowledge of the Greek, that he was acquainted with its minutest peculiarities, and its most refined elegancies. The love of study did not, however, extinguish in the bosom of Guidubaldo, that thirst for military glory, by which his ancestors had been uniformly characterized; and if his health had not been impaired by the gout, at an early period of life, he would probably have acquired, in the commotions which soon after this period disturbed the repose of Italy, a still higher reputation. In his biographers and panegyrists he has been peculiarly fortunate; the learned Pietro Bembo has devoted a considerable tract to the celebration of his merits, and Baldassare Castiglione, in his admirable *Libro del Cortegiano,* Vol. 1. M has *(a) Castiglione, lib. del Cortegiano, lib.* i. *(b) P. Bcmbi de Guido-Ubaldo Feretrio, deque Elisabetha Gonzaga Urbini ducibus, liber.* First printed at Venice, under the inspection of the author, in 1530.

Chap. n. has honoured his memory with an eulogium, which will A. D. 1492. probably be as durable as the Italian language itself. His

A.iEt. 17. wife, Elizabetta Gonzaga, is not less the subject of admiration and applause to both these authors; the latter of whom has, in the commencement of his work, given a striking picture of the vivacity, the taste, the elegance, the tempered wit, and decorous freedom, by which the court of Urbino was at this period distinguished.// Giovanna, sister of the duke, had intermarried, in the year 1475, with Giovanni della Rovere, one of the nephews of Sixtus IV. and brother of the cardinal Guiliano della Rovere, afterwards Julius II. on which

occasion, Sixtus had invested his nephew with the principality of Sinigaglia, and the beautiful territory of Mondavia. By him she had a son, Francesco Maria, who was educated at the court of Urbino, and succeeded to his maternal uncle Guidubaldo, whom he, however, resembled much more in his military character, than in his literary accomplishments.

Francesco Gonzaga, marquis of Mantua, had succeeded Francesco Gou-hlS father, Federigo, in the year 1484. Notwithstanding Tm m,arquU the many hazardous expeditions in which he was engaged, the numerous battles in which he held a principal command, and the adverse fortune which he on some occasions experienced, he found time to apply himself to the study of polite lcttcrs; and there is reason to believe, that he was the author of many sonnets, capitoli, and other verses, which have been printed in the collections of the ensuing century.

(a) The union of the duke and duchess of Urbino was not crowned with the expected fruits of marriage, the reasons of which are detailed at great length *by* Bembo, *in Op. v. iv.p.* 299. century. His wife, Isabella of Este, was not less distinguished Chap, n. by her elegant accomplishments and refined taste, which A. D. 1492. led her to collect antique statues, cameos, medallions, and a.iEt. 17. other specimens ot art, some of which are celebrated in the verses of the poets of the time, fa,/ Nor was the court *of* Mantua deprived of those honours, which the favour of the muses could alone confer. Among the men of talents, who either adopted that place as their constant residence, or enlivened it by their frequent visits, Giampietro Arrivabene, and Battista Mantuano, are intitled to particular notice. The former of these eminent men, was the scholar of Francesco Filelfo, who has addressed to him several of his letters, and who transformed his Italian name of Arrivabene, into the Greek appellation of *Eulychius.* That he enjoyed the confidential office of Latin secretary to the marquis Francesco, might be thought to confer sufficient honour on his memo-

ry; but he was also a man of blameless manners, uncommon eloquence, and a considerable share of learning. His principal work is his *Gonzagidos,* a Latin poem in four books, in praise of Lodovico, marquis of Mantua, who died in 1478, and not in 1484, as mentioned by Mazzuchelli. From this work,

M 2 which *(a) V. Tirab. Storia dcUa Let. Ital.* vii. *far.* i. 53. Ariosto has devoted several stanzas in his 37th Canto to the celebration of the praises of the marquis, and Isabella of Este, his wife:

"Di lei degno cgli, e degna ella di lui; "meglio s'accoppiaro unq' altri dui." *Stan.* 11.

That the marquis was distinguished by his literary productions may be conjectured from the following lines:

"Da insieme egli materia, ond' altri scriva, "£ fa la gloria altrui scrivendo viva." *Stan.* 10.

CHAP-which is said to be written in a much more elegant style, a. D. 1492. than from his early age might have been expected, it apA. *At. 17.* pears, that the author had been present at many of the victories and transactions which he there relates.*(a)*

Battista Mantuano may be enumerated among those writers Battista Man-wno nave hac tne good fortune to obtain, for a long time, a reputation superior to their merits.*(b)* The applause which his works excited was not confined to Italy, but extended throughout Europe, where, under the name of *Manluanus,* or Mantuan, he was considered as another Virgil, whose writings might stand in competition with those of his immortal countryman. Nor can it be denied, that the productions of Battista evince a facility of conception, and a flow of language, which prove him to have been possessed of considerable talents. But in admitting that the native endowments of Battista might bear some comparison with those of his great predecessor, we are compelled to acknowledge, that he was strangely defective in the method of employing his abilities to the best advantage. Of all authors, there are perhaps few, or none, who have been less satisfied with their own productions,

than the Roman bard.

However *(a)* This poem was first printed by Meuschenius, in the beginning of the third volume of his collection, imilled *Vitce summorum dignitate et eritditione virorum.— Coburg,* 1738. In the preface, the editor observes, that the poem is written " elegan"tiori modo, quam a sua adhuc inculta aetate vix aliquis expectare poterat." *Mazzuchelli, Scrittori d'ltal.* ii. 1138. *Tirab.* vi. 2. 230.

(b) It is generally believed that Battista was of illegitimate birth; but the attention paid by his father, Pietro Spagnuolo, to his improvement, enabled him not only to make an early and considerable proficiency in polite literature, but to arrive at the rank of general of his order. Respecting the circumstances of his birth, different opinions have however been entertained, which the reader will find fully stated in the *Mmagiana, vol.* i. *p. 273.*

However we may estimate the powers of his imagination, Chap, n. or the melody of his verse, his taste was still superior to his A. D. *U9i* other accomplishments; and his efforts were unremitting, a. iEt. *17.* to arive at that standard of perfection, which he had conceived in his own mind.*(a)* It is well known, that after having bestowed the labour of twelve years on his immortal poem, the conviction which he felt of its imperfections determined him, in his last moments, to order it to be committed to the flames; and it was only by a breach of his solemn testamentary injunction, that this work has been preserved for the admiration of posterity. To the conduct of the ancient poet, that of the modern, was an exact reverse; and if they originally started from the same ground, they bent their course in opposite directions. Of the productions of Battista, the earliest are incomparably the best, and as these seem to have gratified his readers, so it is probable they delighted himself. As he advanced in years, he poured out his effusions with increasing facility, until he lost even the power of discriminating the merit of his own productions. From his long poem, *De Calamitatibus tempo-*

rum, the historian might hope to select some passages, which might elucidate his researches; but in this he will be disappointed; the adhe .. rence *(a)* "Amici, familiaresque P. Virgilii, dicere eum solitum ferunt, parere se versus more "atque ritu ursino. Namque, ut illa bestia foetum ederet ineffigiatum informemque, lam"bendoque id postea, quod ita edidisset, conformaret et fmgeret, proinde ingenii quoque "sui partus recentes rudi esse facie et imperfecta: sed deinceps tractando, coleadoque, "reddere iis se oris et vultus lineamenta." *Aul. Gel. lib.* xvii. *cap.* 10.

(b) " Divus Augustus carmina Virgilii cremari contra testamenti ejus verecundiam "vetuit; majusque ita vati testimonium contigit, quam si ipse sua carmina probavisset." *Plin. lib.* vii. *cap.* 30. P. Crinitus, *De Poett's Latinis, lib.* iii. M *op. p.* 447-has cited a beautiful copy of veries addressed to Augustus on this subject. CHAP. IT.

A. D. 1492.

A. iEt. 17.

rence of Battista to the track of the ancients, having prevented him from entering into those particulars, which would have rendered his works interesting; whilst the heavy commentary in which they have been enveloped, by Badius Ascenscius, presents them in so formidable an aspect to the modern reader, as fully to account lor that neglect, which they have for a long time past experienced.

Lodovico Sl'orza encourages men of talents.

Lionardi

Vinci.

The tranquillity which had now for some years reigned in Italy, had introduced into that country an abundance, a luxury, and a refinement, almost unexampled in the annals of mankind. Instead of contending for dominion and power, the sovereigns and native princes of that happy region, attempted to rival each other in taste, in splendor, and in elegant accomplishments; and it was considered as essential to their grandeur, to give their household establishments a literary character. Hence their palaces became a kind of polite academy, in which the nobility of both sexes found a constant exercise for their intellectual talents; and courage, rank, and beauty, did not hesitate to associate with taste, with learning, and with wit. In this respect, the court of Milan was eminently distinguished. By the ostentatious liberality of Lodovico Sforza, who then held, in the name of his nephew Galeazzo, but directed at his own pleasure, the government of that place, several of the most distinguished artists and scholars of the time, were induced to fix their residence there. Among the former of these, the celebrated Lionardo da Vinci deservedly holds the most conspicuous place. This extraordinary man, who united in himself the various qualifications of a painter, a sculptor, a poet, a musician, an architect, and a geometrician, and who in short, left untouched very few of those objects, which have engaged the attention of the human faculties, CHAP-nwas born about the year 1443, at the castle of Vinci in Val-A. D. 1492. darno. After having given striking indications of superior A-£t' 7talents, he for some time availed himself of the instructions of Andrea Verocchio, whom he soon surpassed in such a degree, as to render him dissatisfied with the efforts of his own pencil. His singular productions in eveiy branch of art, had already excited the admiration of all Italy, when he was invited by Lodovico, in the year 1492, to fix his residence at Milan. By his astonishing skill in music, which he performed on a kind of lyre of his own invention, and by his extraordinary facility as an *Improwisalore,* in the recitation of Italian verse, no less than by his professional talents, he secured the favour of his patron, and the applauses of the Milanese court. Lodovico had, however, the judgment to avail himself of the opportunity afforded him by this great artist, to enrich the city of Milan with some of the finest productions of his pencil; and if the abilities of Lionardo were to be estimated by a single effort, his panegyrist might perhaps select his celebrated picture of the last supper, in the refectory of the Dominicans, as the most valuable of his works. In this piece it was doubtless the intention of the painter to surpass whatever had before been executed, and to represent, not merely the external form and features, but the emotions and passions of the mind, from the highest degree of virtue and beneficence in the character of the Saviour, to the extreme of treachery and guilt in that of Iscariot; whilst the various sensations of affection and veneration, of joy, and of sorrow, of hope, and of fear, displayed in the countenances and gestures of the disciples, might express their various apprehensions of the mysterious rite. In the midst sits the great founder, dispensing CHAP-n-dispensing with unshaken firmness, from either hand, the a. D. 14s?, emblems of his own approaching sufferings. The agitation A. iEt. 17. of the disciples is marked by their contrasted attitudes, and various expressions. Treachery and inhumanity seem to be concentered in the form and features of Judas Iscariot. In representing the countenance of Christ, he found, however, the powers of the artist inadequate to the conceptions of his own mind. To step beyond the limits of earth, and to diffuse over these features a ray of divinity, was his bold, but fruitless attempt. The effort was often renewed, and as often terminated in disappointment and humiliation. Despairing of success, he disclosed his anxiety to his friend and associate, Bernardo Zenale, who advised him to desist from all further endeavours; in consequence of which, this great work was suffered to remain imperfect. Nor did Lionardo, in acknowledging with Timanthes, the inefficacy of his skill, imitate that artist in the method which he adopted on that occasion. Agamemnon conceals his face in his robe, and the imagination of the spectator is at liberty to supply the defect; but in marking the head of his principal figure by a simple outline, Lionardo openly avows his inability, and leaves us only to regret, either the pusillanimity of the painter, or the impotence of his art.faj

In *(a) Vasari, in vita at Lionardo. BorgMni, il Riposo.* 368, *Sf seq.* Notwithstanding the assertions of the above authors, and that of M. Mariette in later times, *Lettere sul/a Pittura, SfC. vol.* ii. *let.* 84. that Lionardo left the head of Christ in an unfinished state, Richardson assures us, that their information is false, and that such part of the face as yet remains intire, is highly finished, *Traite de la peinture, fyc. vol.* iii. The account given by Richardson is, in like manner, accused of being grossly incorrect, by the author of a modern description of Italy, in 4 vols. 8vo. *London,* 1781. As it can scarcely be imagined, that any of these authors would be guilty of wilful misrepresentation on a subject of such a nature, and in which their testimony would be always exposed to contradiction, may we

In a mind devoted to ambition, all other passions and CHAP 11 pursuits are only considered as auxiliary to its great object; A. D. 1492. and there is too much reason to suspect, that the apparent A-W. solicitude of Lodovico Sforza for the promotion of letters J" and the arts, was not so much the result of a disposition of MUansincerely interested in their success, as an instrument of his political aggrandizement. That the supplanting the elder branch of his family, and vesting in himself and his descendants, the government of Milan, had long been in his contemplation, cannot be doubted; and it is therefore highly probable that, after ingratiating himself with the populace, and securing the aliance and personal friendship of foreign powers, he would endeavour to strengthen his authority by the favour and support of men of learning, who at this time possessed a more decided influence on the political concerns of the country than at any other period. But by whatever motives Lodovico was actuated, it is allowed, that whilst the state of Milan was under his control, the capital was thronged with celebrated scholars, several of whom adopted it as their permanent residence. On Bernardo Bellincione, a Florentine, he conferred the title of his poet laureat; and in the works of this author, printed at Milan in 1493, are inserted some stanzas which have been attributed to Lodovico himself. Among those who at this period contributed by their talents to give splendor to the court of Milan, were Antonio Vol. 1. N Cornazzano, we not reasonably suppose that, according to the united testimony of all the elder writers, the head was left unfinished; but that in the course of the repairs which the picture has undergone, some sacrilegious hand has dared to trace those features, from which the modest genius of Leonardo shrunk in despair? This suggestion appears highly probable from the notes on the *Lettere sulia Pittura, fyc. vol. ii.p.* 183.

CHAP-n-Cornazzano/a Giovanni Filoteo Achillini/ Gasparo a. D. 1492. Visconti,fcJ Benedetto da CingOli, Vincenzo Calmeta,f/ A. *A.* 17. an(j Antonio Fregoso. Nor were there wanting distin guished *(a)* A native of Piacenza, who, having adopted a military life, held a respectable rank under the celebrated Venetian general Bartolommeo Coglioni, of whom he has left a life, written in Latin, and published by Burman; but a great part of his time was passed at Milan, where he was highly favoured by the family of Sforza. His works, both in Italian and Latin, in verse and in prose, are very numerous, and his poem *De re MUUari,* in nine books, *in terza rima,* has frequently been printed. His sonnets and lyric pieces, are however considered as the most valuable of his works, and are acknowledged by Quadrio to be among the best in the Italian language—" delle migliori che abbia "la volgar poesia."—In the latter part of his life he quitted the court of Milan for that of Ferrara, where he terminated his days; having enjoyed the patronage of the duchess, Lucrezia, of whom he makes frequent and honourable mention in his works. *Cornazzano, de re militari.* Ven. 1526. *Sonetti e Canz. Veil.* 1508. *Tiraboschi i. par. ii. p.* l60. *(b)* Author of an Italian poem *in ottaxa rima,* intitled, *II Viridario,* printed at Bologna, 1513, and of several other works. He also distinguished himself by his knowledge of Greek and Latin, his proficiency in music, and his acquaintance with medals, statues, and other monuments of antiquity, of which he had formed a large collection. He died in 1538, at 72 years of age; but his poet-

ry, of which specimens appear in sundry collections, has all the characteristic rusticity of the 15th century, when, says Crescimbeni, " andb spargendo gemme tra'l fango." *(c)* A nobleman of Milan, who married Cecilia, the daughter of the celebrated Cecco Simoneta, and died at 38 years of age, in 1499. His sonnets and other verses were published at Milan in 1493, and obtained him such reputation, that he was considered, for a time, as not inferior to Petrarca; but posterity has formed a different judgment. *Tirab,* vi.*par. ii. p.* 253. *(d)* Benedetto da Cingoli, and Vincenzo Calmeta, are enumerated by Quadrio, II. 211. among the poets who at this time honoured the city of Milan by their residence, and whose verses are found in the collections of the times. The works of the former were also collected and published with those of his brother, Gabricllo, at Rome, in 1503. *Tirab. i. par. ii. p.* 159 *(e)* Called also *Tulgoso* and *Campqfregoso.* From his love of solitude, he also assumed the name of *PMleremo.* His chief residence was at the court of Milan, which he quitted on the expulsion of Lodovico Sforza, and retired to his villa at Colterano. His *Cerva Bianca,* guished scholars in the graver departments of literature; of CBAP-nwhich number were Bartolomeo Calchi and Giacopo Antiqua-A. D. 1492. rio, celebrated not only for their own acquirements, but for A-iEu *17'* their liberality in promoting the improvement of others; Donato Bossi, commemorated both as an eminent professor of laWj and an industrious historian;*(a)* Dionysius Nestor, whose early labours highly contributed to the improvement of the Latin tongue *(b)* and Pontico Virunio, deservedly

N 2, held *Bianca,* is an Italian poem of considerable extent, written with great facility, and occasionally interspersed with beautiful description, and genuine poetry. For his adoption of the *ottaca rima* he apologizes by the example of Lorenzo de' Medici, and Agnolo Politiano. This poem has been several times re-printed; particularly at Venice, 1521, 1525. The first of these editions is intitled *Opera nova del magnifico Cava-*

liero Messcr Antonio PMlcremo Fregoso, intitulata CervA Biancha. His *Dialogo di Fortuno,* consists of 8 *capitoli, in terza rima,* Ven. 1531. Besides these, he is also the author of another poem, *Jlriso di Democrito, e il pianto a" EracUto,* in 30 *Capitoli;* but this work has hitherto eluded my researches. *(a)* His chronicle of the principal events, from the earliest records to his own times, is of occasional use, particularly with respect to the affairs of Milan. This work was printed at Milan in 1492, by Antonio Zaroti, and is dedicated to the reigning duke Giovan-Galeazzo; not however without great commendations of Lodovico, whose *loyalty* and *fidelity* the author particularly celebrates. *(b)* He was a native of Novara, and a descendant of the noble family of Avvenada, of the order of the Minorites. His vocabulary of the Latin tongue, printed in folio at Milan, in 1483, and afterwards at Venice 1488, may be considered as one of the first attempts in modern times to facilitate the study of that language, and displays an intimate acquaintance with the writings of the ancients, which are diligently cited as authorities throughout the work. To the earliest edition is prefixed a copy of Latin verses addressed to Lodovico Sforza, and towards the close are several poems of the same author, both Italian and Latin. The following colophon concludes the book: *Opus Mediolani impressum per Leonardum Pachel et Ulderiaim Sinczenceler, de Alemannia Socios, Anno Domini* M.cccc.lxxxiii. *pridie nonas Januarias.*

The lines to Lodovico Sforza, which celebrate his importance and recount his exploits, from this rare work, are given in the Appendix, No. XX.

Chap. n. neld in great esteem, both as a scholar and a statesman, and A. D. 1492. who will demand more particular notice in the transactions A.iEt. 17. 0f the succeeding century.

The Bentivogli of Bologna.

From the commencement of the century, the city of Bologna had endeavoured to maintain its independence against the superior power of the dukes of Milan, and the continual pretensions of the pontifical see. The chiefs of the noble family of Bentivoglio were regarded by their fellow citizens as the patrons and assertors of their liberties, and after various struggles, in which they had frequently been expelled from their native place, they concentered in themselves the supreme authority, under limitations which secured to the people the exercise of their ancient rights. This authority had now, for nearly half a century, been conceded to Giovanni Bentivoglio, who was only two years of age when his father Annibale was treacherously murdered by the rival faction of the Canedoli, in the year 1445, and who frequently occurs to notice, both in the political and literary annals of the time. The merit of Giovanni, as a friend and promoter of learning and of art, was however eclipsed by that of his three sons, Hermes, Annibale, and Galeazzo, all of whom are frequently commemorated in the writings of their contemporaries; and particularly in those of Antonio Urceo, usually denominated Codrus Urceus, who by his CodTM utcens. scientific and critical acquirements, deservedly held a high rank among the scholars of Italy.

This author was born at Rubiera, in the year 1446. His appellation of *Codrus* was derived from an incident that occurred to him at the city of Forli, where happening one day to meet with Pino Degli Ordelaffi, then Lord of that place, place, who recommended himself to his favour, " Good Chap. n. "heavens," exclaimed the poet, " the world is in a pretty A. D. 1492. "state when Jupiter recommends himself to Codrus. " Dur-A.JJU17. ing his residence at Forli, where he was intrusted with the education of Sinibaldo, the son of Pino, he met with a disaster which had nearly deprived him of his reason.fa Having incautiously left his study without extinguishing his lamp, his papers took fire, by which many literary productions, which stood high in his own estimation, were destroyed; and particularly a poem entitled *Pastor*. In the first impulse of his passion he vented his rage in the most blasphemous imprecations, and rushing from the city, passed the whole

of the day in a wood in the vicinity, without nutriment. Compelled by hunger to return in the evening, he found the gates closed, and took up his lodging for the night on a dunghill. When he again obtained admission into the city, he shut himself up in the house of an artificer, where for six months he abandoned himself to melancholy and grief. After a residence of about thirteen years at Forli he was invited to Bologna, where he was appointed professor of grammar and eldquence, and where he passed in great credit *(a)* Codrus survived both his patron and his pupil, the latter of whom was deprived of his territories by Girolamo Riario, in the year 1480, after his family had possessed them upwards of 150 years; and has devoted the following epitaph to their memory.

"Tertius armorum pacis quoque gloria Pinus
"Ordelaphus, per quem nomina sanguis habet.
"Hie nati gremioSinibaldi continet ossa;
"Ossa ducem quinto mense sccuta patrcm.
"Jquus uterque fuit princeps tibi, Livia, post quos
"Ordelaphi sceptris mox cecidere suis." CHAK Ir-credit the remainder of his days. Of his extraordinary a. D. 1492. learning it might be considered as a sufficient proof, that PoA.jex. 17. litiano submitted his Greek epigrams, and other writings, to his examination and correction.; but his talents and acquirements more fully appear in his own works, which consist of *Sermones,* or essays; of letters to Politiano, Aldo, and others of his learned friends, and of poems on a great variety of subjects; among which the praises of the family of Bentivoglio form the most conspicuous part. He died in the year 1500. After his death his productions were collected by the younger Filippo Beroaldo, who had lived with him in friendly intimacy, and published at Bologna in the year 12)02, with a preface, in which he highly extols the poetical effusions of his friend. Succeeding critics have however been less indulgent to his fame: Giraldi,

whilst he admits that the writings of Codrus are sufficiently correct, denies to them the charm of poetry, and Tiraboschi is of opinion, that neither his prose nor his verse can be recommended as models of elegance. That the poems of Codrus are not entitled to the highest rank among those of his contemporaries will sufficiently appear from the lines addressed to Galeazzo Bentivoglio, as an acknowledgment for the honour done to the poet in placing his portrait amongst those of the o learned men which Galeazzo had collected. Such a subject was certainly calculated to call forth all his powers, but those efforts which were intended to justify, will perhaps be thought rather to impeach the judgment of his patron .*(a)*

Among the men of talents who at this period contributed *(a)* As the works of Codrus are not of common occurrence, this piece is given in the Appendix, No. XXI.

buted to support the literary character of Italy, it would Chap.ii. be unjust to omit Piero Ricci; or, as he denominated A. D. 1492. himself according to the custom of the times, *Petrus Crini*-A.Jtt.17. *tiis..* This,notice of him is the more necessary, as little is P61"150TM"'"'to be found respecting him in those works of general informationj where he ought to have held a conspicuous rank, and that little is for the most part erroneous.fa He was descended from the noble and opulent Florentine family of the *Ricci,fb)* and had the good fortune when young, to avail himself of the instructions, and to obtain the friendship of Politiano. Hence he was introduced into the family of the Medici, and became an associate in those literary and convivial meetings at the palace of the Medici in Florence, or at their different seats in the country, which he has himself occasionally celebrated in his writings. It is not therefore surprising, that on the death of Lorenzo the Magnificent, he honoured his memory in a Latin ode, which he addressed to Pico of Mirandula; but it. is remarkable, that in this production (if indeed it was written at the time to which it relates) he has predicted in forcible terms the approaching calamities

'(a) The notices of Crinitus by Tiraboschi, founded on the equivocal testimony of Jovius and Negri, are peculiarly brief and unsatisfactory.

(b) Jovius, absurdly enough, informs us, that Piero derived his name from the curled locks of his father, *dolt intorta inanellata capillatura del padre;* but from whatever cause the family appellation might originally arise, it was of much greater antiquity than Jovius supposed. The *Ricci* being called by Negri, *Fanuglia antichissima 8f nobilissima.* The latter author however, with no less absurdity than Jovius, adds, that Crinitus was, on account of his own curled locks *(arriciata bionda sua CapigUera)* called *Pietro di crispa chioma,* which he transformed into the Latin name of *Crinitus.* But it is apparent that this name is only his family appellation latinized. *(c) V. lAfeqf Lor.de' Medici,* ii. 140. *4to. ed.*

Chap, L calamities of Italy,*(a)* After this event, Crinitus still contiA. D. 1492. nued to enjoy at Florence the society of Pico and of Politiano, A.iEt. 17. till the death of these distinguished scholars, which happened within two months of each other, in the year 1494.*fb)* It may serve as an instance of the negligence with which literary memoirs are often written, and of the necessity of a more intimate acquaintance with the general history of the times, to notice some of the errors to which the Life of Crinitus has given rise. By one author we are informed, that after the death of Politiano, Crinitus was intrusted by Lorenzo de' Medici with the instruction of his children, and that this example was followed by the principal nobility of Florence, who rejoiced in having obtained such a successor to so accomplished a preceptor. fcj If this were true, Crinitus would be intitled to our more particular notice, as one of the early instructors of Leo X. but when we recollect, that at the time of the death of Politiano, Lorenzo had been dead upwards of two years, we are compelled to reject this information as wholly groundless. Another author, who was a contemporary with Crinitus, has however

informed us, that at the death of Politiano, Crinitus continued to deliver instructions *(a)* At tu mcesta novis patria lachrymis

Indulge; nec enim cernere adhuc potes Quantum mox miseris civibus imminet Fatorum gravis exitus.

Nania, de obitu Law. Med. Crin. op. p. sZ9. (b) Crinitus has also consecrated a Latin poem to the memory of each of his friends, *in. op. p.* 532, 563.

(c) "Quel gran Mecenati de' virtuosi, Lorenzo de' Medici, non dubitb confidare alla di "lui direzionc nelle lettere i suoi figliuoli, dopo la morte del Poliziano; e fu seguitato il di "lui esempio da tutta la nobile gioventii, clie lo gode successore d'un si valente maestro." *Negri, Scrittori Fiorent. p.* 462. structions to the younger branches of the Medici family, and CHAF-IXothers of the Florentine nobility; fia forgetting that the A. D. 1492Medici were, about the time Of the death of Politiano, ex-A.iSt. 17. pelled from Florence, and became fugitives in different parts of Italy, where they could not avail themselves of the precepts of Crinitus, and where indeed they had other occupations than the studies of literature. It is therefore more probable that Crinitus, after this period, quitted his native place, and took an active part in the commotions which soon afterwards occurred; as he frequently refers in his writings to the labours and misfortunes which he has sustained, arid avows his determination to return to his literary studies.f£j That he passed some part of his time at Naples may be presumed, not only from his intimacy with Bernardo Caraffa, Tomaso Fusco, and other Neapolitan scholars, but from the particular interest which he appears to have taken on behalf of the house of Aragon, and the vehemence with which he inveighs against the French in his writings. In this respect his opinions were directly opposed to those of his friend Marullus, who openly espoused the cause of Charles VIII. It may also be conjectured that he passed a part of his time at Ferrara, where having, by accident, fallen into the Po, and escaped with safety, he addressed an ode of gratitude to the *riv-*

er.(c) We are informed by Negri, that Crinitus died about the close of the fifteenth century, at the age of thirty Vol. 1. o nine *(a)* Morto il Politiano, meritb (Crinito) d'essere in grado di compagno, e di precettore appresso quei giovani *de' Medici* & d'altri nobili, che davano opera alle buone lettere. *Giovio, Iscritt. p.* 106. (b) *De sua quiet e post mult as calamitatcs. Crin. op. p.* 531. (c) *Carmen Charisticon, ad Eridattam Jlvvium, pro recepta salute, cum in cum decidissef. vp. Crin. p.* 543.

Chap. n. nme years .(a) but his writings refer to many events beyond A. D. 1492. that period; and his dedication of his treatise *De Poetis K.xx.17-Latinis,* to Cosmo de' Pazzi, then bishop of Arezzo, and afterwards archbishop of Florence, nephew of Lorenzo the Magnificent, is dated in the year 1505, which period, it is however probable, he did not long survive. We are also informed that his death was occasioned by the irregularity of his conduct and the licentiousness of his friends, one of whom, in the frolics of a convivial entertainment, at the villa of Pietro Martelli, poured over him a vessel of water, with the disgrace of which he was so greatly affected, that he died in a few *dzys.(bj* Not to insist merely on the improbability of such a narrative, a sufficient proof that the life of Crinitus was not terminated by any sudden accident, appears in his beautiful and pathetic Latin ode on his long sickness and approaching death, from which we find, that he had struggled with a tiresome feverish indisposition, which had baffled the skill of his physicians, and in which he resigns himself, to his untimely fate; at the same time asserting his claim to the esteem of posterity from the integrity of his life and conduct.fcj From the same piece we also learn, that he intended to have written a poem on the descent of the French into Italy, but this, with many other works, was left unfinished. After the death of Politiano, Crinitus assisted his friend Alessandro Sarti, in collecting the works of that great scholar, for the edition printed by Aldo Manuzio, in 1498. The principal work of Crinitus, *De Honesta Disci-*

plina, as (a) Negri, Scrittori Fiorent, p. 462.

(b) Negri, ubi. sup. Giovio Iscritt, 106.

(c) This poem of Crinitus is given in the Appendix, No. XXII. as well as his treatise on the Latin poets before-men-CHAP-11 tioned, demonstrates the extent of his learning and the ac-A. D. 1492. curacy of his critical taste,fa,) and in these respects are not A-l7unworthy the disciple of his great preceptor.f His poetry, all of which is in the Latin language, is also entitled to commendation, and will occasionally be adduced in the following pages, as illustrating the public transactions of the times in which he lived. t

It may not be improper to close this general view of the state of literature in Italy, in the year 1492, with some account of a person, whose incalculable services to the cause of sound learning, obtrude themselves upon our notice at every step, and the productions of whose skill are at every moment in the hands of the historian of this period. This can only be referred to the eminent printer Aldo Manuzio, to whom the world is indebted, not only for the works of many of the ancient authors, which he either first discovered, or first published in a correct form, but for those of many of his contemporaries, which without his unparalleled industry would not have been preserved to the present day. At this precise time he was making preparations for his laudable o 2, purpose, (a) He was the first who pointed out the mistake of the learned respecting the supposititious elegies of Cornelius Gallus; a subject which has given rise to great diversity of opinion. r. Menagitmo, tom. i. p. 336.

(b) A few Letters of Crinitus appear in the works of Politiano, Ep. lib. xii. and in those of Giovanni Francesco Pico of Mirandula, p. 839 Andreas Dactius has commemorated him in the following epitaph:...

"Heus audi, properes licet Viator,
"Criniti, tumulo teguntur isto,
' Dilecti cineres sacris camcenis.
"Hoc scires volui. Recede foelix."
CHAP-n-purpose, and had determined to devote his learning, his reA. D. 1492.

sources, his industry, and his life, to the service of literaa.iEt. 17. ture. But before we advert to the measures which he adopted for this great and commendable end, it cannot be thought uninteresting briefly to commemorate the previous events of his life.
r
Aldo Manuzio was born about the year 1447, at Bassiano, Aido Main»io. a viuage within the Roman territory, whence he styles himself Aldus Manutius Bassianus; but more frequently Aldus Romanus.fa) Maittaire justly observes, that it was a fortunate circumstance, that the birth of so skilful an artist should have happened at the very time when the art itself was first meditated. Respecting his education, he has himself informed us, that he lost a great part of his time in acquiring the principles of Latin grammar by the rules of Alessandro de Villadei, the book then commonly used in the schools; but this disadvantage was soon afterwards compensated by the instructions which he obtained, in the Latin tongue, from Casparo Veronese at Rome, and in both Latin and Greek, from Battista Guarino who then resided at Ferrara, at which place (a) In the scarce edition of the Thesaurus Cornucopia, of Varino Camerti, printed by Aldo in 1496, he stiles himself Aldus Manutius Bassimtus Romanus. (b) This grammarian lived in the early part of the thirteenth century. His work is written in barbarous Latin verse, which the pupils were compelled to repeat by memory. Manni has given, from a MS. copy in his own possession, a specimen of this pedantic, hut once celebrated production, which thus commences;::

"Scribere clericulis paro doctrinale novellis
"Pluraque doctorum sociabo scripta meorum,
"Jamque legent pueri pro nugis Maximiani
4' Ouae veteres sociis nolebant pandere caris." &c.
Manni, vita di Aido, p. 7. ed Ven. 1759. place Aldo also took up his abode, (a) Under such tutors the proficiency of such a scholar was rapid, and at an early

age Aldo became himself an instructor, having been entrusted with the education of Alberto Pio, lord of Carpi, who was nearly of his own age.fty With this young nobleman he contracted a friendship which proved throughout his life of the greatest service to him, and which was afterwards manifested by his disciple conceding to him the honourable privilege of using his family name, whence Aldus has often denominated himself Aldus Pius Manutius. CHAP-II. a. D. 1492. a. iEt. 17.

In the year 1482, when the safety of Ferrara was threatened by the formidable attack of the Venetians, Aldo retreated to Mirandola/cj where he contracted a strict intimacy with the celebrated Giovanni Pico. His intercourse with these two men of distinguished rank and learning continued with uninterrupted esteem, and Alberto had expressed an intention of investing him with the government of a part of his territory of Carpi; but this project was relinquished for one which proved more honourable to Aldo, and more useful to mankind. In the friendly interviews which

His acquaintance with Alberto Pio, Lord of Carpi, and Pico ofMirandola.

(a) Aldi Manutii prcef. ad Thcocritum, SfC. Ven. 1495. (b) The subsequent commotions of Italy, in which Alberto acted an important part, have probably deprived the world of the fruits of his literary studies. Such at least, is .the.inference which arises from the following passage, in the dedication to him of the Aldine edition of Lucretius, at the time when he was engaged as the Imperial envoy at the court of Rome: "Deus perdat perniciosa haec bella, quae te perturbant, quae te tamdiu avertunt "a sacris studiis literarum; nec sinunt ut quiete, et, quod semper cupivisti atque optasti, "fruaris otio, ad eas artes, quibus;l puero deditus fuisti, celebrandas; jam aliquem fruc"tum dedisses studiorum tuorum utilem sane et nobis et posteris: qua te privari re, ita "moleste fers, ut nullam aliam ob causam, credendum sit, nuper te Romae tarn gravis ." morbo laborasse, ut de salute tua et timerent boni omnes et angerentur." (c) Aldi Ep.

in Ep. Polit. lib. vii.

Chap. n.

A. D. 1492-

A. At. 17.

which took place among these individuals, the idea was giudually formed of the great undertaking which Aldo was destined to carry into effect, and in which, as it has been with great probability conjectured, he was to have the support and pecuniary assistance of his two illustrious friends.

Motives of Aldo, for undertaking to print and publish the works of the

Of the liberal motives by which Aldo was actuated, he has left to posterity abundant evidence. "The necessity "of Greek literature is now," says he, " universally ac"knowledged, insomuch, that not only our youth endeavour to acquire it, but it is studied even by those advanced in years. We read but of one Cato among the Romans who studied Greek in his old age, but in our times we have many Catos, and the number of our youth, who apply themselves to the study of Greek, is almost as great as of those who study the Latin tongue; so that Greek books, of which there are but few in existence, are now eagerly sought after. But by the assistance of Jesus Christ, I hope ere long to supply this deficiency, although it can only be accomplished by great labour, inconvenience, and loss of time. Those who cultivate letters must be supplied with books necessary for their purpose, and till this supply be obtained I shall not be at *rest."(a)* 11

Establishes his press at Venice, and founds an academy there.

But although the publication of the Greek authors appears to have been his favourite object, and always occupied a great part of his attention, yet he extended his labours to other languages, and to every department of learning. The place *(a) v. Aldi Eput. Aristoteti Organ* 1495, *prcefixam, ct Maittaire. Annul, i. 69.* His magnanimity and public spirit appear also from many other passages in his own writings.

place which he chose for his establishment was Venice, al-CHAP-nready the most distinguished city in Italy for the

attention A. D. 1492. paid to the art, and where it was most probable that he 17. might meet with those materials and assistants which were necessary for his purpose.fa,) In making the preparations requisite for commencing his work he was indefatigable;*(b)* but the more particular object of his wishes was the discovery of some method, by which he might give to his publications a greater degree of correctness than had been attained by any preceding artist. To this end he invited to his assistance a great number of distinguished scholars, whom he prevailed upon by his own influence and that of his friends, or the stipulation of a liberal reward, to take up their residence at Venice. That he might attach them still more to the place and to each other, he proposed the establishment of a literary association, or academy, the chief object of which was to be the correcting the works of the ancient authors, with a view to their publication in as correct a manner as possible. Of this academy Marcus Musurus, Pietro Bembo, Angelo Gabrielli, Andrea Navagero, Daniello Rinieri, Marino Sanuto, Benedetto Ramberti, Battista Egna zio, *(a)* If this city has not produced many authors of the first eminence, it has compensated the world by multiplying and perpetuating the works of others. Yet Venice is not without its panegyrists: thus Battista Mantuanus— "Semper apud Venetos studium sapiential et omnis "In pretio doctiina fuit; superavit Athenas

"Ingeniis, rebus gestis, Lacedemona et Argos." *(b)* Maittaire conjectures, that he was employed in these preparations four or five years; but from the preface of Aldus to the *Thesaurus Cornucopia* of Varino Camerti, printed in 1496, it appears that he had been occupied in this undertaking from the year 1489, "Postquam suscepi hanc duram provinciam (annus enim agitur jam septimus) possem "jurejurando affirmare, tot annos ne horam quidem solidae habuisse quietis." CHAP-zio, and Giambattista Ramusio, were the principal ornaa. D. 1492. ments, and will be entitled to our future notice. For the a. iEt. 17. more effectual establishment of

this institution, it was his earnest wish to have obtained an Imperial diploma; but in this respect he was disappointed; and the Venetian academy, which ought to have been an object of national or universal munificence, was left to depend upon the industry and bounty of a private individual, under whose auspices it subsisted during many years in great credit, and effected, in a very considerable degree, the beneficial purposes which its founder had in view.

Progress and ing.

Such were the motives, and such the preparations for ugicsa tutu success of this great undertaking; but its execution surpassed all the 1.1s midcrtak-expectations that its most sanguine promoters could have formed of it. The first work produced from the Aldine press, was the poem of Hero and Leander, of Musaeus, in the year 1494 *(a)* from which time, for the space of upwards of twenty years, during which Aldo continued his labours, there is scarcely an ancient author, Greek or Latin, of whom he did not give a copious edition, besides publishing a considerable number of books in the Italian tongue. In the acquisition of the most authentic copies of the ancient authors, whether manuscript or printed, he spared neither labour nor expense; and such was the opinion entertained of his talents and assiduity by the celebrated Erasmus, who occasionally assisted him in revising the ancient writers, that he has endeavoured to do justice to his merits, by *(a)* This work is not marked by the date of the year in which it was printed, and Mauni seems to doubt its claim to priority, but Maittaire had before sufficiently shewn that this opinion was well founded. *Annal. typ.* i. 70.

by asserting in his *Adagia,* "that if some tutelary deity had CHAP: "promoted the views of Aldo, the learned world would A. D. 1492. "shortly have been in possession, not only of all'the Greek A, el.i7.' "and Latin authors, but even of the Hebrew and Chaldaic; "insomuch, that nothing could have been wanting, in this "respect, to their wishes. That it was an enterprize of "royal munificence to re-establish polite letters, then al"most extinct; to discover what was hidden; to supply "what was wanting; and to correct what was defective." By the same eminent scholar we are also assured, that whilst Aldo promoted the interests of the learned, the learned gave him in return their best assistance, and that even the Hungarians and the Poles sent their works to his press, and accompanied them by liberal presents. How these great objects could be accomplished by the efforts of an individual, will appear extraordinary; especially when it is considered, that Aldo was a professed teacher of the Greek language in Venice; that he diligently attended the meetings of the academy; that he maintained a frequent correspondence with the learned in all countries; that the prefaces and dedications of the books which he published were often of his own composition; that the works themselves were occasionally illustrated by his criticisms and observations; and that he sometimes printed his own works: an instance of which appears in his Latin grammar, published in the year 1507. The solution of this difficulty, may however, in some degree be obtained, by perusing the inscription placed by Aldo over the door of his study, in which he requests his visitors to dispatch their business with him, as expeditiously as possible, and begone; unless they come, as HerVol. 1. p cules Chap, n. cules came to Atlas, with a view of rendering assistance a. D. 1492. in which case there would be sufficient employment, both for A. iEt. *17.* them, and as many others as might repair thither.

QUISQUIS ES ROCAT TE ALDUS ETIAM ATQUE ETIAM,

UT SIQUID EST QUOD A SE VELIS, PERPAUCIS AGAS,

-DEINDE ACTUTUM ABEAS J NISI, TAMQUAM HERCULES,

DEFESSO ATLANTE, VENERIS SUPPOSITURUS HUMEROS:

SEMPER ENIM ERIT QUOD ET TU AGAS, ET QU0TQU0T

HUC ATTULERINT PEDES.

CHAP. Ill 1492—1494. 'THE cardinal de Medici returns to Florence—Death of Innocent VIII.—Election of Alexander

VI.—Ambitious views of Lodovico Sforza—Invites Charles VIII. into Italy—League between the pope, the duke of Milan, and the Venetians— Observations on the respective claims of the houses of Anjou and Aragon— Charles accommodates his differences with other slates—Negotiates with the Florentines—Alexander VI. remonstrates with him on his attempt—The king of JVaples endeavours to prevail on him to relinquish his expedition—Prepares for his defence—Alfonso II. succeeds to the crown of JVaples —Prepares for war—Views and conduct of the smaller states of Italy—Charles VIII. engages Italian stipendiaries—Unsuccessful attempt of the JVeapolitans against Genoa—Ferdinand duke of Calabria, opposes the French in Romagna—Charles crosses the Alps—His interview with Gian-Galeazzo, duke of Milan—Hesitates respecting the prosecution of his enterprize— Piero de Medici surrenders to Charles VIII. the fortresses of Tuscany—The cardinal de' Medici with his brothers Piero and Giuliano expelled the city—Pisa asserts its liberties—Hetreat of the duke of Calabria before d'Aubigny—Charles VIII. enters Florence—Intends to restore Piero de Medici—Commo lions in Florence and treaty with Charles VIII. —Charles enters the territories of the church—The states of Italy exhorted by a contemporary writer to oppose the progress of the French.

Scarcely had the cardinal de' Medici gone through the Chap. m. ceremonies of his admission into the consistory, than he A D 1492 received intelligence of the death of his father, which hap-A. *Jex.* 17. pened on the eighth day of April, 1492-His sensations on eMcl this occasion are strongly expressed in his letters to his bro-returns to ther Piero; *fa)* but not satisfied with epistolary condolence Florence and *(a) v. Life of Lor. de' Med.* ii. 247. *Appendix, No Ixxx.* Another letter written soon after this event, and hitherto unpublished, is given in the Appendix to this vol. No. XXIII.

Chap, in. ancl advice, he prepared to pay a visit to Florence, for A. D. 1492.

the purpose of supporting, by his presence, the credit and a. iEt. 17-authority of the Medici in that city. In order to give him additional importance on this occasion, the pope appointed him legate of the patrimony of St. Peter, and of the Tuscan *state.fa)* Before his arrival, the magistrates and council had, however, passed a decree, by which they had continued to Piero all the honours which his late father had enjoyed. The general disposition of the inhabitants was indeed so highly favourable to the Medici, that the authority of Piero seemed to be established on as sure a foundation as that of any of his ancestors, with the additional stability which length of time always gives to public opinion.

During the residence of the cardinal at Florence, he distinguishcd himself amongst his fellow-citizens, not only by the decorum and gravity of his conduct as an ecclesiastic, but by his munificence to those numerous and eminent scholars, whom the death of his father had deprived of their chief protector. To his favour Marsilius Ficinus was indebted for the respectable rank of a canon of Florence; and his liberality was yet more particularly shewn to Demetrius Chalcondyles, from whom he had formerly received instruction, and to whom he afforded pecuniary assistance, not only for his own purposes, but for the promotion of his numerous offspring. In these, and similar instances, his conduct corresponded with the sentiments professed by him, in the assertion which he made, that the greatest alleviation, which he could experience of his recent loss, would be to have it in his power, to promote the interest of those *(a) Fabronii, vita Leon.* x. *p.* 13. *adnot.* 10. *-rfppeiulix No. XXIV.* those men of learning, who had been the peculiar objects of the affection and regard of his father. *fa)* In the mean time the health of the pope was rapidly declining, and the cardinal received information, which induced him to hasten with all possible expedition towards Rome. On this occasion the magistrates of Florence directed their general, Paolo Orsino, to accompany him to that city, with a body of horse; but before his arrival there, he received intelligence of the death of the pontiff, which happened on the twenty-fifth day of July, 1492.

If the character of Innocent were to be impartially weighed, the balance would incline, but with no very rapid motion, to the favourable side. His native disposition seems to have been mild and placable; but the disputed claims of the Roman see, which he conceived it to be his duty to enforce, led him into embarrassments, from which he was with difficulty extricated, and which, without increasing his reputation, destroyed his repose. He had some pretensions to munificence, and may be ranked with those pontiffs to whom Rome is indebted for her more modern ornaments. One of the faults with which he stands charged, is his unjust distribution of the treasures of the church among the children who had been born to him during his secular k(b).. but (a) Fabronii, VitaLeon. x. p. 14.

(bj These children were illegitimate, as appears from the evidence of Burchard, who denominates Francesco Cibb—" Filius Papae, etium bastardus, prout Domina Theodorifia.'' Burcard. Diar. ap. Notices des MSS. du Roi. i. 93. Nor was incontinency the only crime of this pontiff, if we may judge from the epigram of Marulhis.

"Spurcities, gula, avaritia, atque ignavia deses,

"Hoc, Octave, jacent quo tegeris, tumulo."

Chap. nr. but everl in this respect his bounty was restrained within mO A. D. 1492. derate limits. Instead of raising his eldest son, Francesco Cibdi A. Mx. 17. to an invidious equality with the hereditary princes of Italy, he conferred on him the more substantial, and less dangerous benefits of great private wealth; and although to these he had added the small domains of Anguillara and Cervetri, yet Francesco, soon after the death of his father, divested himself of these possessions, for an equivalent in money, and took up his abode at Florence, among the kinsmen of his wife, Maddalena de' Medici.

On the death of the pope, his body was carried to the church of St. Peter,

attended by the cardinal de' Medici, and four others of equal rank. His obsequies were performed on the fifth day of August, and on the following day the cardinals entered the conclave, amidst the tumults of the people, who, as usual on such occasions, abandoned themselves to every species of outrage and licentiousness/a/ The chief contest appeared to subsist between Ascanio Sforza, whose superior rank and powerful family-connexions gave him great credit, and Roderigo Borgia, Who counterbalanced the influence Of his opponent, by his long experience, deep dissimulation, and the riches amassed from the many lucrative offices which he had enjoyed. With such art did he employ these advantages, that Ascanio him self, seduced by the blandishments and promises of Roderigo, not only relinquished his own pretensions, but became the (a) Per Roma scorrevano a schiera i ladroni, gli omicidarii, i banditi, ed ogni pessima sorte d'uomini; ed i palazzi de' cardinali havevano le guardie di schioppettieri, e delle bombarde, perchS non fossero saccheggiate. Conclavi dc' Pontef. Rom. v. i. p. 133. the most earnest advocate for the success of his late oppo-Chap, Hi. nent. So openly was this scandalous traffic carried on, that A. D. 1492. Roderigo sent four mules, laden with silver to Ascanio, a.iEt. 17. and presented to another cardinal a sum of five thousand gold crowns, as an earnest of what he was afterwards to rectWe.fa) On this occasion, the cardinal de' Medici had attached himself to the cardinals Francesco Piccolomini, (afterwards Pius III.) and Oliviero Caraffa, men of great integrity and respectability, but who were induced to relax in their opposition to the election of Roderigo, by the exertions of Ascanio Sforza, Of twenty cardinals who entered the conclave, we are informed there were only five who did not sell their votes.fo)

On the eleventh day of August, 1492, Roderigo, having assumed the name of Alexander VI. made his entrance, as supreme Pontiff, into the church of St. Peter. The ceremonies vi. and processions on this occasion exceeded in

pomp and expense all that modern Rome had before witnessed; and whilst the new pontiff passed through the triumphal arches erected to his honour, he might have read the inscriptions which augured the return of the golden age, and hailed him as a conqueror and a god.(d) These pageants being terminated, Alexander underwent the final test of his qualifications,

Vol. 1. Q which

Election of

Alexander

(a) Burchard Diar. ap. Notices des MSS. du Roi. i. 101.

(bj Jovius, in vita Leon. x. p. 15. fcj BurcA. Diar. ap. Not. da MSS. du Roi. i. 101. fdj Of these, the following may serve as a sufficient specimen.

"Caesare magna fuit, nunc Roma est maxima, Sextus

"Regnat Alexander; ille vir, iste deus."

"Alexandro

Chap. in. which, in his particular instance, might well have been disa. D. 1492. pensed with,faj and being then admitted into the plenitude a.iEt. 17. 0f power, he bestowed his pontifical benediction on the people. "He entered on his office," says a contemporary historian, " with the meekness of an ox, but he adminis"tered it with the fierceness of a lion."(b)

The intelligence of this event being dispersed through Italy, where the character of Roderigo Borgia was well known, a general dissatisfaction took place, and Ferdinand of Naples, who in his reputation for sagacity stood the highest among the sovereigns of Europe, is said to have declared to his queen with tears, from which feminine expression of his feelings he was wont to abstain even on the death of his children,

"Alexandre) invictissimo, Alexandre pianissimo, Alexandre magnificentissimo, "Alexandre in omnibus maximo, honor et gratia."

"Scit venisse suum, patria grata, Jovem."

Other instances of preposterous adulation may be found in Corio, Storia di Milano, par. vii. p. 888. fyc. If, however, all the enormities recorded of him be true, one of the Roman poets of antiquity would have furnished him with a much more appropriate motto.—

"Attulerat secum liquidi quoque monstra veneni,

"Oris Cerberei spumas, et virus Echidnae,

"Erroresque vagos, caecaeque oblivia mentis,

"Et scelus, et lachrymas, rabiemque, et caedis amorem,

"Omnia trita simul."— *Ovid. Met. lib.* iv. *v.* 499.

(a) " Finalmente, essendo fornite le solite solenniti *in Sancta Sanctorum,* e domesti"camente *toccatogli i testicoli,* e data la benedizione, ritornb al palagio." *Corio, Storio di Milano, par.* vii. *p.* 890. Respecting the origin of this custom *v. Shepherd's Life of Poggio BraccioUni, p.* 149. *Note(b). f.b)* " Entrb nel Pontificato Alessandro vi. mansueto come bue, e l'ha amministrato "come leone. " *Corio, ut sup. p.* 890. children, that the election of this pontiff would be destruc-CHAP-m tive to the repose, not only of Italy, but of the whole re-A. D. 1492. public of Christendom: "a prognostic," says Guicciardini, a.JSuif. "not unworthy of the prudence of Ferdinand; for in Alex

"ander VI. were united a singular degree of prudence and

"sagacity, a sound understanding, a wonderful power of per

"suasion, and an incredible perseverance, vigilance, and

"dexterity in whatever he undertook. But these good qua

"lities were more than counterbalanced by his vices. In his

"manners he was most shameless; wholly divested of sin

"cerity, of decency, and of truth; without fidelity, without

"religion; in his avarice immoderate; in his ambition in

"satiable; in his cruelty more than barbarous; with a most

"ardent desire of exalting his numerous children, by what

"ever means it might be accomplished; some of whom (that

"depraved instruments might not be wanting for depraved

"purposes) were not less detestable than their father."

Such, in the opinion of this eminent historian, was the man, whom the sacred college had chosen to be the supreme head of the christian church.

The elevation of Alexander VI. was the signal of flight to such of the cardinals as had opposed his election. Giuliano della Rovere, who to a martial spirit united a personal hatred of Alexander, insomuch, that in one of their quarrels, the dispute had terminated with blows, thought it prudent to consult his safety by retiring to Ostia, of which place he was bishop. Here he fortified himself as for a siege, alledging, that he could not trust *the traitor,,* by which appellation he had been accustomed to distinguish his ancient adversary.

Q 2 The *(a) Guicciardin. Storia d' Ital. lib. i.* ....j.u *(b) Muratori Annttli d' Italia, v.* ix. *p.-566.'* views of Lodovico Sfcrra.

Chap, in. *The* cardinal, Giovanni Colonna, sought a refuge in the island A. D. 1492. of Sicily; and the cardinal de' Medici, equally inimical, but A.*£t.* 17. less obnoxious to Alexander, retired to Florence; where he remained till the approaching calamities of his family compelled him to seek a shelter elsewhere/aj

No sooner was the new pontiff firmly seated in the chair Ambitious of St. Peter, than those jealousies, intrigues, and disputes, among the potentates of Italy, which had for some time past almost ceased to agitate that country, began again to revive, and prepared the way, not only to a long series of bloodshed and misery, but to events which overturned in a great degree the political fabric of Italy, and materially affected the rest of Europe. During the minority of his nephew, Gian-Galeazzo, Lodovico Sforza had possessed the intire direction of the government of Milan, as guardian and representative of the young prince./ Gratified by the exercise of the supreme authority, he looked forwards with vexation and with dread, to the time when he was to relinquish his trust into the hands of his rightful sover-

eign; and having at length silenced the voice of conscience, and extinguished the sense of duty, he began to adopt such measures as he thought most likely to deprive his nephew of his dominions, and vest the sovereignty in himself. For this purpose he intrusted the command of the fortresses and strong *(t) Ammirato,. Rifratti d'uomini Ulnstri di Casa Medici. Opiuc. vol.* iii. *p.* 64. *(b)* From the ancient chronicle of Donato Bossi, printed at Milan, 1 4 2, it appears, that the Milanese government at this time included the cities and districts of Milan, Cremona, Parma, Pavia, Como, Lodi, Piacenza, Novara, Alessandria, Tortona, Bobbio. Savona, Albingauo, Viatiiuiglia, and the whole" territory of the Genoese. strong holds of the country to such persons only, as hc knew Chap, *m* were devoted to his interests. The revenue of the state, A. D. 1492. which was then very considerable/aj became in his hands a. J. 17. the means of corrupting the soldiery and their leaders. All honours, offices, and favours, depended upon his will; and so completely had he at length concentrated in himself the power and resources of the state, that, if we may give credit to an historian of those times, the young duke and his consort Isabella, the daughter of Alfonso, duke of Calabria, were nearly deprived of the common necessaries of life.*(b* With all these precautions the authority of Lodovico was yet insecure, and the final success of his purpose doubtful. The hereditary right of Gian-Galeazzo to his dominions, was unimpeachable, and he was now of age to take upon himself the supreme authority. His wife Isabella of Aragon, was a woman of a firm and independent spirit, and by her he had already *(a)* Corio states the ducal revenue at this period, at 600,000 ducats. *Storia di Milano. lib.* vii. *p.* 883. *(bj* " Ed in tal forma fu ristretta la corte Ducale, che a fatica Giovanni Galeazzo, ed "Isabella sua moglie, potevano havere il vitto loro." *Corio, Storia di Milano, bb.* vii. *f.* 583. *(c)* It appears, however, from Summonte, that Lodovico had pretended a legal right to the sovereignty, on the plea, that Galeazzo, the father of the young dufce, was bor n before the time that his father Francesco had obtained the dominion of Milan; whereas Lodovico Was the eldest son born after that acquisition, and consequently, as he asserted, entitled to the succession. *Swnmonte, Storia di Napoli, v.* iii. *p.* 497. It is however remarkable, that Donato Bossi, in his chronicle, printed in 1 492,. and dedicated to, GianGaleazzo, expressly commends the fidelity and loyalty of Lodovico to his sovereign. — "Opus autem ipsum annalium, circa quod jam ultra tria lustra versatus sum, tibi Joanni "Galeazio Sfortiae, Vicecomiti, penes quem, hommum divorumque consensus, justissimi"que principis patrui tui Ludovici fides et probitas, Mediolanensis principals, reliquaM rumque excelsarum urbium, regimen esse voluit, dedico et dono." '....

Chap, in. already several children. Under these circumstances it A D. 1492. was scarcely to be supposed, that Lodovico could divest his *A.xx. 7.* nephew of the government without incurring the resentment of the princes of the house of Aragon, who might probably also excite the other states of Italy to avenge the cause of an injured sovereign. That these apprehensions were not without foundation, he had already received a decisive proof. The degraded state to which Isabella and her husband were reduced, had compelled her to represent by letter to her father Alfonso, their dangers and their sufferings, in consequence of which, a formal embassy had been dispatched from the king of Naples to Lodovico, to prevail upon him to relin quish the supreme authority into the hands of his lawful *r'mct.(b)* This measure, instead of answering the intended purpose, served only to demonstrate to Lodovico the dangers which he had to apprehend, and the necessity of forming such alliances as might enable him to repel any hostile attempt.

In turning his eye for this purpose towards the other states of Italy, there was no place which he regarded with more anxiety than the city of Florence; not only on account of the situation of its territory, which might open the way

to a direct attack upon him, but from the suspicions which he already entertained, that Piero de' Medici had been induced to unite liis interests with those of the family of Aragon, in preference *(a)* " La dicte fille," says Commines, speaking of Isabella, "estoit fort courageuse, "et eust volontiers donne" credit a son mari, si elle eust Pu! mais n'estoit gueres

"sage, et rfiveloit ce qu'elle lui disoit" *Mem. de Com. lie.* vii. *p.* 188. *ed. Lyons* 1559.

. *(b) Corio, Storia di Milan, lib.* vii. *p.* 883. where the letter from Isabella to her father is given. ference to the house of Sforza; a suspicion not indeed without foundation, and which some circumstances that occurred A. D. 149?. at this period amply confirmed. a. Ja. 17.

On the elevation of Alexander VI. it had been determined to dispatch an embassy from Florence to congratulate the new pontiff. As a similar mark of respect to the pope was adopted by all the states of Italy, it was proposed by Lodovico Sforza, that in order to demonstrate the intimate union and friendship which then subsisted among them, the different ambassadors should all make their public entry into Rome, and pay their adoration to the pope on the same day. This proposition was universally agreed to; but Piero de' Medici, who had been nominated as one of the Florentine envoys, proud of his superior rank, which he conceived would be degraded by his appearing amidst an assembly of delegates, and perhaps desirous of displaying in the eyes of the Roman people an extraordinary degree of splendor, for which he had made great preparations, felt a repugnance to comply with the general determination. Unwilling, however, to oppose the project openly, he applied to the king of Naples, requesting him, if possible, to prevent its execution, by alledging that it would rather tend to disturb than to confirm the repose of Italy, and to introduce disputes respecting precedency which might eventually excite jealousy and resentment. The means by which this opposition was effected, could not however be

concealed from the vigilance of Lodovico, to whom it seemed to impute some degree of blame, in having originally proposed the measure; while it served to convince him, that a secret intercourse subsisted between Ferdinand and Piero de' Medici, which might prove highly dangerous to his designs.

This CHAP. III.

A. D. 1492.

A.Mt. 17.

This event was shortly afterwards followed by another, more clearly evincing this connexion. It had long been the policy of the Neapolitan sovereigns, always fearful of the pretensions of the holy see, to maintain a powerful interest among the Roman nobility. On the death of Innocent VIII. his son, Francesco Cibo, preferring the life of a Florentine citizen, with competence and security, to that of a petty sovereign, without a sufficient force to defend his possessions, sold the states of Anguillara and Cervetri, to Virginio Orsino, a near relation of Piero de' Medici, and an avowed partisan of Ferdinand of Naples, at whose instance the negotiation was concluded, and who furnished Virginio with the money necessary to effect the purchase. As this measure was adopted without the concurrence of the pope, and evidently tended to diminish his authority, even in the papal state, he not only poured forth the bitterest invectives against all those who had been privy to the transaction, but pretended, that by such alienation, the possessions of Francesco had devolved to the holy *see.fa)* Nor was Lodovico Sforza less irritated than the pope, by this open avowal of confidence between Piero de' Medici and the king of Naples, although he concealed the real motives of his disapprobation, under the plausible pretext, that such an alliance formed too preponderating a power for the safety of the rest of Italy.

In endeavouring to secure himself from the perils which Lodovico Sforza he saw, or imagined, in this alliance, Lodovico was induced,tviTchlrils Dy ms rest-less genius, to adopt the desperate remedy of vm. into inviting Charles VIII. of France, to make a descent upon

Ilay Italy, for the purpose of inforcing his claim, as representative *(a) Gukciardin. Storia a" Italia, lib.* i.

tative of the house of Anjou, to the sovereignty of Naples; Chap-hi. an attempt, which Lodovico conjectured, would, if crowned A. D. U93. with success, for ever secure him from those apprehensions, A..tt. is. of which he could not divest himself, whilst the family of Aragon continued to occupy the throne of their ancestors.

League between the

With this view, Lodovico, in the early part of the year 1493, dispatched the count di Belgioioso, as his confidential envoy to France; but as the interference of the French Pope, the , 1 1 t 1 1 r duke of Mi monarch was regarded by him only as a resource in case of, andtlie necessity, he did not neglect any opportunity of attaching Venetians, to his interests the different sovereigns of Italy. His endeavours were more particularly exerted to effect a closer union with the pope, who, besides the public cause of offence which he had received from the king of Naples, was yet more strongly actuated by the feelings of wounded pride, and of personal resentment. From the time of his elevation to the pontificate, the aggrandizement of his family became the leading motive of his conduct; and very soon afterwards, he had ventured to propose a treaty of marriage between his youngest son, Geoffroi, and Sancia of Aragon, a natural daughter of Alfonso, duke of Calabria, with whom he expected his son would obtain a rich territory in the kingdom of Naples. Alfonso, who abhorred the pontiff, and whose pride was probably wounded by the proposal of such an alliance, found means to raise such obstacles against it, as wholly frustrated the views of the pope. The common causes of resentment which Lodovico Sforza and the pontiff entertained against the family of Aragon, were mutually communicated to each other, by means of the cardinal Ascanio Sforza, who had been promoted by Alexander to the important office of vice-chancellor of the holy Vol. 1. R see;

Chap. Hi. see. anti on the twenty-first

day of April, *1493,fa)* a league A. D. 14y3. was concluded between the pope, the duke of Milan, and

A. *Mx.* is. the Venetians, the latter of whom had been induced by the solicitations of Lodovico Sforza, to concur in this measure. By this treaty, which gave a new aspect to the affairs of Italy, the parties engaged for the joint defence of their dominions. The pope was also to have the assistance of his colleagues in obtaining possession of the territories and fortresses occupied by Virginio Orsino. But although the formalities were expedited in the name of Gian-Galeazzo, the rightful sovereign of Milan, yet an article was introduced for maintaining the authority of Lodovico as chief director of the state.-i.'. -.

As these proceedings could be regarded by the family of Aragon, in no other light than as preliminaries to direct The Florentines hostilities, they excited great apprehensions in the mind of and the king dittand, who was well aware how little cause he had to of Naples unite their rely on the assistance of his nobility and powerful feudatories, in resisting any hostile attack. The direct consequences of this league were, however, such as to induce a closer union between the family of Aragon and the state of Florence; in consequence of which, Piero de' Medici, as the chief of that republic, no longer hesitated to avow his connexions with Ferdinand. In the first impulse of resentment, it was proposed between Piero, and Alfonso, duke of Calabria, that they should join with Prospero and Fabrizio Colonna, in a design formed by the cardinal Giuliano della Rovere, the avowed adversary of Alexander, for attacking '.':»:.'. '.' the interests.

the city of Rome; an enterprise to which the sanction of the fJHAP n1, Orsini, with whom Piefo de' Medici possessed great in-A. n. 1493. fluence, would, in all probability, have given decisive sue-A.iEt. is. cess. In this daring attempt, Ferdinand, however, refused to concur; judging it expedient rather to sooth the resentment, and perhaps, in some degree, to gratify the wishes of his adversaries, than to involve himself in, a con-

test, the result of which he could not contemplate without the most alarming apprehensions. On this account he.not only determined to withdraw his opposition to the pope, respecting the possessions of Virginio Orsino, but found means to, renew the treaty for an alliance between his own family and that of the pontiff. To these propositions Alexander listened with eagerness, and the marriage, between Geoffroi Borgia and Sancia of Aragon, was finally agreed upon; although, on account of the youth of the parties, a subsequent period was appointed for its consummation./

No sooner was the intelligence of this new alliance, and the defection of the pope, communicated to Lodovico Sforza, than his fears, for the continuance of his usurped authority, con(iue,t increased to the most alarming degree, and he determined to f hasten, as much as possible, the negotiation, in which he was already engaged, for inducing Charles VIII. to attempt the conquest of Naples. This young monarch, the only son of Louis XI. had succeeded, on the death of his father in 1483, to the crown of France, when only twelve years of age. Although destined to the accomplishment of great undertakings, he did not derive from nature the characteristics of a hero, either in the endowments of his body, or in the quali

R *2* ties

Charles resolves to undertake *(a)* This treaty was concluded on the 12th day of June, 1493. *Murat. An* ix. 569.

Chap. in. ties 0f nis mind. His stature was low, his person ill-proA. D. 1493. portioned, his countenance pallid, his head large, his limbs A.iEt. is. slender, and his feet of so uncommon a breadth, that it was asserted he had more than the usual number of toes. His constitution was so infirm, as to render him, in the general opinion, wholly unfit for hardships and military fatigues. His mind was as weak as his body; he had been educated in ignorance, debarred from the commerce of mankind, and on some occasions he manifested a degree of pusillanimity which almost exceeds *belief.fa)* With all these defects, both natural and acquired, Charles was not destitute of ambition; but it was the ambition of an impotent mind, which, dazzled by the splendor of its object, sees neither the dangers that attend its acquisition, nor the consequences of its attainment. On a character so constituted, the artful representations of Lodovico Sforza, were well calculated to produce their full effect; but as the prospect of success opened upon Charles, his views became more enlarged, till at length he began to consider the acquisition of Naples, as only an intermediate step to the overthrow of the Turks, and the restoration in his own person, of the high dignity of emperor of the east. This idea, which acted at the same time on the pride and on the superstition of the king, Lodovico encouraged to the utmost of his power. In order to give greater importance *(a)* Commines gives us to understand, that Charles was not displeased at the death of his son, at three years of age, because he was, " bel enfant, audacieux en parole, & ne "craignoit point les choses que les autres en fans sont accoutum6s a craindre," and the king it seems was therefore afraid, that if the child lived, he might diminish his consequence, or endanger his authority; " car le roi ne fut jamais que petit homme de corps, "et pcu etendu; mais etoit si bon, qu'il n'est pas possible de voir meilleure creature." *Mem. de Com. lib.* viii. *p.* 248.

portance to his solicitations, he dispatched to Paris a splendid CHAF-membassy of the chief nobility of Milan, at the head of which A. D. 1493 he placed his former envoy, the Count di Belgioioso. With A.iei. 18 great assiduity and personal address, this nobleman instigated the king to this important enterprize, assuring him of the prompt and effectual aid of Lodovico Sforza, and the favour or neutrality of the other states of Italy; and representing to him the inefficient resources of Ferdinand of Naples, and the odium with which both he and his son Alfonso were regarded by the principal barons of the realm; a truth which was confirmed to Charles by the princes of Salerno and Bisignano, who had sought, in the court

of France, a refuge from the resentment of Ferdinand. These solicitations produced the effect which Lodovico intended, and Charles not only engaged in the attempt to recover the kingdom of Naples, but, to the surprize of all his courtiers, he determined to lead his army in person.(ty

The respective claims of the houses of Anjou and Aragon upon the crown of Naples, were, in the estimation of sound sense and enlightened policy, equally devoid of foundation. In all countries, the supreme authority has been supposed to be rightfully vested only in those who claim it by Claimj of hereditary descent, or by the consenting voice of the people; housesof Ahbut with respect to the kingdom of Naples, each of the contend-jou ing parties founded its pretensions on a donation of the sove-«owi f N»reignty to their respective ancestors. The origin of these contentions, is to be traced to a remote assumption of the holy see, *(a) Guicciard. Sloria d' Ital. lib.* i. *Murat. Annali.* ix. *passim. Corio, Storia di Milan, par.* vii. *p.* 8J)0. *fyc.*

Chap. in. seg5 *yy* which it was asserted, that the kingdom of Naples A. Dj 1493. was held by its sovereigns as a fief of the church,, and in cer

A.iEt. is., tain cases, on which the pontiffs arrogated to themselves the right of deciding, reverted to its actual disposal. That dominion, which the sovereign had received as the gift of another, it was supposed that he could himself transfer by his voluntary act; the consent of the church being all that was necessary to render such transfer valid; and to this pernicious and absurd idea, we are to trace all the calamities which destroyed for several, centuries the repose of Italy, and rendered it, on various occasions, the theatre of massacre, of rapine, and of *blood.faj* . ki;.:.

To balance against each other, pretensions which are equally;unsubstantial on any principle of sound policyi or even of acknowledged and positive law, may seem superfluous. If long prescription can be presumed to justify that which commenced in violence and in fraud, the title of the

house of Anjou may be allowed to have been confirmed by a possession of nearly two.centuries, in which the reins of government had been.held by several monarchs who had preserved the rights and secured the happiness of their subjects. On the. expulsion of Renato, in 1442, by Alfonso of Aragon, the family of Anjou were divested of their dominions; and. by several successive bequests, which would scarcely have had sufficient authenticity to transfer a private inheritance from one *(a)* Should the reader wish for more particular information respecting the claims of the contending parties to the crown of Naples, he may peruse with great advantage the acute and learned observations of Mr. Gibbon on this subject, published in the second volume of his miscellaneous works, under the title of *Critical researches concerning tie title of Charles VIII. to the crown of Naples.* one individual to another, in any country in Europe, the CHAP-Inrights of the exiled sovereigns became vested in Louis XI. A. D. 1493. from whom they had descended to his son Charles VIII. The A-A.18title of Ferdinand was, on the other hand, Open to formidable objections; the illegitimacy and usurpation of his ancestor Manfredo, the deduction of his rights by the female line, the long acquiescence of his family, and the circumstances of his own birth, afforded plausible pretexts for the measures adopted against him; but it must be remembered, that the same power, w;hich had conferred the kingdom on the family of Anjou, had, on another occasion, bestowed it on Alfonso, the father of Ferdinand; and the paramount authority of the Roman see, to which both parties alternately resorted, must, in the discussion of their respective claims, be considered as decisive. Alfonso on his death had given it to his son, who, whether capable or not of hereditary succession, might receive a donation, which had been transferred for ages with as little ceremony as a piece of domestic furniture; and if a nation is ever to enjoy repose, Ferdinand might, at this time, be presumed to be, both *de jure* and *defacto,* king of Naples.

In the discussion of questions of this nature, there is, however, one circumstance which seems not to have been sufficiently attended to, either by the parties themselves, or those who have examined their claims, and which may explain the mutability of 'the Neapolitan government better than an appeal to hereditary rights, papal endowments, or feudal customs. The object of dominion is not the bare territory of a country, but the command of the men who possess that country. These, it ought to be recollected, are intelligent beings, capable of being rendered happy or miserable by the virtues or the vices of a sovereign, and acting, if not always under

Chap, ni. under the influence of sober reason, with an impulse resulta. D. 1493. ing from the nature of the situation in which they are a.iEt. is. plaCed. Whilst the prince, therefore, retains the affections of his people; whilst he calls forth their energies without rendering them ferocious, and secures their repose without debasing their character; the defects of his title to the sovereignty will disappear in the splendor of his virtues. But when he relinquishes the sceptre of the king, for the scourge of the tyrant, and the ties of attachment are loosened by reiterated instances of rapacity, cruelty, and oppression, the road to innovation is already prepared; the approach of an enemy is no longer considered as a misfortune, but as a deliverance; the dry discussion of abstract rights gives way to more imperious considerations; and the adoption of a new sovereign is not so much the result of versatility, of cowardice, or of treachery, as of that invincible necessity, by which the human race are impelled to relieve themselves from intolerable calamities.

The resolution adopted by Charles VIII. to attempt the conquest of Naples, was no sooner known in France, than it gave'rise to great diversity of opinion among the barons and principal counsellors of the realm; many of whom, as well as his nearest relations, endeavoured to divert him from his purpose, by representing to him the impolicy of quitting his own dominions, the dangers to which he must infallibly expose him-

self, and, above all, the depressed state of his finances, which were totally inadequate to the preparation of so great an armament. They reminded him of the prudent conduct of his father, who was always averse to the measure which he now proposed to take, and unwilling to involve himself in the intricate web of Italian politics; of the long established authority authority of Ferdinand of Naples, confirmed by his late tri-Chap, Iii. umphs over his refractory nobles; and of the high military A.d. 1493. reputation of Alfonso duke of Calabria, whose expulsion of A.i».i8. the Turks from Otranto, had ranked him amongst the greatest generals in Europe. The die was however cast; the measure of prosperity in Italy was full; and instead of listening to the remonstrances of his friends, Charles bent his mind on the most speedy means of carrying his purpose into execution. The grandeur of the object called forth energies which none of his courtiers supposed that he possessed. The ardour of the king communicated itself to the populace, whose favour was still farther secured, by representing the conquest of Naples, as only the preliminary step to that of the capital of the Turkish empire, and to the diffusion of the catholic faith throughout the eastern world. An ignorant people are never so courageous, or rather so ferocious, as when they conceive themselves to be contending in the cause of religion. Charles had the artifice to avail himself of this propensity, and to represent his expedition as undertaken to fulfil a particular call from heaven, manifested by ancient prophecies, which had promised him, not only the empire of Constantinople, but also the kingdom of Jerusalem./ From all parts of his dominions, his subjects of every rank, voluntarily presented themselves to share his honours, or to partake his dangers; and, including some bands of mercenaries, he found himself in a short time at the head of an army, the numbers of which have been very differently estimated, but at the time of his Vol. 1. s departure, (a) This expedition was the subject of several publications in France, some of which are cited by M.

Foncemagne, in his *Eclaircissemens historiques sur quelqucs circonttanoei du voyage de Charles VIII. en Italie. v. Mem. de VAcademic dcs Inscrip. tom.*

Charles accommodates his

Chap, in. departure, it could not, in its different detachments, have A. D. 1493. consisted ofless than fifty thousand men.

A. £t. 18. '.

Before Charles could, however, engage with any reasonable degree of safety in his intended expedition, some important difficulties yet remained to be overcome. The countenance, or the acquiescence of the principal sovereigns of Europe was indispensably necessary; but although he was on terms of amity with the king of England (Henry VII.) he was differences involved in quarrels with Ferdinand of Spain, and with MaxTand of imilian, king of the Romans. The former of these mbnarchs, Spain. having had occasion to borrow a sum of one hundred thousand ducats, had proposed to Louis XI. that on his advancing the money, he should be secured for its due return by the possession of the counties of Perpignan and Roussillon, which were accordingly surrendered to him; but when, some years afterwards, Ferdinand offered to repay the money, Louis, being unwilling to relinquish a district which adjoined his own dominions, refused to perform the stipulations of the agreement. This undisguised instance of perfidy, gave occasion to complaints and remonstrances on the part of Ferdinand, *torn.* xvii. *p.* 539. In one of these intitled *La proplietie du roy Charles fmitieme de ce nomy par maitre GuUbochc de Bowdeaux,* is the following passage:...

"Il fera de si grants batailles;
"Qu'il subjugera les Ytailles..."
"Ce fait, d'ilec il s'en ira
"Et passera dela la mer.
"—Entrera puis dedans la Grece,
"Ou, par sa vaillant prouesse,
"Sera nomme le roi des Grecs;
". En Jerusalem entreri),
. "Et mont Olivet montera." *kc.*

dinand, to which neither Louis nor his successor had hitherto CHAP nL paid the least regard. But no sooner had Charles determined A. D. 1493. on his expedition into Italy, than he proposed to restore these A-£t-18 provinces to Ferdinand, in such a manner as seemed most likely to secure his future favour. By an embassy dispatched for this purpose, he represented to the Spanish monarch, that whilst the crown of France had been attacked on all .' sides by powerful enemies, and compelled to defend itself at the same time against the late.emperor Frederic, the king of England, and the dukes of Burgundy and Britany, both he and his father had retained these provinces, notwithstanding the threats and remonstrances of the. court of Spain' but that having now repulsed or conciliated all his enemies, and having nothing to apprehend from any hostile attack, he had resolved to restore these contested territories, without any other compensation than the friendship and alliance of Ferdinand. The restitution accordingly took place, and was soon followed by a treaty between the two sovereigns, in which Ferdinand solemnly engaged, that he would not interfere in the concerns of Naples, notwithstanding the near degree of relationship which subsisted between him and the sovereign of that kingdom and his family, to whom he was connected by the ties of both consanguinity and affinity./ Charles did not, however, consider this treaty, which he concluded with the ambassadors of Ferdinand;at Lyons, as an effectual security for his neutrality; for he soon afterwards dispatched his envoys to Madrid, who required and obtained the personal and solemn oath, not only of Ferdinand himself, but of

S3 his."'"'''. ..' (a) The two sovereigns were brothers children, and Ferdinand of Naples had married, for his second wife, Joanna, the sister of Ferdinand of Spain.

Chap. m. his queen Isabella, and their son John, prince of Castile, then A. D. 1493. of mature age, to the same effect. A. JEx. 18.

And with the Emperor elect, Maxi

The disagreement between Charles and Maximilian, king of the Romans, was of a much more delicate nature.

During the life of his father, Charles had been betrothed to Margaretta, the daughter of Maximilian, who was accordingly sent to France whilst an infant, to be educated among her future subjects; but when the time approached that the nuptial ceremony should have taken place, circumstances occurred which induced Charles to change his intentions, and to disregard his engagements. Francis, duke of Bretagne, who then held his rich and extensive domains as an independent prince, finding himself at open war with the French monarch, had been led, by the hopes of a powerful alliance, td engage his daughter Anna, in marriage to Maximilian. After the death of the duke, Charles persevered in his hostilities, and notwithstanding the interference of Henry VII. of England, who sent a body of troops to the relief of the young duchess, the greater part of her territories was occupied by the French troops, and the duchess herself, besieged in her capital of Rennes, was at length obliged to submit to the terms imposed by the conqueror. The youth and beauty of the duchess, and the important advantages which Charles foresaw from the union of her dominions with his own, induced him, notwithstanding his engagements with Margaretta of Austria, to make her proposals of marriage, and her consent being with some difficulty obtained, the nuptials were accordingly carried into immediate effect. Nor can it be denied, that this union, politically considered, was highly judicious; as it secured to Charles the command of a country naturally formed to be governed with his own, and at the same time, prevented the powerful family of Austria from esta-CHAP-inblishing itself in the vicinity of the French dominions. A. D. 1493. But with respect to Maximilian, the conduct of Charles in-a.JSt.is. eluded tw6 indignities of the most unpardonable nature: the repudiating his innocent daughter, and the depriving him of his betrothed wife. Maximilian was not, however, prepared for hostile measures; and the animosity to which these events gave rise, soon became a matter of negociation, in which Lodovico Sforza in-

terposed his good offices. In the month of June, 1493, a treaty was concluded between the two sovereigns, by which it was agreed, that Margaretta should be restored to her father, with her intended dowry, and that Charles should be released from his contract. The disappointment of Maximilian, Lodovico alleviated by recommending to him his niece, Bianca Maria, whom Maximilian soon afterwards took to wife; whilst his daughter Margaretta found a husband in John, prince of Castile, the son of Ferdinand and Isabella, and presumptive heir to the Spanish monarchy; after whose death, in 1497, she married Filiberto, duke of Savoy. '. '.

Nor did Charles VIII. in preparing for his Neapolitan expedition, implicitly rely upon the representations of Lodovico Negotiates with Sforza, with respect to the disposition of the other states of Italy. On the contrary, he dispatched his emissaries, with directions to obtain, if not the assurance of their assistance, at least the knowledge of their intentions. The principal argument on which he relied, for conciliating their favour, . (a)Memoire sur k manage de Charles Dauphin, §c. inserted in the collection of Du Montt vol. iii. par. ii. p. 404. Bacon. Hist. Hen. VII. The events above related gave rise to many singular discussions, of which some account may be found in the Appendix, No. XXV. (b) Corio, Storiadi Milan, par. vii. p. 898. the Florentines for their Chap. ni. favour, was the avowal of his determination to attempt the A. ». 1493. recovery of Constantinople, and the duty imposed upon all

A. £t. is. Christendom, to assist'him in so magnanimous and pious an enterprize. In order to obtain greater credit to these assert tions, he assumed the titles of king of Sicily arid Jerusalem His chief endeavours were, however, employed to prevail upon the Florentines and the pope, to. withdraw themselves froin their alliance with Ferdinand. The answer which he obtained frorn the forme, was equivocal and unsatisfactory. Whilst they assured the king, in private, of their good wishes, they excused themselves from a public avowal of.

them, lest they should incur the resentnierit of Ferdinand of Naples, who, by turning his arms against the Tuscan territory, mighj render it the seat of the war. Such were the sentiments of the Florentine government, as sanctioned by Piero deMedici; but the intelligence of the intentions of the French monarch was received with inconceivable joy, by a considerable number of. the most powerful inhabitants of Florence, who were hostile to the views of Piero, arid conceived, that in the commotions likely to arise from such a contest, they should find an opportunity of divesting him of his authority. Among these, the most distinguished by their wealth and rank were, Lorenzo and Giovanni, the sons of PierFrancesco de' Medici, and grandsons of the elder Lorenzo, the brother of Cosmo, *Pater Patria.* These young men, jealous of the superior authority of Piero and his brothers, in the-'affairs of Florence, had endeavoured, by their liberality arid affability, and above all, by avowing a decided attachment to the liberties of the people, to establish themselves in the favour of the public, in which attempt they had not been wholly unsuccessful. From them and their friends, the envoys of Chai'les received a secret assurance, that if he would CHAP. III.

would persevere in his intentions, they would not only promote his views to the utmost of their power, but would A. D. 1493. also undertake to supply him with a large sum of money, A-*m-1St*owards defraying the expenses of his expedition. The conduct of the two brothers was, however, regarded with a suspicious eye. They had already shewn a decided partiality to the French king, by accepting honorary appointments in his household; and certain information having been obtained of a secret correspondence with Charles, their persons were seized upon by the orders of Piero de' Medici, who has been accused of having entertained private causes of resentment against them, and of wishing to avail himself of this opportunity of gratifying his enmity, by depriving them of their *lives.fa)* Their misconduct was, however, apparent, and after a long dis-

cussion, and the interference of many powerful friends, they were ordered, by a lenient sentence, to remain at their villas in the vicinity of Florence; but they soon broke the conditions imposed on them, and fled to France, where, by their personal interference, they encouraged the king to persevere in his claims. .,

In order to palliate these proceedings to the French king, and to conciliate, if possible, his indulgence and favour, . Gentile, *(a)* Nardi gives us. reason to believe, that there were very sufficient grounds for the proceedings against the two brothers, which he adverts to, as having fallen within his own knowledge, many years afterwards, " Ma havendo io saputo, dopo mohi anni, per "qualche altra via, che poi il detto Giovanni de' Medici era stato honorato del titolo del "Maestro di hostello, cio& Maestro di casa, del Re di Francia, Carlo VIII. non perb per "alcuna altra instante cagione, che per haver proccacciato, forse in tempo troppo alieno, la "gratia del Re di Francia, allora inimico della citti, ho potuto facilmente credere, che da '.' questo fosse proccduta la suspitione & diffidentia, e consequentemente l'odio che in 41 questo fatto si dimostrb a questi duoi fratelli." *Nardi, Hist. Ftor. lib.* i. *p.* 10.

Dismisses their ambassadors in displea

Chap, in. Gentile, bishop of Arezzo, and Piero Soderini, afterwards A. D. 1493. Gonfaloniere for life, were dispatched as ambassadors of the a. *At.* is. republic to France. They, found the king in the, city of Thoulouse, where, being admitted to an interview, they intreated him not to press the citizens of Florence to take an immediate and decided part in the approaching contest, and represented to him the dangers which they must inevitably incur by such a measure. They artfully extolled the greatness of his name, the extent of his dominions, and the numbers and courage of his troops; but they also suggested to him, that he was separated from Italy by the formidable barrier of the Alps, and that, whilst he was hastening to the protection of the Florentines, they might

fall a sacrifice to the merited resentment of Ferdinand of Naples. At the same time they assured him, that as soon as he should have surmounted these obstacles, and made his appearance in Italy he should find them disposed to render him every assistance in their power. The purport of this discourse, was too obvious to escape the animadversion of Charles, whose indignation it excited to such a degree, that he not only drove the ambassadors from his presence, but threatened instantly to seize upon the property of all the Florentines within his realm, and to expel them from his dominions: and although he was prevented, by his advisers, from carrying this purpose into execution, he ordered that the agents of Piero de' Medici, should instantly be sent from the city of Lyons, where the family had carried on the business of bankers for a long course of years; thereby clearly manifesting from what quarter he conceived the opposition to *dLr'ise.fbJ*

For *(a)* Ammirato, *Istorie Florentine,* iii. 190.

(b) Gtticciard. *Storia d'ltal. lib.* i. 1. 32. with liim on his attempt.

For the purpose of ascertaining the views of Alexander Chap, in. VI. Charles had dispatched a second embassy to Rome, at A. D. 1+93; the head of which was his General and confidential friend A-18i ...... 1-11 1 Alexander VI.

D'Aubigny. The success of this mission was highly desna-rfn,omtrate3 ble to him; as its principal object was to obtain from Alexander, by promises on the one hand, or by threats on the other, the formal investiture of the kingdom of Naples. If, as it has been asserted by many historians, Alexander had before concurred in inciting the king to this undertaking, he did not scruple, on the present occasion, to change his sentiments, and his reply was not favourable to the hopes of Charles. He intreated him to remember, that the kingdom of Naples had been three times conceded by the holy see to the family of Aragon, the investiture of Ferdinand having expressly included that of his son Alfonso; that these adjudications could not be rendered void, unless it appeared judicially that Charles had a superior right, which could not be affected by these acts of investiture, in which.there was an express reservation that they should not prejudice the rights of any person; thaf the dominion of Naples, being under the immediate protection of the holy see, the pontilf could not persuade himself that his most Christian majesty would so openly oppose himself to the church, as to hazard, without its concurrence, a hostile attack on that kingdom; that it would be more consistent with his known moderation and dignity, to assert his pretensions in a civil form; in which case, Alexander, as the sole judge of the right, declared himself ready to enter upon the discussion of the claims of the respective parties. These remonstrances he afterwards more fully inforced in an apostolic brief, in which he exhorted the French monarch to unite his arms with those of the other sovereigns of Europe, against the common Vol. 1. T enemies

Chap, m. enemies of Christendom, and to submit his claims on the A. D. 1493. kingdom of Naples to the decision of a pacific judicature.

a. Et. is. Instead of altering the purpose, these admonitions only excited the resentment of the king, who in return, avowed his determination to expel Alexander from the pontifical throne, (ty

The answers obtained by the envoys of the king, from the duke of Savoy, the republic of Venice, and other dXfVcr5 governments of Italy, expressed in general terms their great respect for the French monarch, and their reluctance to engage in so dangerous a contest; but the duke of Ferrara, although he had married a daughter of Ferdinand, king of Naples, actuated, as has been supposed, by the hope of availing (a) Although Guicciardini, Rucellai, and other contemporary authors, expressly assert,that Charles VIII. was incited by Alexander VI. to attempt the conquest of Naples, in which they have been implicitly followed by subsequent writers, I have not ventured to adopt their representations in my narrative; I. because Commines, who has related, at great

length, the motives by which Charles VIII. was induced to this undertaking, adverts not, in the most distant manner, to any invitation from the pope on that subject; on the contrary, he attributes the determination of the king solely to the persuasions of Lodovico Sforza, and informs us, that he sent Perron de Basche, as his ambassador to Rome, apparently to try the disposition of the pontiff, whom he erroneously names Innocent, v. Mcmoires, Ho. vii. chap. 2. II. In the letter from Lodovico Sforza to Charles VIII. as given by Corio, p. 891, the pope is not even mentioned, although several other sovereigns are specified as being favourable to the intended enterprize. III. In the apostolic brief issued by Alexander, and inserted by the same author in his history, we discover no reason to infer that the pope had, at any previous time, entertained a different opinion from that which he there professes, and which is decidedly adverse to the interference of the king in the concerns of Italy. Guicciardini, actuated perhaps by his abhorrence of Alexander VI. has not discussed this subject with his usual accuracy; and the reader finds it difficult to discover, even in his copious narrative, the real predisposing causes of an enterprize, which gave rise to all the important events recorded in his history.

(b) Benedetli, Fatto d'arme del Tarro, tradotto da Domcnkhi, p. 5. Ed. Vcn. 1545. ing himself of the aid of the French against his powerful CHAP-nrenemies the Venetians, did not hesitate to encourage the A. D. 1493. French monarch, in the most open manner, to persevere in A-£u 18 his claims./

The negotiations and precautions resorted to by Charles, Indecision of preparatory to his Italian expedition, were such as a wise Chrie,vra' adviser would have suggested, and a prudent commander would not fail to adopt. He was also assiduous in collecting those necessary supplies of wrarlike stores, ammunition, and artillery of various kinds, the use of which had then been lately introduced, and on which he chiefly relied for the success of his undertaking. Yet, if we may believe a writer, who himself acted

no unimportant part in the transactions of the times, the conduct of the French monarch was a

T 2, series (a Respecting the conduct of the duke of Ferrara, on this occasion, some discordance of opinion appears among the historians of Italy. Muratori asserts, that he exerted his efforts to dissuade Lodovico Sforza from his imprudent design of inviting the French into Italy. "Fu adoperato Ercole duca di Ferrara, per rimuovere Lodovico dalla pazza "sua risoluzione di tirar l'armi Franzesi in Italia, n& egli omise ufficio alcuno per ottener "l'intento." &c. Annali ix. 569-But Guicciardini, on the contrary, informs us, that Ercole abetted the enterprize, and assigns his motives for it at length. In deciding between these eminent historians, of whom the one was a contemporary, and the other has in general drawn his information from the documents of the times, it becomes necessary to resort to further evidence. Benedetti, in his Fatto d'artne del Tarro, expressly asserts, that Charles was invited into Italy by Lodovico Sforza, Ercole duke of Ferrara, the cardinal Giuliano della Rovere, and Lorenzo (the son of Pier-Francesco) de' Medici; assigning as a reason for it (which strongly confirms the idea that Alexander VI. was uniformly hostile to the measure) that the aversion in which the pope was held by some of the cardinals, induced them to wish for a change in the pontificate, v. p. 5. And from the history of Ferrara, by Sardi, it appears, that Ercole accompanied Lodovico Sforza to meet the king at Alexandria. "Passb Carlo in Italia," says he, " incontrato "dal Moro, e dal duca Ercole, in Alessandria." Sardi, Hist. Far. lib. x. p. 194. From all which, it may be clearly inferred, that the duke of Ferrara took an activ part in bringing the French into Italy.

Chap. ni. series of obstinacy, folly, and indecision.(a) "The king," a. D. 1493. says he, " had neither money nor talents for such an enter

A..fit is. "prize; the success of which can only be attributed to the "grace of God, who shewed his power most manifestly on "this occasion." And again,

" The king was very young, "weak in body, obstinate, surrounded by few persons of prudence or experience; money he had none, insomuch, "that before his departure, he was obliged to borrow one "hundred thousand francs from a banker at Genoa, at an "enormous interest, as well as to resort to other places for "assistance. He had neither tent nor pavilion, and in this "state he began his march into Lombardy. One thing only "seemed favourable to him; he had a gallant company, con"sisting chiefly of young gentlemen, though with little disci"pline. This expedition must therefore have been the work "of God, both in going and returning; for the understand"ing of its conductors could render it very little service; "although it must be acknowledged that it has terminated "in the acquisition of no small share of honour and glory "to their master. "(ft/ Even at the moment of departure, although the king was unceasingly pressed by the envoys of Lodovico Sforza, he displayed a strong disinclination to commence his journey: and as he fluctuated according to the advice of his counsellors, he changed his purpose from day to day. At length he determined to set forwards on his expedition; "but even then," says Commines, " when I had begun my

"journey (a) Memoires de Commines. liv. vii. c/tdp. 4. p. ip2.

(bj It appears from Giustiniani, Annaii di Genoa, p. 24,9, that the Genoese banker was Antonio Sauli, who first advanced to the king 70,000 ducats, and afterwards 25,000 more, at Rome. If we may judge of the supposed risk of loss, by the rate of interest, it was regarded as a hazardous adventure; such interest being no less than cent per cent.— "dgros interest pour cent de foirc en foire." Commin. liv. vii. proem, p. 184.

"journey I was sent back, and told that the attempt was re-Chap. m. "linquished.'Y How then shall we reconcile the external A. D. 1493. demonstrations of perseverance, prudence, and magnani-a.JS.18.' mity, to which we have before adverted, with these internal marks of imbecility, and weakness of mind? In truth, the history of mankind

is susceptible of being represented under very different aspects; and whilst one narrator informs us of the ostensible conduct of sovereigns and their agents, on the public stage of life, another intrudes himself behind the curtain, and discovers to us by what paltry contrivances the wires are played, and by what contemptible causes those effects, which we so highly admire, are in fact produced.

Whilst preparations were thus making by Charles for of his intended expedition, the sagacious mind of Ferdinand of Naples enNapleS had maturely compared the probable impulse of the attack, with the known practicability of resistance, and the to relu6 result of his deliberations was such as to occasion to him no pedinon. small share of anxiety. He well knew, that the arms of the French king were not only superior to any force which he, with his utmost exertions, could oppose to them, but in all probability, to that of all the Italian states united. On his allies he could place no firm reliance; and if he did not suspect their duplicity, or dread their inconstancy, he could only expect them to act as circumstances might prescribe; or in other words, to attach themselves to the conquering party. From his relative, the king of Spain, he could hope for ho assistance; for he had solemnly disavowed and abjured . (a) " A la fin le Roy se delibera de partir; & montay & cheval des premiers, esperant "passer les monts en moindre compagnie. Toutefois je fus remande, disant que tout "etoit rompu." Mem. de Com. liv. vii. chap. 4. p. 193.

Chap. m. jured his cause; and if he resorted to the aid of his own subA. D. 1493. jects, he only saw, on every hand, the indications of tumult A. Ax. is. and rebellion, the natural consequences of a severity, which had alienated the affections of his barons, and reduced his people to servitude. Under these circumstances, he resolved to try whether it might not yet be possible, by prudent negotiation and timely submission, to avert the dangers with which he was threatened; and in this respect he proposed to avail himself of the interfer-

ence of Carlotta, the daughter of his second son Federigo, who was related to Charles by consanguinity, and had been educated in his court.faj He also dispatched, as his ambassador, Camilla Pandone, who had formerly been his representative in France, with offers to Charles, of a considerable annual tribute, if he would relinquish his enterprize; but the humiliation of Ferdinand, rather excited the hopes, than averted o the purpose, of his adversary, and his ambassador was re manded without a public hearing. In his applications to Lodovico Sforza, although he met with an exterior civility, he was, in fact, equally unsuccessful; nor could he, indeed, reasonably hope for any satisfactory engagement with that ever-variable politician, who, in weaving the web for the destruction of others, was at length entangled in it himself.

Nor was Ferdinand, whilst he was thus endeavouring to avert, by negotiation, the dangers with which he was threatened, remiss in collecting together such a force as his own states afforded for his defence. A fleet of about forty galleys was speedily prepared for action, and by great exertions

Prepares for bis defence.

(a) Federigo of Aragon married Anna, daughter of Amadcus, duke of Savoy, who was brother of Carlotta,, queen of Louis XI.

Death of Ferdinand.

..i

Alfonso II. suc cxertions and expense, a body of troops was collected, which, CHAP-raincluding the various descriptions of soldiery, amounted to A. D. 1494 about seven thousand men. But whilst Ferdinand was thus a.jst. 19. endeavouring to secure himself from the approaching storm, he found a more effectual shelter from its violence in a sudden death, hastened, perhaps, by the joint effects of vexation and fatigue, on the twenty-fifth day of January, 1494, when he had nearly attained the seventy-first year of his age.'/aj

The stipulations entered into between Ferdinand and Alexander VI. had, however, for the present, effectually secured the favour of the pontiff, which, on this occasion, was of the ceeds to the greatest importance to Alfonso, the son and successor of jTM Ferdinand, who found no difficulty in obtaining the bull of investiture. He was accordingly crowned, with great pomp, at Naples, on the seventh day of May, 1494, by Giovanni Borgia, nephew of the pope, and cardinal of Monreale, who was sent from Rome to perform that ceremony. Immediately after his accession to the crown, Alfonso appointed the celebrated Pontano his chief secretary; nor, if we may judge from the commendations bestowed on him by the Neapolitan scholars, (a) Burcardo, who made a journey to Naples, soon after the death of the king, relates, that Ferdinand, having found himself indisposed at his villa of Trapergola, returned to Naples, where, in dismounting from his horse, he fell senseless, and died on the following day, without either confession or sacraments. His confessor cried out to him, in vain, to repent of his sins and his opposition to the church, for he gave not the slightest symptom of contrition. *Burcard. Diar. ap. Not. des MSS. du Roi,* 1. 108. Bernardino Rota has honoured his memory by the following lines:—

"Fernandas fueram, felicis conditor aevi,

"Qui pater heu patriae, qui decus orbis eram;

"Quem timuere duces, reges coluere, brevis nunc

"Urna habet; humanis i modo fide bonis."

Carm. illustr. Poet. ltd. viii. 156.

Chap. in. scholars, was this the only instance in which he shewed his a. D. 1494. respect for literature. A.iEt. 19.

Soon after the ceremonial of the coronation, the nuptials

Marriage of of Geoffroi Borgia, with Sancia of Aragon, were celebrated,

Geoff oiBor-tne Dride being at that time seventeen, and the husband only gia, with San-0 _ cia of A agon thirteen years of age. The magnificence of these formalities, was as ill suited to the alarming situation of the Aragonese family, as the expense was to their necessities. The pope and the king seemed to contend with each other which should

be most lavish of his bounty; but Alexander dispensed only the favours and dignities of the church, whilst

Alfonso *(a)* To this period we may refer the bsautiful Latin verses of Sanazzaro, which celebrate the life and actions of Alfonso, and advert to many circumstances either not noticed, or imperfectly related by the historians of the times, it. *Sanaz. Eleg. lib.* ii. *El.* 1. His accession to the crown is also commemorated by Cariteo, in a Canzone, which the reader w-ill find in the Appendix, No. XXVI. and wherein he particularly refers to the meditated invasion of Naples by the arms of the French; to which circumstance he also alludes in other parts of his works, with that indignation and contempt of Charles VIII. to which the occasion may readily be supposed to have given rise; as in the following SONETTO.

"Cantan di chiari autor' le sacre carte,

"Che li giganti stolidi, una volta,

"Con temeraria voglia, audace, e stolta,

"Tentar salir nella supenia parte.

"Onde non col favor del ferreo Marte,

"Ma con la man di Giove, armata, e sciolta,

"Gli fu la vita, con l'audacia, tolta;

"E'l sangue e membra lor per terra sparte. "Dal seme de li quai, produtta in terra,

"*La Simia* fu; che i superi beffeggia,

"Imitando i paterni impii costumi.

"Non e dunque miracol che si veggia

"*Un brutto animaletto* ancor far guerra,

"Col fero volto, a li celesti numi."

Alfonso sacrificed the revenues of his states, and diminished Chap, m. those pecuniary resources of which he stood so greatly in A. D. 14.94. need. Lodovico, the son of Don Henry, natural brother of A-19 the king, was, on this occasion, received into the sacred college, and was afterwards known by the name of the cardinal of Aragon; and the pope released Alfonso, during his life, from the nominal tribute, so constantly, but ineffectually, claimed by the holy see from the sovereigns of Naples. On the other hand, the king invested Giovanni Borgia, eldest son of the pope, already

created duke of Gandia, with the principality of Tricarica, and other rich domains in the kingdom of Naples, of the annual value of twelve thousand ducats; to which he also added the promise of the first of the seven great offices of state, that should become vacant. Nor was Caesar Borgia, the second son of Alexander, forgotten on this occasion; another grant of a considerable income from the kingdom of Naples, being thought necessary to enable him to support the dignity of his rank, as one of the cardinals of the church. Two hundred thousand ducats were expended in the dowry and paraphernalia of the bride; and tournaments and feasts, continued for several days, seemed to afford both the people and their rulers a short respite from their approaching calamities.

The alliance and support of the pope being thus secured, Alfonso prepared for war; and as a proof that he meant, in Aiioum p«the first instance, to resort to vigorous measures, he dismissed from his capital the Milanese ambassador, at the same time sequestrating the revenues of the duchy of Bari, which had been conferred by his father on Lodovico Sforza. By a secret intercourse with the cardinal Fregoso, and Obietto da Fiesco, who then enjoyed great authority in Genoa, he at

Vol. 1. u tempted

Chap. in. tempted to deprive the duke of Milan of his dominion over A. D. 149. tnat state» arm at nothing might be wanting on his part to a.ja. 19. secure himself against the impending attack, he dispatched ambassadors to the sultan Bajazet, to represent to him, that the avowed object of the French king was, the overthrow of the Ottoman empire, and to request that he would immediately send a strong reinforcement to his relief.fflj The lessons of experience, which form the wisdom of individuals, seem to be lost on the minds of rulers; otherwise Alfonso might have discovered, that his most effectual safeguard was in the affections of his people, who, if his conduct had entitled him to their favour, would have been found sufficiently powerful for his defence;

M'hilst, on the contrary, the.aver 7 sion of his own subjects, accumulated by repeated instances of a cruel and unrelenting disposition, both before and after his accession to the throne, was an internal malady which no foreign aid could remove.

The opinions, debates, and negotiations, to which the views and con-intended expedition gave rise among the smaller states of duct of the italy5 each of whom had their ambassadors and partisans constantly employed, combined to form such an intricate tissue of political intrigue, as it would be equally useless and tiresome to unravel. It is not, however, difficult to perceive, that these petty sovereigns, instead of uniting in any great and. general plan of defence, were each of them labouring to secure his private interests, or to avail himself of any circumstance in the approaching commotions, that might contribute to his own aggrandizement. In the conflagration that was speedily to involve the fabric of Italy, the contest, therefore, was *(a) Gukciard. Storia d'ltd. Ub.* i. 1. 34.

was not, owho should most assist in extinguishing the flames, Chap, nr. but who should obtain the greatest share of the spoil. A. D. 1494. a. *m.* 19.

The determination of Charles VIII. to attempt the con-Char,es *x* engages ita quest of Naples, now became every day more apparent. ii»n stipenD'Aubigny, one of the most experienced commanders in the dia"e'' service of the French monarch, had, after his interview with the pope, been directed to remain in Italy; where he had already the command of a small body of French troops, which had been assembled in the territories of Milan *:fa)* and by the assistance of Lodovico Sforza, and his brother, the cardinal Ascanio, several of the Italian nobility and condottieri, regardless to whom they sold their services, undertodk to furnish the king with a stipulated number of cavalry, or men at arms. Among these mercenaries, were some of the chief barons of the Roman state, and particularly those of the families of Colonna, Orsini, and Savelli./ This daring instance of insubordination

in the Roman nobility, alarmed the pontiff, and afforded too plausible a pretext for those severities which he afterwards exercised against them.

In order to concert together the means for their common defence, it was proposed, between Alfonso and the pope, that they should meet at the town of Vico, about u 2 twenty *(a)* Commines, who calls him " un bon et sage chevalier," says, that he had " quelques "deux cens hommes d'armes." *lib.* vii. *chap.* 5. but Corio, a writer of equal credit, says that he had " mille cavalli Francesi. " *StoriadiMilan, par.* vii. *p.* 927. This faithful soldier, and judicious counsellor, to whom the success of the expedition may be chiefly attributed, was of Scottish origin, and is denominated by Summonte, in his history of Naples, *vol.* iii. *p. 5l6.* 7orr. 580.) "Everardo Estuardo," (Everard or Edward Stuart) "Scozzese, per sopra nome, detto Monsignore di Obegni.'' *fbj* These auxiliaries are enumerated by Corio, *Storia di Milan, par.* vii. *p.* 923.

Chap, nx twenty miles from Rome, whither Alexander accordingly A. D. 1494. repaired, accompanied by many of the cardinals, the Ve a. *£x. 19.* netian and Florentine legates, and about five hundred horse.

He was there met by Alfonso, who, with unavailing humility, professed his willingness to rest his cause on the decision of the sacred college, and the ambassadors of the neutral *courts.fa)* After this interview, Alexander returned in haste to Rome, with the resolution of suppressing the Roman nobility, who were now in arms, and openly avowed their attachment to the cause of the French; but he found them so posted, and their numbers so considerably increased, that he thought it advisable to relinquish the attempt for the present, and to reserve his vengeance for a future day..;,k

Alfonso now determined to take the command of his army in person, and appointed his brother Federigo, admiral of his fleet. With the former, it was his intention to advance into Romagna, and oppose himself to the threatened hostilities of D'Aubigny; whilst the latter was

directed to proceed to Genoa, for the purpose of affording the citizens of that place an opportunity of freeing themselves from the dominion of the house of Sforza.ffy

The cardinal Fregoso and his nephew, with Obietto da

Fiesco, *(a) Corio,Sioria di* MHan. *parte* vii. *p.* 925.
(b) The exertions of the monarch were celebrated by the eminent scholars who adorned his court; and Sanazzaro, at this juncture, produced one of his finest Italian poems, in which he has endeavoured to inspire his fellow soldiers with courage and resolution, in defence of their sovereign and their country. This canzone is given in the Appendix, No. XXVII.

Fiesco, and other Genoese exiles, accompanied the armament of Federigo, which was provided with materials for burning, in case of resistance, the fleet, in the harbour of Genoa, and for destroying the preparations which the French had, for some time past, been making there. About the end of the month of June, the Neapolitan flotilla sailed from Civita Vecchia, having on board four thousand soldiers, and being provided with a considerable quantity of artillery and stores. Its arrival in the gulf of Spezia, was immediately announced to Louis, duke of Orleans, who had preceded Charles in his expedition into Italy, and had arrived at Asti, where he was employed in concerting with Lodovico Sforza, the measures to be adopted in commencing the war. Selecting for his purpose, a body of two thousand infantry and five hundred light-armed horse, he repaired to Genoa, where the partisans of the French had prepared for service seven large ships with heavy artillery, besides several smaller vessels, on which they had embarked six hundred men, under the command of the French general DUri6.*(a)* Detachments from Gen?a were also sent to protect the coast; and, in an attempt made by the Aragonese, to possess themselves of Porto Venere, they were repulsed with some loss, and retired to Leghorn, to repair their damage. They soon, however, proceeded again towards the coast of Genoa, and effected a landing at Rapallo, where they began to intrench themselves; but the duke of Orleans, having assumed the command of the Genoese fleet, which had been re-inforced by four large ships, and having taken on board about a thousand Swiss mercenaries, hastened towards that place; whilst a body of troops, under the command of Anton-Maria da San sev-erino, CHAP. III.

a. D. 1494. a. *JEX.* Iflt Unsuccessful ex-pedition of the Neapolitans *(a)* Called by Corio, "Monsignore Orfeo." *Storia di Milan, par.* vii. *p.* 927.

Chap. m. severino, and Giovanni Adorno, were directed to proceed A. D. 14y4. along the coast, and co-operate with the duke.*fa)* On the

A. *Jex.* 19. first attack, the Swiss troops were repulsed by the Neapoli-tans; but the detachment by land arriv-ing to their assistance, the engagement M as renewed; and the Neapolitans, conceiving themselves likely to be sur-rounded, took to flight, and abandoned their enterprize, with the loss of about two hundred men killed, besides a con-siderable number of prisoners. To this victory, the heavy artillery of" one of the French ships, which was brought to bear upon the Neapolitan troops, greatly contributed./ Such of the fugitives as fell into the hands of the Genoese, after being plundered, were suffered to es-cape; but the Swiss shewed no mercy to the vanquished; and notwithstanding the remonstrances of their allies, *(aj Giustiniani, AnnalidiGenoa. lib. . p. 2iQ. b..* (bj It belonged to Commines, who denominates it " une grosse galeace (qui etoit mienne) "qui patron-isoit un appelle Albert Mely, sur laque-lle etoit le diet due et les prlnclpaux. 'Et la "dicte galeace avoitgrande artillerie, et grosses pieces, (car elle etoit puis-sante) et s'approcha "si pres de terre que l'artillerie deconfit presque l'ennemi, qui jamais n'en avoit veu de "sem-blable, et etoit chose nouvelle eB Italic" *liv.* vii. *chap. 5. p.* 194. The use of ar-tillery was, however, known in Italy, about the year 1380, in the wars be-tween the Genoese and the Venetians. *Summonte, Storia di Napoli.* iii. 497-

Corr. 563.) *Malacolti, Storia di Siena, p.* 170. *Gvicaardini, lii. 'i.* The latter au-thor, however, acknowledges that the French had brought this diabolical im-plement—" questo piu tosto diabolico che "umano instrumento"—to much greater perfection, and employed it with more celerity and effect, than had be-fore been done. Cornazzano, in his po-em *De re Militari,* narrates the discov-ery of' fire-arms at considerable length. The' larger pieces were denominated *Bombardi,* the smaller *Scopetti,* and *Spingarde.*

"Nacque cosl madonna la bombarda,
"Di quel che venne le cose iterando;
"Et dui figli hebbe, schiopetto e spin-garda." Relating the effects of the first of these implements (the bombarda, or cannon)(he adds: — "——— dove va in persona, li Ogni edifizio gli Fa riv-erenza." *Cornaz. de re Milk. lib.* iii. *p.* 58. *fyc.* allies stormed and plundered the town of itapallo, where, Chap, in. among other enormities, they slaugh-tered even the sick in A. D. 1494... the hospitals. The indignation which this cruelty excited A-9« at Genoa had near-ly effected that which the Neapolitan, armament had failed to accomplish, On the return of the troops to that cjty, the populace rose apd massacred several of the Swiss soldiery; and the duke of Or-leans, instead of returning from his ex-pedition in triumph, was under the ne cessity of taking precautions for his safety before he ventured to disembark. /?/

Ferdinand.duic

In the mean time» it became neces-sary to check the progress of D'Aubigny, who, having now collected a considerable force, had entered Ro-magna, and wa6 proceeding, of Cal-abria, without interruption, towards the territories of Naples. The. e command of the detachment intended for this pur-pose, was relinquished by Alfonso to his son Ferdinand, duke of Calabria, who, at the head of a body of troops, superior in number to the French and their allies, took his station between the branches of the Po. He there presented himself for some hours in order of bat-tle, and by his courage and promptitude,

conciliated to his cause no small share of popular favour. For some time, the French and Neapolitan armies were en-camped within a mile of each other; but D'Aubigny prudently declined a con-test. As the enemy increased in force, Ferdinand in his turn, was compelled to retreat. The intelligence of the disaster at Rapallo, and the certainty *(a) Gius-tiniani, Antudi di Genoa, lib.* v. *p.* 250. *fb)* At this time, Cariteo endeavoured to incite the states of Italy to concord and confidence in each other, and to an unit-ed defence against the common enemy, in an energetic canzone, which will be found in the Appendix, No, XXVIII.

Chap, in. certainty of the approach of Charles VIII. had contributed to A. D. 1494. dispirit the Neapolitan troops; and at the moment when the

A. *xx.* 19-duke of Calabria, ought, by the vigour and decision of his measures, to have confirmed the wavering minds of the Italian potentates, he gave the omen of his future ruin, by retiring un-der the walls of Faenza; where, instead of attempting offensive operations, he was satisfied with fortifying himself against an attack.*fa)*

On the twenty-second day of August, 1494, Charles took Charles vni. hs de-parture from Vienne; and, passing through Grenoble, crossed the Alps, and arrived at Turin; where he was received with great honour by Bianca, widow of Charles, duke of Savoy. Of the splendid appearance of the duchess and her court, a particular description is given by one of the attendants of the French monarch.(ty Such was the profusion of jewels displayed on this occasion, that Charles, whose resources were not very ample, conceived that a favourable *(a) Gukciardini. lib.* i. *vol. i.p.* 48.

(b) Andr& de la Vigne, was secretary to Anne of Bretagne, queen of Charles VI-II. and accompanied the king on this ex-pedition, of which he has left a journal, in prose and verse, entitled, *Le Vergier d'honneur,* which has been attributed, in part, to Octavien de St. Gelais, bishop of Angoulfeme; but the French critics have determined, that the complaint on the death of Charles VIII. and his epi-taph, are the only parts of the work to

which the bishop has any pretensions. Of this work there are two editions, both printed in Gothic characters at Paris, but without date, the one in folio, the other in quarto; the former of these, which has been consulted on this occasion, is entitled— -Le Vercier D' Honneur, Nouvellement Imprime A Paris, *de Vinterprinse et voyage de Naples. Anquel est comprins comment le roy, Charles huytiesme de ce nam, a banitre deployee, passa et repassa, de journee en journee, depuis Lyonjusques a Naples, et de Naples jasques a Lyon. Ensemble plusieurs auUres chases, faictes et composees par reverend pere en dieit Monsieur Octavien de Sainct Gelais, evesque d'' Angovlesme, et par Maistre Andry de la Vigne, secretaire de la royne, et de Monsieur le due de Savoye, avec autires.* favourable opportunity was afforded him for improving CHAP-Inthem; of this he accordingly availed himself, by borrow-A. D..149. ing a great part of these superfluous ornaments, which he A-*9'* immediately pledged for a sum of twelve thousand ducats. During his residence at Turin, he was entertained by such exhibitions as were then esteemed the most extraordinary efforts of ingenuity. fa,J On the sixth day of September, he quitted that city and proceeded to Chieri, where his progress was again retarded for some days, by the amusements and representations which had been prepared for him, in which the most beautiful women of Italy were selected to congratulate him on his approach, and to crown him *Champion of the honour of the fair.(b)* On his arrival at Asti he was met by Lodovico Sforza, accompanied by his duchess, Beatrice of Este, the splendor of whose dress and equipage astonished his followers. The attention of Lodovico had here provided him with a number of beautiVol. i. x ful *(a)* These exhibitions are thus described by Andre de la Vigne:—

"Labeur y vis bien dehait en pourpoint;

"Et pastoreaulx chanter de contrepoint

"Petis rondeaulx faits dessus lcurs hystoires;

"Inventions de la loi de nature.

"Pareillement de cette descripture

"Bien compassees furent tllic a flac

"Noe, Sem, Cham, y vis en portraiture,

"Et de la loi de grace leur figure;

"Puis Abraham, Jacob, et Isaac,

"Plusiers histoires de Lancelot du lac,

"Celle d'Athenes du gran Cocordillac." &c. *fbj Champion de Vhonncur des dames.* Of the taste of the monarch, and of the delicacy of his female attendants, some idea may be formed from the account given of these representations; one of which was a pretended *accouchement.* This exhibition is described in the rude verses of Andre de la Vigne. It is only to be regretted, that from the nature of things, the curiosity of the monarch could not be gratified by his performing, in reality, the principal part on such an occasion himself, r. *Appendix, No. XXIX.*

Chap, in. ful courtesans from Milan, who were honoured by the notice, a. D. 1494.. and rewarded by the liberality of the French monarch.

A. iEt. ig. At, this place his expedition, had however, nearly been brought to a premature termination; for he was seized with a. disorder, which confined him for some days to his chamber, and is said to have endangered his *lik.fb)*

Whilst the king remained at Asti, he received information of the success of the duke of Orleans at Genoa, and of the retreat of Ferdinand of Aragon before the arms of D'Aubigny. He did not, however, quit that place before the sixth day of October, when he proceeded to Casale, the capital city of the marquis *(a)* " Lodovico Sforza, mahdo al Re molte formosissime matrone Milanese, con alcune » delle quali pigHò amoroso piacere, e quelle presento di preciosi anelli. D'indi per la 'mutation dell'aere Carlo s'infermò di varuole." &c. *Corio, Storia Milanese, lib.* vii.

fbj Historians have represented this disorder as the small pox. Malavolti, in his history of Siena, says, that Charles was detained at Asti about a month; "ritenuto da "quel male che da noi e domandato *Vajuolo.*" par. iii. p. 99. Commines also denominates the disorder of the king, "la petite verole," and adds, that his life

was in danger. Benedetti, in his *Fatto d'arme sul Tarro, p.* 7, informs us, that from change of air, Charles was seized with a fever, "e mando fuori alcuni segni che si chiamano *epinittide;* "(' tmrvxriia, night pimples)* i nostri le chiamano *Vajuole.* " From the extreme licentiousness in which the king had indulged himself, it is not, however, improbable that his complaint was of a different nature, and that the loathsome disorder, which, within the space of a few months afterwards, began to spread itself over Italy, and was thence communicated to the rest of Europe, is of royal origin, and may be dated from this event. In favour of this supposition it may be observed that this disease was much more violent in its symptoms, on its first appearance, than in after times, and that its resemblance to the small-pox probably gave rise to the appellation by which it has since been known.

"Protinus informes totum per corpus achores

"Rumpebant, faciemque horrendam, et pectora fade

"Turpebant; species morbi nova; pusrula summae

M Glandis ad effigiem, et pituita marcida pingui."
Fracastor. Syphil. lib. i. /. 349.

duke of Milan. marquis of Montferrat. At this place he met with a recep-CHAP mtion similar to that which he had experienced at Turin, and A. D. j4)4. repaid it in a similar manner, by borrowing the jewels of the Amarchioness, who was the mother of the duchess of Savoy, upon which he raised at Genoa a further sum of money. He then hastened with his army to Pavia, where some jealousy arose between him and Lodovico Sforza; who consented, as a pledge of his fidelity, to place the fortress of the city in his hands. On this occasion, Charles had an interview with his Hu. if7iew with Gian near relation GianGaleazzo, the unfortunate duke of Milan, Galeazzo, who then lay at the point of death, a victim to the ambition of his uncle Lodovico. The duchess Isabella, availed herself of this opportunity, to throw herself at the feet of the monarch, to intreat his interference on behalf of her husband, and his forbearance towards her father and family; but the importunities of a daughter, a wife, and a mother, were lost on the depraved mind of Charles, and served only to excite the unfeeling remarks of his barbarian attendants. The duke did not long survive this interview; and Lodovico, having attained the height of his wishes, was saluted by. a band of venal partisans, and a corrupt populace, as duke of Milan. His wife, Beatrice, daughter of Ercole, duke of Ferrara, who had long and arrogantly contended with Isabella for precedence in rank and honours, now enjoyed a complete, but temporary triumph over her rival, who was driven from the court of Milan, and obliged, Avith her children, to take refuge in an obscure and sickly cell of the castle of Pavia.1 x 2 On (a) " Elle avoit meilleur besoin," says Commines, "de prier pour son mari et pour elle, qui etoit encore belle dame et jeune." *lib.* vii. *chap.* vi. *p.* 196. (b) " Isabella co i poveri figliuoletti, vestiti di lugubri vestimenti, come prigioniera si richiuse CHAP. III.

A. D..1494.

A. *M. 19-*

Hesitates respecting the

of his enterprise.

On the arrival of Charles at Piacenza, a few days after this interview, he received intelligence of the death of the duke, Gian-Galeazzo; and although he had not the generosity to interfere on his behalf, he was shocked at a catastrophe which he had taken no measures to prevent, and celebrated his obsequies with great state and formality. That the duke died by poison, administered to him at the instance of Lodovico Sforza, was the general opinion; and Theodoro of Pavia, an eminent physician, who had accompanied *the* king of France, in his interview with the duke, declared, that he had perceived manifest symptoms of its effects. A sudden panic seized the French monarch. The perpetration of such a crime, filled him with apprehensions for his own safety. He had already entertained wellgrounded suspicions of the fidelity of Lodovico Sforza, and Jrad experienced considerable difficulties in obtaining the necessary supplies

for his troops. In this situation, he began seriously to hesitate on the expediency of prosecuting his expedition; and his doubts were increased by a communication from his general and grand-ecuyer D'Urfe, then at Genoa, advising him to be on his guard against treachery. Such of his attendants as had been the first to encourage him to this undertaking, were now the most earnest in advising him to abandon it; and had not the Florentine exiles, and particularly richiuse in una camera, e gran tempo stette giacendo sopra ladura terra, che non vide aere. "

Corio, Hist or. Milanese, part. vii. *p. 936.* This unfortunate princess, is introduced by

Bernardo Accolti, as thus lamenting her misfortunes:

"Re padre, Re fratel, Duca in consorte

"Ebbi, e in tre anni, i tre rapl la morte."
Accolti. Op. ven. 1519. *(a) Commines, Mem.Ub.* vii. *chap.* vii. *p. 179 (Corr. 197.) (b) Gtticciardin. lib. i. p.* 49.

ticularly Lorenzo and Giovanni, the sons of Pier-Francesco de' Medici, actuated by the hopes of supplanting the rival branch of their family, at this critical juncture, interposed their solicitations, and offered their services to the king, it is probable, that Italy might yet have been saved from her impending calamities/a,!

Having recovered from his alarm, Charles quitted Piacenza, on the twenty-fifth day of October. A question of great moment now presented itself for his consideration: whether he should proceed through the Tuscan and Roman territories directly to Naples, or by forcing a passage through Romagna, and the March of Ancona, enter that kingdom by the district of Abruzzo. The judicious determination of the king and his advisers on this occasion, was of the utmost importance to the success of his enterprize. In relinquishing the track through Romagna, he was not deterred by the opposition which he might there meet, from the duke of Calabria, who had already retreated before the arms of D'Aubigny; but he prudently considered, that unless he could either secure

the alliance of the pope and the Florentines, or disable them from resistance, he might, during his contest with Alfonso, in Naples, be exposed to the hostile attack of these adjacent states-Instead, therefore, of directing his course towards Bologna, he ordered the duke de Mompensier, one of the princes of the family of Bourbon, to proceed with the advanced guard to Pontremoli, a town on the river Magro, which divides the Tuscan territory from that of Genoa; to which place, Charles followed with the remainder of his army, having passed the Appenines, by the mountain

Determines to proceed *by* way of Florence to Rome.

(a) Mem. de Commines, Bo, vii. *chap.* vii. *p. iff?.* mountain of Parma. From Pontremoli, Mompensier proceeded through the district of Luigiana to Fivizano, a fortress belonging to the Florentines; and being there joined by the Swiss mercenaries, who had returned from Genoa, and brought with them several heavy pieces of artillery, the French attacked the castle, which they carried by storm, and put both the garrison and inhabitants to the sword. The town of Sarzana, which had been acquired by the prudence, and fortified under the directions of Lorenzo the Magnificent, next opposed their progress; and, although the number of soldiers employed in its defence was small, and the commander of little experience, or reputation, yet such was the situation and strength of the place, and of the adjacent citadel of Sarzanella, that the carrying them by force, was regarded as a matter of considerable difficulty. Nor could the French army long retain its position, in a situation between the sea and the mountains, where, from the sterility of the district, they could scarcely hope to obtain supplies. To proceed forwards, whilst these formidable positions remained in the hands of an enemy, was equally inconsistent with the honour and the safety of the *kmg.fa* Piero de' Medici surrenders to Charles VIII. the fortresses of Tuscany.

In this emergency, the unhappy dissentions which prevailed among the citizens of Florence, again relieved the

French from their difficulties. From the time that the approach of the king had been announced, the resentment of the inhabitants had been chiefly directed against Piero de' Medici, whom they considered as the principal cause of the dangers which they were likely to incur. On his part, Piero had *(a) Guicciard. lib. i. Mem. de Comtmnes, lib. vii. chap. 7- v. i. p. 50, 51.*

had endeavoured to regain their confidence, by active pre-CHAP IIi. parations for resisting the enemy; to which end he had A. D. 1494. strengthened the city of Pisa, and other fortified towns of the A-m-19' republic, and had, particularly, provided for the defence of Florence. These preparations, were not, however, effected without expense, and the levies imposed upon the citizens, became an additional cause of dissatisfaction. He then endeavoured to avail himself of the voluntary contributions of the richer classes; but, instead of the necessary aid, he obtained only reproaches and threats. Alarmed and dispirited, he adopted the hasty resolution of repairing in person to the French camp, for the purpose of endeavouring to conciliate the favour of Charles, by such timely concessions as circumstances might require. He therefore privately quitted the city, and hastened to Empoli, a few miles distant from Florence; whence he addressed a letter to the magistrates, which is yet preserved, and which fully explains the motives of his conduct at this period, so critical to the fortunes of himself and his family.*fa)*

"Magnificent and honoured Fathers,

"I shall not attempt to apologize for my sudden de"parture, because I can scarcely think myself culpable "for taking a measure which, according to my weak judg"ment, appears to be the best remedy for restoring "the tranquillity of my country, and which, at the same "time, is attended with less danger and inconvenience "than any other, both to the public and to individuals; "excepting only myself. I therefore intend to present "myself in person, before his most christian majesty "of France; as I may probably thus be enabled to "appease *(aj The original is given in*

the Appendix, No. XXX.

Chap. in. n appease the resentment which he-has conceived against a. D. 1494. "this city, for the conduct which it has hitherto been

A. iEt.19. "obliged to adopt, in consequence of its engagements with "other states; it appearing to be only his majesty's wish, "that an alteration should take place in this respect. I, who "have been blamed as the cause of this animosity, will, "therefore, either exculpate myself to his majesty, or shall "be ready to receive due punishment, rather in my own per"son, than in the body of the republic. Of this course of "conduct, particular instances have been given in my own 4 family; but I consider myself as under much greater obli"gations to exert myself, than any of my predecessors have "been; because I have been honoured much more beyond "my merits than any of them; and the more unworthy I am ". of those honours, the more I feel myself bound to engage in "my present attempt, and not to shrink from labour, inconvenience, or expense, or even the sacrifice of my life, which "I would willingly resign, for each of you in particular, and "much more for the whole republic. This I shall probably "manifest on the present occasion, on which I shall either "return to the satisfaction of yourselves and the city, or lose "my life in the attempt. In the mean time, I intreat you, by "the fidelity and affection which you owe to the ashes of your "Lorenzo, my late father, and the kindness which you have "shewn to me, who, in reverence and affection, am not less "your son than his, that you will remember me in your "prayers. I also have further to request, that you will "accept my recommendation of my brothers and children, "whom, if it should be the will of God that I should not "return, I bequeath wholly to your care. I shall begin my "journey from this place to-morrow.; *In Empoli, 26 October, 494. Piero De' Medici."*

From

From Empoli, Piero proceeded to Pisa, whence, on the CHAP-111 following day, he addressed a letter to his private secre-A. D. 1494. tary, Pietro da

Bibbiena, in which he directs him to Aassure the Neapolitan ambassadors at Florence, of his unalterable attachment to Alfonso and the house of Aragon, from whom he intreats a favourable, construction of the measures which he has unfortunately been compelled to adopt. If his letter to the magistrates contain, as might be expected, only the more plausible and popular motives of his conduct, in this private communication, he explicitly acknowledges, that he has been abandoned by all the citizens of Florence, as well his friends as his enemies; and that he has neither resources nor credit to support the war, in which he has involved himself and his country, by his adherence to his engagements with the royal house of Naples. *(a)*

Under these discouraging impressions, Piero de' Medici presented himself, with a few attendants, at the French camp before Sarzana. On his arrival, two of the confidential officers of Charles, Monsieur de Piennes, his chamberlain, and the general Brissonet, were appointed to treat with him. Their first request was, that the fortress of Sarzana should be surrendered to the French arms, with which Piero instantly complied. They then insisted on Pisa, Leghorn, and Pietrasanta, being also delivered up to the king, on his promise to restore them, when they were no longer necessary to the success of his enterprize; and to this demand Piero also assented. The readiness with which he thus delivered up places of such strength and importance,

Vol. 1. Y astonished *(a)* For the letter to BibbJena, *v. Appauhx, No. XXXT.*

Chap. in. astonished the French, who seem to have despised his A. D. 14.9 +. weakness and ridiculed his credulity *.(a)* As he held no A. A:u 19. ostensible rank, they gave him the title of // *gran Lonibardo;* it being in those times customary to designate all the Italians by the general name of Lombards.

This unfortunate transaction, in which Piero de' Medici The Florentines professedly imitated, but with mistaken application, the exasperated *J x* at the con-example of his father in his voyage to Naples, gave u,ct f,Pl-CTO irremediable offence to the citizens of Florence; who, de' Medici.' although they had refused to assist him in opposing the progress of the French, conceived that he had made a wanton sacrifice of their interests. It may, however, well be doubted, whether this was so much the reason as the pretext for the resentment of the Florentines, many of whom had become impatient of the authority of the Medici, and, being prompted by the violent harangues of Savonarola, sought only for an opportunity of exciting the populace to second their views. A new deputation was nominated, consisting of five citizens, among whom was Savonarola, who were directed to proceed to Lucca, where the king had now arrived, and to intreat him to moderate the severity of the terms agreed on. Charles gave them an attentive audience; but neither the persuasions nor the threats of the priest, who represented himself as a messenger on the part of God, could induce the king to relax from his former (a) " Ceux qui traictoient avec le diet Pierre, m'ont compte, et k plusieurs autres "l'ont dit, en se raillant & moquant de lui, qu'ils etoient ebahis comme si tot accorda si "grande chose, et k quoi ils ne s'attendoient pas. " Mem. de Comm. liv. vii. chap. vii. p. 19S. The circumstances of this interview are also related by Andr& de la Vigne in his Vergier d'honnenr, with his usual insipidity.

fbj Nardi, Hist. at Fiorenza. lib. i. p. 11. former stipulations. This measure, was, however, a suf-Chap. Hl ficient indication to Piero de' Medici, of the dissatisfaction A. D. 1494. which his conduct had occasioned, and of the necessity of A.ir. 19. securing himself against the effects of that animosity, which would probably be excited against him. He therefore engaged his near relation, Paolo Orsini, who then commanded a body of troops in the service of the republic, to accompany him towards the city, intending to suppress the outrages of the populace by force of arms, and, as his adversaries have conjectured, to take upon himself, the uncontrolled dominion of the state; to which he is supposed

to have been incited by his wife, Alfonsina, and her relations of the Orsini *family.(b)* On his arrival, he proceeded with a few attendants to the palace of justice, apparently for the purpose of explaining to the citizens the reasons of his conduct; but Luca Corsini, Giacopo de' Nerli, and other magistrates, met him at the gates, and with many reproaches, opposed his admission. This circumstance occasioned a general clamour and commotion, in which the friends of the Medici, who attempted to suppress the tumult, were insulted and plundered; whilst Piero, with difficulty, escaped the resentment of the populace.

In the mean time, the cardinal, less obnoxious to the people than his brother, endeavoured to conciliate their 11,6 C8rdinal r r de' Medici, favour by pacific remonstrances, and by the cry of *Palle,* withhisbro*Palle,* in reference to the arms of his family. But the charm *lheTM'¥TM*

» and Ginliano, which had lasted so many years, was now broken; and these expelled the words, which had seldom been heard without producing a

Y 2, favourable

"(a) Nardi, Hist. di Fiorenza, lib. i.p. 11. (b). Nardi, Hist. di Fiorenza. lib. i. p. 12.

Chap. nx favourable effect, only served to excite additional indignaA. D. 1494. tion. The clamour and violence of the populace increased;

A. £x. 19. the alarm-bell rang; the prisoners were set at liberty; the farther progress of the cardinal was prevented by impenetrable crowds, whilst Piero and his attendants were threatened with an attack of stones, from the windows and roofs of the houses. The fate of the Medici hung on the decision of a moment; and Piero had to determine, whether he would try the event of arms in the bosom of his native place, or abandon the city, and seek a refuge in some other part of Italy. Of these expedients, he adopted the latter; but, by an unaccountable fatality, instead of resorting to the French camp, where he would probably have obtained the favour and protection of Charles, for having complied with whose requisitions he had

been obliged to quit the city, he passed with his brother Giuliano, through the gate of S. Gallo, and took the road to Bologna. The cardinal, either not equally alarmed at the danger, or more reluctant to quit his native place, was the last of the brothers who left the city. Finding, however, that the populace were proceeding to the utmost extreme of violence, he divested himself of the insignia of his rank, and, assuming the habit of a Franciscan, passed, without being recognized, through the midst of the exasperated multitude, to the convent of S. Marco, where he hoped to find a temporary shelter, in a building erected and endowed by his ancestors. In this, however, he was disappointed; the monks having, with singular ingratitude, refused to admit him within their gates. Repulsed from the only quarter on which he relied for. protection, he immediately abandoned the city, and hastening (a) This event occurred on the ninth day of November, 1494. *Nardi, lib. i. p. 13.* hastening into the secret recesses of the Appenines, effected CHAP-m his retreat, and joined his brothers at Bologna. A. D. 194.

A. M.t. 19.

No sooner had the Medici quitted the city, than the The Palace of rage of the populace broke out in open acts of violence, the Medici The palace of the Medici, and the houses of several of the plundered, chief officers of the state, who were supposed to be favourable to their party, were attacked and plundered. The residence of the cardinal, in the district of S. Antonio, experienced a similar fate; but a circumstance which cannot fail to excite the regret of every friend of the arts, is the destruction of the garden of S. Marco, established by the liberality and personal attention of Lorenzo the Magnificent, as an academy for the promotion of sculpture; the repository of the finest remains of antiquity, and the school of Michael Angelo. We might have pardoned the expunging of the figures of the rebels, painted on the walls of the palace, in the year 1434, or the obliteration of the labours of Andrea del Castagno, commemorating the conspiracy of the Pazzi, in 1478; but the destruction of this collection, was an irreparable misfortune to the progress of true taste, as yet in its earliest infancy; and was poorly compensated by the figure of Judith, executed by Donatello, at the request of the Florentines; and placed at the gate of the palace, as an emblem of the destruction of a tyrant.

On *(a) Ammirato, Ritratti a Ttuomini di Casa Medici. Opusc. v. iii. p. 65.* To the short period which elapsed between the death of Lorenzo and the expulsion of his son Piero, we may refer the Latin poem of Lorenzo Vitelli, intitled *Arborea;* in which, under the allegory of a vigorous and fruitful tree, he describes the flourishing family of the Medici; not aware of the sudden blight which it was shortly to experience, *v. Carm. illustr. Poet. ltd. vol.* xi. *p. 366. -.*

(b) Ammirato, Istorie Florentine, vol. iii. *p. 223.* The dispersion of the library of

Politiano

Pisa asserts it liberties.

Chap, ni. Qn same day that the brothers of the Medici were a. D: 1494. compelled to abandon their native place, an event occurred *A.st. 19.* m the city of Pisa, which, although in its origin, of small comparative importance, became, in the event, a fruitful source of contention and bloodshed; and served, when the terrors of a foreign enemy were removed, to disturb the repose, and protract the calamities of Italy. Irreconcilably adverse to the Florentine government, the citizens of Pisa were, at all times, ready to avail themselves of any opportunity to assert their ancient liberties. This restless and unconquerable spirit, afforded a reason, or a pretext for additional cautions and severities on the part of the Florentines; which, without subduing the courage, excited the resentment of the people. No sooner had Charles, after quitting Lucca, arrived at Pisa, than he was surrounded by a tumultuous assemblage of the inhabitants, who, with affecting lamentations, and grievous complaints against their oppressors, intreated the king to free them from their *yoke.fa)* The earnest and repeated solicitations of the multitude, made a powerful impression on some

of the favourite attendants of the king, who observed to him, that the request Politiano, followed soon after the exile of the Medici. The learned admirers of this great man, will, perhaps, be gratified with the inventory of the MSS. and other effects, found in his possession at the time of his death, taken by the celebrated and learned Greek,

Joannes Lascar, and which has not before been printed, *v. Appendix, No. XXXII.*

(a) " Par grans monceaulx lecommun populaire

"De$a, dela, c'etoit voulu assire,

"Pour hault crier en amour voluntaire;

"Voire si hault qu'ils ne pouvoyent taire,

"*Iabertate, Libertate,* chier sire;

"Qui en Francis vault autaht comme dire,

"*Hclas, sire, donnez nous liberti."* Sec.

And. de la Vigne, Vergier d'honneur. quest of the citizens was just and reasonable; whereupon Chap, ia Charles, acting under the impulse of his immediate feelings, A. D. 149, and forgetful or regardless of his solemn engagement, to A-. restore the city of Pisa to its former governors, signified his assent to their request. This hasty and inconsiderate assurance, was received by the citizens of Pisa, as a full emancipation from their servitude, and their exultation was displayed, by the immediate demolition of the arms and insignia of the Florentines throughout the city. The Florentine commissioners, were at the same time expelled from Pisa, not without great apprehensions of violence to their persons, which was prevented only by the authority of the king and his attendants.

Whilst Charles was thus hastening, without interruption, towards the object of his destination, his general,.

D'Aubigny, had made a considerable progress in Romagna, duke of c»where he had attacked and taken several fortresses, and had 7"

'toe arms *ot* compelled Caterina Sforza, widow of Girolamo Riario, who D Aubignj. then governed the states of Imola and Forli, in the name of her infant son Ottaviano, to relinquish the al-

liance into which she had entered with the pope and the king of Naples. His approach towards Faenza, with the additional troops which had joined his standard, alarmed the duke of Calabria, who, quitting his intrenchments, proceeded with his army, by the most retired and difficult paths, to Cesena. He was there informed of the commotions which had arisen in Florence, and of the surrender of the chief fortresses of the Tuscan state to the French arms; in consequence of which he again broke up his camp, and hastily retreated towards Rome. By these pusillanimous measures, the power of the French, which, like a small stream, might have rence.

Chap. in. have been successfully checked in its commencement, was A. D. 1494. suffcrcd to proceed in an uninterrupted course, and, by a A.Et. 19. continual accession, to bear down all possibility of resistance.

On the eleventh day of November, Charles left Pisa, and proceeded to Empoli, intending to enter the city of Flocharies vm. rence; but on his arrival at Signa, about six miles distant, city of no-ne received information of the expulsion of the Medici, in consequence of the surrender of the fortified towns of the republic to his arms. Conceiving it therefore, not improbable that he might meet with resistance, he ordered D'Aubigny, who was no longer opposed in Romagna, to join him with a part of the troops under his command. This measure greatly alarmed the inhabitants of Florence, who began to suspect that Charles intended to possess himself of the city by force.*fa)* Nor were there wanting among his followers, many who advised him to this measure, and who even endeavoured to prevail upon him to deliver it up to be plundered by the soldiery, on the pretence of its being the first *(a)* The intention of the king to attack the city, is also thus adverted to by Andrd de la Vigne:—

"Au pont du Signe fut des jours cinq ou six;

"Car Florentins mutines et perdus

"S'estoient contre Pierre de Medycys,

"Qui leurs chateaulx avoit au roy rendus.

"Dessus les champs mises ses guettes
et gardes,

"Et leur monstra de si bon remise,

"Que tost apres vindrent les ambas-
sades

"De Florence, de Sene, etde Venice:

"Fait assembler avoit ja tous ses gens,

"Et amener toute l'artillerie,

"Pour a Florence, sans etre negligens,

"Y aller faire quelque grand dyab-
lene." first place that had resisted his
arms, and as an example to CHAP-111
the rest of *Italy.fa)* The Florentines
were, however, inces-A. D. 1494, sant
in their embassies and representations
to Charles; and A-»? perhaps the rich
presents and delicate viands, with which
they supplied his camp at Signa, might,
in some degree, mitigate his resentment.
Nor did they neglect the best precautions in their power to secure themselves against hostilities, in case the
king should prove irreconcilable. Great
numbers of armed men from different
parts of the Tuscan territory, entered the
city under various pretexts, and were secretly lodged in the houses of the citizens. The *condottieri,* in the service of
the republic, distributed their troops in
the most convenient stations, and held
themselves in readiness for action, on
the tolling of the great bell of the palace
of justice. These alarms, however, soon
subsided, and on the seventeenth day of
November, Charles made his peaceable
and public entry into the city on horseback, under a rich canopy, supported by
some of his younger nobles, and attended by his barons and men at arms. He
was met on his approach, by the magistrates and principal inhabitants, who
Vol. 1. z accompanied *(a) Guicciardini,
lib.* i. *v.* i. *p.* 58.

(b) On the same day died at Florence,
in the thirty-second year of his age, the
accomplished Giovanni Pico, of Mirandula, and, if we may credit the report of
Savonarola, had the good fortune to obtain a situation in purgatory. This intelligence, the preacher thus announced to
his audience at the conclusion of one of
his sermons, a few days after the death
of that eminent man. "lo vi voglio riv-
elare un secreto, 'che insino a qui non

ho "voluto dirlo, perchfi non ho avuto
tanta certezza come ho avuto da diece
hore in quiL "Ciascuno di voi credo che
cognoscesse il conte Giovanni della Mirandola, che stava qui "in Firenze, ed
e morto pochi giorni sono. Dicovi che
l'anima sua, per le orationi "de' frati, ed
anche per alcunc sue buone opere, che
fece in questa vita, e per altre ora"tioni,
h nel purgatorio— *orate pro* eo—lui fu
tardo a non venire alla religione in vita
sua, "come era spirato, e perb e in purgatorio." The verses of Marullus, on the
death of Pico, are more appropriate, although less known, than the ostentatious lines inscribed on his tomb in the
church of S. Marco, at Florence, *v. Op.
Mar.* 53.

Chap. in. accompanied *him* to the
church of S. Maria del Fiore, where A.
D. 1494. he paid a visit to the great
altar; alter which he proceeded *K.JEx.
19.* to tlie palace the Medici, which was
magnificently prepared for his reception./ His nobility and chief officers
were lodged in the.princely houses of
the richer inhabitants; and the illumina-
tion of the city, which continued every
night during the stay of the king, contributed no less to its peace and security,
than to the honour of its royal guest.
Conciliated by these attentions, Charles
passed several days in partaking of the
amusements prepared for him. Among
these was the *Rappresentazione* of the
annunciation of the virgin, which was
exhibited, with great splendour and me-
chanical ingenuity, in the church of S.
Felice, and with which the king was so
greatly delighted, that he requested to
be gratified by a second exhibition.

No sooner had the three brothers of
the Medici quitted the city, than Lorenzo and Giovanni, the sons of
PierFrancesco, returned to Florence,
and were restored to their possessions
and their rights; *(c)* but the name of the
Medici was *(a) Nardi, Hist. Fior. lib.*
i. *p.* 14. The entrance of the king into
Florence is one of those topics on which
his poetical annalist, De la Vigne,
dwells with particular satisfaction. On
this occasion he enumerates the'whole
array of the French army, and all the attendants of the king. *v. Appendix, No.*

XXXIII. fbj Nardi, Hist. Fior.-lib. i. *p.* 15.
fcj Lorenzo, the son of Pier Francesco,
appears to have emulated Tiis relations
of the elder branch of his family, in the
love of literature and patronage of
learned men. Politiano has addressed to
him his Sylva, entitled Manto, in terms
of great esteem:— "Ferreus sim," says
he, "si tibi quid denegem, tam nobili
adolescenti, tam probo, tam "mei amanti, tanto denique eam rem studio efflag-
itanti." The beautiful introductory stanzas to this piece, have been elegantly
translated, by the Rev. Mr. Greswell, in
his *Memoirs of Politiano, SfC. p.* 92.
Lorenzo di Pier-Francesco, was also the
great patron of was now become odious,
and with a despicable servility, which
has been imitated in subsequent times,
they relinquished their family appellation, and adopted that of *Popolani;* at
the same time, removing from their residence, the insignia of their arms, and re-
placing them by those of the republic.

In the mean time, Piero and his brothers,
in their retreat to Bologna, had not experienced that friendly reception which
they had reason to expect from Giovanni Bentivoglio, who then held the chief
authority in that place, and whose obligations to their father, were supposed to
be a sufficient pledge for his favour.
Expecting from others that fortitude
which, in the moment of adversity, he
did not exhibit himself, Bentivoglio, instead of consoling them in their misfortunes, or encouraging their hopes, re-
proached them for having pusillani-
mously quitted a place, where they had
such influence and resources, not only
without the death of a single adherent,
but without even the unsheathing of a
sword, or the slightest effort in their
own defence. As this remonstrance
could now be of no avail, the brothers
considered it as a sufficient indication,
that Bologna would not *z 2,* fong

Piero de' Medici retires to Venice,
and the cardinal to Castello.
of the poet Marullus, who has inscribed
to him, at different times, his four books
of epigrams, several of which, are devoted to his praise, hi one of these he is
thus addressed:—..

"Felix ingenii, felix et gratiae opumque, "Laurus, et antiquis nonleven-omen avis,

"Quaerenti cuidam num plura his optet'? ut, inquit,

"Et prodesse queam pluribus, et cupiam. "

Marullus also addressed to Giovanni, the other son of Pier-Francesco, a copy of Latin verses, in praise of Caterina Sforza, the widow of Girolamo Riario, whom Giovanni afterwards married, and by whom he had Giovanni de' Medici, captain of the *bande nere,* and usually called *Ilgran diavolo,* father of Cosmo I. grand duke of Tuscany.

v. Epigr. lib. i.p. 54.

Chap, m. long De a place Gf safety. Piero, disguised in the habit of a A. D. 1494. valet, hastened to Venice, where he met with an honourable

A.iEt. 19. reception from the senate, who permitted him to wear his arms in the city, and to be attended by fifteen or twenty of his adherents. The cardinal, shortly afterwards, retreated to Pitigliano, and from thence to Castello, where he found an hospitable shelter with the Vitelli, then the lords of that place, and the ancient friends of his family./a)

Among the nobility who attended the French king on ci.aries intends his expedition, there was no one who enjoyed, a greater to reinstate

Pierode Me-share of his confidence, than Philip de Bresse, uncle to the dlcl young duke of Savoy, and who succeeded at no distant period to the sovereignty of that state. On the arrival of the army at Florence, this nobleman had taken up his residence at the house of Lorenzo Tornabuoni, a near relation of Piero de' Medici, who found the means of influencing him in favour of the exiled family; insomuch that De Bresse did not hesitate strenuously to advise the king to recall Piero, and restore him to his former authority in Florence. Nor was Charles averse to a measure which was recommended to him no less by the recent compliance of Piero with his request, at so critical a juncture, than by the remembrance of the connexion which had so long subsisted between their families, and the many services

rendered by the Medici to himself and his ancestors. Dispatches were accordingly sent to *(a) Ammirato, Ritratti d'huomini illustri di casa Medici.* 52, 65. Philip de Commines was at Venice when Piero de' Medici arrived, and seems to have taken an interest in his misfortunes; for, says he, "j'avois aime le pere." Piero, in recounting his disasters, particularly dwelt on the unkindness of one of his factors, who refused to furnish him with apparel, to the amount of one hundred ducats, for the use of himself and his brother. So true is it, that ingratitude is the sting of misfortune.

to Bologna, requesting Piero to return into the vicinity of Florence, and assuring him of the speedy restoration of his former authority; but these letters did not arrive till he had already taken his departure for Venice, to which place they were forwarded by the cardinal. Instead, however, of complying with the requisition of the king, Piero imprudently laid this communication before the members of the senate, desiring their opinion on the measures which he ought to pursue. The advice which they gave was such as suited their own interest, rather than the circumstances of their guest. Neither the promotion of the views of the French, nor the tranquillity of the state of Florence, were desirable objects to the Venetians. They therefore represented to Piero, the hazards which he would incur by his implicit confidence in the assurances of the king, and flattered him with promises that, when occasion offered, they would themselves assist in effecting his restoration. Influenced by their representations, Piero lost the only opportunity which ever occurred, of being restored to his native place; whilst the state inquisitors of Venice, directed that he should be narrowly watched, so that he might not quit the city without their consent./ CHAP. III.

A. D. 1494.

A. At. 19.

But although the favourable intentions of the king towards Piero de' Medici, were thus rendered ineffectual, the rumour of such a design excited a

violent alarm in the city, which was increased by the king's avowing his determination to establish a civil authority, and to exercise, by his

Commotions in

Florence, and treaty with

Charles VUl

(a) Guicciardiiti, lib. i. v. i. *p.* 59.

(b) Gukciardini, lib. i. *v.* i. *p.* 57. 59-*Nardi, Hist. di Tior. p.* 15.

Chap, Hi. j1ls own magistrates, a paramount jurisdiction. On this oca. *Tk* 14944 casion, the citizens of Florence gave a decisive proof, that.

A.iEt. 19. tnev were no less resolute in defending their liberties, than they were solicitous, by every reasonable concession, to conciliate the good will of the king. The magistrates expressed their determination to resist, to the utmost extremity, rather than submit to conditions which they conceived, would for ever deprive them of their rights, and afford 3 pretext for the monarchs of France to consider them as their vassals. The populace, animated with the same spirit, thronged to the palace; the French soldiers were under arms; the Swiss, guards had already attacked the *Borgo dogni Santi* on pretence that the king was»»» danger, but had been repulsed.by the populace, and discomfited by showers of stones thrown from the roofs and windows. The tumult had continued for an hour, and the whole city was on the point of becoming a dreadful scene of massacre and bloodshed; when some of the French chiefs, and a deputation from the magistrates, made their appearance, and hy their united efforts and conciliating assurances, succeeded in restoring the public tranquillity. This vigorous opposition induced the king to relax in his pretensions; but whilst he consented to relinquish all interference in the municipal concerns of the Florentines, he insisted on the payment of a large sum of money, as the price of their exemption. On this occasion, the courage of an individual completed what the spirit of the people had begun. The conditions proposed *(a)* Guicciardini, whilst he admits that the citizens and the French soldiery lived in mutual apprehension and distrust of each other, asserts, that they did not proceed to acts of violence.—" Niuno assaltava I'altro o provocava;" but Nardi, who was also a Florentine and a contemporary, and whose history is chiefly confined to the internal transactions of the city, informs us, that this affray lasted more than an hour. *Nardi, Hist. dilior. lib. i. 15.* ty the king, had been read by his secretary, who declared, CHAP-m that they were the ultimate and only terms to which he A. D. 1494. would accede; when Piero Capponi, one of the four deputies a.iEt.19. who had been authorized to negotiate the treaty, stepped forwards, and seizing the paper from the hands of the secretary, tore it in the presence Of the king; at the same time exclaiming—" If these be your terms, you may sound your trumpets, and we shall ring our bells. *"(a)* This act of open defiance, from a citizen of acknowledged ability and integrity, and who was well known to Charles, having resided as an ambassador in his court, had an immediate effect on the king; who probably considered, that although he might succeed in subduing the inhabitants and destroying the city, the consequences of such a measure, would be the ruin of his expedition. Affecting therefore, to receive in good part this daring remonstrance, he directed that Capponij who had quitted the room in apparent anger, should be recalled; and the treaty was concluded without further difficulty. The principal heads of the convention, were a participation of mutual privileges between the two countries; that to his title of king of France, Charles should add that of *Restorer and protector of the liberties oj Florence;* that as a mark *(a)* Machiavelli has recorded this event in his first Decennale:—

"Lo strepito dell'arme e de' cavalli,
"Non pote far che non fosse sentita;
"La voce *d'un Cappon* fra *cento Oalti.* "Tanto che'l re superbo fe partita,
"Poscia che la cittate esserc intese;
"Per mantener sua libertate unita." *(bj* II re fattolo richiamare indietro, perche era suo familiare, essendo stato oratore in Francia appresso di sua maesta, sorridendo disse. *Ah Ciappon, Ciappon, voi*

siete vn mal Ciappon. Nardi, Hist. Fior. lib. i. p. 15. This royal equivoque, is not worth a translation.

Chap, in. mark of gratitude, the republic should present the king A. D.. 1494. with a free-gift of one hundred and twenty thousand florins; a.iEt. 19. fat the fortresses and places surrendered to the French, should be restored, on certain specified conditions; that the citizens of Pisa, on receiving their pardon, should return to their former obedience; that the sequestration of the effects of the cardinal de' Medici, and his brothers Piero and Giuliano, should be annulled, excepting that the hereditary property of the two younger brothers, should remain liable to the debts of the elder. That none of the brothers should approach within a certain distance of the city, which, with regard to Piero, was limited to two hundred miles, and with respect to the cardinal and Giuliano, to one hundred; and, lastly, that Alfonsina Orsini, the wife of Piero, should be allowed to enjoy her dowry, for her separate support. The treaty thus agreed on, was ratified on the following day, being the twenty-sixth of November, in the church of S. Maria del Fiore, where a solemn mass was celebrated, and Charles swore *on the-word of a king,* faithfully to observe the conditions of the contract/a,/

The stipulations between Charles and the Florentines being concluded, the citizens expected his immediate depar,rTTI ture from Florence; where the conduct of himself and

Charles VIII.

enters the his followers continued to excite great apprehensions. He IhToTnT did not, however, appear to be in haste to prosecute his expedition; and Savonarola was again deputed to request an interview *(a)* " Sub verbo regis. "—*Nardi Hist. Fior. lib. i. p.* 16. The original treaty yet subsists in the *Bibliotheca Naniana,* at Venice, under the title of, *Capitula et conventions tnter Carolum VIII. regent Francorum et popvlvm Florentimtm. Florentue, die XXVI. Novembris MCCCCXCIV. jnrata in Eccltsia catbedrali, per ipsnm regem, et priores dictee civitatis, apud altare*

rnajus, post missa: celcbrationem. v. MorellU, MSS. Lat. Bib. Naniana. p. 125. *Ven.* 1776. interview with him, and endeavour to prevail upon him to Chap, m. quit the city. The arguments of Savonarola on this occasion, A. D. *19.* were of a very peculiar kind. He reminded the king, that A.ct. 19. during the four preceding years, he had himself, predicted his arrival in Italy; that God had called him to this undertaking, for the reformation of the church; but that unless he manifested greater zeal and activity in the accomplishment of his labours, he would not be found worthy of carrying them into effect, and God would provide other instruments for that purpose *.(a)* These remonstrances might, perhaps, have lost their effect, had they not been seconded by the earnest solicitations of the vigilant and faithful D'Aubigny, who complained to the king of his imprudence, in neglecting to avail himself of the advantages afforded him, and in allowing his adversaries so fair an opportunity of preparing for their defence. Convinced of the expediency of the measure, Charles immediately prepared for his departure, and on the twenty-eighth day of November quitted the city, to the great joy of the inhabitants, having a few days before issued a manifesto, in which he not only asserted his rights to the kingdom of Naples, but avowed his intentions, after the acquisition of that kingdom, of avenging the injuries which the christian world had sustained from the depredations and cruelties of the Turks.l From Florence the king proceeded to Baroncegli; and afterwards, passing through Certosa and Poggibonzi, arrived at Siena, where he spent several days, indulging himself in splendid banquets and licentious amours. On quitting the Florentine territories, Vol. 1. A A the *(a) Nardi, Hist or. Fior. lib. i. p.* 17. *(b) Ltinig, Codex diplomat. ltd. 1.* 1 302. *(c) Nardi, lib.* i. *p.* 17.

Chap-in. the French army had defiled through the pass of Valdarno, A. D. 1492. where it became practicable to estimate its numbers with

A. ift. 19. tolerable accuracy; and it

was the common opinion that, including cavalry, infantry, and followers of every description, it amounted to sixty thousand persons/a/ From the Tuscan state, the king advanced without opposition, into the territories of the church; and possessing himself of quapendente, Viterbo, and other places, despoiled and plundered the inhabitants. At this juncture, Piero de' Medici, having eluded the vigilance of his Venetian guards, hastened through Ancona and Romagna, and made his appearance in the French camp; where he was received with kindness by the king, among whose courtiers, he had obtained no inconsiderable share of favour and interest.(b) .. The facility with which Charles was thus permitted to itaiTlex-proceed through the centre of Italy, on an expedition so honed to op-hostile and dangerous to its repose, was not unobserved by pel of the many of those eminent literary characters with which it French. abounded. In particular, the inactivity of the state of Venice, which was then at its highest pitch of power and splendor, excited the surprize of all the true friends to the ancient independence of their country. Nor were these sentiments wholly confined to silent lamentation and unavailing regret. About the time that Charles quitted the territory of Florence, an attempt was made by an anonymous individual, (a) Alessandro Benedetti, in his *Fatto d'arme del Tarro, p. 6,* states the French army at only twenty-five thousand, viz. Horse, five thousand, Flemish and Swiss, fifteen thousand, and the remainder, infantry of various nations; but besides these, he admits, that there was a considerable number of Italian auxiliaries. *(b) Nardi, lib. i. p.* 17. individual, to rouse the Italian states to a proper sense of CHAP-ratheir own dignity, and the dangers of their situation. But A. D. 1494.

his efforts, at this juncture, were necessarily confined only A-9-

to remonstrance and exhortation, and these he chose to express in the animated language of poetry. His production yet remains, and throws considerable light on the circumstances of the times. It is written in *terza rima,* and is addressed to the doge of Venice, Agostino Barbadico. The Italian governments are distinguished by the devices of their arms. "The serpent of the house of Sforza, has changed

"the current of the Tesino, and mingled it with that of

"the Reno. The Florentine lion, like a dog that has un-

"dergone correction, declines his head; and the wolf of

"Siena has wandered from her usual path." He then calls on the Venetian state to assist the common cause.

Italia, once the praise of every tongue,
Now scarcely drags her languid steps along;
But let thy glorious standard, wide unfurl'd,
Tremendous wave before the shrinking world;
And bid thy winged lion, at whose sight
The forest tenants seek the shades of night,
Spread his broad vans, distend his serried jaws,
Shake his strong mane, and ope his sheathed claws;
Ferrara's Hercules shall strive in vain,
Nemean like, to stretch him on the plain;
Though to thy matchless glory adverse still,
His power is only wanting to his will.

The lamentations of the different cities of Italy, are followed by a spirited exhortation to a vigorous and united defence, and the alliance and protection of Alfonso, are

Vol. 1. A A *2,* particularly particularly recommended to the chief of the Venetian republic..

Assertor of Italia's rights and laws,
Do thou defend *Alfonso's* sacred cause,
Nor trust barbarian hordes, whose hearts of steel,
Relenting pity never taught to feel;
From.foes like these, intent on spoil and strife,
Defend thy country's freedom with thy life;
Nor let the serpent with his scaly train,
Nor Gallic cock, thy native seats profane.

Although the name of the author of this poem be lost, it sufficiently appears, from several passages, that he was one of the Italian *condottieri,* who had been engaged in the service of the state of Venice; and that he had been, on some occa sion, (a) This poem remained in manuscript until the year 1738, when it was given to the public, by the learned Giovambattista Parisotto, in the Opuscoli of Calogera, *tom,* xviii. accompanied with an introductory letter and notes by the editor. He is, however, mistaken, in supposing, that the poem was written *qfler* Charles VIII. had possessed himself of the kingdom of Naples; it appearing, from several passages, to have been written whilst Charles was on his way through Italy. I. The author mentions Allbnso as king of Naples; but he had abdicated the crown before the arrival of Charles. II. He expressly says, that the French are yet in Tuscany, and proceeding towards Rome:

"———— e gia son sopra l'Arno,
"E van per ruinar il Coloseo."
And again,
"fulminando va con gran tempesta,
"Verso l'antico suo seggio Romano."
When the author laments the condition of Romagna——
"Lacerata dal vulgo, aspro e feroce."

He seems to advert to the progress of the French arms in Romagna, under D'Aubigny, and not to the tumults of the people, or the tyranny of the rulers, as supposed by the editor. With these observations, I shall submit the poem and notes to the reader, at the close of the volume, *v. Appendix, No. XXXIV...'*

Chap. m.

sion, a long time prisoner at Milan. That this composition, CHAP-mshould, of itself, produce any evident effect on the conduct A. D. U94. of the Italian governments, is not to be supposed; but the A-4-'9opinions of an individual, on great public occasions, are seldom peculiar to himself; that which is expressed by one, is frequently thought by thousands; and at such times, the publication of a single person, is the manifestation of a general sentiment, and often leads to important consequences. It is certain, that from this time, the Ital-

ian states began to consider with more attention, the consequences of this expedition, and to adopt precautions for securing themselves against its effects. And although the king still continued his progress without interruption, yet a combination was speedily formed for intercepting him on his return to France, which, had it been properly conducted, might have caused him to expiate his temerity with the loss, not only of his reputation, but of his hfe. *CHAP. IV. 1494—1495. ENTRY of Charles VIII. into Rome—Treaty between Charles and the pope—Alfonso II. abdicates the crown of Naples—Indignation of his subjects—Accession of Ferdinand II.— Charles enters the territories of Naples—Ferdinand is betrayed by Trivulzio—Charles VIII. enters the city of Naples, and assumes the government—Contemporary opinions on that event— Charles reduces the fortresses of Naples—Endeavours to obtain from Ferdinand a surrender of his rights— Conduct of Charles at Naples—The exiled family resort to the aid of Ferdinand of Spain—League between the Italian states and the Spaniards—Dissatisfaction of the Neapolitans with Charles VIII.—Coronation of Charles VIII. at Naples—Charles resolves to return to France—Arrives at Viterbo— Siena— Interview with Savonarola at Pisa—Eager intreaties of the inhabitants to obtain their liberties—Louis, duke of Orleans claims the duchy of Milan—Massacre of the inhabitants at Pontremoli—Charles passes the Appenines—Is opposed by the allied army under the marquis of Mantua—Prepares for an engagement—Battle of the Taro—Ferdinand II. returns to Naples—Contests between the French and Neapolitans—Expulsion of the French from the kingdom of Naples— Charles VIII. forms a new alliance with Lodovico Sforza, and returns to France—Consequences of the expedition of Charles VIII. into Italy.*
Vni. inlo Rome.

As Charles advanced towards Rome, he found that the _ terror of his arms had every where preceded his approach,

A. n. 1494. and that he had little to dread, either from the force of AMt-19' the allies, or the opposition of the inhabitants. The unex-Eniry orchard ampled serenity of the season, seemed also to concur in favouring his views: whilst the dissensions between the pope and the powerful barons of the Roman state, had induced the latter openly to espouse his cause. Inferior in number, and dispirited by their retreat, the Neapolitan troops had intrenched themselves under the walls of Rome, when Vol. 1. B B Alexander CHA-IV-Alexander VI. alarmed at the approach of the king, and unA.d. 1494. willing to risque his safety on the event of an attack, disa.Et. 19. patched the bishops of Concordia and Terni, and his confessor Gratiano, with proposals to treat, on the part of Alfonso and himself, for a cessation of hostilities. These overtures, as far as regarded the king of Naples, were instantly rejected by Charles, who now saw no difficulty in the accomplishment of his primary object, the expulsion of the house of Aragon; but the favour of the pope was of no small importance, and he therefore sent the duke De la Tremouille, and the president Guenay, to treat with him, as to his own separate interests. The French deputies were accompanied by the cardinal Ascanio Sforza, and Prospero Colonna. The rejection of his first propositions, had however induced Alexander to take measures for the defence of the city, and before their arrival, he had admitted the duke of Calabria, with the Neapolitan troops, within the walls. The cardinal and Colonna were committed to prison, and in the commotions to which these measures gave rise, the French deputies were also seized upon, but were speedily liberated by the orders of the pope. The efforts of Alexander, for the defence of the city, were, however, fruitless. Already the chief nobility had joined the standard of the French monarch. Even Virginio Orsino, grand constable of Naples, whilst he continued in the service of the Aragonese, allowed his son to negotiate with Charles, for the reception of the French into the territories of his family, and for provid-

ing them with the necessary supplies. Influenced by the united apprehensions of external force and internal faction, Alexander renewed his treaty with the king, for admitting him with his troops into Rome. The deliberation was short; and the terms being concluded, Charles entered the Charles and the pope. city on horseback, at the head of his army, on the last day of Chap, Iv. December, 1494. Alexander had offered to obtain from A. D. 194. Charles a safe conduct for the duke of Calabria, through the a.iEt. g. ecclesiastical state; but Ferdinand rejected the proposal as an indignity, and at the very hour that the king entered the city, by the gate of S. Maria del Popolo, the duke evacuated it with his troops, by that of S. Sebastiano.

Notwithstanding the assurances of Charles, that he would treat the pontiff with all the reverence which his ancestors Treaty between had been accustomed to pay to the holy see, Alexander could not, on this occasion, divest himself of his fears; but flying to the castle of S. Angelo, accompanied by the cardinals Orsino and Caraffa, sought to secure his personal safety. This imprudent timidity had nearly cost him his tiara; as it afforded an opportunity to his adversaries, and particularly to the cardinals, della Rovere and Sforza, of influencing the mind of the king, by representing to him the shameful traffic by which the pope had obtained his high dignity, the scandalous enormities of his private life, and his treachery in refusing to surrender the castle of S. Angelo; for which, and similar reasons, they contended, that to depose him would not only be an excusable, but a commendable act, and would entitle the king to the gratitude of the christian world. Twice was the artillery of the French brought out to attack the castle; but the crafty pontiff, at length found means to pacify the resentment of the monarch; and after long deliberation, a treaty was concluded, which was to be the basis of future union and mutual defence. By this treaty, the pope consented, that Charles should retain possession of Civita

B B *2,* Vecchia, CHAP-nr-Vecchia, and other fortresses in the Roman state, until he A. D. 1495. had accomplished the conquest of Naples; and promised to

A. *M.* 20. dismiss all resentment against the Roman barons, who had espoused the cause of the French. In return, the king engaged to restore the pope to his authority in Rome, to perform personal obedience to him, and not to require from him the possession of the castle of S. Angelo. As a pledge for the performance of this treaty, it was further agreed, that Caesar Borgia, cardinal of Valenza, should accompany the king on his expedition; and that Zizim, the brother of the sultan Bajazet, should be consigned to the care of Charles, who should place him in safe custody at Terracina; but the annual payment of forty thousand ducats, transmitted to the pope by the sultan, as a compensation for keeping his brother at Rome, was expressly reserved to the pontiff.fizj Alexander now ventured to quit his place of refuge, and an interview took place between him and the king, in the gardens of the pontifical palace. On the approach of the pontiff, with his cardinals, Charles twice bent his knees, but the pope pretended not to see him; when, however, he was about to repeat once more this act of submission, the pope, taking off his cap, hastened and prevented him, at the same time saluting him with a kiss. The king then being uncovered, the pope would not replace his cap, until the king had restored his hat to its station, for which purpose the pope, with great civility, applied his hand to it, and they both covered themselves at the same moment. At this meeting it was observable that Charles did not kiss either the *faj* The minutes or heads of this treaty are given by Liinig, *Cod. ltd. Diplomat.* ii. 795. Du Mont, *Corps diplomat. tom.* iii. *par.* ii. *p.* 318. A copy is also preserved at Venice, which appears to be different from that which has been published, *v. Morellii, Cod. MS. Bib, Naniana. p.* 126".

the feet, or the hand, of the pontiff, and there can be no CHAP-1V doubt, that Alexander had so contrived it, that he might A. D. 1495. not be under the ne-

cessity of demanding from the king a A-*Mt*-20 species of homage, which in the relative situation of their affairs, it was probable that he might not be inclined to pay.

A subsequent interview was, however, appointed for the public reception of the king, at which Charles performed, with due humiliation, the usual ceremonies, and professed, as a dutiful son of the church, his submission and obedience to the holy *see.(a)*

During the negotiations between the two sovereigns, Charles had endeavoured to prevail upon the pope to grant him the investiture of the kingdom of Naples; but, although Alexander had, under the first impressions of terror, incautiously assented to this request; yet he afterwards excused himself from complying with it, alledging that it affected the rights of others; and only promised that he would consult the college of cardinals, and do all in his power for the satisfaction of the *king.fb) (a* These, and many other particulars respecting the conduct of the king and the pontiff, are related by Burchard in his Diary, an extract from which is given in the Appendix, No.XXXV.

(b) These circumstances also explicitly appear from the diary of Burchard above cited, and may serve to correct an error of Guicciardini, who asserts, that the pope consented to invest Charles with the sovereignty of Naples, "investissilo il pontefice del Regno di Na"poli," *lib.* i. *v.* i. *p.* 64. The long negotiations which afterwards took place on this subject, and which Guicciardini himself relates, and the silence of the treaty on this head, are a full confirmation, if any were yet wanting, of the veracity of Burchard. Respecting the investiture of the French king, it may be proper further to observe, that in the dissertation of M. de Foncemagne, on the expedition of Charles VIII. into Italy, *Mem. de V academie des Inscriptions, tom.* xvii. *p.* 539, tnat writer has endeavoured to shew, that at the time the pope delivered up the Turkish fugitive, he also invested the French king, with the title of *Emperor of Constantinople.* In confirmation of this circumstance, not

adverted to by any contemporary historian, he has produced and published a document, which purports to be the Chap. rv.

A D. 1495.

A..Et. 20.

Alfonso II. abdicates the crown of Naples.

During the time that Charles remained at Rome, which was about the space of a month, he appears to have considered himself as complete master of the city, and to have punished offenders and executed criminals by his own authority. Brissonet, one of his chief favourites, and bishop of St. Maloes, was, at this time, honoured with the hat of a cardinal; and we may readily credit Commines, when he informs us, that the residence of the king at the palace of S. Marco, was the constant resort of all the dignified ecclesiastics, and most eminent officers of the *chy.(b)*

It might have been presumed, that the long and frequent delays of the king, in the progress of his expedition, would have been injurious to the success of his cause; but his negligence was no less favourable to him than his exertions; and the act of a notary public, transferring the empire of the east, from Andrea Paleologus, to Charles'; said to have been first discovered by the duke De St. Aignan, the French ambassador at Rome, and presented by the pope, to Louis XIV. M. de Foncemagne, considers it as a French lawyer would a contract for the sale of a house; and not being able to discover, *that the king appeared before the notary to affirm the contract,* is inclined to doubt its validity. These doubts are increased by the discovery, that six years afterwards, Paleologus made his will, and bequeathed his empire to Ferdinand and Isabella, of Spain, which *he could not have done,* had the previous disposition been effectual. I shall only remark, on one suspicious circumstance, respecting this investiture, viz: that it purports to bear date, on the eighth day of September, 1494, nearly four months before the arrival of Charles at Rome, and whilst the pope was avowedly hostile to his views. In the present day, when kingdoms are transferred without sufficient ceremony, it may, however, be of use to the gentlemen of the long robe, to have *a precedent* for *conveying* an empire, by the act of a notary public! This document will be found in the Appendix, No. XXXVI.

(a) Soon after his arrival, some of his suite were insulted by the Jews, in consequence of which he ordered the Mareschal de Gies to inquire into the subject, and six of them were hanged in the Campo di Flora. He also erected gallows in different parts of the city, and executed several malefactors: "Par quoi Ton peut noter

"Que sa puissance etoit bien singulier." *Vergier d'Honneur. (b) Mem. de Commines, lib.* vi. *chap.* x. xii. and whilst he was enjoying his honours and his pleasures in CHAP-nr

Rome, the inhabitants of many of the districts of Naples, A. D. 1495.

and particularly those of Aquila and Abruzzo, had erected A-20 his standard, and only waited his approach to join his arms. At the same time, Fabrizio Colonna, one of his Italian stipendiaries, had occupied, in his name, the territories of

Albi and Tagliacozza. But an event yet more important occurred at Naples; where Alfonso, being informed of the approach of the French, and the retreat of the Neapolitan army from Rome, and alarmed at the universal symptoms of disaffection amongst his subjects, resolved to relinquish his crown to his son Ferdinand, and to seek his own safety by flight. He accordingly dictated to Pontano, in the presence of his brother Federigo, and some of the chief barons of the state, the instrument of his renunciation ;*(a)* after which, he secretly withdrew himself from the city; and accompanied only by a few confidential attendants, repaired, under the most evident symptoms of terror, to the harbour, where four gallies were provided for his reception, in which he had privately embarked his most valuable effects. With these he proceeded to the island of Sicily, and arrived at Mazara, a villa which had been given by Ferdinand of Spain, to his sister, the queen dowager of Naples, the mother-in-law of

Alfonso; where, in the consciousness of being secure from the pursuit of his enemies, he consoled himself for the loss of his reputation, his country, and his crown.

As Alfonso had, on many occasions, given undoubted proofs of his courage, and by his expulsion of the Turks from Otranto, in the year 1481, had obtained the character of one of the greatest generals of his time, his sudden flight astonished

Indignation of hit subjects.

(aj Giannone, Storia di Napoli. lib. xxix. *v. Hi.* 385.

Chap. rv. nished all Italy. By some it was conjectured, that he hv A. D. 1495. tended to proceed to Constantinople, to solicit the aid of the

A. iEt.20. sultan Bajazet, who, as well as himself, was the avowed object of the resentment of the French monarch. With greater probability, others imagined, that he had been induced to this measure, by the consciousness of his own misconduct and cruelty, and the hope that his son Ferdinand, who had not yet attained the twenty-fourth year of his age, and had given no such causes of offence, would be enabled to conciliate the affections of the people; but the opinion of Commines was, that he relinquished his crown through mere pusillanimity, for which he assigns, as a reason, that—" no "cruel man was ever courageous *"fa)* and in this opinion, he was probably followed by a great majority of those Who reasoned on the subject./ No sooner, indeed, was the place of his retreat discovered, than the indignation of the Neapolitans was excited to the highest degree; and in particular those distinguished scholars, who had celebrated his triumphs, *(a)* " Mon avis," says honest Commines, " fut toujours, que ce fut par vraye las"chetd; *car jamais homme cruel ne fut hardi." lib.* vii. *chap.* 2. *p.* 205.

fbj It was a common opinion (if, says Guicciardini, we may be allowed not altogether to despise such reports) that the ghost of Ferdinand, the late king, had appeared thrice to the chief surgeon of the court, and on his first visit had

mildly requested, but afterwards commanded him with threats, to announce to his son Alfonso, that all attemps to resist the French arms were hopeless; and that it was destined, that after various misfortunes, and the loss of their kingdom, their family should become extinct. The ghost, it seems, explained also the reason of this calamity, which was intended as a just retribution for the enormities committed by the Aragonese against their subjects; and particularly for the cruelty of Ferdinand, in having, at the instigation of Alfonso, put to death, in the church of S. Leonardo, at Chiaia, near Naples, many of his barons, whom he had long detained in prison. There was, however, no need of a ghost to excite in the mind of Alfonso those terrors, which were the consequences of his guilt, and which, as Guicciardini informs us, with more probability, tormented his dreams with the spectres of those whom he had slaughtered, and with the ideas of an enraged populace dragging him to punishment. *Guicc. lib.* i. *v. i.p.* 65, *66.* triumphs, and immortalized his name in their works, en-Chap. iv. deavoured to expiate their error, and prove their abhorrence A. D. 1495. of his misconduct, by the severest reprehensions. The fol-a.iEt.20. lowing production of Sanazzaro, although not expressly applied to this event, in any edition of his works, sufficiently marks the subject on which it was written. SONNET.

O thou, so long the Muses favourite theme,

Expected tenant of the realms of light;

Now sunk for ever in eternal night,
Or recollected only to thy shame!
From my polluted page thy hated name

I blot; already on my loathing sight

Too long obtruded; and to purer white Convert the destin'd record of thy fame.

On thy triumphant deeds far other strains

I hop'd to raise; but thou defraud'st the song; Ill-omen'd bird, that shun'st the day's broad eye.

Go then, and whilst the Muse thy praise disdains,

Oblivion's flood shall sweep thy name along,

And spotless and unstain'd the paper lie.*fa*)

Antonio Tebaldeo has also adverted to this event in one of his sonnets, more remarkable for good sense than poetry: "If," says he, "a kingdom could have been defended by "immense treasures, strong walls, powerful armies, or a '" commander of acknowledged talents, Alfonso might yet "have maintained his sovereignty; but he who would "reign in safety, ought to know, that it must be by the love

Vol. 1. c c "of *(a)* The original, with another sonnet, apparently on the same occasion, are given in *the* Appendix, No. XXXVII.

CHAP. IV.

A. D. 1495. a.iEt.20.

"of his subjects, and not by their dread of him; and whoever "adopts a different maxim, will, in the end, discover his "error." Then, rising to a higher strain, he exclaims— "Eternal disgrace to Italy! shall it then be read, that so "powerful a kingdom, could not resist the French arms for "a single month! When Saguntum was attacked by Han"nibal, she defended herself to the last extremity; for "death itself is sweet on behalf of a good prince."fo Whilst some were thus expressing their resentment against the fugitive monarch, others were equally earnest in soliciting Charles to hasten his approach. In the Latin verses of Marullus, Italy is represented as mourning his long delay; and Greece, languishing under the scourge of barbarians, expecting with impatience her promised deliverer.

Accession of Ferdinand II. who prepares for his defence.

Ferdinand II. began his reign in a manner the best calculated to secure himself from the dangers with whiich he was threatened. He set at liberty such of the nobles as his predecessor had imprisoned; he restored to every person the domains of which he had been arbitrarily deprived, and granted new and extensive privileges to the citizens of Naples. But, whatever might have been the effect of these conciliatory mea-

sures, if sooner adopted, they were now too late. The partisans of the French, among whom were most of the chief officers of the government, had pledged themselves too far to retreat; and the hourly expectation of the approach of the enemy, had a more powerful effect on the public mind, than either the liberality or the remonstrances of the new sovereign. Ferdinand, however, collected together *(a)* v. Appendix, No. XXXVIII. *(b)* For the poem of Marullus, addressed to Charles VIII. on this occasion, v. Appendix, No. XXXIX. gether a body of about six thousand infantry, and fifty troops Chap, Iv.

of cavalry, the principal command of which he intrusted to A. D. 145. Giovanni Giacopo TrivUlziO, an Italian *condottiero* of great A-20, eminence, and Nicolo Orsino, count of Pitigliano. With these, he proceeded to S. Germano, which, from its situation, between steep mountains on the one side, and impassable marshes on the other, with the river Garigliano in front, was esteemed one of the keys of the kingdom. At the same time, he also occupied, by a detachment, the pass of Cancella, and gave every indication of his resolution to make a vigorous defence. Nor is it improbable, that if the shameless cowardice, or yet more shameless perfidy of some of his principal officers, had not frustrated his efforts, he might have made an honourable, if not an effectual resistance. At this juncture, Crinitus wrote a Latin ode, in which he deplores the want of unanimity among the states and people of

Italy, and anticipates the approaching calamities of Naples.

Ah why the hated theme recall,
Or bid me sing th' imperious Gaul?
Already tears enough are shed; '"
Of slaughter'd friends, enough have bled;
Yet, most disgraceful of our woes,
We too, confed'rate with our foes;
Our wealth, our strength, to them resign;
And with their hostile standards join.
As thus extends the direful pest,
We perish, by ourselves opprest;

c c 2, And

Chap, iv. And victims of a mutual hate,

A. D. 1495. Each from the other, meet our fate.

A-*£u 20'* Meanwhile, his bands the conqu'ror calls,

And points to Rome's defenceless walls;
And menaces the sacred band,
That round her holy altars stand;
Whilst the fierce soldier, stain'd with blood,
Hurls his proud spear in Tyber's flood.
O ancient worth, for ever fled!
O manes of th' illustrious dead!
Thro' your pale bands what horror moves,
Whilst Jove, the adverse cause approves!
Hence what streams of blood shall flow,
What ills shall rise, what fires shall glow;
Whilst Naples mourns to future times,
The victim of another's crimes!
And sinks the Aragonian star,
Before the blazing god of war!
Tis he directs th' o'erwhelming flood,
And scorns Italia's dastard brood.
Trembling, I mark the dread decree:
—Ah, hapless Naples, woe to thee!

In the mean time, Charles had quitted Rome, and procharks enters ceeded on his route towards Naples, having received inriel ofNa formation of the abdication of Alfonso, at the moment when rles-he took his departure from the city. A short time after wards, his captive Zizim, terminated his unfortunate life, in consequence, as some have conjectured, of poison, administered to him by the orders of Alexander VI. before he was delivered up to the king; whilst others have asserted, that that his death was occasioned by the inattention of Charles Chap, Iv. VIII. to his personal accommodation/aj On the arrival of A. D. 1495. the French, at Velletri, it was also discovered, that Caesar A.ieuso. Borgia, had eloped from the army and returned to Rome: and although the pope protested, that he was a stranger to this proceeding, and offered to the king any further assurances for his fidelity, it was the general opinion, that this event was only preparatory to a change of conduct in the pope, whenever his interest might seem to require it.

The march of the French army towards Naples, was marked by cruelty, rapine, and blood. The fortresses of Montefortino and Monte S. Giovanni, for a short time retarded (a) Sagredo, in his *Memorie istorichc de monarchi Ottomani,* informs us, that Zizim lived only three days after he was consigned to Charles, and died at Terracina, having been poisoned by Alexander VI. who was induced to commit this crime, by the promise of an. immense reward from the Sultan Bajazet. "La cieca gentiliti" says the historian, "adoro piii idoli; a nostri giorni l'idolo univerṣale e l'interesse." *p.* 97. Guicciardini also informs us, that *he* was poisoned at the instance of Alexander VI. but mentions Naples as the place of his death, in which last circumstance, Corio agrees with him; but accounts for it by the negligence of the French monarch—" per la indiligenza di Carlo." *Stor. Miian. par.* vii. *p.* 939-This latter account is also confirmed by the testimony of Burchard, who ascertains, not only the cause, but the day of his death:—15 *Feburier, h Jils du grand Turc, mourut a Naples—ex esu sive polu non contenienti natura; sum if consueto.* On this subject, some curious documents remain, from which it appears, that the pope had applied to Bajazet, to assist him in repelling the attack of the French, and had represented to him that Charles intended to obtain the custody of Zizim, in order to promote his views upon the Ottoman state. In the reply of Bajazet (if so atrocious a production can be considered as authentic) he intreats that the pope will have the goodness to put his brother Zizim to death, in such way as he may judge best, and thereby translate his soul to another state, where he may enjoy greater repose. For this deliberate murder, Bajazet solemnly promises to pay to the pope three hundred thousand gold ducats to enable him to purchase a domain for his sons, and to allow the christians a free intercourse in his dominions. On another occasion

Bajazet recommends to the pope a proper person to be honoured with the rank of a cardinal. Such was the fraternal intercourse which at this period subsisted between the Mahometan chief and the head of the Christian church! *v. Appendix, No. XLI.*

Ferdinand i» betrayed by Trivukio. and escapes to Ischia.

Chap, rv. tarded their progress; but the attack of their artillery was A-D. 1495. irresistible, and the soldiers employed in the defence of these

A.Et. 20. places, were indiscriminately put to the sword. Apprized of the approach of the French, and apprehensive that his retreat to Naples might be cut off by a detachment under the command of the mareschal De Gies, whom Charles had dispatched for that purpose, Ferdinand abandoned his camp at S. Germano, and retired to Capua, so cl6sely pursued by Charles, that he left on the road a part of his artillery, and the intrenchments which he had quitted in the morning, were occupied by the French in the evening. On his arrival at Capua, he received information, that an insurrection had taken place in-Naples, which required his personal interference. Committing, therefore, the chief command of his army to Trivulzio, he hastened to his capital; intending to return the following day; but no sooner had he left the place, than Trivulzio entered into a treaty with Charles, to surrender the city to him, and join his arms. This act of treachery, which stamps the character of this eminent soldier with indelible disgrace, decided the fate of the kingdom. The Neapolitan troops, throwing off all obedience, and eager to anticipate the plunder of the French; licentiously sacked the place; and the count of Pitigliano, and Virginio Orsino, who had, under a safe-conduct from the king, retired to Nola, were made prisoners. On his return from Naples, Ferdinand *fa)* " Celuy jour mesme, par maniere subtille,

"Fut prins a Nosle le domp seigneur Virgile;

"Semblablement le conte Petilenne,

"Qui aux Frangoys cuydoit faire de l'asne." *Vergkr d'honntw.* dinand was

met, at the distance of two miles from Capua, Chap, Iv. by a deputation of the inhabitants, who apprized him of the A. n. 1495. calamities which they had suffered. The surrender of this A.iEt.20. place, was followed by that of the other principal cities of the kingdom, which seemed ingloriously to vie with each other, which should first make its submission to: the conqueror. Betrayed by his commanders, and abandoned by his subjects, Ferdinand retired to his residence at *Castelnuovo;* where, having assembled together many of the principal inhabitants of Naples, he explained to them the motives by which he had been actuated in assuming the royal authority, and lamented that his endeavours to remedy the effects of the severity and misconduct of his ancestors, had been. prevented by the calamities of the house of Aragon. He then released them from the oath of fidelity and homage which they had so lately taken to him as their sovereign, and gave them his permission to negotiate with the French monarch, for their safety and privileges, in such manner as might seem expedient to them. These sentiments were not heard by the populace without compassion; but all hopes of resisting the approaching torrent, had now vanished; and Ferdinand, being informed that the insurgents in the city had attacked his palace, and being also apprehensive that attempts would be made to seize his person, and deliver him a prisoner to Charles, privately withdrew from the castle, and, accompanied by his uncle Federigo, the queen dowager of Naples, widow of Ferdinand I. and her daughter Joanna, effected his retreat to the harbour, whence he proceeded to the island of Ischia, at the distance of about thirty miles from Naples. Adversity is the natural parent of resignation, and as the prospect of his native place vanished from his sight, the fugitive monarch was frequently heard

Chap. iv. heard to repeat with the Psalmist, "Unless God keep the A. D. 1495. " city, the vigils of the keepers are vain" *fa) A.AX.30.*

On his arrival at Ischia, an incident occurred which shewed that, notwithstanding his misfortunes, Ferdinand was not devoid either of courage or promptitude. On his demanding admission for himself and his followers into the castle, his lieutenant, Giusto della Candina, who had already held secret intelligence with the French, refused to receive them within the walls. A parley took place, in which Candina at length consented that the king should enter alone; probably with an intention of securing his person. The gates were accordingly opened to him; but the lieutenant no sooner made his appearance, than the king, drawing a carbine from beneath his cloak, shot him dead upon the spot. The soldiers, alarmed at the fate of their commander, and awed by the courage of the king, submitted to his authority; and his followers immediately possessed themselves of the garrison,..

On the twenty-second day of February, 1495, Charles chaiei vnt VIII. entered the city of Naples, amidst the rejoicings and dtyof Na-acclamations of the inhabitants. On this occasion, it was pie«, and as-observed, that the adherents and favourites of the Aragonese Tclment family, who had existed by their liberality, and been exalted of the king-hy their kindness, were the first to express their attachment to the new sovereign/cj But similar situations have, in all countries, (a) "Nisi dominus custodierit civitateffl, frustra vigilat qui custodit eam." v. Guicciard. lib. i. l'. 70. (b) Guicciard. lib. i. 1. 71. Mem. de Comminet, to. vi. chap. 13. (c) Verier d'honneur. Muratori states the number of his army on his entering Naples, dom.

countries, produced similar instances of ingratitude; and it CHAP-IV;can occasion no surprise, that the creatures of a court or a A. D. 1495. faction, who are actuated by no motives but those of their a. Mx. 20. own interest, should, under every change, adhere to the same rule of conduct. Before his departure, Ferdinand had committed the command of the Castel-nuovo to Alfonso Davalos, marquis of Pescara; who, amidst the defection of all the rest of the Neapolitan nobility, continued to defend the place with unshaken fidelity; and Charles,

therefore, after visiting the cathedral, was conducted to his apartments in Gastel-Capuano, the ancient residence of his ancestors of the house of Anjou. Here he received the homage of his new subjects. The Neapolitan barons expressed to him an uniform obedience. The remoter cities and provinces sent deputations to acknowledge their submission to his authority; and, in the course of thirteen days from the time of his departure from Rome, Charles had the satisfaction of finding himself the acknowledged sovereign of the kingdom of Naples.

The intelligence of this important event, was received with very different sensations, by the different states of Italy. In Florence, whither the king had sent the new cardinal Brissonet, to solicit the pecuniary aid of the government, it was celebrated with formal processions and ostensible rejoicings. Whatever were the feelings of Alexander VI. he betrayed no external symptoms of dissatisfaction; but contented himself with sarcastically observing,

Vol. 1. D D that

Contemporary opinions on that event.

Naples, at thirty thousand men; independent of the troops he had left in the Tuscan fortresses, in the states of the church, and the other cities of the Neapolitan state. Amtali. vol. ix. p. 579'

Chap. iv. that the French had overrun Italy with wooden spurs, and cona. D. 1495. quered it with chalk; alluding to a custom prevalent among

A.iEt.20. their officers, who, when riding out for their amusement, used only pointed wood instead of spurs; and to the practice of their foragers, who marked with chalk such houses as were fixed upon for the habitations of the soldiery. The pusillanimous conduct of the Italian states, received, however, a severer reprehension from the pen of Antonio Tebaldeo; who, with honest indignation, has thus recorded the degradation of his country; SONNET.

Not with so prompt a foot fierce Hannibal

Rush'd o'er thy fields; nor e'er amid th' alarms

Of Gothic fury and barbarian arms,

Didst thou so tame and unresisting fall.

Ah whence these terrors, that thy sons appall,

Inglorious Italy! whilst forward springs l

The Gallic cock, and claps his conqu'ring wings;'

Nor hears the voice of answering vengeance call?

Just is thy doom: for now that honour'd earth,

That gave to Scipio and Camillus birth,

Sardanapalus, Midas, Crassus claim.

Once, in thy better days, a cackling goose,

From the Tarpeian rock could scare thy foes;

— Now eagles, serpents, lions—all are tame.f

. But (a) Nardi, Vita di Antonio Giacomino Tebaldini Makspini, p. 18. Fior. 1597.

(bj This rude production of a contemporary poet, may at least serve to call to recollection, the elegant sonnet of Vincenzo Filicaja, written about two centuries afterwards,

But although Charles VIII. had thus succeeded in his CHAP-nr enterprize against the kingdom of Naples, much yet remained A. D. 1495 to be done to secure his acquisitions. The Castel-nuovo, A. iEt. 20.

and Castello deWUovo, both fortresses of uncommon strength, Char,e reduce» , the fortresses yet retained their allegiance to their former sovereign. The of Naples. first attack of the French artillery, was upon the Castelnuovo which surrendered in a few days. The Castello deWUovo made a longer resistance; but the impetuous cannonading of the French, who discharged three hundred balls against it in the space of three hours, at length reduced the garrison to the necessity of a capitulation, by which they were suffered to depart in safety, on the thirteenth day of March.(a) The valuable effects contained in these fortresses were distributed by the king amongst his followers, without discrimination; it having been sufficient to ask, in order to obtain a share of the spoil.(b) D D 2 Nor during the war of the Spanish succession, when the French and the

Imperialists made Italy once more the theatre of their hostilities. For these sonnets v. Appendix No. XLII. SONNET.

Italia '. thou to whom in evil hour,

The fatal boon of beauty nature gave,

Yet on thy front the sentence did engrave, That ceaseless woe should be thy only dower!

Ah were that beauty less, or more thy power!

That he who now compels thee to his arms,

Might gaze with cold indiffrence on thy charms, Or tremble at thine eye's indignant lower!;

Then shouldst thou not observe, in glitt'ring line,

From the high Alps embattled throngs descend, And Gallic herds pollute thy Po's clear wave;

Nor, whilst encompass'd close by spears not thine,

Should'st thou by foreign hands thy rights defend,

Conqu'ring or conquer'd, evermore a slave. (aj Vergkr d'honneur. fb) " II les donna" says Com/mines, " a «ux qui les demandoyent." Mem. liv. vii. ch. 13.

Chap. rv.

a. D. 1495. A-vEt. 20.

Charles endeavours to ob

Ferdinand a surrender of Us rights.

Nor was Charles yet at rest; in his new possessions. Whatever might be his pretensions to the crown, the title by which he immediately held it, was his sword; and Ferdinand, by relinquishing his dominions only to a superior foi ce, was justified in attempting their recovery, whenever an occasion should present itself. Aware of these circumstances, Charles became desirous of entering into a negotiation for the purpose of obtaining from Ferdinand a voluntary resignation of his rights. He therefore addressed a letter to Federigo, uncle of the king, then at Ischia, re? questing an interview with him at Naples, and offering four hostages for his return. Federigo accordingly proceeded to Naples, where Charles proposed, that, if the king his nephew would relinquish his crown, he would grant him a territory in France, with a considerable revenue, and would also honourably provide for

Federigo, and the rest of the family of Aragon. In reply to this proposition, Federigo did not hesitate to assure the king, that he was sufficiently acquainted with the sentiments of his nephew, to know that he would assent to no conditions that would deprive him of his crown, or remove him from his subjects. That if these preliminaries could be conceded, he should be ready to enter into further negotiations, but that Ferdinand was determined cither to live or die a king. After a second interview, equally fruitless, though conducted with circumstances of apparent respect and civility, Federigo took his departure, and returned to announce the result of his voyage to his nephew, who yet remained at Ischia to wait the issue of t.fa)

Conduct of

Charles at

V spies.

Of the manner in which Charles employed his time during his residence at Naples, an exact diary has been preserved served by his faithful attendant, Andre de la Vigne. But Chap. Iv: the observation of this humble annalist, has seldom pene-A D. 1495 trated beyond the external ceremonies and common oc-A.Et.20. currences of the day. We may, however,.discover, that the king displayed a rigid punctuality in paying his devotions every morning in some of the churches of Naples, and that he occasionally diversified his amusements, by an excursion to Poggio Jieale,fa) a seat of the Neapolitan sovereigns, situated at a small distance from the city. The king appears also to have been highly delighted with the wonderful display of courage and agility exhibited by a daughter of the duchess of Melfi; who, in the presence of her mother, rode her courser at full speed, and afterwards went through the various exercises of a cavalier; insomuch, that the annalist assures us, it was a miracle to see a young lady perform such "outrageous feats;" nor can he believe that the warlike dames who opposed the Grecians, at the siege of Troy, could have performed one hundredth-part of what was then represented. On the twenty-third day of April a solemn.tournament was

proclaimed; which was daily renewed 'till the first of May; and was attended by many distinguished persons, as well from Florence as other parts of Italy, and honoured by the presence of the ladies of Naples.(ty The royal hand (a) " II alloit quelquefois" says Commines, translating the appellation into French, 44 au Mont imperiale:" which has led his commentator, Denis Sauvage, to conjecture, .that he went en manteau imperiale, pour venir a ce qu' aucuns disent quil fut couronne 44 pour empereur de Constantinople." Such is the authority on which an Historiogra'pher du tres Chritien Roi, Henri II. would imply the pretensions of the French monarchs to the empire or the east! Mem. de Comm. lib. vii. chap. 14. This palace was built by Alfonso, duke of Calabria, on his return from his successful expedition against the Turks at Otranto. A very curious account of It is given in the Vergier d'Honnenr of Andr6 de la Vigne. v. Appendix, No.XLIII. (b) 41 Etapres disner alla le roy aux lices, ou se devoyent faire les joustes, et la trouva "le

Chap. rv.

a. D. 1495. A. iEt.20. hand was however employed with more safety, if not with more efficacy, in touching those affected with the evil, who sought, in the condescension of the king, a remedy for their sufferings. Thus prone have the sovereigns of the world generally been, to disregard those calamities which they might have alleviated, and to attempt the relief of those which are beyond their power to cure. On paying his devotions in the church of St. Januarius, the head of the martyr was exhibited to him, and the vessel produced which contained a portion of his blood, which appeared consolidated, like a stone; but on being touched by the king with a silver wand, and placed on the altar before the head of the saint, it began to dissolve, grow warm, and boil, to the astonishment of Charles and his attendants, who were assured that this blood was privy to the secrets of heaven, and never dissolved but at the prayers of the just.faj

Whilst the French monarch was thus

consuming, in the Tte exiled fa-most abject superstition, or the most puerile amusements, AeUistwe that tmle which he ought to have devoted to the regulation of Ferdinand and government of his newly acquired dominions, Ferdi0f spam. nan(j had proceeded from the island of Ischia to Sicily, to consult with his father Alfonso, on the most likely measures for restoring the fortunes of the family. He found him at Messina, in a convent, surrounded by monks, passing his

"le roy plusieurs grans seigneurs, tant de Florence que d'ltalie, & des dames du pays," "especiellement de Napples; & furent faites les dictes joustes en une grant rue, pres le "chasteau-nouve, devant une eglise, fondee des rois de Cecille; (Sicily) c'est a scavoir de "ceulx d'Anjou. Et durerent les dictes joustes des le Mecredy, xxm. jour d'Ayril, "jusques au premier jour de Mai. Et se nommerent lestenans du dedans des dictes joustei "*Chastillon et Bourdilkm. " Vtrg. cCHonneur. (aJ Vergier d'Hmnenr.* a. *JEX.* 20.

his days in abstinence, and his nights in prayer. The result Chap, Iv. of their deliberations was such as appeared likely to answer A. D. 1495. the immediate purpose for which they were intended, the expulsion of the French from the kingdom of Naples; but, in dangerous situations, there is nothing so much to be apprehended as the recurring to expedients which are worse than the existing evil; and a serious consideration would have shewn them, that of all the means of assistance, the support and interference of Ferdinand of Spain was the most to be deprecated. The motives by which they were induced to have recourse to his protection, are not indeed difficult to be discovered. Ferdinand was already possessed of the island of Sicily *fa)* and the vicinity of so powerful a neighbour as the French monarch, who was avowedly meditating fresh conquests, could not fail to excite in his mind apprehensions for its ultimate safety; whilst the near relationship that subsisted between him and the royal house of Naples, might be supposed to induce him to take a personal interest

in their misfortunes. But, whilst the abdicated and exiled monarchs were thus flattering themselves with the advantages to be derived from his support, they ought also to have considered, that this ambitious and politic prince was the unquestionable legitimate heir of Alfonso I. king of Aragon, Sicily, and Naples; and that he might naturally regard as a derogation Of his hereditary rights, the bequest of the crown of Naples by Alfonso, to his illegitimate son Ferdinand I. the grandfather of its last possessor. It is true he had not only long » acquiesced *(a* Dr. Robertson is mistaken in asserting that Ferdinand " acquired the kingdoms of "Naples and *Sicily,* by violating the faith of treaties, and disregarding the ties of blood." *HUt. of Charles V. book* i. Ferdinand having succeeded to the undisputed sovereignty of Sicily, on the death of his father John, king of Aragon and Sicily, the brother of Alfonso I.

Chap. rv. acquiesced in this separation of the dominions of his house, a. D. 1495. but had married his sister to his cousin Ferdinand I. But as

A. *JEx.20.* the fortunes of the Neapolitan branch declined, the strength and resources of the Spanish house had increased, and it might therefore justly have been suspected, that its representative might now assert his claims, which had been suffered to remain so long dormant, not perhaps from his moderation, but from his inability to inforce them. These obvious suggestions were however overlooked, or disregarded, in the panic occasioned by the invasion of the French; and the fatal resolution was adopted of applying to Ferdinand of Spain for his assistance. Bernardo Bernaudo, secretary to the king of Naples, was the ambassador employed on this occasion. He was received with great attention. The Spanish monarch had not observed with indifference the progress of the French arms in Italy, but had already intimated to Charles, that he should consider his attack on the kingdom of Naples as an act of hostility against himself! He had indeed engaged by a solemn oath not to interfere in this contest; but on ex-

amining the purport of this engagement it was discovered, that it contained a reservation of the rights of the church, which it was contended would be materially affected by the proceedings of Charles VIII. and besides, the restriction against the interference of the Spanish monarch was on condition, that Charles was rightfully entitled to the crown of Naples; a proposition which it was as easy to deny as to assert. A powerful armament was therefore provided, the command of which was given to Gonsalvo Fernandez, a native of Cordova, of the family of Aguilar, a commander of acknowledged talents, courage, and experience; who immediately repaired to Sicily, to be in readiness to act as circumstances might require; and, by his subsequent subsequent victories, converted the appellation of *The great* Chap, Iv. *Captain,* originally used by his countrymen merely to A. D. 1495. designate his authority, into a title which has ever since A-£t-2' been attached to his name, as expressive of his superior abilities and virtues.

Nor was the progress of the French arms regarded with-h out jealousy and dread by the other states of Italy; and par-state ticularly by the person who had been the first and most ac- Fct tive promoter of the enterprize, the restless Lodovico Sforza. The extraordinary talents of this misguided politician, like sharp implements in the hands of an awkward artificer, not only defeated his intended purpose, but in the result generally proved injurious to himself. Could he have been contented with the rank and influence which he had acquired among the states of Italy, without soliciting the interference of the French; or, after the arrival and success of Charles VIII. had he maintained his fidelity and assisted the king in securing his new acquisitions, and returning in safety beyond the Alps; in either case, he might, in all probability, have enjoyed without interruption his ill-acquired authority; but there seems to exist in some persons such a propensity to evil, as induces them to overlook the plainest dictates of their own interest, if they happen to be, as they generally are, in unison with morality and good-faith. Even before the arrival of Charles at Naples, Lodovico had entered into negotiations with the senate of Venice, for intercepting and cutting him off on his return to France; and on the last day of March, 1495, a league was concluded at Venice, among the Italian states, under the specious pretext of the defence of their dominions, and the protection of Christendom against the Turks, but in fact to oppose the French monarch on his reVol, 1. Ee turn

Chap, iv. turn from Naples. This combination, which was called A. D. 1495. the holy league, the most formidable that Europe had then

A.jei.20. seen, was acceded to, not only by the states of Venice and of Milan, but by Alexander VI. who eagerly availed himself of any opportunity that might protect him against the dreaded power of the French. The emperor elect, Maximilian, and Ferdinand of Spain, were also parties to the convention; and those ideas of a balance of power, by which the Italians had long regulated their respective governments, were thus extended to the countries beyond the *Alps/bJ* But whilst the ostensible views of this powerful combination were industriously laid before the world, it was secretly proposed, that they should unite their forces in divesting Charles VIII. of the conquest which he had so easily obtained. To this end it was agreed that the Spanish monarch should assist his relations of the house of Aragon, in the recovery of their dominions; that the Venetians should send a powerful naval *(a)* Machiavelli thus animadverts on the conduct of Lodovico, on this occasion, in his first *Decennale:*

"Conobbe allor la sua stultitia certa;
"£ dubitando cader nulla fossa
"Che con tanto sudor s'havea aperta,
"Ne' li bastando sua natural possa,
"Fece quel Duca, per salvare il tutto,
"Co'l Papa, Imperio, e Marco, testa grossa."

It is amusing to observe with what simplicity Philip de Commines, who was then ambassador of the French king at Venice, relates the manner in which he was imposed upon by the artifices

of the Venetian Doge and senators, who flattered him with personal attentions, and assurances of amity, till this formidable league, which he had the mortification to see proclaimed with extraordinary magnificence at Venice, was fully completed. This narration, which occupies the 15th chapter of his seventh book, is highly interesting, and deserves an attentive perusal.

(bj This treaty is preserved in *Ltinig, Codex Italics diplomat tens, tom.* i. *p.* 111. naval armament to occupy the ports of the kingdom of Naples; and that Lodovico Sforza should oppose the arrival of further succours to the French through the states of Milan. It was also stipulated, that considerable sums of money should be advanced to Maximilian and Ferdinand of Spain, to enable them to carry an effective war into the provinces of France. To the completion of this league, the concurrence of the other states of Italy was highly desirable; but the duke of Ferrara, with true Italian policy, whilst he permitted his son Alfonso to join the allies at the head of a body of horse, as a stipendiary to the duke of Milan, professed his determination to adhere to his former engagements; and the Florentines, well aware that, in case of hostilities, they would be the first to experience the resentment of the French monarch, and not less jealous of the power of the Venetians than of the success of the French, refused to become parties to the convention. CHAP. IV. a. D. 1495. A. *At.* 20.

The exultation which the Neapolitans had expressed on the arrival of a new sovereign, was not of long continuance. Notwithstanding the privileges and exemptions granted by Charles to particular cities, which had been the first to acknowledge his authority, the people soon perceived their err ror, in exchanging the well regulated, though severe government of the house of Aragon, for the licentious misrule of the French. The great barons of the realm, instead of receiving those favours which they expected, as the reward of their ready submission, were deprived of their offices and their domains, which, with the ex-

ception of two or three instances, were conferred by Charles, with indiscriminate liberality,

E £ *2* upon

Dissatisfaction of the Neapolitans with Charles VIII.

(a) Guicciard. Storia d'ltal. lib. ii. 1. 89. Chap, iv. upon his ablest generals, and his most worthless depenA. D. 1495. dants/aj The French soldiery, dispersed through different

A. *Ax.* 20. parts of the country, were restrained by no considerations of either humanity, honour, or decency , and the Italian writers have complained, that even the sanctuaries of religious chastity were not always a sufficient protection against their brutal violence./ Under these circumstances it can occasion no surprize, that the Neapolitans should have conceived a speedy aversion to their new governors; and Guicciardini might with safety have rested their dissatisfaction on the general principles of human nature, without seeking for it in the levity and instability of the people. That the indications of this disposition were cautiously expressed under the immediate pressure of a military government, may well be conceived; yet the voice of complaint was not wholly silent, and the following lines of Crinitus, addressed to Bernardo Caraffa, one of the chief nobility of Naples, may be considered as the expression of a national sentiment :*(d)* ODE *(a)* " Tous etats et offices" says Commines, "furent donn£s aux Francois, a deux on "trois. " I suspect that Giannone has misunderstood this passage, when he says "Tutte "le autorita, e carichi furono conferiti a due, o tre Franzesi." *Storia di Napoti lib.* xxix. *chap.* 2.

(b) Cork, Storia di Milano. parte vii. *p.* 939. *Benedetti, Fat to d'arme sul Tarro. p.* 9. . *(c)* 44 Tale £ la natura de' popoli, inclinata a sperare piu di quel che si debbe, ed a tole44 rare manco di quel che *i* necessario, e ad avere sempre in fastidio le cose presenti; e 44 specialmente degli habitatori del regno di Napoli, i quali, tra tutti i popoli d' Italia, 44 sono notati di instability, e di cupidita di cose nuove." *Guicciard. lib.* ii. *v. i. p.* 90.

For a very just account of the general character of the French in their conquests, *v. Robertson's History of Scotland, b.* ii. *vol.* i. *p.* 128.

(dj v. Appendix No. XLIV. ODE. Chap. IV. a. D. 1495. Thy sad lament, my friend, forbear; A.JB.20.

Nor longer pour the fruitless tear.
Enough to patriot sorrows given,
Think not to change the doom of heaven.
We feel the fates, and own their sway,
Whilst Naples sinks, a hapless prey;
Her iron bondage doom'd to mourn,
Till that auspicious hour return,
When, to his native soil restor'd,
She hails again her former lord;
Him who recalls her ancient fame,
And vindicates her honour'd name.
Yet when that happier dawn shall rise,
My mortal vision ill descries;
And dubious is the voice divine,
Responsive from Apollo's shrine.
But, hark! along the sounding poles,
Signal of hope, the thunder rolls;
And soon th' avenging bolt shall fall
That checks the fury of the Gaul.

No sooner did Charles receive information of the formidable league, so unexpectedly formed between the princes of coronation of Italy and the other European states, than he instantly be-,, N8-plet came sensible of the dangers of his situation, and was no less impatient to quit his newly acquired dominions, and return to France, than he had lately been to possess himself of the crown

Chap. iv. crown of Naples. He now perceived that the treaties, which a. D. 1495. he had with so much precaution and by so many sacrifices, A. At. 20. concluded with the European sovereigns, had served no other purpose than to lead him into a snare, from which he could not expect to extricate himself without great difficulty. The desertion of Lodovico Sforza convinced him that no reliance was to be placed upon his Italian allies, and that his only hopes of safety must rest on the courage of his army, in forcing his way through the hostile states of Italy. Critical, however, as his situation might be, he was unwilling to quit the city of Naples without the ceremony of a coronation. With

this view he dispatched an envoy to the pope, to endeavour, by the assurance of his protection and favour, to detach him from his new allies, and induce him to grant the bull of investiture. But Alexander, who had refused to assent to his request, when he occupied Rome at the head of a victorious army, was not likely, after the alliances which had lately been formed, to comply with his wishes.*(a)*

This *(a)* Summonte, *Storia di Napoli. lib.* vi. *p.* 517 (581) and after him Giannone, *(lib.* xxix. *cap.* ii. *p.* 3S9) positively assert, that the pope, alarmed by the threats of the king, expedited to him the bull of investiture, and appointed a legate, who performed the office of coronation. It is, however, highly probable, that these two judicious and national historians, have on this occasion fallen into an error. Benedetti, in his *Fatto d'arme sid Tarro,* asserts, that Alexander positively refused to comply with the request of the king; in consequence of which Charles, forgetting his expedition to Jerusalem, threatened to overturn the governments of Italy, and the dominion of the pope. *p.* 9-The negative opinion is also strongly confirmed by the French annalists. Commines coldly informs us that the king was crowned, *liv.* vii. *chap.* 14; and Andr6 de la Vigne, although he minutely describes the ceremony in which Charles swore to maintain the rights of the people, and enumerates the chief of the French nobility who were present on that occasion, neither notices the papal investiture, nor even asserts that any coronation took place. The subsequent flight of Alexander, on the second visit of the king to Rome, may also be

This disappointment did not, however, deter Charles from Chap. rv. displaying to the Neapolitans, before his departure, a splen-A. D. 1495. did pageant. On the twelfth day of May, the princes A-20and chief nobility, both of France and Naples, and the great barons from other parts of Italy, assembled at *Poggio Imperials,* and accompanied the king in a solemn procession into the city of Naples, where he made his public entry, as king of France, Sicily, and Jerusalem.

He was clad in an imperial mantle; the crown on his head; in his right hand he held the ball of gold, the proud symbol of universal empire; in his left the sceptre. The canopy was supported by some of the first nobility of Naples. The duke de Mompen sier appeared as lieutenant-general, and viceroy of the kingdom. Among those who were habited in royal mantles, as related to the king, were Philip de Bresse, afterwards duke of Savoy, Monsieur de Foix, Monsieur de Luxemburg, and Monsieur de Vendosme. As he entered the city, he was met by great numbers of the nobility and chief inhabitants, with their wives, who presented to him their children, from the age of eight to sixteen, requesting that he would grant them the order of knighthood, with which he readily complied. Jean Daunay performed on this occasion the office of champion; he was drest in complete armour, and was mounted on a horse richly caparisoned. If we may believe de la Vigne, the citizens of Naples confessed they had never before beheld so accomplished a cavalier. Proceeding to the cathedral, the king approached the great altar, where he promised, under the sanction of a solemn oath, to maintain the rights of his new be admitted as an additional proof, that he had not complied with the wishes of the king in granting his sanction, for the coronation.

Chap, It. new subjects, and was gratified by the temporary assurances A. D. 1495. of their loyalty and allegiance.! On this occasion the celea.iEt.20. brated Pontano is said to have addressed the king, as the orator of the people of Naples; and the tenor of his discourse, which was supposed to inculpate the unfortunate monarchs of the house of Aragon, by whom he had been uniformly favoured and protected, has stained his character with the indelible blot of ingratitude. As this oration has not reached the present times, it is not easy to determine how far the accusation against him is well founded; but the circumstance, if true, is itself unfavourable to the fame of the Neapolitan scholar; and it may readily be inferred, that if he undertook an office so inconsistent with his own honour, he would not display much delicacy in its execution.

But although Charles did not think proper any longer to hazard his own person, in the defence of his newly acquired dominions, he judged it expedient to leave a part of his troops, under the command of his most able generals, in *(a)* The narrative of this transaction, from the Vergier d' Honneur, is given in the Appendix, No. XLV.

(h) It was most probably also on this occasion, that RafFaello Brandolini, called *IJppo Brandolini U giovane,* made a panegyric oration before die king, which he immediately turned into verse; on which Charles is said to have exclaimed, *Magnus orator, summus poeta.* It is certain that the monarch conferred on Raffaello, a pension of one hundred crowns, and gave him an honourable diploma, which bears date at Castel Capuano, the 18th May, 1495; in which he assigns as a reason for his bounty, the services which Raffaello had rendered, and might yet render to the king, and that he might be enabled to pursue his studies to advantage. In this diploma he is said to have been *cxcus a nativitate;* but Mazzuchelli conjectures from his appellation of Lippo, that he was not born blind. *v. Mazz. Scrittorid' Italia, vol.* vi. *p.* 2018. *tit. Brandolini.* It is indeed not improbable that Brandolini, and not Pontano, made the oration before the king on his coronation at Naples.

Charles resolves to return to France.
in possession of the capital, and of the fortresses of the king-Chap, Iv. dom, with assurances, that he would not only supply them A. D. 1495. with the necessary means of defence, but would shortly A-20return into Italy, at the head of a more powerful army. Of all the measures adopted by Charles on this expedition, and which Commines uniformly represents as a series of errors and absurdities, this, upon which he makes no comment, was the most imprudent, and proved in the event the most destructive. Had he concentered his strength in Naples, and endeavoured to obtain the speediest reinforcements, either by the passes of the Alps, or by means of his

fleet, it would have given confidence and security to his adherents, and enabled him to defend himself against the meditated attack. Or, had he determined to relinquish his conquests as untenable, he might have returned at the head of his troops, if not with honour, at least with safety, to his own dominions; but by dividing his forces, he exposed his own person to the danger of. an attack from the superior numbers of his enemies, which had nearly proved fatal to him, and left the remainder of his troops to support a hopeless and destructive contest with the arms of the allies, and the partisans of the house of Aragon. On quitting the capital, he intrusted the command of his forces to the duke de Mompensier; who, notwithstanding his indolence, or his levity, had served his master on all occasions with courage and fidelity.) D'Aubigny, who had been recompensed for his labours with the states of Acri and Squillazzo, and the title of grand constable of Naples, was appointed to the chief command in Calabria. The strong holds of the Vol. 1. F F kingdom *(a)* " Bon chevalier et hardy," says Commines, "mais pen sage. II ne sc levoit ' qu'il ne fut midi." *Man. liv.* viii. *chap. i.* p. 217. CHAP. IV. A. D. 1495.
A. iEt. 20.
kingdom were intrusted by Charles to his most experienced commanders. Of the Italian nobility, the family of Colonna availed themselves the most effectuallv of his bounty, and were appointed to the chief offices of the state; and it was supposed to be at their request, that Charles retained as prisoners the count of Pitigliano and Virginio Orsino, the chiefs of the rival family of that name, who had been arrested whilst under the sanction of a safe conduct from the king. These favours did not, however, secure the fidelity of his Roman allies, who had already entered into a secret correspondence with his enemies, and on his departure were the first to oppose his authority; not perhaps, as Commines asserts, without cause; but because they were aware that the king, by the imprudent division of his forces, had deprived that authority of its necessary support,

fa)
Proceeds with his army through the Roman territories.

On the twentieth day of May, 1495, Charles quitted Naples, and proceeded directly towards Rome. He was accompanied by Gian-Giacopo Trivulzio, at the head of one hundred lances, three hundred Swiss infantry, one thousand French, and an equal number of Gascons. Commines estimates his force at nine thousand men; all of whom, as he informs us, were young and in high spirits, fully persuaded that they should meet with no opponents able to take the field against them. Alexander VI. was too sensible of the offences which he had committed, in joining the alliance, and refusing the bull of investiture, to trust for his safety to the assurances of the king; and, being apprized of his approach, quitted the city two days before the arrival of the *(Man. de Commines, liv.* viii. *chap.* i. *p.* 217, 218.

the French, and fled to Orvieto, leaving the cardinal S. Chap. iv. Anastasio, as his legate, to receive the French monarch with A. D. 195. due honour. The rest of the college of cardinals accom-a.JEt.20. panied the pope; who was also escorted by two hundred men at arms, one thousand light horse, and three thousand infantry, Charles, after paying his devotions at the great altar of St. Peters/ speedily quitted the city without offering any violence to the inhabitants, and directed his course towards Viterbo; in consequence of which the pope left Orvieto, and passed on to Perugia, whence it was his intention, if the king approached, to retire to Ancona, and take shipping for some other part of Italy.

Charles arrived at Viterbo, on the fifth day of June, and remained there until the eighth day of the same month, ArriTej at during which time he availed himself of the opportunity of viterbo. seeing the body of S. Rosa, which the priests shewed him in real flesh and blood, assuring him, she was only in a trance. He here received intelligence that his advanced guard had met with some resistance at Toscanella, a fortified town belonging to the pope, in consequence of which they had taken the place by storm, and plundered it, with the slaughter of about six hundred of the inhabitants; an event which is said to have given him great dissatisfaction; f F 2 as *(a) Guicciard. lib.* ii. Pi i. *p. 94.*

(bj " Lundy premier de Juing le roy entra dedans Romme, et fut log6 au palais "du cardinal Sainct Clement, » et incontinent qu'il fut a Romme, ainsi que "bon et loyal catholique, il alia en l'eglise de Monsieur Sainct Pierre de Romme, faire "ses oftrandes." &c. *Vergier d' Honneur.*

(c) " Et apres la grant messe alla veoir le corps de madame Saincte Rose, qui repose "au dit Viterbe en chair et en os, et n'est que transie." *lb.*

Arrives at
Siena.

Chap. iv. as he was desirous of passing through the territories of the

A. D. 1495. church in as pacific a manner as possible.

A. *At.* 20.

On the approach of the king towards Siena, he was met by a deputation of the chief inhabitants, who conducted him into the city; where he was received with great honour, and remained for several days, attracted by the charms of female beauty, and gratified by the sumptuous banquets prepared for him. He had here an interview with his ambassador, Philip de Commines, then just arrived from Venice; whom he questioned with apparent jocularity, but perhaps not without real anxiety, as to the preparations made for opposing his *return.fa)* The answer of Commines was not calculated to allay his apprehensions. He assured the king that he had been informed by the senate, that the united army of the Venetians and the duke of Milan, would amount to forty thousand men; but that they were intended to act only on the defensive, and would not pass the river Oglio, unless the king should attack the states of Milan. Commines availed himself of this opportunity to intreat the king to hasten his departure, before his enemies could have assembled their forces, or received succours from the emperor elect, who was reported to be raising considerable levies; but Charles suffered himself to

be detained by a negotiation with the deputies Of Florence, who met him at Siena, and solicited, with the utmost eagerness, the restoration of Pisa, offering not only to pay the contribution stipulated in the treaty, but to advance him seventy thousand ducats as a loan, and to dispatch their *Condottiero* Francesco Secco, with three hundred men at arms, and two thousand *(a) Commines, Ho.* viii. *chap.* ii. *p.* 218.

thousand infantry, to attend him, until his arrival at Asti. The more prudent part of his followers earnestly advised the king to accede to so advantageous a proposal; but the prince de Ligny, a young man, his cousin and favourite, having observed, that it would be a pity to deliver up the people of Pisa into the power of their tyrants, Charles, acting under the impulse of his feelings, and disregarding at once his interest and his oath, rejected the *oSer.fa)* In like opposition to the advice of his most judicious counsellors, but at the request of some of the inhabitants of Siena, he appointed the prince de Ligny, governor of that place; who deputed his authority to Monsieur de Villeneuve as his lieutenant, with whom the king left an escort of three hundred men; thereby diminishing his forces at this critical juncture, without the possibility of deriving from it the slightest advantage. In fact the governor and his attendants were expelled the city in less than a month from his departure. CHAP. IV.

A. D. 1495.

A., fix. 20.

It appears to have been the intention of Charles to have proceeded from Siena to Florence; for which purpose, he advanced as far as Campana, a small town at no great distance from that *ciy(c)* but on his arrival there, he found, that although the Florentines had made preparations to receive him with due honour, they had collected a considerable number of troops, and had filled the city with armed men. These precautions were perhaps not so much to

Interview with
Savonarola at
Pisa.

(a) Mem. de Commutes, lie. viii. *chap.*

ii.p. 220.

(b) Ibid. fcj Andre de la Figrie, Vergier d'honneur.

Chap. iv. to be attributed to their apprehensions from the king, as to A. D. 1495. their dread of the restoration of the authority of the Medici. A. *m.* 20. They were already apprized that Piero had attached himself to the cause of the French, and that he was then actually in the camp *fa)* and they justly feared, that if he were admitted within the walls, he might avail himself of their assistance to regain his former ascendency. Unwilling to engage in a contest, Charles changed his intentions, and directed his course towards Pisa. In his route he passed through the town of Poggibonza, where he had an interview with the monk Savonarola, who had been sent by the Florentines, for the express purpose of prevailing upon him to deliver up to them the city of Pisa, and the other fortified places of Tuscany, which had been conditionally intrusted to him. The persuasions of Savonarola were accompanied by threats and denunciations, that if the king violated the oath which he had sworn, with his hand on the evangelists, and in the sight of God, he would incur the wrath of heaven, and meet with a merited punishment; but these representations, although urged by the fanatic with his usual vehemence, seem to have been little regarded by Charles; who at some times undertook to restore the places, and at others alledged, that prior to his oath, he had promised the citizens of Pisa to maintain their liberty *fb)* thus availing himself of the inconsistent engagements made with each of the contending parties, to frustrate the requisitions of both.

On the arrival of Charles at Pisa, the same solicitations and *(a) Gutcctard. lib.* ii. v. i. *p.* 98.

(b) Ibid. and intreaties, with-which he had been assailed in his route towards Naples, were again renewed with additional importunity, and no measures were omitted, which might induce him to take the inhabitants under his protection, and enable them to throw off the hateful yoke of the Florentines. In fact, the spirit of political independence

was never more strongly evinced by any people than by the inhabitants of this place; who already began to manifest that inflexible disposition, which supported them through the long and severe trial which they were destined to undergo. The streets of the city were lined with escutcheons, and bannerets of the arms of France; the principal citizens, with all their attendants, were ready to receive the king; and the children, drest in white satin, embroidered with the *Jleurs de h/s,* saluted him with exclamations of *Vive le RoL—Vive la France.* As he proceeded towards the bridge, an emblematical exhibition was prepared, on a scaffold decorated with rich tapestry, which represented a figure mounted on horseback, completely armed, so as to resemble a king of France. His mantle was strewed with lilies, and in his hand he held a naked sword, the point turned towards Naples. Under the feet of his horse, were the figures of a lion and of a large serpent, intended to represent the states of Florence and of Milan. On the following day the king was formally requested, by a large body of the inhabitants, to take them under his safeguard; but his answer was, as usual, equivocal and unsatisfactory. Those assurances, which the citizens could not obtain, were next solicited by their wives and daughters; who, cloathing themselves in mourning, proceeded, bare-footed, through the streets towards the apartments of the king; and, being admitted to his presence, supplicated, with loud cries and CHAP. IV. a. D. 1495. a. *fix.* 20.

Eager intreaties of the inhabitants to obtain their liberties.

and exclamations, his compassion on their husbands, fathers, and children, intreating him to protect them against their oppressors. In his reply, Charles assured them of his affection for the inhabitants of Pisa, and promised so to arrange matters, that they should have reason to be perfectly satisfied. The method which he took for this purpose, was to garrison the citadel with French soldiers, the command of whom he intrusted to D'Entraghes, one of the most profligate of his followers; who, with-

out regarding either the honour of his sovereign, or the wishes of the inhabitants, availed himself of the first opportunity of converting his trust to the purposes of his own emolument.

Louis, duke of Orleans, claims the duchy of Milan.

After remaining six or seven days at Pisa, Charles pro ceeded through Lucca and Pietra Santa, to Sarzana.frj On his arrival there, he received information, that the Genoese had shewn a disposition to free themselves from the dominion of the duke of Milan, whereupon he dispatched the duke de Bresse, with one hundred and twenty men at arms, and five hundred infantry, to encourage the attempt; which was also to be supported by the French fleet, which had sailed for that purpose from Naples. The Genoese, however, retained their fidelity; the fleet was wholly defeated and captured *faj Vergkr d'honneur. (b)* " Unappele Entragues, homme bieu mal condkionnfi:" says Commines, *liv. viii. chap.* iii.

(cj At Lucca, says Andre de la Vigne, the king
"Fut festie moult honnorablement,
"En submettant la ville entierement:
"Lcs corps, les bieus des hommes et des femmes,
"A son plaisir et bon commandement,
"Pour le servir de cueur, de corps, et dames."—
captured at Rapallo; and the duke de Bresse with difficulty Chap, rv, effected a junction with the king at Asti, when it was too A. D. 1495. late to render him any service. In the mean time the duke a..fit. so. of Orleans had not only secured the town of Asti, through which Charles was necessarily to pass, but having also captured the city of Novara, a part of the territory of Milan, had begun to set up his hereditary pretensions, as a descendant of the Visconti, to the dominion of that duchy.

The advanced guard of the French army was led by the marshal de Gies, who was accompanied by Gian-Giacopo Massacre of the Trivulzio. In approaching the fortified town of Pontremoli, inhabitants of advantageously situated at the foot of the Appenines, and which

was garrisoned with three or four hundred soldiers, , some resistance was expected; but on the approach of the French, the place was surrendered without the necessity of an attack. On the troops being admitted within the town, a quarrel however arose, between some of the inhabitants and a party of German soldiers in the service of the French, in which about forty of the latter lost their lives; a circumstance which so exasperated the rest of their countrymen, that they not only attacked and massacred the inhabitants, but set fire to the place. By this act of barbarity they consumed a considerable quantity of provisions, of which the French army then stood in the greatest need. This outrage, which it was not in the power of the marshal de Gies to prevent, was highly resented by the king; not only on account of the loss of the necessary supplies, at a time when his troops were almost perishing for want, but of the disgrace which it attached to his arms 5(0 and it was only

Vol. 1. G c in *(a)* " Tant pour la honte, qu'i cause dcs grans vivrej qui y estoient," says Commines,

Chap. iv. in consequence of a most essential service, which the Ger

A. D. 1495. man auxiliaries soon afterwards rendered to him, that they

A. *JEt.* 20. were restored to his favour.

Charles passes

Having quitted Sarzana, Charles now arrived at the foot of the Appenines, near the town of Villa Franca; having the Appe-consumed nearly six weeks in his march from Naples, at a time when his safety chiefly depended upon his passing the mountains, before his enemies had assembled a sufficient force to oppose his progress. The same good fortune, which had attended him on his descent to Naples, seemed, however, to accompany him on his return, and frequently reminded his annalist, Commines, of an interview which he had at Florence, with Savonarola, in whose predictions he appears to have placed great confidence; and who assured him, "That God would conduct the king in safety, f without the loss of his honour; but that, as a punishment "for his neglecting the reformation of the church, and "indulging his soldiers in their licentiousness, he must feel "a stroke of the scourge.'Yoj In ascending the mountains, the army deviated from its former track, and inclined to the right, towards Parma, where they met with steep ac? clivities, which rendered the conveyance of their artillery, of which they had about forty heavy pieces, a labour of extreme difficulty. On this occasion the German auxiliaries offered their services to the king, to transport the cannon by their own labour, provided he would restore them to his favour. Yoking themselves in couples, like beasts of burthen, mines, *liv. viii. chap.* 4. a passage which is perfectly intelligible; although his Coiuukivtator, Sauvages, suggests the alteration of *honte* to *bonte. (a) Commines, Uv, viii. chap.* ii. *p.* 220.

then, one or two hundred to a piece of artillery, and aided CHAP-nrby such horses as could be spared, they at length reached the A. D. 1495 summit of the mountains; but the danger and difficulty of a..fit. 20. descending were not less than those which they had experienced in the ascent, on account of the frequent precipices which they were obliged to pass; and which induced several of the officers to advise the king to destroy his artillery, in order to expedite his progress; but to this he would by no means consent. It is however certain, that without the aid of the Germans, the difficulties of conveying the artillery over these rugged and trackless wilds, would have been wholly insurmountable.

Charles had now passed the summit of those hills, which form the northern extremity of the Appenines, and was winding his array through the steep and narrow defiles of «TMy "«»«» the mountains; when, as the plains of Lombardy opened,f M upon his sight, he perceived, at the distance of a few miles, the tents and pavilions of a numerous army, assembled by the allies, to oppose his progress. Of this army, the chief command was intrusted to Francesco Gonzaga, marquis of Mantua, who was assisted by his uncle Ri-

dolfo, a soldier of acknowledged honour, and great experience. Under the marquis, several of the most celebrated generals in Italy led the different bodies of which the allied army was composed. The number is variously stated by contemporary authors. If we may credit the Italian writers, the amount scarcely exceeded that of the French; but Commines estimated them at the least, at thirty-five thousand men.

The allied army had already occupied an eminence on the banks of the river Taro, one of the numerous streams c c 2, of

Chap. iv. Gf the Appenines, which discharge themselves into the Po, A. D. U95. between Parma and Piacenza.fo At the distance of about

A.iEt. 20. three miles from the Italian camp, the advanced guard of the French took possession of the small town of Fornova. From this place the marshal de Gies dispatched a messenger to the allied army, requesting that the king might be allowed to pass without interruption to his own dominions, and might be supplied with provisions, for which he was willing to pay. On the arrival of the main body of the French army, which encamped on the banks of the river, between that of the allies and the town of Fornova, these demands were repeated; and Commines, who was personally acquainted with the Venetian commissaries, was directed to forward the negotiation. Commines, whilst he undertook the commission, told the king, with great sincerity, that he had little hopes of success, as he had never known two such large armies, so near to each other, quit the field without a trial of their, strength. Nor was he mistaken in this conjecture; for the commissaries, after consulting the chief officers, returned for answer, that they could not consent to any pacification, unless the king would first lay down his arms, and consent to restore to the duke of Milan the city of Novara, and to the pope, the different places in the papal territories which had been occupied by his arms.

A contest *(aj* Cornazzano, in one of his sonnets, enumerates twenty of these tributary rivers; and he might have

recorded as many more:

"Non ti maravigliar se'l Po vien grosso

"A primavera, e cresce in Ferrarese;

"Vinti gran fiumi gli fanno le spese

M Di neve alpestre, che gli scolla adosso,"!Lc.

(b) Mem. de Commutes, /jr. viii. chap. y. p. 227

Preparations for an engagement.

A contest was now unavoidable, and both parties pre-CHAP IVpared for it, with great devotional ceremony and repeated A. D. 1495. exhortations to the soldiery. A party of the *stradiotti*, or a.iEt.20 hussars, in the service of the Venetians, had approached towards the French camp, and falling in with a small detached body, had killed several of them, and dispersed the rest, carrying off the heads of the slain, in triumph, to the Italian camp. The approach of evening however prevented the general engagement till the folloAving day; but a dreadful storm of thunder, attended by a copious fall of rain in the night, seemed to the superstitious multitude, to announce some important event, and struck both armies with terror. "On Monday, the sixth day of July," says Commines, with a simplicity almost ludicrous, " the gal"lant king Charles, in complete armour, mounted his "horse, *Savoy,* which was presented to him by the duke "of Savoy; he was the finest horse I ever saw; his co"lour was black, he had only one eye, was of a middle "size, but well proportioned to his rider, who seemed on "this occasion, to be quite a different being from that for "which nature had intended him, both in person and "countenance; for he always appeared, and is still, timid "in his speech, having been educated among low and effe"minate people; but on this occasion, his horse gave dig"nity to his appearance; his countenance was firm, his "complexion ruddy, and his expressions bold and judi"cious; insomuch that they reminded me of the promise "of Savonarola, that God would lead him by the hand, ' and that his honour would still be preserved to him."

The *(a) Commines, lie.* vii. *chap.* vi. *p.* 227.

Chap, iv. The advanced guard of the French army was first di

A. D. 14c)5. rected to pass the river with the artillery, which was ef

A. i». 20. fected with great difficulty, and by the aid of a considerable

Battle of the numDer of beasts of burden. Next came the *battle,* or

Tan.' cavalry, in the midst of which was the king, accompanied by the duke de Tremouille. The rear of the army with the baggage, was brought up by the count de Foix. As the French army began to pass the river, the Italians were in motion. The marquis of Mantua, following close upon the French, attacked their rear with great impetuosity; whilst the other commanders of the allied army, passing the river in different directions, assailed the French troops on every side. The marshal de Gies, with the advanced guard, maintained the strictest discipline, and proceeded with little annoyance; but the king, being compelled to turn his front, to resist the powerful attack of the marquis of Mantua, found himself suddenly in the midst of the conflict, and was frequently in imminent danger of falling into the hands of his enemies; his relation, the bastard of Bourbon, having been made a prisoner within twenty paces of him. In the confusion that ensued, the commanders lost their authority. Gonzaga, rushing furiously among the enemy, fought his way into the midst of them; and after a considerable slaughter, returned in safety to his followers. The French monarch is also said to have performed the duty of a common soldier/a Whilst the event yet remained doubtful, the count of Pitigliano, and Virginio Orsino, availed themselves of the opportunity of effecting their escape, and announced to the Italians the disorder of their enemies, endeavouring, by every possible means, to stimulate their countrymen *(a) Muratori, AnnaUd ' Italia, vol.* ix. *p.* 581.

countrymen to continue the battle, and to avail themselves Chap, rv. of this occasion to destroy for ever, the influence of the A. D. 1495. French in Italy. Their exhortations were, however, of little A-20avail. More intent on plunder than on

victory, the Italian soldiery were inspired with no other emulation than that of acquiring the greatest share of the immense booty which the French had brought with them from Naples, of which having possessed themselves, they deserted their standards, and took to flight in every direction; and Charles, collecting his scattered army, was suffered to proceed on his march. The royal standards, with the pavilion of the king, and a profusion of spoil, fell into the hands of the allies *(a)* but the French having effected their passage, claimed the honour of the victory. The number slain on the part of the Italians was also much greater than on that of the French. Among them was *(a)* Among this booty were some singular articles:—" Vi fu trovato un libro, nel quale, 11 sotto diversi habiti ed et., al naturale erano dipinte molte femine per loro violate in molte M città, e seco il portavano *per memoria." Corio, Storia di Milcmo.* 949. Benedetti asserts, that he saw this invaluable treasure:—" Vidi io un libro, nel quale erano "dipinte varie imagini di meretrici, sotto diverso habito ed et6, ritratte al naturale; "secondo che la lascivia, e l'amore l'aveva tratto in ciascuna cittj: queste portava egli "(il Re) seco dipinte *per ricordarsene* poi." *Fatto d'arme del Tarro,* p. 31. *(b)* Summonte asserts, that two thousand of the French, and four thousand Italians were slain in this engagement; *Storia di Napoti, vol.* iii. *p.* 582; but the number is exaggerated. The slaughter of the Italians was in the proportion of more than ten to one of the French, who lost only from two to three hundred men. This is in a great degree to be attributed to the cruelty of the French, who massacred all those who fell into their hands, without making any prisoners, whilst such of the French as were taken by the Italians were well treated, and soon afterwards obtained their liberty. In an interview, which Commines had soon after the battle, with the marquis of Mantua, that commander recommended to him the prisoners, and particularly his uncle Ridolfo, whom he supposed to be living; "mais je savoye bien," says Commines, "le contraire; toutefois je

l'as"seuroye que tous les prisonniers seroyent bien traitez, et luy recommanday le Bastard de

"Bourbon

Chap. iv. was Ridolfo Gonzaga, with many other noblemen and officers a. D. 14.95. of distinguished rank. Unaccustomed to the profuse sheda.Et.20. ding of blood in battle, the Italians seem to have considered this as a dreadful engagement. An historian of great authority admits that the event was doubtful, and that it diminished the fear which the Italians had entertained of the French; but Commines represents it as an encounter of no great importance. "It was not however," says he, " like the battles "to which the Italians had been accustomed; which some"times continued a whole day, without either party gaining "the victory."

In judging of this engagement, which has been described at considerable length, by both the French and Italian Misconduct of.

both parties, historians, and from which such decisive consequences were expected, it is not easy to determine whether the misconduct of the French, or of the Italians, was the greater. The intention of the French monarch, seems to have been to pass the river, and if possible to avoid a battle; in consequence of which attempt, he was not only deprived of the assistance of his advanced guard, in which he had placed almost all his infantry and artillery, but was also exposed, both in flank and 1' Bourbon qu'il tenoit. Les prisonniers par nous detenus estoyent bien ais£s a penser; "car il n'en y avoit point. Ce qui n'advintpar adventure jamais en bataille." *Mem. Ik.* viii. *chap. i.p.* 233. *(a) Thuarnu Hist. sui Temp. lib.* i. *(b) Mem. de Comm. liv.* viii. *chap.* vi. *p.* 231. Machiavelli, in his *Decennale* i. 57 seems to concede the victory to the French:—

"Di sangue il fiume parea a vedello,

"Ripien d'uomini e d'arme, e di cavagli,

"Caduti sotto al Gallico coltello.

"Cosl gli Italian' lasciaro andagli;

"E lor, senza tuner gente avversara

"Giunson in Asti, e senz' altri

travagli." and in rear, to the attack of the allies. If instead of adopting a CHAP-IVmeasure which was equally imprudent and pusillanimous, he A. D. 1495. had opposed his enemies in an open contest, it is easy to per-A-2Jceive, from the consequences of this irregular affray, how fatal the event must have been to the arms of the allies; and that he might afterwards not only have pursued his march without interruption, but in all probability have possessed himself of the whole territory of Milan. Nor was the conduct of the allies less liable to reprehension than that of the French. The superiority of their numbers, and the advantages which they possessed, in attacking an enemy actually on their march, and impeded by the low and marshy banks of the river, ought to have secured to them an easy and decisive victory. But their army was divided into many detachments, under generals who paid little respect to the authority of the chief commander. Of these, some were unable, from the situation of the place, and others unwilling, to take an active part in the engagement. A great number fled at the first report of the French artillery, and of the remainder, the chief part were employed in sacking the French camp, and securing for their private use, as great a share of the plunder a they could obtain. The question is not, therefore, which of the contending parties obtained the greatest honour in this engagement; but which of them incurred the least disgrace.. v

The dread which the Italians had entertained of the French, may in some degree be estimated by the exultation which the event of the battle of the Taro occasioned in Italy. The praises of the marquis of Mantua resounded in every quarter, and the works of contemporary writers yet bear ample testimony to his fame. Ever hostile to the

Vol. 1. H H French,

Chap. rv. French, Crinitus immediately addressed to him a Latin A. D. 1495. ode.faj Battista Mantuano, has celebrated his prowess in t.20. a poetical allusion to his baptismal name;J and Lelio Capilupi has left a copy of Latin verses, intended as an inscription for his

statue/c/ Without prostituting his talents to national partiality, or personal flattery, Fracastorius has also adverted to this engagement, in a few beautiful lines, near the close of the first book of his *Syphilis,* which deserve to be recalled to more particular notice./

No sooner had Ferdinand, the young king of Naples, Ferdinand u received information that Charles had quitted the city, returns to than he made a descent on the coast of Calabria, at the Naples. hea(l. 0f about six thousand troops, hastily raised in Sicily, and supported by a detachment of Spaniards, under . the *(a) v. Appendix, No. XLVI.. (b)* " Dant sua Romanis victae cognomina gentes,. "Et jam patratum testificantur opus: "At nondum victi dederant tibi nomina *Frand,* "Haec tibi venturae nuntia laudis erat." *(c) V. Appendix, No. XLVII. (d)* ". Dii patrii, quorum Ausonia est sub numine, tuque "Tu Latii, Saturne, pater, quid gens tua tantum "Est merita? An quidquam superest dirique gravisque "Quod sit inexhaustum nobis? Ecquod genus usquam "Aversum usque adeo caelum tulit? Ipsa labores, "Parthenope, die prima tuos, die funera regum, "Et spolia, et praedas, captivaque colla tuorum. "An stragem infandam memorem, sparsumque cruorem "Gallorumque, Italumque pari discrimine, quum jam ; "Sanguineum, et defuncta virum, defunctaque equorum "Corpora volventem, cristasque atque arma trahentem "Eridanus pater acciperet rapido agmine Tarrum?" the command of Gonsalvo da Cordova; but the gallant CHAP-TVd'Aubigny, to whom the defence of that part of the king-A. D. 1495. dom had been intrusted, was prepared for their reception; A-20and, in an engagement near Seminara, defeated them with considerable loss. Gonsalvo fled across the mountains to Reggio, and Ferdinand returned

to Messina, after owing his life to the generosity of his page, Giovanni di Capua, brother to the duke of Termini, who relinquished his horse to the king when his own was slain under him, and thereby met with that death which would otherwise have been the fate of his master. At Messina he fitted out a fleet, consisting of numerous, but small and weakly manned vessels, and proceeded towards Naples, where he was in hopes that the inhabitants would have shewn some demonstrations of their attachment to his cause. Disappointed in his expectations, after hovering three days on the coast, he was proceeding to the island of Ischia, when a bark arrived from Naples, with information, that his return was most ardently wished by the inhabitants, who were only prevented by the presence of the French soldiery from manifesting their loyalty; and assuring him, that, if he would make a second descent on the coast, they would be ready to espouse his cause. On the day following that of the battle of the Taro, Ferdinand landed at Madalena, near the mouth of the river Sebeto, within a mile of Naples; and whilst the duke de Mompensier led out the French troops to oppose his progress the inhabitants, tumultuously taking up arms, closed the gates of the city against their conquerors, and opened them only to receive their former sovereign, who entered, amidst the most joyful acclamations, into a place, which he had quitted only a few months before, as an outcast and a fugitive.

H H 2, The CHAP. IV.
A. D. 1495.
a. /Ex. 20.
Contests between the
French and
Neapolitans.

The French, however, still retained possession of the two fortresses of Naples, the *Castel-nuovo,* and *Castel deWUovo,* where the duke de Mompensier for some time resisted the attacks of Ferdinand, till, being at length reduced to extremities, he effected his escape in safety to Salerno. At this place he again raised the French standard, and reinforced his small army by the accession of several powerful partisans; till, conceiving himself sufficiently strengthened to hazard another attack, he approached towards Naples, defeated a considerable body of the Aragonese, and occasioned such consternation in the city, that the king was once more on the point of seeking his safety by flight. A timely reinforcement from the pope, and the powerful assistance of Prospero, and Fabrizio Colonna, at length enabled Ferdinand to repel his enemies; and the provincial cities of Capua and Nola, with many other important places, returned to their allegiance, and acknowledged him as their sovereign. The duke de Mompensier withdrew into the city of Atella, where he strongly fortified himself; whilst d'Aubigny still kept possession of Calabria, in the hope of supporting himself till the promised succours should arrive from France.

Expulsion of the French from the kingdom of Naples.

Amongst the other powers to whom Ferdinand had resorted for assistance in his necessities, he had not neglected the senate of Venice; who, having now avowed an open hostility to the French, sent to his succour a well armed fleet, and a considerable body of troops, under the command of the marquis of Mantua, who had so well established his military reputation at the battle of the Taro. This assistance was not, however, obtained without important sacrifices on the part of the king; and the Venetians were to be put in possession of Brindisi, Trani, Gallipoli, Otranto, and other places places an the coast of the Adriatic, as pledges for the per-Chap, Iv. formance of the conditions on which it was furnished. On A. D. 1495. commencing the attack of Atella, Ferdinand was also joined A-?. by a body of Swiss troops, who had just arrived in Italy to co-operate with the French; but who now turned their arms against their employers, who were no longer able to advance them the stipulated pay. In this emergency, the duke de Mompensier had recourse to d'Aubigny, whom he earnestly intreated to send him immediate succours; and although that gen-

eral, then in an infirm state of health, had to contend with the Spanish troops under the command of Gonsalvo, who had again taken the field, yet he sent a detachment to his assistance, under the command of the count de Moreto, and Alberto Sanseverino. Gonsalvo, however, surprised and defeated the French troops on their march, and made both the commanders prisoners. He then hastened to Atella, and uniting his arms with those of the king, blockaded the place so effectually, that the duke was reduced to the necessity of proposing a capitulation. A truce of thirty days was agreed on; and it was further stipulated, that if within that time a considerable armament should not arrive, the duke should not only surrender the fortress of Atella, but all the other places dependant on the French in the kingdom of Naples. Having secured his own retreat, Charles paid little regard to the safety of the faithful soldiers whom he had left in i?y.(a) The expected succours did not appear, and the treaty was accordingly concluded. But Ferdinand, who had engaged to send the duke and his troops by sea to Provence, led them prisoners, to the amount of about six thousand men, to Naples, whence they were conveyed to the (a) Mem. de Commines, liv. viii. chap. xiii.

Chap. nr. the island of Procida, and other unhealthy places, where A. D. 1495. upwards of two-thirds of them perished by sickness, famine, A. £x. 20. and pestilence. The duke de Mompensier shared the same fate, having died at Pozzuolo, leaving behind him the character of a good soldier, and a faithful subject. D'Aubigny had made some progress in Calabria, but, hearing of the capitulation of Atella, and being again closely pressed by Gonsalvo, he finally withdrew his troops from the Neapolitan territory, and had the good fortune to return with them in safety to France.. ..;......

The capture of Novara by the duke of Orleans, which had been considered as an event highly favourable to the French, proved in the result one of the most humiliating and Charles Viii. destructive incidents, which had occurred

during the war. TMoa Soon after the battle of the Taro, Novara was invested by Lodovico the allies, who possessed themselves of the approaches, and fet 2 so effectually cut off all supplies, that the duke of Orleans, France. with a numerous garrison, was reduced to the utmost extremity of famine. In this emergency, Charles had no resource but to enter into a treaty with Lodovico Sforza, for a temporary cessation of hostilities, which he with great difficulty obtained; and the duke of Orleans and the marquis of Saluzzo, with a small party of their friends, were suffered to visit the king at Vercelli, under a promise of returning to Novara, in case a final treaty was not concluded on. This circumstance led to a more general discussion between the adverse parties, in the course of which, Lodovico again changed his politics, and, without the assent of his allies, entered into a league of perpetual peace and amity with the king, in which, among other articles, Lodovico agreed to allow him to fit out a fleet at the port of Genoa, and and promised to grant him a free passage, on his return to CHAP-IvNaples, and to assist him with money and troops. The bas-A. D. 1495. tard of Bourbon, with the rest of the French, made prisoners A.iEt.20. at the battle of the Taro, were set at liberty, and power was reserved for the Venetians to enter into the treaty within the space of two months, in which case they were to recall their fleet from Naples, and undertake not to afford any assistance to the house of Aragon. The city of Novara was restored to Lodovico; in consequence of which the French garrison, after having lost upwards of two thousand of their number by famine and disease, were led from thence to Vercelli, so exhausted through want of sustenance, that many of them perished on the road, and upwards of three hundred died after their arrival./ty No sooner was the treaty concluded, than Commines was again dispatched to Venice, lo induce the senate to accede to the terms proposed; and Charles, taking the route of Turin, returned in the month of October, 1495, to France, with the remains of his army;

plundered, diseased, and reduced to less than one-fourth of its original number.. ;;..1...

Thus terminated the celebrated expedition of Charles VIII. against the kingdom of Naples; an expedition originating in puerile ambition, conducted with folly and rapacity, and ending in the dissipation of the revenues of his Consequence crown, and in the destruction of his army. That he ac-dition'o"1"" complished his object, is the boast of the French historians; chariesvni.: but it is easy to perceive, that the successes of Charles VIII. are not to be attributed to his courage or to his abilities, but to the weak and irresolute conduct of his adversaries, the;...... selfish (a) The number which quitted Novara was about five thousand five hundred men, of whom not more than six hundred were able to perform duty. *Commiius, liv.* vi-ii. *chap,* x selfish and temporizing policy of the Italian states, and above all, to the odium excited against the house of Aragon, by the cruelties exercised by Ferdinand I. and his son Alfonso, on their subjects. If these advantages could have been countervailed by any misconduct of his own, the defeat of Charles had been certain. Such were his necessities in the commencement of his undertaking, and such the difficulties with which he provided for his soldiery, that he was not only obliged to borrow money at a most exorbitant interest, but even to plunder his friends and allies. The time chosen for his enterprize, could not indeed have been more favourable to his views; for many causes had concurred to disgust the people of Italy with their rulers, and had led them to regard the French, as their friends and deliverers, and as a nation, on whose honour and good faith they could place the most perfect reliance; but this error was not of long duration; and the cruelty and disorder which distinguished the march of the French army, soon convinced their partisans and admirers, that the expected change was not likely to promote their happiness. The irruption of the French, seemed to be the extinction of all literature in *Italy.fa)* The example of a weak and licentious .... monarch, *(a)* "

Nescio quo fato superiore anno evenerit, quo Francorum rex Carolus, Italian! "cum infesto exercitu et instructs copiis invasit, ut principes viri in Uteris, atque in "summis disciplinis clarissimi perierint: hoc est, *Hermolaus Barbarus, Io. Ficus Mi"randula,* et *An. Politianus;* qui omnes in ipso statin! Francorum adventu et conatibus, "immaturo obitu, ad superos concesserunt. Sedcnim literae ipsae, ac studium bonarum "artium, simul cum Italiae libertate, coeperUnt paulatim extingui, barbaris ingruentibus, "cum deessent hi homines, qui illas, suo patrocinio, assiduisque studiis, mirific& foverent. "Qualis inter alios vir summa sapientia *k* egregio animo *Laurentius Medicis* » "Qua? res monere interdum me solet, quam brevi tempore fortunae ratio commuterur, "quamque inique" nunc agatur cum bonis studiis; siquidem pro melioribus disciplinis, "vitia, pro humanitate et'officii, bella et cedes succreverunt." *Crinitus, de honestd discipl. lib.* xv. *cap.* ix.

monarch, corrupted his followers. An incredible degree of Chap. iv. debauchery and prostitution prevailed. The restraints of A., D. 1495. modesty, the ties of morality, the voice of religion, were all a.iEt. 20. equally disregarded; and the hand of providence almost visibly interfered, to punish by the scourge of a loathsome and destructive malady, those enormities which no other motives could restrain. Shocked at the hideous disease, which now first obtruded itself, like a putrid carcase, into the rosy bowers of pleasure, the Italians and the French recriminated on each other the disgrace of its introduction; and the appellations of *mal de Naples,* and *mal Franceze,* were intended by each of these nations, to remove to the other the infamy of its origin. Of all the consequences incident to the expedition of Charles VIII. against the kingdom of Naples, it is probable that this will be the longest remembered. In other respects, this event seems only to have broken down those barriers, which nature had formed to secure the repose of mankind, and to have opened a wider field for the range of ambition, and the destruction of the human race. *CHAP. V.*

I HE death of Alfonso II. the fugitive king of Naples, CHAP-v which happened at Messina on the nineteenth day of No-A.d. 1496.

vember, 1495, had confirmed to Ferdinand the possession of A the crown; and he, being now freed from the apprehen-Marril,«e of sions oi the *t* rench, thought it expedient to enter into the king of matrimonial state. In selecting a bride, he found no great plesdifficulty; having chosen, for that purpose, his aunt Joanna,

the half-sister of his father, then only fourteen years of age,

but highly distinguished by her beauty and accomplishments. This marriage gave great scandal to the christian world; world ;(a) but the dispensation of the pope speedily removed all difficulties. Guicciardini, who supposed that mankind are always actuated by motives of political interest, accounts for this union, by presuming, that Ferdinand wished to strengthen his connexion with the king of Spain; but had the ties of consanguinity been a sufficient title to his favour, Ferdinand already stood nearly related to him; and it is therefore more probable, that the motive of his choice was the gratification of an amorous passion, which he had conceived during their voyage to Sicily. This is rendered yet more probable by the accounts given of the cause of his death; which event took place on the fifth day of September, 1496, and was said to have been occasioned, or accelerated, by the excessive indulgence of his passion for his new bride.() As he left no offspring, he was succeeded in his dominions by his uncle Federigo, a prince of excellent dispositions, and considerable talents; but the ambition of his contemporaries, and the unfavourable circumstances of the times, prevented his people from enjoying that happiness which they might otherwise have experienced under his government.

Before Charles VIII. had quitted Turin, on his return to

Contests re-. specting the France, another interview had taken place between him and dominion of Pisa.

the (a) " Ce me semble horreur," says Commines, "de parler d'un tel marriage; "dont on eu fait ja plusicrs en cette maison." *Mem. de Commines, lib.* viii. *chap.* xiv. *p.* 251. *(b) Summonte, Hist. di Napoli* iii. *lib.* vi. *p.* 583. He is commemorated by the following lines, in the sacristy of the church of S. Domenico, at Naples:

"Ferrandum, Mors saeva, dift fugis arma gerentem;

"Mox positis, quaenam gloria? fraude necas."'

the Florentine deputies; who still pursued him with their Chap. V. solicitations and remonstrances; and by the advance of a A. D. 1496. large sum of money, of which he stood greatly in need, and *A.ft.n.* many unreasonable concessions, obtained from him a definitive assurance that Pisa should again be restored to *them.fa)* Directions were accordingly sent to d'Entraghes to sur-

render to them the citadel; but these directions were" either accompanied by others of a contrary tendency, or d'Entraghes preferred his own interest to the honour and the favour of his master; for, instead of complying with the orders of the king, he sold the fortress to the inhabitants of Pisa, for the sum of twelve thousand ducats; and, having received the money, relinquished it into their hands.

The Florentines, thus deluded in their expectations, had immediate recourse to arms. The citizens of Pisa, on the other hand, not only prepared to defend themselves to the last extremity, but endeavoured, by the most earnest solicitations, to obtain assistance from several of the other states of Italy, and even of Europe; to whom they did not hesitate to offer the dominion of their city, provided they were freed from the yoke of the Florentines. The Venetians, eager to extend the limits of their territories, were among the first to listen to their intreaties. Lodovico Sforza also engaged in their defence. The Florentine army, under the command of Paolo Vitelli, attempted to storm the city; but, after having driven in, with great precipitation and slaughter, the troops employed in the defence, and possessed themselves of the suburbs, they were, in their turn, obliged *(a) Guicciard. Storia d' Italia, lib.* ii. 1. 120.

obliged to retreat by the artillery of the citadel; their commander being wounded, and many of the soldiery killed. Encouraged by their success, the troops of Pisa took the field, and opposed themselves to the Florentines, over whom they obtained some advantages, although no decisive engagement took place.

In this situation of affairs, a new competitor made his appearance, with the intention of terminating at once the pretensions of inferior powers, and of taking the city of Pisa under his own protection. This was no less a personage than the emperor elect, Maximilian; who, induced by the offers of the citizens of Pisa, and the persuasions of Lodovico Sforza, passed, in the month of October, H96, with a party of horse,

and eight regiments of infantry, through the Valteline, into the territories of Milan. After having been splendidly entertained during some days, by Lodovico, he hastened to Genoa, where he embarked, with his troops, for Pisa; but on his arrival there, he found that the Venetians had already occupied the garrison, as auxiliaries to the inhabitants, and, conceiving themselves equal to the defence of the place, did not choose that he should share with them, either in the honour or the spoil. He then sailed to Leghorn, which place he cannonaded for several days, and where he had nearly lost his life by a ball, which carried away a part of the imperial robe. This place was defended by the celebrated Tebalducci, the first of the Florentine *Condottieri* who succeeded in introducing a proper state of subordination and discipline amongst the Italian soldiery. (ty During this contest, the Venetian commissaries admonished *(a) Nardi, Vita a" Antonio Giacomini Tebalducci Malespini. Fior.* 1597. *Mo. passim.* admonished Maximilian to desist, as they had themselves pretensions to the possession of the place. He then determined to attack the Tuscan territories, for the purpose of devastation and plunder; but at this moment, a violent tempest dispersed his fleet. Finding all his purposes defeated, and apprehensive for his own safety, Maximilian abandoned his enterprize, and took the speediest route to his own dominions; where he arrived, full of animosity against the Venetians, and with no small discredit to his character as a military commander.

Chap. v.
a. D. 1496. *A.Mt.* 21.

Whilst the Florentines were thus contending with powerful enemies abroad, and were distracted by discordant opinions, and the inflammatory harangues of Savonarola at home, the brothers of the Medici conceived that a favourable opportunity was afforded for attempting to regain their authority in their native place. For this purpose they formed the project of an attack upon the city, in conjunction with their kinsman, Virginio Orsino, who, after having escaped from the custody of the French king, at the battle of the Taro, had again begun to collect his adherents, in hopes of retrieving the fortunes of his house, by the sale of their services. The Medici were then at Rome; but Virginio having flattered them with the fairest hopes of success, if the necessary resources could be found for the payment of his troops, they exerted themselves in procuring for him large sums of money, with which he continued to increase the number of his followers. The three brothers also employed themselves with great industry, in collecting together their adherents from all parts of Italy. Piero having obtained pecuniary assistance from the Venetians, and being favoured in his enterprize by the pope, raised a considerable vot. 1. K K number

The Medici attempt to regain the city of Florence. .?.' v'.. number of troops within the papal states, with which He: A. D. 1496. advanced through the territory of Siena, to the lake of *A.M.SU*-Perugia, expecting to be joined by such levies as his brother Giuliano had been able to assemble in Romagna. *A* formidable body being thus collected, Virginio and Piero de' Medici passed, in the midst of Winter, into Umbria; and, by a toilsome march through the snow, at length reached the baths of Rapollano. The Florentines had, however, been apprized of the attempt, and had withdrawn a part of their troops from Pisa for their own defence. They had also fortified and strengthened the cities of Arezzo and Cortona, and continued to watch with unremitting vigilance the adherents of the Medici within the walls of Florence. The vigour and promptitude of these precautions, depressed the hopes of the assailants, who had relied more on the exertions of their friends within the city, than on their own force, and supposed, that the appearance of a powerful military body, in the vicinity, would encourage them to declare themselves. No disturbance was however excited; and Virginio, instead of proceeding to the attack, contented himself with plundering the defenceless villages, for the subsistence of his troops. Whilst such was the hopeless state of. the expedition, he received highly advantageous

offers to induce him to relinquish his undertaking, and join the standard of the French, then on the point of being expelled from the. kingdom of Naples. Virginio did not long hesitate between his honour and his interest. Even his animosity to the king of France, who had unjustly detained him as a prisoner, gave way to the hopes of gain; and, notwithstanding the remonstrances of Piero and his friends, he led his troops toward Naples; not, however, without the most solemn promises that as soon as the contest respecting that; :; kingdom Jdngdom should be terminated, he would return to' Tus-Chap-t. cany, with a more powerful armament: promises which, A. D. 149S. if sincere, he. never had an opportunity of fulfilling; for, a. iEt.ft. being captured with the duke de Mompensier, at Atella, he experienced the same fate as that officer, having died whilst a prisoner at Naples, *(a,)* The cardinal de' Medici, and his brother Giuliano, who had in vain endeavoured to prevail upon Giovanni Bentivoglio of Bologna, to assist them in their attempt, were now obliged to retire from that place, and to seek for shelter within the territories of Milan.J

Early in the year 1497, the prosperous fortunes of Lodovico Sforza were interrupted by a domestic disaster, which Death of Be, was only the harbinger of his approaching calamities. His wifeof wife Beatrice, the partner of his ambition, his grandeur, and T'c0 Sforeshis crimes, and of whose councils he had on every occasion availed himself, died in child-bed, after having been delivered of a son, who did not survive his mother./) Though insensible, or regardless of the distress which he had occasioned throughout Italy, Lodovico sunk under his misfortune, in weak and unmanly sorrow; and sought to alleviate his grief, and at the same time, perhaps, to gratify his ostentation,

K K 2, by *(a) Nardi. Histor. Fiorent. lib.* ii. *p.* 28.
(b) Jovii, Vita Leon. x. *lib. i. p.* 17, 19.
(c) The epitaph which Lodovico caused to be placed over the' body of his child, displays his arrogance in the midst of his grief.

"Infelix partus, amisi ante vitam qu.lm in lucem ederer; infelicior quod matri moriens "vitam ademi, et parentem consorte sua orbavi. In tam adverso fato hoc solum mihi "potest jucundum esse, Quod Divi Parentes Me Ludovicus, Et Beatrix, Mediolan
"ENSES DUCES, C.ENUERE. 1497, TEBTIO NONAS Januarh." . ' *Corh, Storta di Milan, par* vii. *p.* 962. 1497.

Chap. v. by the most expensive and splendid obsequies, which A. D. i49r. were repeated, with additional magnificence, on the expiraA.iEt.22. tion of a year from the death of his wife. During this interval, he never seated himself at his table; but was served in a chamber hung with black, from the hands of his attendants.(a) Such a violent and persevering sorrow, caused him to be considered, throughout all Italy, as a paragon of conjugal fidelity; and the poets of the time sought to assuage his grief, by celebrating his affection, and embalming the memory of his wife in their verse.f

Alexander VI. attacks the Roman ba

Alexander VI. being now firmly seated in the pontifical chair, and freed from his apprehensions of the French, began to adopt those vigorous measures for the subjugation of the rons. Roman nobility, and the aggrandizement of his own family, which he pursued with unremitting industry, during the remainder of his life. His eldest son, Giovanni, had been honoured, *(a) Corio, Histor. Milan, parte* vii. *p.* 962.

(b) Among these was the Greek Marullus, vyho has devoted the following hyperbolical lines to her memory:
"Solverat Eridanus tumidarum flumina aquarum; "Solverat, et populis non levis horror erat.
"Quippe, gravis Pyrrhae metuentes tempora cladis,
"Credebant simili crescere flumen aqua.
"Ille dolor fuerat saevus, lacrymaeque futuri
"Funeris, et justis dona paranda novis:
4' Scilicet et fluvios tangunt tua acerba, Beatrix,
"Funera, nedum homines mcestaque corda Viri." *Epigr. lib.* iv.

On the same subject, the learned Pontico Virunio wrote four books of Latin elegies, '4 historiis Graecorum, et fabulis reconditis refertos, pulcherrimaque inventione digestos;" from the perusal of which, Lodovico, it seems, derived great consolation. *Zeno Diss. Voss. vol. ii.p.* 315. These elegies have not been printed.

honoured, by Ferdinand of Spain, with the title of duke of CHAP-vGandia; Caesar, his second son, had been raised to the A. D. 1497. dignity of the purple; and his daughter Lucrezia, who A-22before the elevation of her father, had been married to a Spanish gentleman, was, soon after that event, divorced from her husband, and became the wife of Giovanni Sforza, Lord of Pesaro. The first hostile attempt of the pontiff, was directed against the territories of the Orsini; who had equally disregarded his admonitions and his threats, and had united their arms with those of the French. The command of the papal troops, destined to this expedition, was intrusted to the duke of Gandia; who was accompanied by Guidubaldo da Montefeltri, duke of Urbino, a commander of acknowledged courage and experience. After possessing themselves of some places of inferior importance, they commenced the siege of Bracciano. This event first called into action the mij litary talents of Bartolommeo d' Alveano, then very young, but who afterwards established his reputation, as one of the most accomplished commanders of Italy. In conjunction with Carlo, the illegitimate son of Virginio Orsino, and Vitellozzo Vitelli, he vigorously attacked the papal troops. The engagement continued for several hours; in the result, the Roman generals were completely routed; the duke of Urbino was taken prisoner, with several other noblemen, and officers of high rank; but the duke of Gandia effected his escape, after having been slightly wounded in the thigh. Thus disappointed in his attempt to wrest from the family of Orsini their patrimonial possessions, Alexander had recourse, for the aggrandizement of his offspring, to another expedient. With the consent of the college of cardinals, he separated from the states of the

church, the city of Be'ne vento;
Chap. r. vento; and erecting it into an independent duchy, confer-'
A. D. 1497. red it, with other domains, on his eldest *son.fa)*
A. J£x. 22.

Although Charles VIII. after his return from his NeaRecoTere the politan expedition, had relinquished to the pope, the foratyofOstia. tresses 0f Civita Vecchia, Terracina, and other places within the papal state, which he had occupied by his arms, he still retained the city of Ostia, the command of which he had entrusted to the cardinal Giuliano della Rovere, bishop of that placedJ The expulsion of the French from Naples, by the aid of the Spanish troops, under the command of Qonsalvo, had not only encouraged the pope to attempt the recovering of this important station, but afforded him an opportunity of carrying his intentions into effect, by the aid of Gonsalvo, who being then unemployed, gladly accepted of the lucrative offers of the pontiff, to assist in the attack. Uniting his arms with those of the pope, Gonsalvo proceeded to bombard the fortress; but the cannonading had scarcely commenced, when Menaldo, who held the place for the cardinal, and who by his piratical depredations, had greatly annoyed the navigation of the Tiber, surrendered at discretion; and was led by Gonsalvo, in triumph, to Rome. On his approach to the city, Gonsalvo was met by the sons of the pontiff, the cardinals and prelates of the church, and by an immense concourse of the people, who were *(a)* " Feria quarta, septima Junii, Fuit secretum consistorium, in quo serenessimus D. "noster erexit civitatem Beneventanam in ducatum, et de consensu omnium cardinalium "qui interfuerunt, nullo se opponente, seu minimum verbum contradicente, infeudavi "iliustrissimum dominum Johannem Borgia, dc Arragonia ducem Gandiae, S. R. E. capi"taneum generalem, filium suum carissimum, et omnes successores suosy ex Inmbis "descendentes." &c. *Burchard. Diar. fbj Gvicciard. Storiad' ItaL lib.* ii. 1. 94.
were anxious to see a man, whose ex-

ploits had already *Chap,* V extended his fame through all Italy. He was immediately A. D. 1497. introduced to the pope, who received him with the holy A. iEt.22. kiss, and bestowed upon him, in full consistory, the golden rose, which is annually consecrated by the pontiff, and presented only to sovereigns and great princes, who have merited the favour of the holy *see.fa)* On this occasion Gonsalvo gave a proof of his magnanimity, in prevailing on the pontiff to spare the life of Menaldo; who being set at liberty, was permitted to retire to France. -The exultation of the pontiff on this occasion, was not, however, of long continuance, having been speedily sue-Death of ceeded by a most tragical event, that not only blasted in dia, n of a great degree, the hopes of his family, but branded it with a stigma, which has rendered it peculiarly odious to future times. This was the death of the duke of Gandia; who, after having passed the evening at a splendid entertainment, given by his mother, was, on his return home, assassinated, and his body thrown into the Tiber; where it remained undiscovered for several days. The perpetration of this crime has been imputed by the Italian historians, without hesitation, to Caesar Borgia; who, being disgusted with his ecclesiastical profession, and earnestly desirous of signalizing himself m a military capacity, is supposed to have considered his brother as having pre-occupied the station which he was'desirous of obtaining; and to have been jealous of the superior ascendancy which the duke had acquired, in the favour of the *(a)* Josh, *vita nuigni Gonsalvi. lib.* i. *p.* 222. (b) *Gvicciard. Storia a" Italia, lib. Hi. I. 175.*

Chap, v. the pontiff. In examining these motives, it might indeed a. D. 1497. be observed, that the destination of the elder brother to a A. Mi. 22. secular employment did not necessarily confine the younger to an ecclesiastical state; and that the honours bestowed on the duke of Gandia, did not seem to prevent the pontiff from promoting the interests of his second son, whom he had placed in such a station, as to afford him an opportunity of obtaining the highest dignity in Christendom. Some authors have, therefore, not scrupled to suggest a more pow erful cause of his supposed enmity, by asserting, that he was jealous of the preference which the duke had obtained in the affections of their sister Lucrezia, with whom it is said, that not only the two brothers, but even Alexander, her father had criminal intercourse. Frequently, however, as this charge has been repeated, and indiscriminately as it has been believed, it might not be difficult to shew, that so far from this being, with justice, admitted as a proof, that Caesar was the perpetrator of the murder of his brother, the imputation is in itself, in the.highest degree improbable; and this transaction must therefore be judged of by such positive evidence as yet remains, without presuming the guilt of Borgia from *(a)* " Era medesimamente fama, se pero e degno di credersi tanta enormita, che "nell' amor di Madonna Lucrezia concorressino, non solamente i due fratelli, ma eziandio "il padre medesimo." *Gvkciard. Storia d' Ital. lib.* iii. 1. 182.

"On avoit des preuves convainquantes," says the compiler Moreri, "que Caesar "etoit l'auteur de ce fratricide; car, outre ses interets d'ambition, il ne pouvoit souffrir "que le due de Gandia eut plus de part que lui aux bonnes graces de Lucrece Borgia, leur "sceur, et leur maitresse." *Moreri, art. Cces. Borgia.* Thus to convict a person of one crime, it seems only necessary to accuse him of another equally groundless, and to denominate this *a convincing proof.* from circumstances, which are yet more questionable than CHAP-v the crime of which he stands primarily accused/a A. D. 1497.
a.iEt.22.

The most interesting and particular account of this mysterious event, is given by Burchard; and is in substance, count of tlliJ as follows: "On the eighth day of June, the cardinal of event "Valenza, and the duke of Gandia, sons of the pope, "supped with their mother, Vanozza, near the church of "*S. Pielro ad vinculo,:* several other persons being present at "the entertainment. A late

hour approaching, and the car"dinal having reminded his brother, that it was time to "return to the apostolic palace, they mounted their horses "or mules, with only a few attendants, and proceeded to"gether as far as the palace of cardinal Ascanio Sforza, "when the duke informed the cardinal, that before he re"turned home, he had to pay a visit of pleasure. Dismis"sing therefore all his attendants, excepting his *staffiero,* "or footman, and a person in a mask, who had paid "him a visit whilst at supper, and who, during the "space of a month, or thereabouts, previous to this time, 4; had called upon him almost daily, at the apostolic pa"lace, he took this person behind him on his mule, and "proceeded to the street of the Jews, where he quitted "his servant, directing him to remain there until a certain Vol. 1. L L "hour; *(a)* Gordon, in his Life of Alexander VI. *(hand.* 1720. *fa.* not only asserts, on the authority of Tomaso Tomasi, that Caesar as the perpetrator of this murder, but has given.at great length the private conferences, between him and the assassins hired for this purpose, with as much accuracy, as if he had himself been present on the occasion, *fv. pp.* 153. *fyc)* In the same manner he has also favoured us with the private conversation between Caesar and the duke, on their last interview in the streets of Rome: " Caesar wished him much "pleasure, and so they parted."— A mode of writing, which reduces history below the level of romance.
CHAP V-"hour; when, if he did not return, he might repair to A. D. 1497. "the palace. The duke then seated the person in the mask a.t.22. "behind him, and rode, I know not whither; but in that "night he was assassinated, and thrown into the river. "The servant, after having been dismissed, was also as"saulted and mortally wounded; and although he was "attended with great care, yet such M as his situation, that "he could give no intelligible account of what had befallen "his master. In the morning, the duke not having re"turned to the palace, his servants began to be alarmed; "and one of them informed the pontiff of the evening ex"cursion of his sons, and that

the duke had not yet made his "appearance. This gave the pope no small anxiety; but "he conjectured that the duke had been attracted by some "courtesan to pass the night with her, and not choosing to "quit the house in open day, had waited till the following "evening to return home. When, however, the evening ar"rived, and he found himself disappointed in his expecta"tions, he became deeply afflicted, and began to make inqui"ries from different persons, whom he ordered to attend him "for that purpose. Amongst these was a man named Giorgio "Schiavoni, who, having discharged some timber from a "bark in the river, had remained on board the vessel to "watch it, and being interrogated whether he had seen "any one thrown into the river, on the night preceding, "he replied, that he saw two men on foot, who came down "the street, and looked diligently about, to observe, whe"ther any person was passing. That seeing no one, they "returned, and a short time afterwards two others came, "and looked around in the same manner as the former; no "person still appearing, they gave a sign to their com"panions, when a man came, mounted on a white horse,
"having "having behind him a dead body, the head and anus of CHAF-v"which hung on one side, and the feet on the other side A. D. *U97.* V of the horse; the two persons on foot supporting the A--lEt-22"body, to prevent its falling. They thus proceeded "towards that part, where the filth of the city is usu"ally discharged into the river, and turning the horse, with his tail towards the water, the two persons took "the dead body by the arms and feet, and with all "their strength flung it into the river. The person on "horseback then asked if they had thrown it in, to which "they replied, *Signor, si.* (yes, Sir.) He then looked to"wards the river, and seeing a mantle floating on the "stream, he inquired what it was that appeared black, to "which they answered, it was a mantle; and one of them "threw stones upon it, in Consequence of which it sunk. "The attendants of the pontiff then inquired from Giorgio, "why he had not

revealed this to the governor of the city; "to which he replied, that he had seen in his time, a hun"dred dead bodies thrown into the river at the same place, '! without any inquiry being made respecting them, and "that he had not, therefore, considered it as a matter of any "importance. The fishermen and seamen were then collect"ed and ordered to search the river, where, on the follow"ing evening, they found the body of the duke, with his "habit entire, and thirty ducats in his purse. He was pierc"ed with nine wounds, one of which was in his throat, the "others in his head, body, and limbs. No sooner was the "pontiff informed of the death of his son, and that he had "been thrown, like filth, into the river, than giving way to "his grief, he shut himself up in a chamber, and wept "bitterly. The cardinal of Segovia, and other attendants "on the pope, went to the door, and after many hours

Ll2 "spent spent in persuasions and exhortations, prevailed upon him to admit them. From the evening of Wednesday, till the following Saturday, the pope took no food; nor did he sleep from Thursday morning till the same hour on the ensuing day. At length, however, giving way to the intreaties of his attendants, he Began to restrain his sorrow, and to consider the injury which his own health might sustain, by the further indulgence of his *grief." fa)*

Casar Borgia accused of the murder of his brother without sufficient evidence.

From this account, which is in truth the only authentic information that remains, respecting the death of the duke, it seems probable, that he had for some time been carrying on an amorous intrigue, by the intervention of the person who so frequently visited him in disguise. That the evening on which he met with his death, he had been detected by some jealous rival, or injured husband, and had paid with his life the forfeiture of his folly, his presumption, or his guilt. The cardinal appears not to have had the least share in directing the motions of the duke; nor does it appear from Burchard, that he again left the palace, after he had returned home on the evening, when the murder was committed. Throughout the whole narrative, there is not the slightest indication, that Caesar had any share in the transaction; and the continuance of the favour of both his father and his mother, after this event, may sufficiently prove to every impartial mind, that he was not even suspected by them as the author of the crime.

The brothers of the Medici, disappointed in their first attempt to regain their native place, now formed a more deliberate *(a) The original is given in the Appendix, No. XLVIII.* deliberate and systematic plan for effecting their purpose. Amidst the internal commotions which Florence had experienced since the expulsion of the Medici, the form of its government had undergone frequent changes, until the populace had at length usurped the whole direction of the state, to the exclusion of the higher ranks, and under the influence of Savonarola, had united the enthusiasm of liberty with the fanaticism of superstition. The violent extremes to which they proceeded, soon however, produced a re-action favourable to their opponents. The inability of a set of artisans, who left their stalls in the habits of their occupations, to regulate the concerns of the state, became apparent; the misconduct or negligence of the rulers had been manifested by an alarming scarcity of provisions; and at length, by the exertions of the more respectable inhabitants, the office of *gonfaloniere,* was conferred on Bernardo del Nero, a citizen of advanced age and great authority, whose long and friendly intercourse with the family of the Medici, gave reason to suppose that he was well inclined to their interest. The other offices of government were also filled by persons who were supposed to be adverse to the *fratescki,* or followers of Savonarola. Encouraged by these favourable circumstances, Piero communicated his views to the Venetians, who promised to support him in his attempt. The concurrence of Alexander VI. who was highly exasperated against the Florentines, for the protection afforded to Savonarola, in his free censures of the abuses of the church, was easily obtained; nor did Lodovico Sforza oppose an enterprize, which, by dividing and weakening the Florentines, might afford him an opportunity of availing himself of their dissentions to his own advantage. The military commander chosen by Piero de' Medici, on this occasion, CHAP. V. a. D. 1497. A. iEt. 2.

Second attempt of the Medici to enter the city of Florence.

CHAP-v-occasion, was Bartolommeo a" Alveano, who had acquired A. D. 1497. great honour in the defence of Bracciano, against the arms of A. i£t. 22. the pope. By the credit and exertions of the three brothers, a considerable body of troops was raised, with which d'Alveano, marching only by night, and, through the least frequented roads, proceeded to Siena. He was here met by Piero and Giuliano, who had obtained further succours from the inhabitants of Siena, whose aversion to the Flo rentines, led them to promote every measure that was likely to increase their internal commotions, or to weaken their political strength.*(a)* A communication was secretly opened between the Medici and their friends in Florence. The day was agreed upon, when the Medici should, early in the morning, approach the city, and enter the gates; at which time their adherents would be ready to receive them, and to second their efforts. In their progress towards Florence they met with no interruption; and, arriving within a few miles of the city, they took their stations for the night; intending to reach the walls at the hour appointed, on the following morning. When, however, they prepared to pursue their route, they found their order deranged, and their progress obstructed, by the effects of an uncommon fall of rain, which had continued throughout the night; and which, by postponing their arrival until a late hour of the day, gave sufficient time to their adversaries to be apprized of their intentions. Vigorous measures were instantly adopt ed for the defence of the city. Paolo Vitelli, the *condottiero* of the Florentine troops, who had casually arrived there on the preceding evening, secured the gates, and took the command of those who were ready to join in repelling the attack. *(a) Malavolti, Storia di Siena, par. 3. p. 103.* attack. The partisans of the Medici, some of whom had CHAP-vgiven sufficient indications of their designs, were seized A. D. 1497. upon, and committed to safe custody; insomuch, that when a.iEt.22. the Medici arrived under the walls, instead of finding their friends ready to receive them, they discovered, that every measure had been taken for resistance. Being thus disappointed in their expectation of succeeding in their enterprize, by the aid of their accomplices within the city, they deliberated whether they should attack the gates, and endeavour to carry the place by storm; but, after a consultation of four hours, they concluded that their force was not equal to the undertaking. Bending their course, therefore, towards the papal dominions, d'Alveano and his military associates endeavoured to recompense themselves for their disappointment, by plundering the inhabitants; whilst Piero and his brother Giuliano retired in haste to Siena.

This *(a)* Nardi informs us, that this attempt was made on the twenty-eighth day of April 1497. According to the same author, Piero de' Medici approached so near to the city walls, as to be seen by the inhabitants; who came in throngs, as to a spectacle, to take a view of him and his associates, but gave no demonstrations of attachment to his cause. He remained there about two hours; and being molested by the small arms from the fortress, was obliged to take shelter behind the wall of one of the fountains in. the suburbs of the city. This historian, who was a great admirer of Savonarola, gives a singular instance of the folly of the magistrates, and of his own credulity, in relating, that Girolamo Benivieni, the celebrated Florentine poet, who was himself a warm enthusiast, was dispatched to consult Savonarola, on the event of the attempt made by Piero de' Medici, which had occasioned the magistrates great alarm: When Savonarola, who was engaged in reading, raised his head, and said to

Benivieni—" *Modiae Jidei, quare dubitasti?* Know you not "that God is with you? Go, and inform the magistrates from me, that I shall pray to "God for the city, and that they may entertain no fears; for Piero.de' Medici will come "as far as the gates, and will return without having effected any thing." "And so" says the historian, " it proved." *Nardi, Hist. Fior. lib.* ii. *p.* 37.

Chap, v. This affair did not, however, terminate without blood A. D. 1497. shed. No sooner were the prevailing party within the walls A.iEt.22. apprized of the retreat of the Medici, and the object of Fatal con«s-their visit, than they instituted a strict inquiry as to the tie partisans authors and abettors of the undertaking; in consequence of of the Mewnich, four of the principal citizens, Nicolo Ridolfi, Lorenzo dici within...

the city. Tornabuoni, Gianozzo Pucci, and Giovanni Cambi, were found to be implicated in the conspiracy, and were condemned to death.faj Bernardo del Nero, the *gonjaloniere,* accused of having been privy to their proceedings without disclosing them, was adjudged to a similar fate. The persons thus condemned, appealed to the *consiglio grande,* or general assembly of the people, in conformity to a late regulation in the constitution, introduced by the *frateschi;* but the promoters of this salutary law were the first to infringe *(a)* To Lorenzo Tornabuoni, who was nearly related to the Medici, Politiano had inscribed, in terms of warm commendation, his Sylva, intitled *Ambra;* at the same time applauding him for his proficiency in the Greek language, and exhorting him to persevere in the study of it. His untimely death is lamented in a sonnet of Bernardo Accolti, called *L'Unico Aretino:*
"Io che gil fu tesor de la natura,
"Con man legate, scinto, e scalzo vegno
"A porre il giovin collo al duro legno,
"E ricever vil paglia in sepoltura.
"Pigli exemplo di me chi s'assicura
"In potentia mortal, fortuua, o regno;
"Che spesso viene al mondo, al cielo, a sdegno "Chi la feliciti sua non misura.

"E hi che levi a me gemme, e tesauro,
"La consorte, i figlioli, la vita mesta;
"Che piu poi troverrei un Turco, un Mauro! "Fammi una grazia almen, turba molesta,
"A colei, cui tanto amo, in piatto d'auro,
"Fa presentar la mia tagliata testa." *Opere dAccolti. Ed. Fir.* 1514.

infringe it, and the convenient pretexts of public danger Ohap.v. and state necessity, were alledged by the adherents of Savo-A. D. 1497. narola, as sufficient justifications for carrying the sentence a. *ft.* 23. into immediate execution. The inhabitants of Florence, unaccustomed for a long course of years, to see the political errors of their fellow citizens punished with such sanguinary severity, derived from this transaction additional motives of dissatisfaction; and the death of these citizens, who, whether guilty or not of the crime laid to their charge, were condemned contrary to the established forms of law, was soon afterwards avenged by the slaughter of those who had been most active in their destruction. the Florcatines.

The siege of Pisa still continued to increase in importance, and to augment the number of the contending parties. PaolVitelu In favour of the inhabitants, the duke of Urbino, who had general of purchased his liberty at the expense of thirty thousand ducats, d'Alveano, his late adversary, Paolo Orsini, Astorre Baglioni, and several other commanders of independent bodies of troops, took the field, having been engaged in the cause principally by the wealth and credit of the Venetians: and the command of the whole was intrusted to the marquis of Mantua. The ardour of the Florentines kept pace with that of their enemies. They raised a considerable body of troops within the Tuscan territories; several experienced commanders joined their standard. Paolo Vitelli, who had already rendered many important

Vol. 1. Mm services *(a)* " E quel condusse in su le vostre mura
"Il vostro *gran rilello,* onde ne nacque,
"Di cinque cittadini la sepoltura." *Macchiavcl. Decennale,* 1.

services to the republic, was appointed

chief general, and the *bastone,* or emblem of command, was delivered to him with great solemnity, on a day fixed upon for that purpose, by the rules of astrology. On this occasion all the astrologers in the city, who it seems formed a numerous body, were assembled in the great court of the palace; and whilst one, who was in the immediate service of Vitelli, with the rest of his fraternity, waited with the instruments in their hands to observe the *felice punto,* or fortunate moment, Marcello Virgilio, chancellor of the republic, delivered an oration before the magistrates in honour of their general; when, on a sign being given by the person appointed for that purpose, the orator instantly concluded his speech, and Vitelli, on his knees, received from the *gonfaloniere* the emblem of his authority, amidst the sound of trumpets, and the plaudits of the populace. At the same time the *Madonna deli Imprunata* was carried through the city in a ceremonial procession; a measure which we are told had never been resorted to at Florence without manifest advantage, *(b)*

The Florentines form an alliance with Lodovico

Whilst the adverse parties were thus preparing for a decisive contest, the inhabitants of Pisa dispatched a body of troops, consisting of seven hundred horse and one thousand foot, to levy contributions upon, or to plunder the inhabitants of the district of Volterra. Returning with a considerable booty, they were attacked in the valley of S. Regolo by a party of the Florentines, under the command of the count Rinuccio, and being thrown into disorder, were on *(a) Nardi, Hist. Finr. lib. iii. p. 53.*

(b) dmmirato, Hist. Fior. v. iii. p. 254. on the point of relinquishing their spoil; when a fresh CHAP-vbody of horse arriving from Pisa changed the fortune of the A. D. 1497. day, and the greater part of the Florentine detachment was A. JEt. it. either slaughtered or made prisoners. This disaster was severely felt by the Florentines, who now began to apprehend, that unless they could detach some of their adversaries from the alliance formed against them, they might

eventually, not only fail in their attempt to recover the city of Pisa, but might so far exhaust their strength, as to become themselves a prey to the ambition of their enemies. Of these, the most formidable were the Venetians, who were then in the zenith of their power, and had given decisive proofs of their intentions to extend their dominion into the southern provinces of Italy. In this exigency, the Florentines had recourse to Lodovico Sforza, who, by having so frequently changed the object of his political pursuit, afforded them some hopes, that he might not refuse to listen to their respresentations. Nor were they mistaken in this opinion. Lodovico heard, with attention, the arguments by which they endeavoured to convince him, that in affording assistance to the inhabitants of Pisa, he was only acting a subsidiary part to the republic of Venice, which was already too powerful for the other states of Italy, and would, by the acquisition of Pisa and its territory, become highly formidable, even to Lodovico himself. Induced by these, and similar motives, and actuated by that instability which characterized the whole of his conduct, Lodovico entered into the proposed treaty; and, it was agreed between the parties, that in order to avail themselves of it to greater advantage, no external demonstration of it should immediately take place, but that Lodovico should take advantage of such opportunity of with

M M *2i* drawing drawing his troops, as should appear to be most for the interest of his new *ailies.fa), A*

From the time of the return of Charles VIII. to his own dominions, the Italian states had been kept in continual alarm, by rumours of great preparations, said to be making, for another and more powerful descent upon the kingdom of Naples; but these apprehensions were suddenly dispelled by the death of that monarch, occasioned by an apoplexy, whilst he was amusing himself by the game of tennis, at the castle of Amboise, in the month of April, 1498. The exultation of the Italians on this event, was not, however, well founded, and it is probable that the death of the king,

instead of being favourable to their repose, was the occasion of their being exposed to still greater calamities. Charles had little pretensions, either in body or in mind, to the character of a hero. He had made a hazardous attempt, from the consequences of which he had been extricated with difficulty; and there was no great probability that he would have exposed himself to the dangers of a second expedition. The longer continuance of his life would therefore have prevented, or postponed, the hostile efforts of his bolder and more active successor. This successor was Louis, duke of Orleans, cousin to Charles in the fourth degree, who, under the name of Louis XII. assumed the crown, without opposition, and immediately after his accession, gave a striking proof of his intentions, by taking the additional titles of duke of Milan, and king of the two Sicilies. No sooner had he ascended the throne, than he found a pretext for divorcing his wife, the daughter of Louis XI. who, as he alledged, was so devoid of personal attractions, and of so sickly a constitution, that he had no hopes *(a) Guicciard. Storia d'Ital. lib. iv. 1. 195.*

hopes of progeny from her, and chose in her stead, Anne CHAP vof Bretagne, the widow of his predecessor, Charles VI-II. who A D. 1498. is supposed to have been the object of his affection before her A. *At.* 23, former marriage. As the dispensation of the pope was requisite for this union, Alexander VI. was happy in so favourable an opportunity of gratifying the wishes of the new sovereign; but the king was too impatient to wait the return of his ambassador, and presuming on the success of his mission, celebrated the marriage before the necessary formalities for his divorce had been expedited from Rome. This irregularity was, however, readily pardoned, and Caesar Borgia, who had now divested himself of the rank of cardinal, was deputed to carry to France the dispensation, which was accompanied by the hat of a cardinal for George of Amboise, archbishop of Rouen. The magnificence displayed by Caesar on this embassy, far exceeded that of royalty itself; and the king remunerated his services, by conferring on him the title of duke of Valentinois, in Dauphiny, and by a grant of the annual sum of twenty thousand livres; to which was also added, the promise of a territorial possession in the Milanese, as soon as the king should have completed the conquest of that country, *fa)* About the same time, Lucrezia, the daughter of the pontiff, was divorced from her husband, Giovanni Sforza, lord of Pesaro, and married to Alfonso of Aragon, a natural son of Alfonso II. late king of Naples.

Ever since the brothers of the Medici had been compelled *(a) Guiceiard.lib.* iv. 1. 207. On this occasion Caesar is supposed to have carried with him an immense treasure, and even the horses of his attendants are said to have been shod with silver. His magnificent entrance into Chinon, is described by Brantome. *Mem. v.* 227 *Ed. Ltyde,* 1722. *Gordon i Life of Alex. Pl. p. 180.* The divorce of Louis XII. and his marriage contract with Anne of Bretagne, appear in the collection of Du Mont, *vol. Hi. p. .2. pp.* 404, 405..

Chap. v. pelled to quit their native place, the Florentines had ex A. D. 1498. hibited a striking, instance of the effects of fanaticism, A.iEt.23. in debasing both the intellectual and moral powers of the mind. Absurd and blasphemous pretensions to the peculiar favour of heaven, to the power of working miracles, and of Death of Savo-predicting future events, were asserted by Savonarola and njroi... his followers, who attempted to establish the reign of Jesus Christ, as it was impiously called, by acts of violence and bloodshed. This sudden depression occasioned, however, as sudden a reverse. No sooner were the Florentines convinced of the fraudulent practices of their pretended prophet, than they satiated their resentment by the destruction of the man who had so long been the object of their admiration, after which they committed his body, together with those of two of his associates, to the flames, and scattered their ashes in the river *Amo.fa)* Respecting the character of Savonarola, *(a)* This circumstance is adverted to in

the following sonnet, prefixed to an Italian translation in MS. of the life of Savonarola, from the Latin of Giovan-Francesco Pico, one of his warmest admirers. At the close of the work is a large collection of miracles, attributed to this extraordinary and unfortunate man. The person referred to under the name of *11 Tiranno,* is undoubtedly Piero de' Medici:— »

"Alma città, clie al fuoco, al onda,
"Vedesti in preda i tre martiri eletti, l
E tra le pene acerbe, e tra dispetti,
"Lieti insieme provar morte giocon-da, "Godi, clie d'ogni ben tosto feconda
"Ti mostran di profeti i santi detti;
"E tu, che sei regina de' profeti,
"Ove il fallo abondo, la grazia abon-da. "II tuo ricco, onorato, altiero fiume,
"Che si nasconde il grantesoro in seno, "Di quel sacro divin cenere spar-so,
"Vedra morto *il Tiranno,* spento ed arso
"Ogn 'infidel, e'l vizio venir meno,
"Ed apparir nuova luce, enuovolume.
" For the particulars of the catastrophe of Savonarola, *sttljfc of Lor. de' Medici, vol, ii.p.* 569. vonarola, a great diversity of opinions has arisen, as well in Chap, V. subsequent times, as in his own; and whilst some have consi-A. D. 1498. dered him as a saint and a martyr, others have stigmatized A-£u 23him as an impostor and a demagogue. It requires not, however, any great discernment to perceive, that Savonarola united in himself those exact proportions of knavery, talents, folly, and learning, which, combined with the insanity of superstition, compose the character of a fanatic; the motives and consequences of whose conduct, are perhaps no less obscure and inexplicable to himself, than they are to the rest of mankind.

The secret treaty between Lodovico Sforza and the state of Florence, was much more detrimental to the Venetians, vietin captures than it would have been if publicly avowed. By his solici-Vico Pis tations, several of the Italian leaders, who had engaged in the defence of Pisa, were induced to enter into the service of the Florentines; and the army of the republic, under the command of Paolo Vitelli, at length took the field,

with a considerable body of horse, and a powerful train of artillery. Having hastily passed the Arno, Vitelli first bombarded the castle of Buti, where the Venetians attempted to oppose his progress. This place he carried by assault on the second day. Thence he proceeded towards Pisa, and having stationed several bodies of troops in the vicinity, so as to prevent the approach of supplies to the city, he turned his artillery against Vico Pisano, a fortress in the neighbourhood of Pisa, where, having made a breach in the walls, he compelled the garrison to capitulate, and proceeded, by regular approaches, to reduce the city to submission.

In *(a) Guicciard. Storia dltd. lib.* iv. 1. 199.

Third attempt of thc Mcdici to re

Chap. v. In the mean time the exiled brothers of the Medici, conA D. Hps. ceiving that another opportunity was now afforded them for A. *Jex.?.3.* attempting the recovery of Florence, requested the Venetian senate to admit them as associates in the war; representing to them, the practicability of sending a body of troops through the passes of the Appenines, where they would be gain their na-joined by the numerous friends of the Medici in that quartive place. ter whose assistance they might attack the city before it could be provided with the means of defence. The Venetians, at this time closely pressed by Vitelli, willingly accepted the offer; and a large body of infantry was immediately collected, the command of which was given to the duke of Urbino and Astorre Baglioni, of Perugia. Piero de' Medici, with his brother Giuliano, and his cousin Giulio, having united their troops with those of Bartolommeo d'Alveano and Carlo Orsino, joined the Venetians in the Val de Lamone, and possessed themselves of the small town of Marra. They soon, however, found themselves opposed by the Florentines, with whom Lodovico Sforza had now united his arms; but the duke of Urbino pressed forwards, and having captured the town of Bibbiena, descended into the sterile district of Casentino, through which the Arno continues its course to

Florence; and, although his operations were retarded no less by the severity of the weather, than by the efforts of his enemies, his approach filled the inhabitants of Florence with consternation. They, therefore, directed their commander Vitelli to fortify, in the best manner he could, the places which he had occupied near Pisa, and to proceed immediately to oppose the Medici, in Casentino. The courage and experience of the duke of Urbino, and the ardour and rapidity of d'Alveano, were opposed by the vigilance and caution of Vitelli. With inconceivable industry dustry he fortified thè passes by which alone the troops of CHAP-vthe Medici could approach; he restrained their excursions A. D. 1498. on every side; he weakened their forces in various skir-a.ifit. 23. mishes, and harassed them by cutting off their supplies. Unable either to procure subsistence, or to change the situation of their troops, the Venetian commissaries, with the brothers of the Medici, secretly deserted their army, and fled for safety to the town of Bibbiena. The soldiers themselves were compelled to undergo that last of all military disgraces the compulsory surrender of their arms; after which they were permitted by their conquerors to retire, dejected, emaciated, and disgraced, to their own country. It was probably on this disastrous event, that the anguish of Piero de' Medici burst forth in the following sonnet; Vol. i. N N which, (a) This production is now first printed from the original, in the Laurentian library; which appears there in a very rude and imperfect state: SONETTO.

"Non posso far che gli occhi non m'inacqui,
"Pensando quel ch'io sono, e quel ch'io ero;
"D'aver diletto mai più non spero
"In alcun nido com' in quel ch'io nacqui. "Per certo ch'a fortuna troppo spiacqui,
M E chi'l cognosca credi che'l sia 'l vero;
"Sofert' ho in pace, e già non mi dispero, "Con tutto che con l'ira il viso imbiacqui.
"Io m'assomiglio al legno in alto mare,;.

"Che per fortuna l'arbore sta torto,
"Cangio le vele e sto per annegare. _,. -'"
"Se non perisco ancor, guignerò in porto.
"Fortuna sa quel ch'ella sa ben fare,
"Sana in un punto chi è quasi morto.
"Io ion fuor del mio orto,
"Dice il proverbio; odi parola adorna
"Che chi non muor qualche volta ritorna."
CHAP. V.
which, although incorrect and unpolished, may be consi a. D. 1498. dered as the genuine expression of his feelings.

A. *JEt.* 23.
SONNET. When all my sorrows past I call to mind,
And what I am, with what I was compare;
No more allow d those dear delights to share,
Alone to thee, my native spot, confin'd,
   Tears dim my eyes. Yet tho' with looks unkind
Vindictive fortune still pursues me near,
Firm as I may her injuries I bear;
In spirit ardent, but with heart resign'd.
   Like some storm-beaten bark, that o'er the deep
Dismantled drives, the sport of every blast,
I speed my way, and hourly wait my doom.
   Yet when I trace the many dangers past,
   Hope still revives; my destin'd course I keep,
And trust to fate for happier hours to come.

During the contest respecting the city of Pisa, the FloThe contest re-rentines lia(j at various times made overtures to the Vene specting Pisa submitted to tians and their allies, for compromising the differences to of Ereoie0" which it had given rise; but the senate, conscious of their duke of Fer-superiority, and desirous of reducing the territory of Pisa under their own dominion, had, under various pretexts, refused to listen to any terms of pacification. The disgraceful defeat of their troops in Casentino, and the vigour with which Vitelli carried on the siege of Pisa, at length induced them

to relax in their pretensions; and, by the intervention of Lodovico Sforza, it was, after long negotiation, agreed, that all differences between the contending parties should be finally finally decided by Ercole,' duke of Ferrara. Having under-CHAP-vtaken the office of mediator, and heard the various rep re-A. D. 1499. sentations of the different envoys, he published his deter-A-.Et-24mination on the sixth day of April, 1499; by which he ordered, that the Venetians should immediately withdraw their troops from the Florentine and Pisan territories. That the Florentines should pay to them one hundred and eighty thousand ducats, by stated payments of fifteen thousand in each year, as an indemnity for the expenses of the war; and that the city of Pisa should return to its obedience to Florence, under certain restrictions, by which the administration of justice, both criminal and civil, and the public revenue of the state, were secured to the inhabitants.

His interference

This determination, instead of reconciling the contending parties, was received with disapprobation by all. The ineffectual. Venetians, disappointed in those views of aggrandizement with which they had entered into the war, considered the payment of an annual sum as no alleviation of their vexation and disgrace. The Florentines murmured, that after the enormous expenses which they had already sustained in the defence of their long established rights, they should be compelled to reimburse the Venetians to so large an amount; whilst their dominion over the city and territory of Pisa was mutilated and restricted, so that they could not indemnify themselves in that quarter for any part of their expenditure. But above all, the citizens of Pisa exclaimed against the decision of the duke; which they contended, would in effect, deliver them once more into the absolute power of their oppressors, who would soon find a pretext

N-N 2, tO (a) Gukciard. Storia d' Ital. lib. iv. 1. 220.
CHAP. V.
A. D. 14.99.

A. iEt. 24.

to deprive them of their immunities, and to reduce them to the same disgraceful state of vassalage, under which they had so long laboured. It was to no purpose, that the duke attempted, by an additional decree, to obviate these objections. The continuance of the war was resolved upon; and measures were resorted to for the renewal of hostilities, with greater violence than before.faj

The inhabitant! of Pisa resolve to de sclves.

In some respects, however, the contest took a different aspect. From some indications in the course of the treaty, the citizens of Pisa began to suspect, that the Venetians might at length accommodate their differences with the Florentines, and that their city might be considered as the price of reconciliation; whilst the Venetians, affecting to be dissatisfied with the conduct of the inhabitants, withdrew their troops from the defence of the city, for the purpose, in fact of securing the possession of such parts of the territory as they might be enabled to occupy. The citizens saw, without regret, the departure of their doubtful allies; and with the aid of a few mercenaries, who had been introduced within the walls by the Venetians, and who had agreed to join in their defence, they resolved to maintain their independence to the last extremity. The walls of Pisa were of uncommon strength. The fortresses were well provided and garrisoned. The inhabitants were numerous and courageous; many of them were respectable by their rank and talents; and an unremitting warfare of several years, had habituated them to military fatigues. Above all, their aversion to the government of the Florentines was inextinguishable; tinguishable; and this sentiment alone would have supplied every deficiency.

On the other hand the Florentines lost no time in availing themselves of the successes which they had already obtained. Besides a considerable body of horse, their army was now increased to ten thousand foot; with which, and the aid of twenty large pieces of artillery, Vitelli attacked the fortress of Stam-

pace, on which the citizens of Pisa chiefly relied for the defence of the city. The exertions of the besieged to repair the breaches, although both sexes, and all descriptions of persons united in the labour, were ineffectual, and an unremitting cannonade of ten days, at length levelled a great part of the walls. Of those engaged in the defence, many were slaughtered; the rest took refuge in the city, and were closely pursued by the Florentine troops, who at that moment might in all probability have possessed themselves of the prize for which they had so long contended. Vitelli, however, either did not perceive, or did not choose to avail himself of the opportunity afforded him for terminating the war. Satisfied with the success of the day, in thc acquisition of the fortress, and conceiving that the city would now become an easy prey, he restrained the ardour of the soldiery, and allowed the inhabitants to recover from their panic. But although Vitelli had omitted to storm the city, he persevered with the utmost vigilance in such measures as were most likely to compel the inhabitants to surrender; and, in the various means which he adopted for reducing the place, gave striking proofs of those abilities, by which he had obtained his military reputation. The constant use of artillery, had again effected a breach in the walls; the soldiers, inflamed with the hopes of plunder, were

Chap. v.
a. D. 1499. A. iEt. 24.

Vitelli effects a breach in the walls, but neglects to of his advantages.

o

Chap. v. were earnest for the attack; the Florentine commissaries a. D. 1499. remonstrated with Vitelli on the injudicious and dangerous.a.iEt.24. delays which he manifested in all his proceedings, and a time was at length fixed upon for storming the place, which it was agreed should be the twenty-fourth day of August. But, whilst the fruits of his labours were thus ripening, and seemed only to court his hand, a sudden blight deprived Vitelli of his expected prize. The low and marshy district in the vicinity of Pisa, had combined with the

slaughter of the soldiery, to occasion a pestilential distemper in the Florentine camp, which in the course of a few days, made so rapid a progress, that at the time appointed, a sufficient number of troops could not be collected to proceed to the attack. Fresh levies of soldiers were poured in by the Florentines; but the destructive malignity of the disorder, destroyed them more rapidly than they could be replaced.(a) Smitten like the Greeks before Troy, by an invisible hand, the Florentine troops were compelled to abandon their enterprize, in order to secure a retreat, before the further progress of the disease should so far debilitate them, as to render them an easy conquest to the exasperated and vindictive inhabitants. Vitelli therefore embarked his artillery on the Arno, for the purpose of conveying it to Leghorn; but by an unfortunate fatality, the greater part of it fell into the hands of the enemy. Quitting with the remainder of his troops, the contagious precincts of Pisa, he *(a) Guitciard. Storia d' ltd. Ub. iv. 1. 235. Muratori Annali cC Ital. ix. 597.* Macchiavelli also alludes to this circumstance in his first Decennale:

"Lungo sarebbe narrar tutti i torti,

"Tutti gl' inganni corsi in quell' assedio,

"E tutti i cittadin, per febbre morti."

he proceeded through the Via Marrana towards Cascina. CHAP-vOn his arrival at this place, he was met by a deputation A. D. 1499. from the citizens of Florence, by whom he was made a a. ifiLS. prisoner and conducted to that city, where he was put to the "Jf" torture, for the purpose of inducing him to confess that he and decapihad conducted himself with treachery towards the republic.,ated' Among other charges against him, it was alledged, that he had held an interview with the Medici in the war of Casentino, and that he had intentionally suffered them to escape, although he had it in his power to have sent them prisoners to Florence, to have received the due reward of their rebellion against their country. His conduct before Pisa was, however, a still more grievous cause of offence; and although no acknowledgment of either guilt or error could be obtained from him, he was ordered to be decapitated; and the sentence was on the same night carried into effect. His brother Vitellozzo, although at that time labouring under sickness, had the good fortune to effect his escape, and fled to Pisa, with as many of his followers as he could prevail *(bj Nerli, Commcntarii. lib. iv. p.* 84. The unhappy fate of Vitelli is commemorated by Ant. Fr. Ranieri, in the following, not inelegant, lines:

"Urbis ut ingratae scelus, et victricia Pauli "Audiit immiti colla resecta manu, "Scipiadum major, tua quid benefacta, Vitelli,

"Quid valuere mea? ah, dixit et ingemuit.

Nardi informs us, that although no charge, but that of disobedience, could le proved against Vitelli, before his execution, many of his letters were afterwards discovered, which manifested his treachery. *Hist. Fior. lib. iii. p. 6l.* This mode of executing a person first, and obtaining the proofs of his guilt afterwards, is not greatly to be commended, and affords too much reason to conjecture, that the documents were fabricated, for the purpose of justifying an act of odious and illegal severity.

Chap. v. vaii upon to accompany him. He was received with great a. D. 1499. exultation by the inhabitants, who by their own resolution, A.Et.24. an(j a fortunate concurrence of events, were at length freed from their adversaries, and once more indulged themselves in the hope of establishing the ancient independence of their republic.

CHAP. VI. 1499—1503. LOUIS XII. resolves to attempt the conquest of Milan and Naples—Forms an alliance with Alexander VI. and the Venetians—The cardinal de' Medici quits Italy—Travels through various parts of Europe—Louis XII. possesses himself of the duchy of Milan—Casar Borgia attacks the cities of Romagna—Imprisonment and death of Lodovico Sforza—The cardinal de' Medici arrives at Rome—The Florentines again attack Pisa—Casar Borgia perseveres in his hostilities against the Italian states—The Medici attempt a fourth time to effect their return to Florence—Casar Borgia threatens that city— Treacherous combination between Louis XII. and Ferdinand of Spain—Federigo king of JVaples is deprived of his dominions—He retires to France—Gonsalvo betrays the young duke of Calabria—Casar Borgia captures the states of Piombino, Camerino, and Urbino—Pietro Soderini preserves Florence from the attacks of Borgia—Is appointed Gonfaloniere for life—Alliance between Casar Borgia and Louis XII. The Italian nobles oppose the proceedings of Borgia—Several of them treacherously put to death by him at Sinigaglia—He seizes on their territories—Death of Alexander VI.—Remarks on his character and conduct.

Vol. i. o o WHILST Italy continued to be thus agitated by internal commotions, another storm was gathering beyond the Alps, which soon burst with additional violence on that unhappy country. The attack of Charles VIII. upon the kingdom of Naples, was the effect of a puerile ambition; but Louis XII. was a courageous and a politic prince; and the personal experience which he had acquired during the expedition of Charles VIII. in which he had himself born a principal part, rendered him a still more dangerous enemy. After having openly asserted his pretensions to the crown of o o 2, Naples, CHAP. VI.

a. D. 1499a. *£x.* 24.

Louis XII. resolves to attempt the conquest of Milan, and Naples.

Chap. vi. Naples, and the states of Milan, he began to negotiate with A. D. 1499 the other powers of Europe, and in particular with the A.iEt.2. Italian governments, for their assistance or neutrality in the approaching contest.

Forms an alliance with

In gaining over Alexander VI. to his interests he found but little difficulty. That ambitious pontiff, incessantly Alexander aiming at the exaltation of his family, and desirous, beVp Zt If yona" mea-sure, of establishing his authority in the kingdom Venice. of Naples, where he had already obtained considerable influence, had proposed to Federigo the marriage of Caesar Borgia with one of his daughters, whose dowry he expected should be the. extensive principality of Taren turn. This union was, however, rejected in the most decisive terms by Federigo; who, although he was not ignorant that his refusal would draw down upon him the resentment of the pontiff, chose rather to abide its consequences, than assent to an alliance, which he considered as still more dangerous. Thus disappointed in the hopes of aggrandizement, which he had so warmly cherished from this quarter, Alexander was prepared for any propositions from the French monarch, which might enable him to gratify his resentment against the king of Naples. A reciprocation of favours had already commenced between Louis XII. and the pope, by which both parties had been highly gratified; and this connexion was speedily strengthened by the marriage of Caesar Borgia with Carlotta, daughter of John d'Albret, king of Navarre, and nearly related to Louis XII. and by the promotion of the brother of that princess to the purple. The marriage took place on the twelfth day of May, 1499; and from this period Alexander considered himself as devoted to the interests of France, and was ready to to employ both his spiritual and temporal arms in her service. The Venetians, disgusted with the irresolute and treacherous conduct of Lodovico Sforza, had already been induced, by the promise of being put into possession of the city of Cremona, and the district of Ghiaradadda, to enter into a league with Louis XII. to assist him in the recovery of Milan, in which a power was reserved to Alexander VI. to become a party.*(b)* Of this privilege the pope soon afterwards availed himself; having first stipulated, among other articles, that the states of Imola, Forli, Faenza, and Pesaro, then under the government of their respective lords, should be conquered by the arms of the allies, and united under the sole dominion of Caesar Borgia.

CHAP. VI. a. D. 1499A. iEt. 24.

These portentous transactions were not regarded with an inattentive eye by the cardinal de' Medici. He had now attempted, in conjunction with his brothers, at three different times, to effect the restoration of his family to their native place. The ill fortune or misconduct of Piero had defeated

The cardinal de' Medici quila Italy, and travels thro' various part of Europe. *(a)* When the news of the marriage of Caesar Borgia, and of his being honoured by Louis XII. with the order of St. Michael, was received at Rome, great rejoicings took place; which, if we may believe Burchard, were conducted in a manner highly discreditable to the pontiff" and the apostolic see. "Feria quinta vigesima tertia "Maii, venit cursor ex Francia, qui nunciavit Sanctissimo Domino nostro Caesarem Va"lentinum Oucem filium suum, olim cardinalem, contraxisse matrimonium cum magni"fica Domina de Allebretto, a die praesentis mensis; et illud Dominica duodecima ejusdem 4 consununasse. Venit alius annuncians quod in die "pentecostes nona decima hujus, Rex Franciae assumpsit Ducem pncdictum in confra41 trem confraternitatis Sancti Michaelis, quae est regia et magni honoris. Fuerant prop"terea ex mandato Pontificis facti multi ignes per urbem in signum laetitiae; sed in "magnum dedecus et verecundiam Sanctissimi Domini nostri, et ejus sancta? sedis.'' *Burchard. Diar. v. Appendix to Gordon's life of Alexander VI. (b)* This treaty, formed at Blois, and bearing date the fifteenth day of April, 1499, is given in the Corps Diplomatique of Dumont. *v.* iii. *par.* ii. *p.* 406.
Chap. vi. defeated all their endeavours, and eveiy new attempt had A.d. 1499. only served to increase the violence of their enemies, and to A.-Et. 24. Dar the gates of Florence more firmly against them. During five years he had been compelled to avail himself successively of the protection of the ancient friends of his family, in different parts of Italy; but as the hopes of his restoration to Florence diminished, he began to be regarded as an exile and a fugitive, and in the approaching disturbances of Italy, it was not easy to determine in what part he might find a secure asylum. The city of Rome, which ought to have afforded him a safe and honourable residence, was rendered irksome to him by

the vices, and dangerous by the animosity of the pontiff; whilst the Florentines, in order to secure themselves during the approaching commotions, had acceded to the league with France, and thereby cut off from the Medici all hopes of deriving assistance from that power on which they had hitherto relied. Impelled by these circumstances, and perhaps also actuated by the laudable desire of visiting foreign countries, the cardinal determined to quit Italy, and to pass some portion of his time in traversing the principal kingdoms of Europe, till events might arise more favourable to his *views.fa)*

This design he communicated to his cousin Giulio de' Medici, and it was agreed to form a party of twelve friends; a number which they considered sufficiently large for their mutual security in the common incidents of a journey, and too small to afford any cause of alarm. Discarding, therefore, the insignia of their rank, and equipping themselves in an uniform manner, they passed through the states of....Venice, *(a) Ammirato, Ritratti cFhuomini Ulustri eft Casa Media. Opusc. vol.* iii. *p. 66.*

Venice, and visited most of the principal cities of Germany; CHAP-VIassuming in turn the command of their troop, and partak-A. D. 1499. ing of all the amusements afforded by continual change of A-24place, and the various manners of the inhabitants. On their arrival at Ulm, their singular appearance occasioned their being detained by the magistrates; but, on their disclosing their quality and purpose, they were sent under a guard to the emperor Maximilian, who received the cardinal with that respect and attention, to which, from the celebrity of his ancestors, and his high rank in the church, he was so well entitled. Far from interrupting their progress, Maximilian highly commended the magnanimity of the car dinal in bearing his adverse fortune with patience; and his judgment and prudence, in applying to the purposes of useful information, that portion of his time, of which he could not now dispose to better advantage. Besides furnishing him with an honourable passport through the

German states, Maximilian gave him letters to his son Philip, then governor of the low countries; recommending the cardinal and his companions to his protection and favour. After having passed a considerable time in Germany, the associated friends proceeded to Flanders; where they were received by Philip, not only with hospitality, but with magnificence. The cardinal then intended to have taken shipping, and proceeded to England; but the danger of the voyage deterred his friends from the undertaking; and at their intreaties, he relinquished his *design.fa)* They, therefore, bent their course towards France. On their arrival at Rouen they were again *(a)* " Dal qual finalmente partendo, *h* Terrovana su' 1' oceano si condusse; con "pensiero di veder Inghilterra, se da compagni non fosse stato dissuaso; paurosi oltre ' modo de' flutti di quel vasto e profondissimo mare." *Amrnk. Ritratti. in Opusc. vol.* iii. *p. 66.*

Chap, vi. again seized upon, and detained in custody; and, although A. D. 1499. the cardinal, and his cousin Giulio, made an immediate dis

A. Mx. 24. covery of their rank, and represented the object of their journey to be totally unconnected with political concerns; yet, in the state of hostility that had then commenced between the kings of France and of Naples, there appeared to be too much ground for suspicion, to admit of their being speedily released; nor was it until''letters were obtained from Piero de' Medici, then in the French camp at Milan, that they were enabled to procure their discharge. Having again obtained their liberty, they proceeded through France, visiting every place deserving of notice, and examining whatever was remarkable, till they arrived at Marseilles; where after a short stay, they determined to proceed by sea immediately to Rome. The winds being, however, unfavourable, they were compelled to coast the Riviera of Genoa, where having been driven on shore, they thought it advisable to relinquish their voyage, and to proceed by land to Savona. On their arrival at this place, they met with the cardinal Giuliano della Rovere, who had fled thither to avoid the resentment of Alexander VI. A common enmity to that profligate pontiff, and a similarity of misfortunes, rendered their meeting interesting; and three refugees sat at the same table, all of whom were afterwards elevated to the highest dignity in the christian world. The two cousins of the Medici gave an account of the objects which they had met with on their journey; and related the difficulties which they had surmounted by land, and the dangers which they had encountered by sea. The cardinal della Rovere recapitulated in his turn, the events which had taken place in Italy since their departure, and in which they were so deeply interested. rested. From Savona the cardinal de' Medici repaired to Chap. vi.

Genoa, where for some time he took up his residence with A. D. 1499. his sister, Madalena, the wife of Francesco Cibo, who had A-2fixed upon that city as the place of his permanent abode/aj

During the absence of the cardinal from Rome, a very considerable change had taken place in the political state of Lm»»xn. posItaly. The French army under the command of d'Aubigny *TeL »* had crossed the Alps; and, forming a junction with the of troops of Gian-Giacopo Trivulzio, who had now obtained the rank of marshal of France, occupied several of the principal towns in the Milanese, and at length captured and sacked the capital. It was not without difficulty that Lodo vico Sforza effected his escape into the Tyrol. Louis XII. informed of the success of his arms, hastened to Milan, which he entered as sovereign on the sixth day of October, 1499, amidst the acclamations of the people; who, wearied with the tyranny of the usurper, regarded the French as the avengers of his crimes, and the assertors of their rights/ On this occasion the rightful heir to the supreme authority fell into the hands of Louis XII. who tore him from his mother Isabella, and sent him into a monastery in France; whilst Isabella herself, having witnessed the destruction of her husband and children at Milan, returned to Naples to behold that of her whole family. The arms of the French and their al-

lies in Italy, having thus far been successful, the conquering parties began to divide the spoil. The states of Milan and of Genoa were received into the

Vol. 1. p p allegiance *(a) Ammxr. Ritratti, Opusc. vol.* iii. *p. 66. (b) Muratori, Annali a" Italia, vol.* ix. *p. 600.*

Chap. vi. allegiance of the king of France, fa The city and district A. D. 1499. of Cremona were surrendered up to the Venetians, as had a. *Jex.* 24. been previously agreed on; and it only remained to gratify the wishes of Alexander, and his son Caesar Borgia, by obtaining for the latter the dominion of the several states in Romagna, which had been promised to him as a recompence for the concurrence of the pope in the league with France.

Caesar Borgia, now no longer called the cardinal of Cssm Borgia Valenza, but duke of Valentinois, having obtained a attacks the 1 1 ckieaofRo-considerable body of French troops, and united them with the papal forces, proceeded to attack the city of Imola, which he soon compelled to capitulate. The fortress of Forli was defended with great courage by Caterina Sforza, the mother of the young prince Ottaviano Riario; but all resistance to so superior a force being ineffectual, she was at length obliged to surrender; and, being made a prisoner, was sent to the castle of S. Angelo, at Rome. She was, however, soon afterwards liberated in consequence of the representations of Ivo d' Allegri, who commanded the French troops in the service of Caesar Borgia, and who was induced not less from admiration of her courage, than compassion for her sex, to interest himself in her behalf. The further progress of the united armies, was prevented by new disturbances in the Milanese, in consequence of which, d'Allegri returned with the troops under his command, into that district; and Caesar, hastening to Rome, entered the city on the twenty-sixth day of

February, *(a) v. MacchiavcUi, lib. del Principe, p. 6.* erf. 550.

February, 1500, with extraordinary pompYaJ A carnival Chap. vi. was soon afterwards celebrated, in

which he displayed his A. D. 1500. magnificence at an incredible expense; and, as a reward for *A-25,* his achievements, the pope presented him with the golden consecrated rose, and dignified him with the title of *Gonfaloniere* of the holy Roman church.

Imprisonment and death of

The period was now fast approaching in which Lodovico Sforza, the author of so many calamities to his country, and to mankind, was to meet with the retribution that LodoTico awaited his misdeeds. After having attempted, in vain, to procure the assistance of the emperor elect Maximilian, he resorted to the mercenary aid of the Swiss, from whom he engaged an army of eight thousand men. With this force, and such additional troops as his own exertions, and those of his brother, the cardinal Ascanio, could raise, he suddenly descended into Italy, and passing by the lake of Como, possessed himself of the adjacent city. The commencement of his undertaking was prosperous. The cruelties and enormities practised by the French, had already convinced the people of the error into which they had been led, by a too favourable opinion of their conquerors. The cities of Milan opened their gates to their former sovereign; whose government, though severe, appeared to them kind and lenient, in comparison with the tyranny of the French. Louis XII. was, however, unwilling to relinquish his conquest without further efforts. Fresh troops were poured over the Alps; the principal part of which consisted also of Swiss mercenaries, who, to the number of ten thousand, p p 2, engaged *(a)* The particulars of this splendid procession are fully given by Burchard. *v. Appendix. No. XLIX.*

Chap. vi. engaged to oppose their own countrymen; and who, joined a. D. 1500. to six thousand French troops, under the command of the A.iEt.25. duke de Tremouille, again threatened the destruction of the family of Sforza. The contest between the two armies was concentred at the city of Novara, from which Lodovico had expelled the French; who still, however, kept possession of the fortress. Whilst the event of the war yet remained uncertain, that treachery, of which Lodovico had so often set the example, was now employed to his own destruction. A secret intercourse had already taken place between the Swiss troops in his service and the French commander. At the moment when he expected to avail; himself of their assistance, they suddenly deserted his standard, alleging that they would not oppose their countrymen in battle; and, with the privity and concurrence of the French, took the direct road towards their own country/a In attempting to effect his escape, Lodovico was, on the tenth day of April, 1500, made prisoner, with several of his nobility and friends/ His own crimes afforded a pretext to Louis XII. for treating him with a degree of cruelty, which, in fact, only served to gratify the resentment of the king, for the opposition given to his pretensions, and which changed the remembrance of the misconduct of Lodovico into compassion for his misfortunes. Conveyed to the castle of Loches, in the duchy of *Berri,fc)* he was there *(a)* The treacherous conduct of the Swiss on this occasion was notorious, and is commemorated in the works of several of the writers of the time, v *Appendix. No. L. (bj* On the same day that Sforza was made prisoner, the poet Marnllus lost his life, in attempting to pass the river Cecina, in the district of Volterra. His untimely fate was a subject of regret to several of his learned friends, v. *Appendix. No. LI, fcj Cuicdard. lib.* iv. 1. 252. *Marat. Annali. vol.* ix. *p. 605.* there inclosed in a dark and lonely chamber; where, daily Chap.vt. furnished witlr the means of life, but deprived of all that A. D. 1500. could render life tolerable, he languished in solitude and a.Ja.25. misery the remainder of his existence; a space of ten years. Scarcely does the history of mankind exhibit a spectacle of equal commiseration. Pain and privation, racks and chains may agonize the body; but the indignant reaction of a mind conscious of its rectitude, opposes a barrier to their effects; whilst death, a ministering angel, is ever at hand to ward off he last extremes of suffering. This, alas, was not the fate of Lodovico:

with sufficient understanding to: be aware of his errors, and with sufficient sensibility to be convinced of his guilt, the sufferings of his mind were probably yet more acute than those of his body. The human ruin was complete. Other calamities may be tolerated, "but a wounded spirit, who can bear?".

The cardinal de' Medici

Rome.

Such were the events that had taken place in Italy, during the absence of the cardinal de' Medici, and which speedily prepared the way to still more important altera-returns to tions. From Genoa the cardinal hastened to Rome, in the expectation, that amidst the changes and commotions to which the pretensions of Louis XII. and the ambition of Caesar Borgia incessantly gave rise, an opportunity might yet occur of restoring the Medici to their former authority in the city of Florence. On his arrival at Rome, the moderation of his conduct, and the respectability of his life, seemed to have effected a change in the disposition of the pope; who, from this time, appears to have laid aside his illwill, and to have treated the cardinal with the respect and attention due to his rank. But, although this alteration in the conduct of the pope was sufficiently observable, it was not supposed,

Chap. vi. supposed, by those who had the best opportunities of forma. D. 1500. ing a just opinion of these very opposite characters, that a. *£x.* 25. Alexander was sincere in his professions of esteem, for one whom he had so lately marked as an object of his displeasure. On the contrary it was conjectured, that the crafty pontiff was only desirous of avoiding the imputation of having such a man as the cardinal for his enemy, and of screening himself from the odium which he justly deserved, by inducing a belief, that he lived with him on terms of intimacy and confidence. It is thus that vice sometimes associates itself with virtue, that it may with less danger of detection pursue its criminal purposes./

The award of the duke of Ferrara for terminating the xiie Fioren-war respecting the city of Pisa, having been ren-

dered inttsck the effectual by the dissent of all the parties, the Florentines city of Pisa, hacl begun to take measures for repairing their former dispuised by asters; and, as they had concurred with the Venetians and the iniMbi-the pope, in the league with France, they conceived that they were also entitled to derive some advantage from the successes of the allies, towards which they had contributed by sending to the aid of the king a considerable body of troops./ These pretensions were urged with great eager ly " Cum enim vitam moresque tuos ab ineunte aetate consiJero, cum castissimd 4' superatam adolescentiam, juventutem actam gravissime atque sanctissimd, cum praterea "intueor quanta animi fortitudine atque constantia, paupertatem, diutumumque milium "toleraveris; qui prudentia, errore fortasse aliquo, gravem tibi adversarium Alexandrum "pontiiicem maximum, eb deduxeris facilitate tua et suavissimis moribus, ut non modo "odium dissimulare vellet, sed etiam ad deciinandam invidiam, se tibi cuperet haberi amt14 cissimum," &x. *Greg. Cortesii Ep. ad Leon.* x. *inter ejusd. ep.fam. p.* 24-9. *Ven.* 1573.

(b) Guicciard. lib. v. *vol.* i. *p.* 254. The frequent introduction of the " siege of "Pisa," may perhaps remind the reader of the sarcasm of Boccalini, where he pretends, that ness; insomuch, that the cardinal of Rohan, who governed Chap, Vl the Milanese states on behalf of Louis XII. was at length A. D. 1500. prevailed upon to furnish the Florentines with a body of A-Et-25 six hundred horse, and eight thousand Swiss soldiers, accompanied by a formidable train of artillery, and a supply of ammunition, for the purpose of reducing the citizens of Pisa to obedience/aj With this aid, and a considerable additional body of Italian mercenaries, the Florentines again assaulted that unfortunate city; which the inhabitants had fortified to the utmost of their power. The besieged did not, however, wholly rely either on the strength of their ramparts, or on their own courage; but had recourse to artifice and negotiation, for mitigating the violence, or obviating the ef-

fects of the threatened attack. To this end, they dispatched their envoys to the French governors in Milan and Genoa, as well as to Beaumont, the commander of the French troops destined for the assault, proposing to deliver up the city to the French king, provided he would receive them as his subjects, and afford them his protection: To this offer Ravestan, the governor of Genoa, expressed his assent; but Beaumont still persevered in the attack; and, having at length succeeded in demolishing a part of the walls, he ordered his troops to commence the assault. An ill-disciplined and tumultuous body ...... of that the Laconic senate condemned an unfortunate author, who had been convicted of using three words, where two were sufficient, to read once overthewarofPisabyGuicciardini; but that the culprit, after having with great agony laboured through the first page, requested his judges would send him to the gallies for life, rather than compel him to go through with his labour. *Boccalin. Ragguag.* vi. Guicciardini enjoys his reputation and the critic his jest. *(a) Nardi, Hist. Fior. lib. iv. p. 55, IfC. (b) Guiceiard. lib. v. vol. ii. p. 256.* Chap. vi. Qf horse and foot rushed towards the city; but, although a. D. 1500. the walls were destroyed, an immense trench, which the in.

A.iEt.25.'. dustry of the inhabitants had formed within them, with an additional rampart, unexpectedly opposed their further progress./iz/ In one moment the daring assailants were converted into astonished spectators, and the remainder of the day was passed without any effort to surmount the difficulty. The offers made to the king of France, now began to: produce their.effects. Many of the French officers were favourable to the cause of the inhabitants. An amicable intercourse soon took place between them, and they who had been repulsed as enemies, were now admitted as friends. By this communication, and the long delay to which it gave rise, the discipline of the besieging aimy was wholly destroyed. A general mutiny took place, in which the soldiery seized upon the supplies intended

for the siege, sacked the camp, and took prisoner the Florentine commissary, Luca d'Albizi, on a pretext that the arrears of their pay had not been duly discharged. No sooner was the besieging army dispersed, than the troops in the city sallied out, and proceeding to Librafatta; a garrison town on the Tuscan frontier, with great intrepidity, scaled the walls and possessed themselves of the place; which was of the utmost importance to their safety, as it opened to them all the country towards Lucca. Nor did the misfortunes of the Florentines terminate here. Louis XII. exasperated beyond measure at the dishonour which the French arms had sustained in this enterprize, accused the

Florentines *(a) Nardi. Hist. Fior. lib. iv. p. 56. (b) Guictiard. lib. v. vol. i. p. 257.*

Florentines of having rendered it abortive by their own Chap, Vi. parsimony and imprudence. The Florentines were earnest A. D. 1501. to justify themselves; for which purpose they dispatched A. 26two ambassadors to the king; one of whom was the celebrated Nicolo Macchiavelli but their representations were of little avail; and it was only by the payment of an additional sum, for the support, as the king pretended, of the Swiss troops on their return to Milan, that they were again received into favour. The resentment of the monarch being thus pacified, he once more proposed to afford them his assistance. But the Florentines suspecting, perhaps, that he had himself designs upon the city of Pisa, or being already so far exhausted, as to be unable to bear the expenses which a new attempt must inevitably occasion, thought proper to decline his further aid.

In the mean time Caesar Borgia persevered in his attempt to subdue the cities of Romagna. By the assistance of the c«sar Borgia French troops, he soon possessed himself of Pesaro, the ff"™"" *1 1 _* his attempts patrimony of Giovanni Sforza; and of Rimini, then subject on the Italian to Pandolfo Malatesti. The conquest of Faenza was an sUtes" undertaking of greater difficulty. Such was the attachment of the inhab-

itants to their young sovereign, Astorre Man fredi, then only seventeen years of age, that the utmost efforts of the assailants were unable to reduce the place until the following year, when the city surrendered to the French and papal arms. Even then the possession was only obtained under the sanction of an honourable capitulation, by which the young prince, who had already distinguished himself by his military talents, was to hold a respectable Vol. 1. o Q rank *(a) Nardi. Hut. Fior. lib. iv. p. 67.* CHAP. VI. a. D. 1501. A..fit. 26.

The Medici attempt a fourth time to effect their rank in the service of Caesar Borgia. No sooner, however, had that implacable tyrant secured his person, than he sent him, accompanied by his natural brother, to Rome; where they were both put to death.*(a)* He then turned his arms against Bologna, where he had already a secret communication with some of the principal citizens, whom he had seduced to espouse his cause; but Giovanni Bentivoglio, who then held the supreme authority, having discovered the intrigue, seized upon several of the conspirators, who were immediately slaughtered by his adherents; and, having diligently attended to the defence of the city, prevented, for a time, the further progress of the usurper, who had intended to constitute Bologna the capital of his new government; of which the pope had already granted him the investiture, by the title of duke of Romagna.

Whilst Caesar Borgia, thus checked in his career, was hesitating against whom he should next lead the formidable body of troops, of which he had obtained the command, the Medici conceived that a favourable opportunity was once more afforded them, of regaining their former authority in the city of Florence. The want of ability and energy in the government of that place became daily more conspicuous. The city, exhausted of its wealth, was distracted by tumults; whilst the Tuscan territories were disgraced by dissentions and feuds among the principal families. In this situation of affairs, Piero de' Medici, encouraged by the Venetians, and supported by the Orsini, and by Vitellozzo Vitelli, whose animosity to the Florentines on account of the the death of his brother Paolo, was unextinguishable, hast-Chap, Vi. ened to the camp of Caesar Borgia, and endeavoured to A. D. 1501. convince him of the advantages which he would derive a.ift. 26. from marching his troops into the Florentine territory, and effecting a change in the government. At the same time Giuliano de' Medici suddenly presented himself at the court of Louis XII. who was then highly displeased with the Florentines, and, by the promise of a large subsidy for the support of the expedition against Naples, and the assurances of a constant devotion to the French government, obtained from the king, the promise of his support in the intended enterprise. But Caesar Borgia, although he received Piero de' Medici with apparent kindness, and even promised to promote his cause, had no object less at heart than the restoration of the Medici toF lore nee; fo) having already formed designs more conducive to his own interest. He considered, however, that in the deranged state of the affairs of Florence, he could

Q Q 2 not *(a)* " Dux Valentinus fecit mirabilia magna solus in Flaminia, jactaturque vulgo, et "rumor increbrescit, quod ubi Faventiam, Bononiamque expugnaverit, velit ferro "aperire iter *Petro Medici,* ut hie plusquam civis (facinus magnum) tantae civitati im"peritet." *Aug. Vespucci Ep. ad Nic. MaccA. ap. Band. Coll. Vet. Mm. p. 51.*
(b) Guicciard. lib. v. 1. 263.

fc) Guicciardini, on the authority of particular and private information, relates, that Caesar had long lwrn a secret enmity against Piero de' Medici, on account of a circumstance which occurred whilst Caesar was pursuing hi studie at Pisa, before his father was raised to the pontificate; when, having occasion to resort to the assistance of Piero, on behalf of one of his friends, who was implicated in some criminal transaction, he had hastened from Pisa to Florence; but after waiting some hours for an audience, whilst Piero was engaged in

business or amusement, he had returned, not only without effecting his purpose, but without having obtained an interview. Trivial as this incident may appear, it must be remembered, that the resentment of wounded pride is of all others the most violent, and that the soul of Borgia knew not how to forgive. i. *Guicciard. lib.* v. 1. 264. not fail, either of occupying some desirable part of their territory, or of obtaining such terms as might be favourable to the prosecution of his favourite project, the establishment of the duchy of Romagna. Nor is it improbable that he had indulged the hope of availing himself of some fortunate concurrence of circumstances to subjugate to his own authority the whole of the Tuscan state.

Caesar Borgia turns his arms against Florence, bat is ordered to desist by VI

About the beginning of the month of May, 1501, Caesar descended with his army, consisting of seven thousand foot, and eight hundred horse/aj from Romagna, into the district of Mugello, and pitched his camp in the vicinity of Barberino. He was here joined by a body of troops from Bologna, which had been sent to his assistance by Bentivoglio, in pursuance of a treaty concluded between *them.fb)* From Barberino, Caesar dispatched his envoys to Florence, to acquaint the citizens with the purpose of his approach, and to prescribe to them the terms on which alone he would withdraw his troops. Of these proposals, as preserved by Nardi/cJ the principal were, that the Florentines should pay him a considerable stipend, as their *Condottiero;* that they should not interfere with.him in his meditated attack upon the other states of Italy, and particularly that of Piombino, then under the protection of Florence; that they should deliver up to him six of the principal citizens as hostages, to be named by Vitellozzo; and lastly, that they should restore Piero de' Medici to his former honours, or should otherwise make such an alteration in the government, as might secure on their part the performance *(a) Guicciard. lib.* v. 1. 264.
(b) Nardi, Hut. Fior. lib. iv. *p.* 71.

(e) Nardi, Hist. Fior. lib. iv. *p. 72.*
v performance of the proposed treaty. No sooner were these Chap. Vi. propositions heard in the city, than they excited the A. D. 1501. highest indignation; insomuch, that the magistrates, whilst *A.jex.z6.* deliberating on the measures to be adopted, could scarcely be secured from the violence of the people. But, whilst the negotiation was depending, and the result was yet uncertain, Caesar received peremptory orders from the pope, to abstain from any further proceedings against the Florentines. In consequence of this mandate, he unwillingly withdrew his troops; not, however, without obtaining the appointment of *Condottiero* to the republic, with an annual income of thirty-six thousand ducats, and a stipulation that he should not be obliged to serve in person. The motives that induced Alexander VI. thus to interfere in the designs of Caesar Borgia, arose from the representations of Louis XII. who, although he might have consented to the restoration of the family of Medici to their former authority in Florence, was too well apprized of the character of Alexander VI. and his son, to permit them to obtain such an ascendancy in that city, as must have resulted from their being the instruments of such restoration. Nor was it difficult to perceive, that an influence so extensive, as the family of Borgia would then have acquired, might, in case of a rupture with the pope, have formed an effectual barrier against the projected invasion of the kingdom of Naples; on which account Louis had given positive directions to his general d'Aubigny, that in case Caesar did not, on the first representation to him, evacuate the Florentine dominions, he should employ all his forces to compel him to retreat.
Whilst *(a) Guicriard. lib.* v. 1. 265.

Chap, vi. Whilst Caesar Borgia was thus industriously, attempting A. p. mi, by fraud or by force, to establish an independent authority A. Jex. 26. m Italy, another event took place, which surpassed his ducTof crimes, no less in treachery and injustice, than in the rank Louis xn. of the perpetrators, and the extent of the theatre on which rdlfs'ain was transactea-Federigo, king of Naples, had comtoward Fede-menced his reign with the affection of his people; and his Napiek»ing disposition and talents were well calculated to promote their happiness. Even those who had revolted, or quitted the country, under the reigns of Ferdinand I. and Alfonso II. had returned with confidence to their allegiance; and the princes of Salerno and Bisignano, were among the first to salute him as their sovereign. Federigo, on his part, lost no opportunity of confirming the favourable opinion already entertained of him. Instead of persecuting such of the nobility as had espoused the cause of the French, he restored to them their domains and fortresses. He patronized and liberally rewarded the many eminent scholars, by whom the city of Naples was distinguished, and who had been injured or exiled during the late commotions; and, as an indication of the tenor of conduct which he meant to adopt, he struck a medal with a device, alluding to the better order of things which he meant to establish. But, although the reign of Federigo commenced under the happiest auspices, it was not destined to be of long duration; and whilst he supposed that every day gave additional security *(a) Giannone, Storia di Napoli, vol. Hi. p. 391.*

(b) This device represented a book in the flames, surmounted by the crown of Naples, with the motto, Recedant Vetera. The life, character, and conduct of Federigo, are particularly noticed by Sanazzaro, in a Latin elegy, wholly devoted to that purpose: and which merits perusal, no less as an interesting historical monument, than as a beautiful poem. *v. Sanaz. Eleg. lib.* iii. *El. I.* security to his authority, the kings of France and of Spain, Chap, Vi. had, by a secret treaty, divided between them his do-*A. D. 1501.* minions, and formed a scheme for carrying their purpose A-*£t-2fi*into effect. This plan, which has served as a model on subsequent occasions, was, that the king of France should assert his pretensions to the kingdom of Naples, as representative of the house of Anjou; the infallible consequence of which

would be, that Federigo would resort for assistance to Ferdinand and Isabella of Spain, who should send over a considerable military force, under the pretext of opposing the French; but that, as soon as the latter arrived, the Spanish troops should unite their arms with their pretended adversaries, expel the family of Aragon, and divide the kingdom between the two sovereigns. By this treaty the king of France was to possess the city of Naples, the provinces called Terra di Lavoro and Abruzzo, with a moiety of the income arising from the pastures of Apulia, and was to assume, in addition to his titles of king of France and duke of Milan, that of king of Naples and Jerusalem. The districts of Calabria and Apulia, with the other moiety of the income, were allotted to the king of Spain, who was to style himself duke of those provinces. This treaty, which bears date the eleventh day of November, 1500, is yet extant *fa)* and if the moral sense of mankind be not extinguished by the subsequent repetition of such enormities, will consign the-memory of these royal plunderers to merited execration.

Preliminaries being thus adjusted, Louis XII. began openly to prepare for the intended attack, the direction of which, he *(a) Du Mont, Corps Diplomatique, vol.* iii. *par.* ii. *p.* 444.

CHAP VI-he confided to his general d'Aubigny; who commenced his A. D. J50i. expedition, at the head of ten thousand foot, and a thousand A. *Jex.* 26. horse. Federigo was no sooner apprized of this measure than Eonisxn. at-he dispatched information of it to Gonsalvo, the Spanish ritorytf Na-general, who had withdrawn his troops into Sicily, on the pe»-pretence that he might be in readiness, in case his assistance should again be required in the kingdom of Naples. On the arrival of Gonsalvo, the king confided to his care the fortified places in Calabria, which the Spanish general pretended were necessary for the security of his army. Federigo had also raised a considerable body of troops, which had been re-inforced by those of the Colonna; with which, when joined by the Spanish army, he expected

to be enabled to oppose an effectual barrier to the progress of the French. All Italy was in suspense, and a contest far more bloody than had of late occurred, was expected to plunge that country into new calamities. A short time, however, removed all apprehensions on this head. No sooner had the French troops made their appearance in the Roman territories, than the envoys of the allied monarchs met at Rome; where, entering together into the consistory, they notified to the pope and cardinals, the treaty already formed, and the consequent division of the kingdom of Naples. The convenient pretext of the promotion of the christian faith, by a war against the infidels, for the preparations necessary to which, it was asserted, that kingdom afforded the most convenient station, was the mask under which their *most catholic* and *most christian* majesties affected to hide from the world the deformity of their crime.

The stipulations thus agreed upon, met with no opposition from Alexander VI. who had now an opportunity of gratifying gratifying the resentment which he had so long harboured Chap, vi. against the king of Naples. On the twenty-fifth day of A. D. 1501. June, 1501, a pontifical bull deprived Federigo of his a. iEt.26. dominions, and divided them between the two monarchs, in the shares before-mentioned *.fa)* The intelligence of this alliance, and of its consequences, struck Federigo with terror; but Gonsalvo, pretending to discredit it, continued to give him the most positive assurances of his assistance. No sooner, however, had the French army entered the Neapolitan territory, than he avowed his instructions, and immediately sent off from Naples to Spain, in vessels already provided for that purpose, the two dowager queens, one of whom was the sister, and the other the niece of the Spanish king. Federigo persevered in the defence of his rights; and, intrusting the command of the city of Naples to Prospero Colonna, determined to make his first resistance at Capua,*fb)* D'Aubigny had, however, already possessed himself of the adjacent country; the king was obliged to return with his army from Aversa to Naples; and Capua, being taken by assault on the twenty-fifth day of July, was sacked by the French with circumstances of peculiar cruelty, and unexampled licentiousness. fo) The loss of Capua was speedily followed by the capitulation of the city of Naples, which purchased an exemption from plunder by the payment of Vol. 1. R R seventy (a) The bull of Alexander VI. by which he divides the kingdom of Naples between the French and Spanish monarchs, is published by Rousset, in his supplement to the *Corps Diplomatique* of DuMont. *vol.* iii. *p.* 1.

(b) To this period we may apply the sonnet of Cariteo:

"Mentre che d'Aragona il sommo honore

"Tra Galli c Cimbri il suo destrier raggira."

Chap. vi. seventy thousand ducats to the invaders. Federigo witha. D. 1501. drew himself into the *Castel-nucvo,* which he refused to

A. £i. 26. surrender till he had effected a treaty with d'Aubigny, by which he was to be allowed to retire to the island of Ischia, and to retain it for six months, and was also to be at liberty to remove from the *Castel-nuovo* and *Castel deW Uovo* whatever he might think proper, excepting only the artillery. In negotiating for his own safety, he did not forget that of his subjects. A general amnesty was to be granted of all transactions since Charles VIII. had quitted the city of Naples; and the cardinals of Aragon and Colonna were to enjoy their ecclesiastical revenues arising from that kingdom. In the commencement of this contest, Federigo had sent his infant son Ferdinand, duke of Calabria, to Tarentum, under the care of the count of Potenza. The rest of the wretched family of Aragon were now assembled on the barren rock of Ischia. This family consisted of his queen Isabella and a numerous train of children; his sister Beatrice, the widow of the great Mattia Corvino, king of Hungary, and his niece, Isabella, the widow of Gian-Galeazzo, duke of Milan; who, already deprived of her sovereign rank, her husband, and her son, now saw the completion of her ruin in that of her royal relations.

This *(a)* The poet Cariteo has paid the last tribute of duty and affection to his unfortunate sovereign, in the second *Cantico* of his *Metamorphosi,* in which he introduces the city of Naples, the lovely Parthenope, lamenting her lost glory and happiness, and contrasting them with the disgraceful state of servitude, to which she was reduced by her conquerors:

"Libera fui gran tempo; hor son captiva;

"In man di feri monstri, horrendi e diri."

A considerable part of the poem is devoted to the commemoration of the female part of the

This deeply meditated act of treachery, to which Fede-CHAP-*Vi*rigo had fallen a victim, whilst it excited in him the highest A. D. 1501. indignation against his perfidious relative Ferdinand of Spain, A-iEt-26inspired him with a disgust of the cares and the dangers of Itetir" t0 royalty, and induced him to seek for repose in a less invidious station. Having therefore obtained a passport from Louis XII. he left his family at Ischia, under the care of the Marquis del Vasto, and proceeding directly to France, endeavoured to conciliate the favour of the king, so far as to afford him the means of fulfilling his wishes. No longer regarding him as a rival, but as a suppliant, Louis acceded to his request, and an annual income of thirty thousand ducats, with the title of duke of Anjou, secured to him opulence and

R R 2 repose the family; four of whom, then living, had sat upon a regal throne, and the fifth had enjoyed sovereign rank as duchess of Milan:

"Ove siete, O Joanne, ambe regine,

"D'Ausonia, e d'Aragonia ambe ornamento,

"Per virtute e bellezze ambe divine?

41 Ove *i* Beatrice; ov' il grande incremento

"Del valor d'Aragon? di re sorella,

"Figlia, e consorte? e di lor gloria augmento?

"Hor per te cresce il duolo, alma Isabella;

"Di Re feconda madre, e di virtute,

"£ di Re guida, orientale Stella.

» »

"Verace ardente amor, constante e fiso,

"Vuol ch' in 1' altra Isabella sempre io pensi,

"Che i thesauri del ciel porta nel viso;

"Duchessa di Milan; di cui gli accensi

"Rai di bellezza efflagran *si* nel volto,

"Che sveglian di ciascun gli ignavi sensi." &c.

Boccalini has selected the example of this last accomplished lady as the most unfortunate on historical record—" unica nelle disgrazie"—on which account he represents her, in his imaginary Parnassus, as reduced to the necessity of supporting herself by selling matches through the streets. *Ragguag. di Parnaso. 75.*

Chap, vt repose during the remainder of his days. Historians have a. D. 1501. accused him of pusillanimity, in thus relinquishing for an a./Et.26 inferior title, his pretensions to a crown, which, in the dissentions that soon afterwards arose between the two successful monarchs, he might in all probability have re-f covered; but Federigo had sufficiently experienced the treachery and ingratitude of mankind; and, having in vain attempted to promote the happiness of others, he perhaps chose a wise part in securing his own.

The regrets of the muses, whom he had so generously protected during his prosperity, followed him to his retreat. Sanazzaro, who accompanied him on his expedition into France, seems to consider the-events that then took place, to be, as indeed they afterwards proved, the final destruction of the Neapolitan branch of the house of Aragon,*fa)*

The *(a)* " O fatum infelix! O sors malefida! quid illic

"Egimus? O tristi mersa carina loco I"
Sannaz. El. lib. iii. *El,* 2.

Federigo died at Tours in the year 1504, at 52 years of age. The Neapolitan historians feelingly regret the loss of a line of monarchs, who had for a long course of years rendered Naples the seat of magnificence, opulence, and learning; and of whom the last was the most deserving, and the most unfortunate.

"Principe cotanto saggio," says Giannone, *(lib. xxix. cap.* iv.) " e di molte lettere adorno, che a lui, non men che a "Ferdinando suo padre, deve Napoli il ristoramento delle discipline, e delle buone "lettere." He was accompanied on his expedition to France, by a few of his faithful adherents; and, among the rest, by Sanazzaro, who, on this occasion, sold the remainder of his hereditary possessions to relieve the necessities of his sovereign, and remained with him to the time of his death j having taken his farewell of his native country, in the following beautiful verses.:

"Parthenope

The last place in Naples that resisted the arms of the Spanish monarch, was the city of Tarentum, whither the young duke of Calabria had been sent by his father, as to a place of security. The command of the castle was intrusted to Leonardo Napolitano, a knight of Rhodes; but he, being reduced to extremities by Gonsalvo, agreed, with the consent of the count of Potenza, to surrender the city and fortress, if succour did not arrive in the space of four months; Gonsalvo binding himself by the solemnity of an oath, on the holy sacrament, that the duke of Calabria should be at liberty to proceed whithersoever he thought proper. On the surrender of Tarentum, the duke expressed his intention to follow his father into France; but Gonsalvo, disregarding his oath, sent him to Ferdinand of Spain, in which country he continued during the life of that monarch, in a sort of honourable captivity./

If CHAP. VI.

a. D. 1501. a. *Mt. 26.*

Gonsalvo betrays the young duke of Calabria.

"Parthenope mihi culta, vale, blandissima Siren; "Atque horti valeant, Hesperidesque tuae;

"Mergillina, vale, nostri memor; et mea flentis

"Serta cape, heu domini munera avara tui.

"Maternae salvcte umbrae; salvete, paternae;

"Accipite et vestris turea dona focis.

"Neve nega optatos, virgo Sebethias,

amnes;

"Absentique tuas det mihi somnus aquas.

"Det fesso aestivas umbras sopor; et levis aura

"Fluminaque ipsa suo lene sonent strepitu;

"Exilium nam sponte sequor. Fors ipsa favebit

"Fortibus haec solita est saepe et adesse viris.

"Et mihi sunt comites musae; sunt minima vatum;

"Et mens laeta suis gaudet ab auspiciis,

"Blanditurque animo constans sententia; quamvis

"Exilii meritum sit satis ipsa fides."

Epigr. lib. iii. *Ep. 7. Ed. Com. fa)* On the accession of Charles V. to the Spanish monarchy, the prince obtained the particular

Piombino.Urbino, and Ca

Chap. *n.* If the descent of Louis XII. into Italy, interrupted the a. D. 1501. progress of Caesar Borgia in effecting the conquest of Ro a. magna, the part which he had taken, in uniting his arms

Caesar Borgia *yyifa* those of the French on this occasion, enabled him to captures the states of return to his former undertaking with a greater prospect of success. The first object, towards which he directed his attention, was the city of Piombino, then held in subjection by Jacopo d'Appiano. To the attack of this place he dispatched two of his generals, Vitelozzo Vitelli, and GianPaolo Baglione. Jacopo did not, however, wait their arrival; but, leaving a garrison in the place, precipitately fled into France, expecting by his representations to Louis XII. to prevail upon that monarch to prohibit the further progress of the papal arms. His endeavours were, however, ineffectual, and Piombino soon afterwards capitulated to the invaders. The territory of Urbino, consisting of four cities and thirty fortified places, next attracted the ambitious views of the conqueror; but the duke Guidubaldo, instead of affording any pretext for hostilities against him, had frequently fought the battles of the church. His courage was indisputable; and his amiable qualities, and excellent

endowments, had secured the affections of his people. Despairing ticular favour of that monarch, by refusing to place himself at the head of the Spanish insurgents in the year 1522. His wife, Mencia di Mendoza, dying without children, Charles gave him, in a second marriage, Gerniana de Foix, niece to Louis XII. of France, and widow of Ferdinand of Aragon; a rich bride, but not likely to bear a progeny. On the death of this prince, which happened in the year 1550, this branch of the family of Aragon became extinct; his two younger brothers and two sisters having all died without offspring. Before the marriage of Federigo king of Naples, with his queen Isabella, he had been married to Anna, daughter of Amadeus, duke of Savoy, by whom he left a daughter, Carlotta, and from her the dukes of Tremouille in France, have claimed their descent; in consequence of which, they have in much later times, asserted their rights to the crown of Naples, *v. Giannone, Storia di NapoU, lib.* xxix. *cap.* iv. *v. 3.p.* 406.

spairing of effecting his purpose by an open attack, Caesar, on this occasion, resorted to treachery. He marched, at the head of a powerful army, to Nocera, avowing his intention of attacking the state of Camerino. Thence he dispatched an embassy to the duke of Urbino, requesting the assistance of his artillery, and as many soldiers as he could furnish. His request was instantly complied with; but no sooner had Caesar deprived the duke of the means of defence, than he turned his own arms against him; and, possessing himself of Cagli, proceeded by rapid marches towards Urbino. Alarmed, not only for his dominions but his life, Guidubaldo, with his nephew Francesco Maria della Rovere, hastily quitted the city in disguise, and, though vigilantly pursued, had the good fortune to escape to Mantua, where he met with his wife Isabella; who, after having accompanied Lucretia Borgia to Ferrara, on the recent celebration of her nuptials with Alfonso d'Este, son of the duke, had passed to Mantua to visit the marquis her brother. Having thus obtained the duchy of Urbino, Cae-

sar attacked the states of Camerino; and, having under pretext of a treaty, gotten into his power Giulio da Varano, *lord* of that country, with two of his sons, he treacherously put them to death, and rendered himself master of their dominions./ CHAP. VI. a. D. 1502. a. *M. 27*
The success which attended Caesar Borgia in all his undertakings, had attracted to his standard many of the most eminent *condottieri,* or military adventurers of Italy. Among these were Vitellozzo Vitelli lord of Citta di Castello, Francesco Orsino duke of Gravina, Pandolfo Petruccj lord of Siena, Paolo Orsino, Gian-Paolo Baglioni, and Oliverotto da Fermo. By the assistance of these leaders, and

Pietro Soderini preserves
Florence from the attacks of Borgia, and
u appointed
gonf'aloniere
% for life.
(a) Muratori, Annali a" Italia, vol. x. p. 9.
Chap. vi. an(1 the exertion of his own unrivalled talents in the art a. D. 1502. of dissimulation, he still continued to extend his conquests. A.yEt.27. Encouraged by the number of his adherents, and the favour of the king of France, he again turned his views towards the territories of Florence, which were suddenly assailed on all sides by his arms. The city of Cortona, the towns of Anghieri and Borgo San-Sepolcro, and even the city of Arezzo, surrendered to the invaders. As the difficulties of the Florentines increased, the hopes of the Medici revived; and uniting their power with their relations and auxiliaries, the Orsini, they joined the forces of Borgia, whose rapid progress left no reason to doubt that the Florentines would soon be obliged to surrender up their city at the discretion of the conquerors. In this alarming emergency the principal inhabitants met together, to deliberate on the most effectual measures for averting the dangers with which they were threatened; when Pietro Soderini had the good sense, to point out the only expedient that could preserve them from ruin. After expatiating on the deplorable state of the republic, and the impractica-

bility of obtaining assistance from any other quarter, he recommended, that an embassy should be dispatched to Louis XII. to request his interference on their behalf, in pursuance of a treaty lately formed between him and the Florentines. He did yet more; he took upon himself the office of ambassador, and, hastening to the king, laid before him such cogent reasons for granting his aid to the republic, as induced that monarch to comply with his request. Messengers were immediately dispatched *(a)* The treaty for protecting the republic, is dated the nineteenth day of November, 1501, at Blois.—*v. Lunig.* 1. 1142.
(b) Ammirato Hist. Fior. lib. xxvii. 3-267. *NarcU Hist. Fior lib.* iv. *p.* 81. patched to the pope and his son, to admonish them against CHAP-vifurther proceedings; and, lest these should be ineffectual, a A. D. 1502. considerable body of troops was directed to enter the Tuscan A.iei. 27 territories, and not only to repel those in the service of Borgia, then under the command of Vitellozzo, but to obtain the restitution of the places which had submitted to his arms/a,) Measures so decisive, from a quarter so powerful, admitted of no opposition. Vitellozzo and the Florentine exiles reluctantly drew off their troops; Soderini was regarded as t the saviour of the republic, and was soon afterwards honoured with a more extensive and durable authority, than any citizen had before enjoyed, under the novel title of *Gonfaloniere for Life.*
As the hopes of Caesar Borgia were principally founded Alliance tiron the favour of Louis XII. he was greatly alarmed at this £a,T unexpected opposition to his projects; and hastening iuu *vx* in person to the king at *Asti,(bJ* he endeavoured to remove the unfavourable suspicions entertained respecting him, by representing the prompt obedience which he had paid to
Vol. i. s s his *(a)* These events are commemorated by Machiavelli, in his Decennale:
"E perchft Valentin havea fatto alto
"Con le sue genti a Nocera, e quindi preso
"II ducato d'Urbin, sol con un salto,'

"Stavi co'l cuor, e con l'alma sospeso,
"Che co'l Vitello e' non si raccozzassi,
"£ con quel fusse a' vostri danni sceso,
"Quando a l'un commando che si fermassi
"Pe' vostri pfieghi il Re di San Dionigi
"A l'altro furo i suoi disegni cassi."
Deceit, lib. i. 65. (bj "E'l Duca in Asti si fu presentato
"Per giustificar se col re LuigL"
Chap. vi. hij. orders, imputing the attempt upon Florence wholly a. D. 1502. to the animosity of Vitellozzo and the Orsini against that *A. &x.* 27. republic, and to the desire of the Medici to be again admitted as chiefs of the city. Satisfied by his protestations, and desirous of conciliating the favour of the pope, in the disputes which had already arisen respecting the partition of the kingdom of Naples, Louis not only received him into favour, but formed with him a treaty of alliance, by which the parties stipulated to afford to each other mutual assistance; and it was particularly agreed, that Csesar should be furnished with a troop of French horse, to enable him to enforce his claims against the feudatories of the church, (ty
The event of this interview occasioned great alarm to Formidable opmany of the principal commanders, who were engaged in position to the service of Borgia, and who held the supreme authority the proceed-# . kgsofBor-in different cities of Italy. A diet was convoked in Perugia, " at which the cardinal, and Paolo Orsino, the duke of Gra vina, Vitellozzo Vitelli, Gianpaolo Baglioni, Oliverotto da Fermo, and others were present; when the conduct of Caesar Borgia was fully discussed, and it was resolved, that decisive measures should be taken for restraining his further progress. As the intelligence of this alliance became public, *(a) Gmcciard. hi.* v. 1. 283.
(b) Machiavelli, the constant apologist of Caesar Borgia, thus characterizes the members of this diet, in his first Deceonale:
"E rivolli fra lor questi serpenti
"Di velen pkn, cainminciaro a ghermirsi,

"£ con li ugnoni a straciarsi e co' denti. "E mal potendo il Valentin fuggirsi,

"Gli bisognb per ischifare il rischio, 44 Con lo scudo di Francia ricoprirsi." *Dec l&. i. p. 66.*
public, the different states which had before submitted to CHAPthe dominion of Borgia, began to oppose his authority; and A.d. 1502. in particular the inhabitants of Urbino, having seized upon A-2?the fortress of that place, disclaimed their dependence on him, and recalled their former prince. Deprived at once of the assistance of his principal commanders, who had suddenly avowed themselves his enemies, and of the greater part of his troops, Borgia retreated for safety to Imola, where his hopes were unexpectedly revived by an embassy from the Florentines; who having been solicited to unite in the league against him, had not only rejected the proposal, but dispatched to him their secretary, Niccolo Machiavelli, to assure him of their assistance against his revolted commanders. The joint efforts of these two accomplished proficients in mischief, could not fail of producing some extraordinary result, and accordingly a plan was adopted for the destruction of their adversaries, to which, in the annals of treachery, it will be difficult to find a parallel. This transaction the Florentine historian has thought deserving of a particular narrative, in which he affects not to conceal the features of guilt under the slightest covering of *decency.faj*
From this narrative we learn, that the troops of Borgia, having been attacked by those of the Vitelli and Orsini, several of the near Fossombrone, were put to the rout; in consequence of ta,ia"nob'es

'-l » Tl treacherously which, Borgia perceiving no possibility of resisting his put to death enemies by force, endeavoured to engage them in a negoti-sL-gaJifa ation. As he was a most accomplished dissembler, he re s s 2 presented *(a) Descrittione del modo tenuto dal Duca Valentino nello ammazzare Vitelozzi Viteili, Oliverotto da Fermo, il Signor Pagolo ed il duca dt Gravina Orsini.*
Chap. vi. presented to them, that the

efforts which he had made in A. D. 1502. subjugating the different states of Romagna, were intended
A. iEt. 27. no less for their interest than his own, and that, provided they would allow him the title of sovereign, the sovereignty itself should remain at their direction. These blandishments were not without their effect, and Paolo Orsino was deputed by his colleagues ta carry on the treaty; but Caesar, instead of relaxing in his preparations, continued by every possible means, to increase the number of his adherents, distributing his new levies, both of horse and foot, in separate detachments throughout Romagna, so as to avoid all cause of suspicion. The arrival of five hundred horsemen from the king of France was a most seasonable reinforcement; but although he might now have contended with his adversaries in the field, he judged it more expedient to proceed in the execution of his plan, and to continue the negotiation already entered into. The terms of amity were at length agreed upon; in consequence of which, he. received his former commanders again into his employ, and agreed to pay, to each of them, four thousand ducats in advance. He also engaged not to molest Giovanni Bentivoglio, who had joined in the league; nor to require the personal attendance of his new allies, in case it might not be agreeable to them. On their part they promised to restore to him the duchy of Urbino, with all the other places which they had occupied; to serve him in all his expeditions; and not to engage in any undertaking, or afford their assistance to any other power, without his assent.
On the conclusion of this league, the duke of Urbino again deserted his capital, and took shelter at Venice, having first dismantled the fortresses within his states, to the end that that they might not be garrisoned by his enemies, for the CHAP-vipurpose of keeping in subjection a people ardently devoted A. D. 1502. to the cause of their sovereign.... A. £.1.27.
This arrangement being completed, and his own troops, with his French

auxiliaries distributed throughout Romagna, Caesar left Imola and proceeded to Cesena; where he met the envoys of his new allies, and deliberated with them towards what part of Italy they should next turn their arms. No decisive measures being concluded on, Oliverotto da Fermo was deputed by these depredators to propose to Borgia another attack upon the Tuscan states; or, if he should not approve of this project, to offer their concurrence in attacking the city of Sinigaglia, then held by Francesco Maria della Rovere, nephew of the duke of Urbino. With the former of these proposals Borgia refused to comply, alledging,that the Florentines were his friends; but the attack on Sinigaglia met. with his entire approbation. That place was accordingly soon invested and captured; but the fortress held out for some time, the commander being unwilling to surrender it to any one but to Borgia himself; for which reason his allies entreated that he would hasten to the place. This circumstance seemed to Caesar, to offer a favourable opportunity for executing his purpose, without giving rise to suspicion; his visit to Sinigaglia appearing to be at the request of his allies, and not from his own choice. Still further to avoid all cause of offence, he dismissed his French auxiliaries. Reserving only one hundred horse, under the command of one of his relations, and quitting Cesena about the end of December, he proceeded to Fano, where he employed all his artifice and sagacity to prevail upon the Vitelli and the Orsini to wait his arrival in Sinigaglia.
Vitellozzo,
Chap. vi. Vitellozzo, who had learnt from the fate of his brother, a. D. 1502. the danger of confiding in those to whom he had once given
A..Et. 27. cause of offence, was extremely averse to this interview; but, being prevailed upon by Paolo Orsino, who had engaged more deeply in the interests of Borgia, he at length consented to wait his approach.
On the thirtieth of December, 1502, the day fixed upon for his departure from Fano, Caesar communicated his

project to eight of his principal adherents, in which number were Don Michele and Monsignor d'Euna, with instructions to this effect; that as soon as the meeting should take place betwixt himself and Vitellozzo, Paolo Orsino, the duke of Gravina, and Oliverotto, who would come out to meet and conduct him into the city, they should divide their number into pairs, and that each pair should single out his man, and take their stations respectively on each side of him, occupy ing his attention till they reached Sinigaglia, when they were not to quit them, till they had delivered them into safe custody at the apartments prepared for the duke. At the same time he ordered his whole force, which consisted of ten thousand foot, and two thousand horse, to take their station at day break on the banks of the Metauro, a river about five miles from Fano, where they should wait his. further orders. All things being thus arranged, Borgia advanced with the whole force towards Sinigaglia, where Vitellozzo Vitelli, Paolo Orsino, and the duke of Gravina, mounted upon mules, and accompanied by a few horse, came forwards to meet him. Vitellozzo was unarmed, and appeared so deeply dejected, as to excite the admiration of those who were acquainted with his courage and past achievements. We are also told, that when he left his dependants to come to Sinigaglia for the purpose of meeting the duke, he he took a kind of last farewell of them; recommend-CHAP-VIing to his chief officers, the fortunes of his house, and A. D. 1502. admonishing his nephews, not to remember the calamities AM-27' of their family, but the courage of their ancestors. Arriving in the presence of Borgia, they respectfully saluted him, and were received by him with apparent kindness, whilst the persons, to whom the charge of them had been confided, took the stations assigned to them. Borgia, perceiving that they were not accompanied by Oliverotto, who had remained with his troops at Sinigaglia, where he had drawn them up in the square, made a signal to Don Michele, to whom the care of Oliverotto had been

committed, to take measures for preventing his escape. In consequence of which, that officer rode forwards, and coming up with Oliverotto, told him it was not a proper time to keep his men from their quarters, as they would, perhaps, be occupied by the soldiers of Borgia, and he therefore advised him to dismiss them, and to accompany him to meet the general. These directions having been complied with, Borgia arrived, and accosted Oliverotto, who approached and paid his respects to him. Proceeding thus to Sinigaglia, they dismounted at the lodgings of Borgia, and were led into a secret apartment, where the unsuspecting victims were all made prisoners.

Borgia immediately mounted his horse, and gave orders for disarming the troops of Oliverotto and the Orsini. Those of Oliverotto were all plundered; but those of the Orsini and Vitelli, being at a distance, and having received information of the ruin of their leaders, had time to collect themselves together, and in a firm body effected their escape, notwithstanding the opposition of their enemies, and of the surrounding inhabitants. The soldiers of the duke, not satisfied with the plunder of those of Oliverotto, Chap. vi. rotto, began to sack the city; and, if Borgia had not repressed A. D. 1502. their licentiousness, by putting many of them to death,

A. iEt. 27. they would have effected their purpose. Night approaching, and the tumult having subsided, he thought it expedient to dispatch Vitellozzo and Oliverotto; and, bringing them together into the same place, he caused them to be strangled. On this occasion neither of them, we are told, expressed themselves in a manner worthy of their past lives; for Vitellozzo intreated that the pope might be applied to for a plenary indulgence of his sins, and Oliverotto, weeping, attributed all his offences against Borgia, to the influence of Vitellozzo. Paolo Orsino and the duke of Gravina were suffered to live until Caesar received information that the pope had secured the persons of the cardinal Orsino, the archbishop of Florence, and Jacopo di Santa Croce, after *igos* which,

on the eighteenth day of January, they were-put to the same kind of death, as had been already-inflicted on their unfortunate associates. Such ' *fa)* Ant. Franc. Raineri has commemorated the death of Vitellozzo in a copy of Latin verses, the substance of which he has compressed into the two following lines:

"Non mare me, non Mars, saeva aut mors perdidit; at me
"Perdidit omnibus his Borgius asperior.
"

Carm. Must. Poet. Ital. viii. 59

And the same event has also afforded a subject for reprobation to Paulo Giovio; who justly denominates Borgia rabidus, barbarus, impotens,

"Humani generis pernicies, atque hominum lues."'

'-*Carm. Must; Poet. Ital.* v. 433.

(b) The cardinal Giambattista Orsino was detained by the pope in the Torre Borgia till the month of February following, when he died by poison, as it is supposed, administered to him by the direction of the pope; who caused him to be carried to the grave uncovered, that it might appear he had died a natural death. *Muratori, Antudi x.* 13. Besides the individuals of the family of Orsini, mentioned by Machiavelli, the pope also seized upon Carlo Orsino, and the Abate d'Alveano, brother of the celebrated general Bartolommeo d'Alveano; but they were soon afterwards liberated. *Nardi, Hist. Tior.f.* 88. Such is the account given of this extraordinary transac-Chap. vi. tion by the Florentine secretary; a transaction upon which A. D. 1503: he has forbom to make the slightest observation, either of A-28 praise or of blame, and which he seems to have considered He on merely as an instance ot superior talents and successful po-rie9 licy.*fa)* Having thus freed himself from all apprehensions from his doubtful allies, Caesar lost no time in proceeding to Citta di Castello, of which place he took possession; the remainder of the family of Vitelli having betaken themselves to flight. He then entered Perugia, which had been in like manner abandoned by Gian-Paolo Baglione, Avho had, however, the good fortune to escape from the snare laid for him at Sinigaglia. Siena was the next place towards which he bent his course; but whilst he was hovering round the city, and had already compelled Pandolfo Petrucci, who then enjoyed the chief authority, to quit the place, he received intelligence from the pope, that the duke of Bracciano, with others of the Orsini family, as well as the nobles of the Savelli, had again taken up arms. He

Vol. *i, T T* was *faj* The presumption that Machiavelli had a principal part in the contrivance of this most iniquitous stratagem, is indeed extremely strong. The Florentines dreaded and abhorred both the Orsini and the Vitelli; the former as relations and adherents to the Medici, the latter for exerting themselves to avenge the unmerited fate of Paolo Vitelli, so cruelly put to death at Florence. Borgia had retreated to Imola, where Machiavelli found him in a state of great dejection, " pieno di paura." No sooner, however, did the Florentine envoy appear, than he took fresh courage, and the plan for the destruction of their adversaries seems to have been agreed on. It is certain, also, that Machiavelli accompanied Caesar to Sinigaglia, and was present at the perpetration of the deed; after which Borgia remarked to him, that " he knew the government of Florence would be gratified by this "transaction." *v. Nardi, Hist. Fior. lib. iv. p.* 85. The Florentine writers acknowledge, that the intelligence of it gave great satisfaction in the city. "Rcstb allora "la cittil, morti costoro, molto sicura da ouelli suoi nemici, che tanto e si spesso la tra"vagliavano." *Nerli, Commcntar. lib. v. p. gi.* The Florentines also sent Jacopo Salviati as their ambassador, to congratulate Caesar on the success of his treachery. *Razii, vita di Pietro Soderini. p. J. Padcrua, 1737*

Chap, Vl was tnerefore obliged to quit Siena; and, hastening into the A. D. 1503. papal territories, again reduced them to obedience. This A. *Iei.* 28. was tne peri0(of the highest power of Caesar Borgia.

In full possession of the extensive territory of Romagna, he regarded with eager avidity the domains of Pisa and of Siena; nor were the citizens of Florence without constant apprehensions from his increasing power; whilst the pope, equally earnest in the aggrandizement of his son, had proposed to the college of cardinals to bestow upon him the title of king of Romagna and Umbria.

But whilst every circumstance thus seemed to conspire in his favour, an unexpected reverse of fortune suddenly overrider vi" turned tne fabric of his greatness. This was the death of Alexander VI. which happened on the eighteenth day of August, 1503. And this misfortune was increased by the effects of a dangerous malady, under which Caesar himself at the same time laboured, and which prevented him from taking those measures for securing his authority which he might otherwise have adopted. The historians of this period, eager to represent both Alexander and his son in the most odious colours, have asserted that the death of the one, and the disorder of the other, were occasioned by poison, prepared by them for the destruction of several cardinals, of whose wealth they intended to possess themselves; but which, by the error of an attendant, was incautiously administered to themselves. That the horrid and detestable practice of destroying persons by poison, was frequently resorted to in these profligate times, is certain; and that Alexander and his son had employed these measures for the gratification of their avarice, their ambition, or their revenge, is positively asserted by many historians; but it by no means accords accords with the acknowledged ability, caution, and pene-Chap, Vx tration of these men, that they would risk their lives upon a. D. 1603. the negligence or fidelity of a servant, or place it in the A-t.28. power of accident to render them the victims of their own crime. If, therefore, the death of Alexander is to be attributed to poison, it was most probably administered to him by some of those numerous enemies whom his rapacity and violence had incited to this deed of revenge; but documents recently produced, and a more dispassionate inquiry, afford sufficient reason to conclude, that the death of the pontiff was not occasioned by poison, but was the effect of a fever, which in a few days hurried him to the grave.faj

T T *2,* Were *(a)* Burchard informs us, that the pope was attacked by a fever on the 12th day of August, 1503; that on (he sixteenth he was bled, and the disorder seemed to become tertian. On the seventeenth he took medicine; but on the eighteenth he became so ill that his life was despaired of. He then received the Viaticum, during mass; which was celebrated in his chamber, and at which five cardinals assisted. In the evening extreme unction was administered to him, and in a few minutes afterwards he died. *Burchard. Diar. ap. Notices de la bibliotheque du lioi, vol. i. p.* 118. Muratori has produced many authorities to shew, that the death of Alexander was not occasioned by poison; among which, that of Beltrando Costabile, then ambassador of the duke of Ferrara, at Rome, seems the most decisive. "The court of Ferrara," adds Muratori, " which was "then the residence of the daughter of Alexander, may be presumed tq have been well "informed of the cause of his death."

That it was, however, the general opinion, at the time of his death, that Alexander perished by poison, appears from numerous contemporary authorities. Thus Guido Postumo, *in Tumulum Sexti:* .

"Quis situs hie? *Sextits.* Quis pectora plangit? *Erynnis.* "Quis comes in tanto funere obit? *Vitium.*
"Undepyra? Ex *crucibus,* quibus Itala pectora torsit.
"Quae laniata genas praefica? *Avaricies.*
"Quis tulit ossa? *Nefas.* Quis longo murmure dixit
"Nate, vale? Mater *Rixa,* paterque *Odium.*
"Qui pressere oculos? *Incendia, Stupra, Rapince.*
"Quis moriar dixit, hoc mbriente? *Dolus*
"Sed quae causa necis? *Virus.* Proh numina! virus
"Humano generi vita, salusque fuit." *Guid. Post. Eleg. p* 36".
conduct and character.

Chap. vi. Were we to place implicit confidence in the Italian hisa. D. 1503.

torians, no period of society has exhibited a character of a. iEt. 28. darker deformity than that of Alexander VI. Inordinate in Remarks on his fllS ambition, insatiable in his avarice and his lust, inexorable in his cruelty, and boundless in his rapacity; almost every crime that can disgrace humanity is attributed to him without hesitation, by writers whose works are published under the sanction of the Roman church. He is also accused of having introduced into his territories, the detestable practice of searching for state offences by means of secret informers; a system fatal to the liberty and happiness of every country that has submitted to such a degradation. As a pontiff he perverted his high office, by making his spiritual power on every occasion subservient to his temporal interests; and he might have adopted as his emblem, that of the ancient Jupiter, which exhibits the lightning in the grasp of a ferocious eagle. foJ His vices as an individual, although

(a) To this period, when truth became a crime, we may refer the origin of the Pasquinades; of which the following lines afford one of the earliest instances.

"Vendit Alexander claves, altaria, Christum.

"Emerat ille prius; vendere jure potest.

"De vitio in vitium, de Mamma transit in ignem;

"Roma sub Hispano deperit imperio.

"Sextus Tarquinius, Sextus Nero, Sextus et isle;

"Semper sub Sextis perdita Roma fuit."

Machiavelli, although more favourable to the family of Borgia than most other writers, accuses him of lust, simony, and cruelty; per aver riposo,

"Portato fu fra l'anime beate
"Lo spirto di Alessandro glorioso.
Del qual seguiro le sante pedate
"Tre sue familiari e care ancille,
"Lussuria, Simonia, e crudeltate."
Decennak i. *p.* 68.

although not so injurious to the world, are represented as yet CHAP-V1more disgusting; and the records of his court, afford repeated A. D. 1503. instances of a depravity of morals, inexcusable in any station, A-iEt. 2Sbut abominable in one of his high rank and sacred of-

fice. Yet, with all these lamentable defects, justice requires that two particulars in his favour should be noticed. In the first place, whatever have been his crimes, there can be no doubt but they have been highly overcharged. That he was devoted to the aggrandizement of his family, and that he employed the authority of his elevated station to establish a permanent dominion in Italy in the person of his son, cannot be doubted; but when almost all the sovereigns of Europe were attempting to gratify their ambition by means equally criminal, it seems unjust to brand the character of Alexander with any peculiar and extraordinary share of infamy in this respect. Whilst Louis of France and Ferdinand of Spain conspired together, to seize upon and divide the kingdom of Naples, by an example of treachery that never can be sufficiently execrated, Alexander might surely think himself justified in suppressing the turbulent barons, who had for ages rent the dominions of the church with intestine wars, and in subjugating the petty sovereigns of Romagna, over whom he had an acknowledged supremacy, and who had in general acquired their dominions by means as unjustifiable as those which he adopted against *them.faj* With respect *la)* Oliverotto da Fermo had obtained the chief authority in the city, from which he derived his name, by the treacherous murder of his uncle, and several of the principal inhabitants, whom he had invited to an entertainment. This atrocious deed was perpetrated on the same day in the preceding year, on which he afterwards fell into the snare of Caesar Borgia The other persons put to death by Borgia, had also supported themselves by rapine, and were the terror of all Italy. The contests of this period may in fact be regarded by posterity, as a combat of wild beasts, in which the strongest and most ferocious animal destroys the rest. *v. Macch. lib. del Principe, cap.* viii *p.* 21, 22.

Chap. vi. respect to the accusation so generally believed, of a criminal a. D. 1503. intercourse between him and his own daughter, which has

A.iEt.28. caused him to be regarded

with a peculiar degree of horror and disgust, it might not be difficult to shew its improbability, and to invalidate an imputation which disgraces human nature itself.

In the second place it may justly be observed, that the vices of Alexander were in some degree counterbalanced by many great qualities, which, in the consideration of his character, ought not to be passed over in silence/a Nor, if this were not the fact, would it be possible to account for the peculiar good fortune, which attended him to the latest period of his life, or for the singular circumstance recorded of him that, during his whole pontificate, no popular tumult ever endangered his authority, or disturbed his *repose, (b)* Even by his severest adversaries, he is allowed to have been a man of an elevated genius, of a wonderful memory, eloquent, vigilant, and dexterous in the management of all his concerns. The proper supply of the city of Rome with all the necessaries of life, was an object of his unceasing attention; and, during his pontificate, his dominions were exempt from that famine, which devastated the rest of Italy. In his diet he was peculiarly temperate, and he accustomed himself to but little sleep. In those hours which he devoted to *(a)*" in Alexandre, ut de Annibale Livius scribit, aequabant vitia virtutes.

"Inerant namque ingenium, ratio, cognitio, memoria, diligentia, eloquentia verb quae"dam natural is, et ad pcrsuadendum apta, ut nemo rem cautius proponeret aut acrius "defensitaret," &c. *Raph Volater. Anthropol. lib.* xxii. *p.* 683. "Fu magnanimo, et "generoso, et prudente, se non che si lascib vincere dall'amore di figliuoli che haveva, "et da troppo cupiditi." *Monaldeschi, Comm. Istor. p.* 148.

(b) Raph. Volater. Anthropol. M. xxii. *p.* 682. to amusement, he seemed wholly to forget the affairs of Chap, Yi. state; but he never suffered those amusements to diminish A. D. 1503. the vigour of his faculties, which remained unimpaired to a.J&.28. the last. Though not addicted to the study of literature, Alexander was munificent towards its professors; to

whom he not only granted liberal salaries, but, with a punctuality very uncommon among the princes of that period, he took care that those salaries were duly *paid.fa)* That he at some times attended the representations of the comedies of Plautus has been placed in the black catalogue of his defects; but if his mind had been more humanized by the cultivation of polite letters, he might, instead of being degraded almost below humanity, have stood high in the scale of positive excellence. To the encouragement of the arts, he paid a more particular attention. The palace of the Vatican was enlarged by him, and many of the apartments were ornamented with the works of the most eminent painters of the time; among whom may be particularized Torrigiano, Baldassare Peruzzi, and Bernardino Pinturicchio. As an architect, his chief favourites were Giuliano and Antonio da San-Gallo; nor does his choice in this respect detract from his judgment. By their assistance, the mole of Hadrian, now called the castle of S. Angelo, was fortified in the *(a)* The cardinal Giovanni Borgia, nephew of the pontiff, was also an encourager of literature, and condescended to receive instructions from Mariano Probo, of Sulmona, who distinguished himself as a Latin poet, and died at Rome in the year 1499. His *PartAenias,* or Life of the Virgin, in six books, was printed at Naples, in 1524. The preface to this rare volume by Nic. Scaevola, contains some curious particulars of the state of learning at Rome, during the pontificate of Alexander VI. *(b)* " Quapropter Comcedias Plautinas ceteraque ludicra, libenter spcctavit." *Raph. Volattr. Ub.* xxii. *p.* 685. Chap. vi. the manner in which it yet remains. In one circumstance a. D. i5o3. his encouragement of the arts is connected with a singular

A. jEt. 28. instance of profaneness, which it is surprising has not hitherto been enumerated among his many offences. In a picture painted for him by Pinturicchio, the beautiful Julia Farnese is represented in the sacred character of the Virgin, whilst Alexander himself appears in the same picture, as supreme

pontiff, paying to her the tribute of his adoration.

DISSERTATION ON THE CHARACTER OF LUCRETIA BORGIa.

If the Lucretia of ancient histoiy has been considered as the glory of her sex, the Lucretia of modern Rome has been alledged as an example of its disgrace and its shame. From her own times to the present, her depravity is on historical record; yet many circumstances concur to raise considerable doubts in the mind of an impartial inquirer, whether the horrible accusations under which her memory labours be well founded. Amidst the licentiousness that characterized the age in which she lived, the most flagrant charges acquire a probability which they could not in another period obtain; and among the vices of the times, calumny and falsehood have in general been at least as active as the rest.

To the present day Lucretia is, for the most part, only known as the incestuous daughter of Alexander VI. the prostitute, in common, of her father and of her two brothers; one of whom is supposed to have assassinated the other from jealousy of his superior pretensions to her vu2 favour. favour. If nothing more had been recorded respecting her than the charges of her accusers, we must have submitted to receive their information as true, with those doubts only which the abominable nature of the accusation must always inspire. But Lucretia Borgia is known, from other sources of information, to have been a woman of great accomplishments, as well of mind as of person, and to have passed the chief part of her life in an eminent station, not only without reproach, but with the highest honour and esteem. If the Ethiopian cannot change his skin, nor the leopard his spots, how are we to conceive it possible, that the person who had, during so many years of her life, been sunk into the lowest depths of guilt and of infamy, could at once emerge to respectability and to virtue? The history of mankind furnishes no instances of such a rapid change; and we are therefore naturally led to inquire upon what evidences such charges have

been made; and as from their nature it can scarcely be supposed that they are capable either of positive proof, or of positive refutation, we must be satisfied to form our belief according to the best evidence of probability.

That accusations of this nature were brought against Lucretia early in life, and during the pontificate of her father, there is great reason to believe. The first traces of them appear in the writings of the Neapolitan poets, who being exasperated against Alexander VI. for the active part which he had taken in the expulsion of the house of Aragon, placed no limits to their resentment.fa/ These imputations might, *(a)* Thus Pontano, in an epitaph for Lucretia Borgia, who, however, survived him upwards pf twenty years.

"Hie jacet in tumulo, Lucretia nomine, sed re

"Thais. Alexandri filia, sponsa, nurus." And might, however, scarcely have deserved a serious reply, had they not received additional credit from the pen of the distinguished historian Guicciardini, who informs us', that "it was rumoured, that not only the two brothers, but even "the father were rivals for the love of Lucretia.'YoJ By these rumours it is probable that he alludes to the writings of the Neapolitan poets, with whose works, it is to be remarked, he was well acquainted, as appears from the manner in which he refers to the small river Sebeto, near Naples, so frequently the theme of their applause.,'

These authorities have been considered as sufficient grounds for future historians to assert the guilt of Lucretia in the most explicit terms; nor have even the writers of the Romish church hesitated to express their conviction of her criminality in the most unqualified manner, and the tale of her infamy has accordingly been admitted into general compilations and biographical dictionaries as undoubted matter of *foct.fc)* It can, therefore, occasion no surprise, that the protestant authors have frequently expatiated on a subject which, as they suppose, reflects

And Sanazzaro thus addresses her:;

"Ergo te semper cupiet, Lucretia,

Sextus.

"O fatum diri numinis, hie Pater est."

And this supposed intercourse is also frequently alluded to, in other parts of the works of the last mentioned writer.

(a) " Era medesimamente fama, se peri) & degno di credersi tanta enormity, che nell' "amor di Madonna Lucretia, concorressino non solamente i dui fratelli ma eziandio il "padre medesimo." *Guicc. Storia d' ltd. lib..ii.* 1. 182. *(b)* " II piccolo piu presto rio che fiumicello, chiamato *Sebtto*; incognito a ciascuno "se non gli havessino dato nome i versi de' poeti Napolitani." *ib. p.* 113. *(c) v. Moreri, Diet. Hist. Art. Casar Borgia, SjC.* fleets such disgrace on the Roman see. In the writings of Henry Stephens/ a,) of *Bale,(b)* and of Gordon/cj this accusation forms a conspicuous feature; nor is it less decisively admitted by the discriminating Gibbon in his Antiquities of the House of Brunswick. "In the next generation," says this author, " the House of Este was sullied by a san"guinary and incestuous race; by the nuptials of Alfonso I. "with Lucretia, a bastard of Alexander VI. the Tiberius of "christian Rome. This modern Lucretia might have assumM ed with more propriety the name of Messalina; since the "woman who can be guilty, who can even be accused, of "a criminal intercourse with a father and two brothers, "must be abandoned to all the licentiousness of venal love."

Such being the evidence on which these charges have been generally believed, it may now be proper to state such circumstances as may throw additional light on the subject. This will perhaps be most effectually done, by taking a brief review of the principal circumstances in the life of Lucretia, as far as they can be collected from the writings of her contemporaries; and by comparing her conduct and character, as it is represented by those to whom she was well known, and by whom she was highly respected, with her conduct and character as represented by those, who have, either directly or indirectly, countenanced imputations against her of so detestable a nature.

Before *(a) Apologiepour Heroddte. liv. i. p.* 559» *Ed.* 1692.
(b) Pageant of popes, p. 173. *Ed.* 1574
(c) life of Alex. VI. and his son Ccesar Borgia, p. 271, *4fc (d) In the second vol. of his Posthumous Works, p.* 689.

Before the elevation of Alexander VI. his daughter Lucretia, not being then of marriageable age, had been betrothed to a Spanish gentleman *(a)* but on his obtaining the pontificate, he dissolved the engagement, apparently with the ambitious view of forming a higher connexion. On the twelfth day of June, 1493, being in the first year of her father's pontificate, she was accordingly married to Giovanni Sforza, lord of Pesaro, a grandson of the brother of the great Francesco Sforza, duke of Milan.fAj With him she resided till the year 1497, when some dissensions having arisen between her and her husband, she quitted him, and the pope afterwards dissolved the marriage; "not being able," as Guicciardini asserts, to bear even a husband as a rival, and having "proved, by suborned evidence, before judges delegated "by himself, that Giovanni was impotent." This separation gave rise to a disagreement between the pope and Sforza, in consequence of which, the latter was in danger of being deprived of his dominions, which he preserved only by resorting to the Venetians for assistance.

If the reason given by Guicciardini, for the interference of the pope on this occasion, be the true one, he soon changed his mind, having shortly after entered into a treaty for a marriage between his daughter and Alfonso, duke of Bisaglia, a natural son of Alfonso II. king of Naples.

(a) NarcUHiit. Fior. lib. iv. p. 75. *(b)* " Le nozze con gran solennita ma con poco onesta, furono celebrate nel pontificio "palazzo nelcQ 12 di Giugno 1493." *Murat. Annul.* f *ItaUa* ix. 569. *(e) Gukciard. Storia d? Italia, lib. iii. v. i. p.* 182. *(d) Murat. Annali. v. ix. p. 590. ples.fa)* This marriage was celebrated in the year 1498, and the pope conferred on his daughter the perpetual government of the duchy of Spoleto, and invested her with the territory of Sermon-

eta, of which he had shortly before deprived the family of Gaetani./ The offspring of this marriage Mras a son, who was born in the month of October, 1499, and named after the pontiff, Roderigo. fe/ The attention paid by Alexander to the education of this child, has been considered as a presumptive proof, that he stood related to him in a still nearer character than that which he avowed ;fd) but when it is recollected, that this son was the future hope of an ambitious and aspiring family, and detached from all criminality, was allied to the pontiff by the near claims of consanguinity, there seems no need to resort to other motives to explain the conduct of Alexander on this occasion. From the explicit evidence of Burchard, who appears to have intruded himself into the most secret transactions of the apostolic palace, we may exonerate the pontiff and his daughter from this heinous charge, and allow that there are ,.. faj ".His diebus venit ad Urbem Illustrissimus Dominus Alphonsus de Aragonia, "Dux Bisiliarum, Princeps Salernitanus, filius naturalis divae memorise Alfonsi secundi "de Aragonia regis Neapolitani,. septemdecim annos natus vel circa, futurns maritus "Lucretiae Borgia;, filiae carissimae S. D. N. uxoris olim Johannis Sforziae' Domini "Pisauri; qui non fuit receptus vel associatus publica pompa, sed tam en a quibusdam "particularisms, perpapam sibiobviam missis." *Burchard, Diar. ap. Gordon.* (b) *Muratori, Annali d'Italia,* ix. 601. *fej* " Feria quinta, ultima Octobris circa horam nonam, Domina Lucretia Papae filia, "peperit filium masculum, quod, ut dictum fuit, de mandato Papae omnibus cardinalibus "et oratoribus et aliis amicis ad eorum domos ante diem est nuntiatum; fuerurit propterea "nuntiantibus donati per singulos cardinales et oratores ducati duo, ac plus vel minus "prout placuit donanti. " *Burch. Diar. ap. Gordon.* (d) *Gordon' Life of Alexander VI. p.* 271. are good grounds to admit, that Alfonso of Aragon was the father of the child.fio

The unfortunate husband did not however long survive this event. In the month of June, 1500, he was attacked on the steps, before the great door of the church of S. Pietro, by a band of assassins, by whom he was dangerously wounded. That the perpetrators of this crime were persons of rank, may be conjectured from their having been escorted out of the gates of Rome by a body of forty horsemen, who protected them in their flight./ Alfonso, yet living, was conveyed into a chamber in the apostolic palace, where he struggled with the consequences of his wounds upwards of two months, and, as Burchard asserts, was then strangled in his bed. The physicians who had attended him, and a person who had waited on him during his confinement, were apprehended and examined, but were soon afterwards libei-ated.(ty The death of Alfonso, like that of the duke of Gandia, has been attributed to Caesar Borgia, but with no

Vol. i. xx other *(a)* " Contraxit deinde post paucos dies matrimonium per verba de presenti cum ipsa "Lucretia; *iUudque carnali copulatione consummavit." Diar. Burch. ap. Gordon.* (b) M Feria quindecima mensis Junii circa horam primam noctis Illustrissimus Do(minus Alphonsus de Arragonia, Dux Bisiliarum, Maritus Dominae Lucretiae Filiae "papae, supra planum scalarum Basilicae Sancti Petri ante primum introitum versus Basili"cam pnedictam, per plures personas aggressus fuit, et in capite et brachiodextro et crure "graviter vulneratus. Invasores effugerunt per scalam Sancti Petri ubi circiter quadra"ginta Equites eos expectarunt, cum quibus equitarunt extra portam pertusam." *Diar. Burch. ap. Gordon.* (c)" Feria tenia, octava decima Mensis Augusti, Alphonsus de Arragonia Dux Bisilia« rumet princeps Salernitanus, qui in serodiei quindecimi Mensis *Juki* proximo preteriti, "graviter fuit vulneratus, et deinde ad Turrim nonam supra cantinam Papae in Horto

"majori other evidence than that which arises from presumptions, founded on the general atrocity of his character, and his supposed criminal attachment to his sister; to which it has been added, that the new connexions which he had formed with Lewis XII. operated

as an inducement with him, to terminate his alliance with a family which he had already devoted to destruction.

A few days after the death of Alfonso, his widow, who has never been accused of having had any share in this horrid transaction, retired for some time to Nepi, for the purpose of indulging her grief.*(b)* On her return to Rome, she was intrusted, during the absence of the pope, with the management of public affairs, for which purpose she was empowered to open all letters addressed to the pontiff, and directed,

"majori palatii apud Sanctum Petrum portatus est, et diligenter custoditus, *cum tum vellet "hujusmodi vulneribus mori, in lecto suo fuit strangulatut.* Circa horam primam noctis "portatum fuit cadaver ad Basilicam S. Petri et ibidem in Capella Beatae Mariae de "febribus depositum. Capti fuerunt *k* ad Castrum S. Angeli ducti Medici defuncti *k* qui"dam gibbosus, qui ejus curam habere consueverat *k* contra eos inquisitio facta: liberati "postea fuerunt." *Burch. Diar. ap. Gordon. (a)* Guicciardini expressly asserts, that the husband of Lucretia, whom he calls Gismondo, was assassinated by Caesar Borgia, "il quale era stato ammazzato dal Duca "Valentino," and Muratori informs us, that Alfonso was first wounded, and afterwards poisoned, and that Caesar Borgia, was supposed to be the perpetrator of the crime; to which he was instigated by his attachment to the French, and his aversion to the family of Aragon. *v. Annali d'Italia vol.* ix. *p. 6o6 (b)* " Feria secunda, ultima Augusti Domina Lucretia olim de Aragonia Filia Papae re"cessit ab urbe, itura ad civitatem Nepesinam, associata a sexcentessimis equitibus vel "ctrea, ut caperet aliquam consolationem propter dolorem et conturbationem quam habuit "diebus praeteritis propter obitum illustrissimi domini Alfonsi de Aragonia Ducis Bisi"liarum, *kc.* mariti sui." *Burch. Diar. ap.. Gordon.* directed, in cases of difficulty, to consult with some of the cardinals in the confidence of the pope. We may agree with Muratori, that this mode of government conferred but little honour on the pontiff,*(a)* but we can scarce-

ly admit it as a proof, as some have been willing to assume, of an incestuous intercourse between the father and the daughter// To a short time subsequent to this period, we may, however, refer those abominable scenes of lewdness, which are said to have been transacted within the precincts of the apostolic palace, and which, however incredible, are recorded by Burchard, not only without a comment, but with as much indifference as if they were only the usual occurrences of the day.fic But it is highly important to our present subject to observe, that throughout the whole narrative of this loquacious master of the papal ceremonies, who seems on no occasion to have concealed what might disgrace either his superiors or himself, there appears not the most distant insinuation of that criminal x x 2 intimacy *(a)* " Questa maniera di Governo, se facesse onore al Papa, poco ci vuole per "conoscerlo." *Murat. Annal.* x. 7. *(bj Cordon's Life of Alexander VI. p.* 173, J-c. *(c)* " Dominica ultima mensis Octobris in sero feccrunt caenam cum Duce Valenti"nensi in camera sua in Palatio Apostolico, quinquaginta Meretrices honestae, Cortegianae "nuncupatae, quae post caenam chorearunt, cum servitoribus et aliis ibidim existentibus, "primo in vestibus suis, deinde nudae. Post caenam posita fuerunt candelabra com"munia mensae cum candelis ardentibus, & projectae ante candelabra per terram castancae, "quas meretrices ipsae, super manibus et pedibus nudae, candelabra pertranseuntes colli"gebant; Papa, Duce, & Lucretia sorore sua, praesentibus Se aspicientibus. Tandem ex"posita dona ultima, diploides de serico, paria caligarum, bireta et alia, pro illis qui "plures dictas meretrices carnaliter agnoscerunt, quae fuerunt ibidem in aula publicd "carnaliter tractate, arbitrio preseutium, Se dona distributa victoribus." *Burch. Diar. ap. Gord.* intimacy between Alexander and his daughter, or between her and her brothers, which if he had known or suspected it to have existed, it is not likely, from the tenor of other parts of his narrative, that he would have been inclined wholly to conceal.

However this may be, the pope, who never for a moment lost sight of the aggrandizement of his family, in the latter part of the year 1501, entered into a negotiation for uniting Lucretia in marriage to Alfonso of Este, the son of Ercole, duke of Ferrara. This connexion was highly flattering to the house of Borgia, as well from the elevated rank of the husband, who was expected shortly to take a respectable station among the sovereigns of Italy, as from his personal character, which had already given rise to expectations, that his future conduct abundantly confirmed. (ty In accounting for an union which has in later times been considered as degrading to the family of Este, some have been inclined to attribute it to the advantageous proposals made by the pope, who besides an immense sum which he expended in jewels and apparel, gave to his daughter on her marriage one hundred thousand gold crowns, and accompanied them with the grant of the territories of Cento and Pieve; whilst others have conjectured, that the princes of Este were rather terrified than allured to such a measure, by their apprehensions from the ambition, rapacity, or resentment of the family of Borgia.fty The marriage ceremony was performed *(a)* "Principe glorioso nel mondo," says Muratori, " che in senno e valore cbbe pochi "pari al suo tempo." *Annali, vol. x. p. 262.*

(bj Nardi, Hist. Fior. p. 75.

"The marriage articles were signed," says Mr. Gibbon *(Antiq. of Brunswick, m posth.* performed at Rome on the nineteenth day of December, 1501, with circumstances of uncommon magnificence, which are related by Burchard, with great minuteness./ Her journey thence to Ferrara, and her splendid entry into that city, on the second day of February, 1502, are dwelt upon at great length by contemporary writers, whose narratives exhibit a curious picture of the manners of the age.)

At this period of the life of Lucretia, when she was finally *posth. works, vol. ii. p. 689.)* " and as the bed of Lucretia was *not then vacant,* her "third husband, a royal bastard of Naples, was first

stabbed, and afterwards strangled "in the Vatican." This is not founded on historical fact, nor as far as I know, asserted by any other writer; the treaty for the marriage with Alfonso of Este, not having taken place till upwards of twelve months after the death of her former husband.

(a) " Feria quarta, nona Decembris, Tibicines et omnia musicorum instrumenta, parata "in piano, super scalas S. Petri, inceperunt magna vehementia sonare, singuli instrumenta "sua, prope domum Dominae Lucretiae, juxta Basilicam S. Petri. Exivit ipsa Domina "Lucretia, in vestibus brocati auri, circumdatis, more hispanico, cum longa cauda, quam "quaedam puellae deferebant; ipsa Domina Lucretia media inter Ferdinandum a dextris, "et Sigismundum a sinistris, Fratres mariti sui. Sequebantur circiter quinquaginta "Romanae pulchrfi vestitae, & post illas Pedissequae Dominae Lucretiae, et ascenderunt ad "primam aulam Paulinam, super portam Palatii ubi erat Papa, cum tredecim Cardina"libus & Duce Valentinensi; finito sermone, fuit posita ante Papam quaedam mensa "sive tabula ad quam accederunt Ferdinandus Frater et Procurator Sponsi, et Domina "Lucretia, cui ipse Ferdinandus procuratorio nomine Fratris sui, imposuit quemdam an"nulum aureum, sive gemmam. Apportati deinde fuerunt per Cardinalem Estensem "etiam Fratrem Sponsi quatuor alii annuli magni valoris, et apportata una capsa super "dictam mensam posita, et de mandato praedicti Cardinalis aperta, qui extraxit ex ea "multa collaria, sive torques, pulcherrimis lapidibus pretiosis et margaritis ornatos. 4' Item quatuor pulcherrimae bruces, &c. oblata Sponsae per Cardinalem Estensem, verbis "ornatissimis. His factis retraxit se Papa ad sequentem aulam sive cameram Paulinam "quem secuta est Domina Lucretia cum mulieribus," &c. *(bj v. Descrittione della nozza di Lucretia Jigliuola di Akssandro VI. ed Alfonso d' Este, inter Muratori, Rerum ltd. Scrip, vol. xxvii. p. 398. .finally re-* moved from the Roman court to the city of Ferrara, which became her residence during the remainder of her life, some

reflections occur on her past conduct. That the daughter of Alexander VI. young, beautiful, and accomplished, educated in the midst of a luxurious city and a profligate court, might, on all occasions, have escaped the general contagion, will not perhaps be readily believed; but with respect to the incestuous intercourse, of which she has been so generally accused, the circumstances of her life and conduct afford no evidence; on the contrary, the anxiety of her father, to avail himself of the first opportunity of uniting her to another husband, must be considered as a strong indication, that his own attachment to her was not of the criminal nature before referred to. Were it also to be granted, that the family of Este was induced to accede to this marriage by the allurements and persuasions, or was terrified into it by the dread of the vengeance of the pontiff, it must still require a considerable portion of credulity to believe, that either Ercole, duke of Ferrara, or Alfonso his son, who were distinguished by their virtues and their talents, both civil and military, beyond any of the sovereigns of the time, would have submitted to have perpetuated their race through the contaminated blood of a known and incestuous prostitute.

The arrival of Lucretia at Ferrara, gave a new impulse to those studies and literary amusements, by which that place had been so long distinguished. Among the many men conspicuous by their talents and their learning, who at this time frequented the court, was the celebrated Pietro Bembo. He had accompanied his father, who had visited that that city in a respectable public character, and the attractions which he had met with in the literary society of the place, had induced him to prolong his residence there. The reputation which Bembo had already obtained by his writings, and perhaps his personal address and accomplishments, early introduced him to the notice of the duchess, who received him with that freedom and affability for which the Italian courts were then remarkable. At this time Bembo was about thirty years of age, and it appears from his letters, that he had twice been the slave of an amorous but unsuccessful passion. The extraordinary beauty, the various endowments, the vivacity, and condescension of the duchess, were attractions too powerful for him to resist, and there is reason to believe, that Lucretia Borgia was destined to complete that amorous servitude of three lustres, or fifteen years, of which he frequently complains. The epistolary correspondence of Bembo, contains several letters addressed to the duchess of Ferrara, to which she frequently replied. But although it might be presumed from her letters, that she was not wholly insensible to the passion *(a)* In the Ambrosian library, at Milan, a manuscript is said to exist, which contains nine letters, in the hand-writing of Lucretia, seven of which are in Italian, and two in Spanish; and at the close, a copy of verses, also in Spanish, all of which are addressed to Bembo. These letters appear to have been folded in the form of billets, and are superscribed, *Al mio carissimo M. Pietro.Bembo.* The writer denominates herself *Lucretia Estense da Borgia,* and the seals of the arms of Este and Borgia are appended to them. At the close of the volume is a canzone in Spanish, of the composition and handwriting of Bembo, and in a folding of white vellum, tied with four ribbands, is a lock of light coloured hair, such as Bembo has frequently described in his poems, and which by constant tradition, has been believed to be that of Lucretia Borgia. From the description of this singular relick, it decidedly appears, that this book formerly belonged to Bembo, who has minuted with his own hand, the dates of the letters, and had probably inserted them in this volume, as a memorial of what he considered as the most elevated and honourable attachment of his early years. *Dmertazione del Dott. Baldassare OltrocM topra iprimi amori di Pietro Bembo. Racolta d'opuscoli di Calogerd. rol. iv. p. 1.*

sion of her admirer, by whose attentions, it is probable she was highly flattered, yet it must be observed, that Mazzufchelli, one of the most judicious critics that Italy has produced, considers

this attachment as having been regulated by sentiments of propriety and honour *fa)* nor is it indeed likely, that a friendly epistolary intercourse would have been continued for so long a time after the termination of a connexion, which could never have been recollected by either of the parties without sentiments of compunction and of shame. In the letters of Bembo to the duchess of Ferrara, which extend from the year 1503, to the year 1516, he at some times communicates to her his own sorrows, and at others congratulates her on the birth of her children; but the warmth of the lover, if it ever existed, soon gave place to the respect of a friend, and the introduction of frequent apologies for his neglect, or omissions, clearly indicates that he had long relinquished that character, which on their first acquaintance, he appears to have been willing to assume.

The attachment of Bembo to Lucretia Borgia, was not, however, so cautiously concealed, as to have escaped the notice of his friends, the two Strozzi, with whom he lived at Ferrara on terms of the utmost intimacy, and at whose villa, in the vicinity of that city, he passed a considerable portion of his time. Tito, the father, has recorded this passion in an enigmatical epigram, which it is not now difficult to explain, and Ercole the son, in confiding to

Bembo *(a) Mazzuch. Scrittorid Ital. in art. Lucretia Borgia. (b)* " Si mutetur in X. C. tertia nominis hujus
"Litera, *Lux* Get, quod modo *Luc* fuerat
"*Retia* subsequitur, cui tu *hoec* subjunge, *paratque;*
"Sic scribens, *Lux hax retia,* Bembe, *parat.*"

Bembo his own amours, adjures him to conceal them with the same secrecy, with which he has himself preserved those intrusted to him by the confidence of his *friend.fa)*

From this period, the conduct of Lucretia Borgia, during the remainder of her life, being an interval of upwards of twenty years, was not only without reproach, but in the highest degree commendable and exemplary. Amidst the disturbances which agitated Italy, and

which frequently threatened Ferrara with destruction, she was intrusted by Vthe duke, during those warlike expeditions in which he so eminently distinguished himself, with the government of the state; in which she conducted herself so as to obtain, not only the approbation of her husband, but the respect and affection of her subjects. By Alfonso she was the mother of three sons, the eldest of whom succeeded to the government of the state of Ferrara, by the name of Ercole *ll.fb)* Towards the close of her life, she became severely .vol. i. Y Y rigid *(a)* " At tu, Bembe, meos quem non celare calores "Debueram, tanti semina disce mali.

"Fas uni tibi nosse, decem quae me usserit annos,
"Quaeque meo jussit corde latere faces.
"Hanc tamen obtestor, ne te sciat indice quisquam;
"Graia tibi servet sic *Telesilla* fidem.'
"Sic mihi, quae dixti, cunctos celentur in annos;
"Nullaque non felix sic eat hora tibi." *Strozz.Jil. Amor. p. 72.*

(b) " Alfonso I." says Mr. Gibbon, " *believed himself* to be the father of three sons. "The eldest, his successor, Hercules II. expiated this maternal stain by a nobler choice, "and his *fidelity* was rewarded by mingling the blood of Este with that of France." *Antiq. of the House of Brunswick, in post, works, vol.* ii. *p. 689.* The doubt which Mr. Gibbon has implied respecting the legitimacy of the eldest son, involves the historian rigid in her religious duties, and devoted herself to works of benevolence and piety. From the official letters of Leo X. it appears, that she had applied to that pontiff, soon after his elevation, for his spiritual advice and consolation, which he conceded to her in the fullest terms, with high commendations of her exemplary *lik.fa)* It is true, that long after she had established a character beyond all just reproach, and when her father was no more, and her brother was driven from Italy, the voice of calumny did not fail to pursue her amidst the splendor of a court; and in the vindictive lines of Sanazzaro, Lucretia is the heifer that wanders disconsolate on the banks of

the Po, lamenting the loss of her *mate.* *fb)* But the motives of these accusations have already been explained, and even if Sanazzaro had been more impartial, the distance of his residence from Rome, would prevent his being considered on such an occasion as an authentic evidence.

But although the charges against Lucretia Borgia, appear to be wholly unsupported, either by proof or probability, it would be unjust to her talents and her character, to close the present inquiry, without adducing some of those numerous rian in some degree of inconsistency. For, if Hercules was not *in fact* the offspring of Alfonso, how can he be said to have mingled the blood of *Este* with that of France?

(a) v. Bembi Ep. nom. Leon. x. *lib.* iv. *Ep* 3. (b) "Juvenca, solos quae relicta ad aggeres

"Padi sonantis, heu malum sororibus
4' Omen, dolentes inter orba populos
"Te te requirh, te reflagitans suum
"Implet querelis nemus; et usque mugiens
"Modo hue, modo illuc furit, amore perdita."
Sauna, lib. i. *Epigr.* 15. rous testimonies in her favour, with which the writings of the most celebrated scholars of the age so frequently abound. In this we need not rely on the applauses bestowed on her by Ercole Strozzi, or Antonio Tebaldeo, who may be considered as the poets-laureate of Ferrara, the former of whom has in particular availed himself of every opportunity of resounding her praise, fa,) Still less must we found our decision on the various poems, both in the Latin and Italian tongue, which Bembo has consecrated to her honor, because he may not be considered as an impartial judge. Yet we cannot pass unnoticed the letter, in which he inscribes to her his romance of the *Asolani,* which he completed and published at her request, and in which he addresses her " As a "princess, who was more desirous of ornamenting her "mind with excellent endowments, than her person with "the decorations of dress. Applying all her leisure hours "to reading or composition.—To the end," says he, "

that "you may surpass other women, as much in the charms of v Y 2 "your *(a)* Several of the principal poems of Ercole Strozzi, as his *VrnationGigantomachia,* are inscribed to Lucretia, whom he also thus addresses at the close of one of his elegies, in which he relinquishes all further interference in public affairs.

"Teque meum veneror, Coelestis Borgia, Sydus, "Qua nullum Hesperio purius orbe micat.
"Tu mihi carmen eris, tu lucida callis ad astra,
"Qui niveas animas lacteus orbis habet;
"Adsertae superis, Juno, Pallasque, Venusque,
"Junoopibus, Pallas moribus, ore Venus.
"Regna tibi meliora, animiquc nitentior ardor,
"Plusque tua igniferi forma vigoris habet.
"Quis neget his ccelum meritis? tua numina quondam
"Neilus, et extrema Baetis honors colent.
"Templa tibi statuent, nec votis templa carcbunt.
"At nostrum, inter tot grandia, majus erit." *Strozi.Jil. E/eg. ad Divam Lucretiam Borgiam Ferrarice Ducem, Strozii op. p.* 53

"your understanding, as you already do in those of external "beauty, and may be better satisfied with your own ap"plause, than with that, however infinite, of the rest of "the world."

The historians of Ferrara, so far from supposing that the family of Este was degraded by their union with Lucretia Borgia, mention her with the highest praise. Giraldi denominates her " a woman of uncommon excellence '*(a)* and Sardi, "a most beautiful and amiable princess, adorned with every virtue.''/ty Yet more honourable is the praise of Libanori; who describes her as " a most beautiful and "virtuous princess, endowed with every estimable quality "of the mind, and with the highest polish of understand"ing; esteemed as the delight of the time, and the treasure "of the age.'Ycj Caviceo, in the year 1508, dedicated to her his work, intitled // *Peregrino,* and adverting to the

celebrated Isabella of Este, daughter of Ercole I. duke of Ferrara, and wife of Francesco Gonzaga, marquis of Mantua, he conceives that he has given her sufficient praise, in asserting that she approaches next in excellence to Lucretia Borgia, *(d)* If the most remote idea had been entertained, that Lucretia had been the detestable character which the Neapolitan poets have represented, is it to be conceived, that this author would have introduced one of the first women *(a)* " Rarissima Donna." *Girald. Comment. delle cose di Ferrara. p.* 181.

(b) " Donna bellissima, gentile, ed ornata d'ogni virtu." *Sardi, Historie Ferraresi. lib.* x. *p.* 198. *(c) MazzucMli Scrittori d' Italia, vol.* v. *p.* 1751. *(dj* " Accede alla tua eccellentia quello lume che extinguere non si pub, di que 11a vera "mortale Dea, Elizabetta Estense di Gonzaga principessa Mantuana, alla quale le Muse "fanno riverentia." *Caviceo, op. Quadrio Storia d' ogni Poesia. vol.* vii. *p.* 70. women in Italy, in point of rank, character, and accomplishments, as only second to her in merit?

The marriage of Lucretia, with Alfonso of Este, was celebrated in a Latin epithalamium by Ariosto; but this may be considered as one of those complimentary tributes, which a youthful poet would be proud to pay to his prince. If however the moral character of the bride, had been so notoriously disgraceful as to render her an object of abhorrence, it is scarcely to be supposed that Ariosto would have had the effrontery, or the absurdity, to represent her, as " rivalling "in the decorum of her manners, as well as in the beauty "of her person, all that former times could boast. "(ty The same author has, however, on a subsequent occasion given a more decisive testimony of his approbation. In the forty-second book of his immortal poem, he has raised a temple of female excellence, the splendid niches of which are occupied by women of the greatest merit and chief distinction in Italy; and among these, Lucretia Borgia assumes the first, and most conspicuous station. It is remarkable, that in the lines devoted to her praise on this occasion, the poet asserts that V Rome ought to prefer the "modern Lucretia to the Lucretia of antiquity, ay *well in "modesty, as in beauty;* a comparison which, if the aspersions under which she has laboured, had obtained the slightest credit, could only have been considered as the severest satire. Each of his heroines are attended by two of the most distinguished poets of Italy, as heralds of their fame, those *(aj "* —— clari soboles Lucretia Borgiae,

"Pulchro ore, *Sc* pulchris aequantem moribus aut quas

"Verax fama refert, aut quas sibi fabula finxit."

Ariost. Epithal. ap. Carm. Must. Poet. ltd. vol. i. *p.* 344.

those assigned to Lucretia Borgia, are Ercole Strozzi and Antonio *Teba.ldeo. fa)*

These commendatory testimonies might be increased to a considerable extent from the works, both in prose and verse, which have been inscribed to her by those authors to whom she afforded encouragement and protection; hut in addition to those already adduced, it may be suffi,, cient *(a) "* La prima inscrittion ch' agli ocelli occorre,

"Con lungo onor *Lucretia Borgia* noma;

"La cui bellezza, e onestil, preporre

"Deve a 1'ant tea la aua patria Roma.

"I duo che voluto han sopra se torre

"Tanto eccellente ed onorata soma,

"Noma lo scrilto, *Antonio Tebaldeo,*

"*Ercole Strozza;* un Lino, ed'uao Orfeo.
"

Can. 42.. *St.* 83.

(b) Antonio Cornazzano, addressed to her his Life of the Virgin, and Life of Christ, both in *terza rima, (Tirab. vol.* vi. *par li.p.* 6l.*)* And Giorgio Robusto, of Alexandria, his poems, printed at Milan, about the year 1500, *(Quadrio, v.* viii.*p.* 65. *)* To these I shall only add another testimony. Father Francesco Antonio Zaccharia, on examining the Jesuit's library of S. Fedele, at Milan, found a manuscript volume of poetry, the author of which, as appears by the dedication, was Luca Valenziano, of Tortona. Zaccharia imagined, that these poems were unpublished, but there is extant a rare edition of them printed at

Venice, by Bernardino de' Vital!, in 1532, 8«-under the title of *Opere volgari di M. Luca Valenziano, Dertonese, ad istanza di Federigo di Gervasio, Napolitano.* The poems in question have great merit, particularly for their pathetic simplicity; and are dedicated in the manuscript copy, but not in the printed work, to Lucretia Borgia, in the following Latin verses: *Ad Divam Lucretiam Borgiam Estensem*;

Lucas Valentianus, Dertonensis.

"Quae tibi pauca damus, tali Lucretia, fronte

"Suscipe nunc, quali grandia dona soles.

"Haec ego dum canerem lacrymis rorantia, dixi;

"Praesideos nostrae, Borgia diva, lyrae.

"O tecum Alphonsus duri post pnelia Martis,

"Otia Musarum quzerere tuta velit.

cient to cite the grave and unimpeachable testimony of one, who, from the respectability of his character, cannot be suspected of flattery, and who indeed, cannot be supposed to have had any other motives for his commendation, than such as he has himself assigned; the favour and assistance which she afforded to every meritorious undertaking, and to every useful art.

The "Sic Caesar, sic Rex Maced&m, sic Hle solcbat,

"Africa cui nomen, victa parente, dedit.

'" Hunc lege; perlectum longo ditabis honore;

"Tutus et a rabido dente libellus erit."

v. *Raccolta* f *Optucoli di Calogerd vol.* xliv.

That Lucretia wrote Italian poetry is believed by Crescimbeni, who informs u that he had been assured by a person deserving of credit, and who was well acquainted with the early literature of Italy, that he had seen, in a collection of poems of the sixteenth century, several pieces attributed to her, but that notwithstanding all the researches made both at Rome and at Florence, no traces of them could now be discovered. The annotator on Crescimbeni is, however, of opinion, that if this had been the case, her works would have been noticed by Bembo in the many letters addressed to her, or by Aldo, in his preface to

the works of the two Strozzi. "She was, however," adds he; a great pa"troness of literature, and by her means the court of Ferrara abounded with men dis"tinguished even in foreign countries; among whom was the before-mentioned Bembo." Mazzuchelli has, however, cited one of the letters of Bembo; from which it appears that she addressed some verses to him; but whether they were in Italian or Spanish, which latter language she frequently adopted in her poetical compositions, he has not ventured to decide. It may, however, be presumed, from the following lines in one of the elegant Latin poems addressed to her by Bembo, that she wrote Italian poetry, and it is not therefore without sufficient reason that both Mazzuchelli and Quadrio have enumerated her among the writers of Italy.

"Te tamen in studio, et doctas traducis in artes,

"Nec sinis ingenium splendida forma premat.

"Sive refers lingua modulatum carmen Hetrusca,

"Crederis Hetrusca nata puella solo;

"Seu calamo condis numeros et carmina sumto

"Illa novem possum scripta decere Deas." &c.

Ad Lucretiam Borgiam. in Bemb. op. tom. iv. *p.* 345.

The person referred to, is the celebrated printer, Aldd Manuzio. From the tenor of his address to her, prefixed to his edition of the works of Tito and Ercole Strozzi, it appears that she had offered, not only to assist him in the establishment of his great undertaking, but also to defray the whole expense attending it. If the sentiments which he attributes to her, were in fact expressed by her, of which there appears no reason to doubt, they sufficiently mark a great and a virtuous mind. "Your chief desire," says he, "as you have yourself so nobly asserted, is to stand ap"proved of God, and to be useful, not only to the present "age, but to future times; so that when you quit this life, "you may leave behind you a monument that you have "not lived in vain." He then proceeds to celebrate in the warmest terms of approbation, her piety, her liberality, her justice and her affability. If Lucretia was guilty of the crimes of which she stands accused, the prostitution of her panegyrists is greater than her own; but of such a degradation several, of the authors before cited were incapable; and we may therefore be allowed to conclude, that it is scarcely possible, consistently with the known laws of moral character, that the flagitious and abominable Lucretia Borgia, and the respectable, and honoured duchess of Ferrara, could be united in the same person.

APPENDIX. APPENDIX.

No-I.

(Vol. i. p. 12.;

Io ho inteso, per una vostra de' 30 di Gennajo, el desiderio avete di Giovanni vostro figliuolo, il che se io avessi inteso avanti la morte del Cardinale di Roana, mi sarei ingegnato No. I. adempire; ma sono ben contento, nei primi benefizj vacanti, fare il meglio che io potrò.

Alla giornata di Ferrara, dove dite haver promesso andare, v'avrei consigliato non andasse punto, ma che guardasse bene tener sicura vostra persona, perchè non conosco e personaggi, nè il luogo dove v'avete a trovare, et v'arei mandato uno imbasciatore di qua in vostra ex cusatione; nientedimancho poichè l'havete promesso, me ne rapporto a voi, e alla buona hora sia et a Dio.

Scripta Aupkm du Parch. Die 17 *Feb.* 1482.

Luv.

N II.

(Voi. i. p. 17.) Ex. orig. in Archiv. Paint. Reipub. Fior ertt. Magnifico Viro motori honorando, Johanni de Lanfredinis, Oratori Fiorentino, Roma.

Magnifice Maior Honorande,

Ho inteso quanto v'ha decto N. S. circa la promotione, e di chi, et respondendo breve

A 2 per per essere occupatissimo, dubitando non essere soprastato ad rispondere per essere stato NO. II. fuori, quando hebbi questo vostro adviso. A me pare, che S. Santità non debbi differire la promotione, se non tanto quanto e' non può più accelerare, perchè giudico,

quando S. Santità lo harà facto, gli parerà essere un' altro Pontefice che fino qui non è stato; perchè dove è stato capo senza membri, sia con quelli; dove è stato facturad'altri, che altri sia fattura sua; et però lo confortate, et importuniate al venire a quella conclusione che debbe, prima che può; perchè periculum est in mora, et nel fare acquisti, et nel differire perde. Sicchè in questa parte usate tutta la vostra auctorità, perche segua questa benedetta promotione, et prima che si può; che avendo mosso la cosa in Collegio non è da allentare, o ritardare senza gravissima perdita della dignità, et commodo di sua Beatitudine.

Quanto al chi, appruovo tutti quelli segnati col punto, et sono quelli medesimi che altre volte mi dicesti. Commendo bene ne metta inanzi molti pct tirare più commodamente quelli che vuole, et se può consolare noi, se ne ricordi. Quando la promotione si differissi per noi, diteli, facci e sua. Se dovessi farne uno solo per cominciarne un tratto a fare, et che paia, che possa; et poi di tempo in tempo col favore di quelli harà fatti, non gli mancherà modi di fare degli altri, et satisfare a ciascuno, et per quella parte del Signor Francesco mi piace la deliberatone di Nostro Signore, et non è da ometterla, perchè è tutta la importantia di questa cosa, et la causa principale perchè si viene a questo acto, et Sua Santità absente come presente può fare quello medesimo; per questo non è da tardare, ne da torsi tempo, poichè Dio gliele prepara tanto oportuno. Questo è el parere mio, aspectando con desiderio dì per di quello seguirà, in che vi prego mettiate diligentia, come solete, et a voi ricordo, che con tutto el cuore rìngratiate Nostro Signore della humanità che usa verso di me, e della fede mi presta benemerita della servitù, et observantia mia verso Sua Santità.

Fiorenti, die xvi. *Junii,* 1488.

Laurentius De Medicis.

N III.

(Voi. i. p. is.;

Innocemtio Vili. Pont. Max.

Sànctissime ac beatissime Pater et Domine. Post pedum oscula beatorum.

Intendendo dall' imbasciatore nostro

che la S. V. è in fermo proposito di fare nuovi cardinali in brevi giorne, me parebbe meritare grandissima reprensione, se io non le ricordassi in questo caso l'honore di questa città et mio anchora, che per sua dementia sono certissimo, secundo secondo mi scrivi l'imbasciatore predetto, che quella se ne ricorda. Ringratio la S. V; di tale sua disposinone, e supplico a quella molto humilmente, se mai sono per ricevere al-N0-TM. cuno rilevato beneficio da quella, si degni abondantemente e con eflècto porgerne il premio della gratia sua, della quale la richieggo questa volta con quella efficacia che farei a N. S. Dio la salute dell' anima mia. Io non credo che in tutto el tempo del pontificato suo laS. V. possa fare cosa che porti seco maggiore obligatione di questa città verso la S. V. perchè come questa dignità è stata molto rara, et per cousequenza da uno tempo in qua molto desiderata, cosi passerebbe con grandissima molestia quando restassi mal contenta. Di me in particolare non parlo, perchè non potrei desiderare più questa cosa che è in eflècto un desiderio a nlentissimo dello honore mio, el quale havendo sempre preposto alla vita propria, può considerare la S. V. quando seguissi altrimente ch'io speri, in che termine mi troveria, che non mi parebbe esser più al mondo. L'imbasciatore nostro è informato a punto de' pensieri miei, dalli quali non sono punto mutato, nè vorrei perdere il bene pe'l meglio, quando il meglio non si possa. Però non potendo obtenersi il primo, supplico la S. V. si degni nell' altro tenere la mano su lo honore mio, ricordando però alla S. V. con ogni hu- miltà, devotione, et fede, che in questo caso quella non ha da havere altra legge o resistentia se non quella che lei medesima vorrà per benignità ed Immanità sua; perchè in arbitrio di V. S. è, et absolutamente in mano sua tutta questa cosa, e conseguendo questo immortale beneficio mi chiamo per sempre satisfacto et obligatissuno. Senza questo non veggo modo come sia in facultà di V. S. di satisfare e ricomperare l'honor mio, e la opinione che quella hà data che io sia nella gratia sua. Raccommandomi humilmente alli piedi di V. B. e supplicola mi habbi per ex-cusato se io non li ho scripto di mano propria, che Io hò facto per darle man-cho molestia, non essendo troppo buono scriptore, et anche perchè me trovo im-pedito da una mano, e sariami stato dif-ficile.

V. S. Humillimus Servitor. Florentia, dit 1. Octb. 1488. Laur. De Medicis.

N-IV.

(Vol. i. *p. Ì8.J Ex Origin, in Arehiv. Palai. Reipub. Florcnt. Rcv. Domino mio Domino Cardinali Sa. Marias in Portici/.*

Rev. Domine mi. Benchè io sia certis-simo, che con fede et amore l'Imbasciadore ostro facci le cose mie, et io non me ne potrei più confidare, pure molte experience" passate mi fan-no havere molti dubi in questa promo-tione di nuovi Cardinali. Confortami la la devotione mia nella Signorìa V. Rev. la quale prieigho con tucto el cuore mio, che N-IV. in questo punto attenta la buona disposinone di N. S. quella non abandoni la servitù mia; ne tanta fede, et speranza quanta io riposo-in quella, resti vana, che mi reputerei sotterrato. La Signoria V. Rev. per experientia ha sempre conosciuto, che io ho preposto lo honore alla vita; et quando questo mio desiderio non succedessi, non so se mi contentassi di più vivere. In somma io raccomando alla Signoria V. Rev. lo honore di questa Repubblica et mio, con quella efficacia, che farei a Dio la salute dell' anima mia. Io non parlo de' par-ticulari, che me ne rimetto all' Imbas-ciadore, et sono fermo in quelli medesi-mi pensieri et non vorrei perdermi el bene pel meglio, quando il meglio non si potessi; non obstante il desiderio, che ne mostra N. S. che sarebbe anche il mio, quando si potessi. Io confido assai nella Signoria V. Rev. laquale prieigho tenga le mani su l'honore mio, et a quel-la me raccomando humilmente.

Laurentius De Medicis. mom pro-pria/. Flurentia, dei primo Decembris. Ex orig. in Archiv. Palat. Repub. Fior. Mortifico Viro motori meo honorando Juhanni de Lanfredinis Oratori Fiorentino, Roma.

CIRCA la promotione, havendo rice-vuta la lettera di Mona. Ascanio, mi pare havere gran pegno di questo desiderio, et speranza mia; con questa sarà la risposta, non quale bisognerebbe, ma seconda che posso, et so fare io. A me piace tra le altre cose, che habbiate bene disposto » ne mai in vero hebbi altra opinione, perchè non li feci mai se non piacere, et honore, et sono apto, et disposto in ogni occasione a fargliene più che mai. Con » non mi pare habbiate facto pocho a fermarlo, che non contradica; se non potete trarne più, mi pare da ringratiarlo di questo, et certificarlo, che per la natura sua quel-lo obligo harò di questo, che con gli altri del favore manifesto; pure quando si potessi, mi sarebbe molto grato el consenso suo. La opera vostra, et l'auctorità di N. S. forse doverrebbono condurlo, pure a ogni modo che questa cosa venga, mi sarà grande, et diarissi-ma. Ricordovi, quando vi pare havere le cose disposte, non mettere dilatione nel fare lo efièeto, et benchè voi mi diate termine in sino a Venerdì, che saremo a di xx, alle volte si sogliono prolungare, et a me parebbe d'assicurarsene il più presto si può, sanza aspectare 4. tem-pora. Voi havete però governato tanto bene questa cosa, che mi pare superfluo a ricordarvi di quà altro.

Lorenzo De' Medici. Florentite, die xv. *Februarii,* 1488—y.

No.

(Vol. i.p. 18J

Ex orig. in ArcUt. Palat. Reipub. Fior. Magnifico Viro ma/ori meo Aonorando Johanni de Lanfrtdinis Oratori Fiorentino, Rome. 10 rispondo con una lettera di mia mano alli Rev. Mons. Vicecancelliere, et Monsign. Ascanio. La lettera, che mi hanno scripta, e le opere, che mi scrivete voi, che tucto dì fa Mons. Ascanio in beneficio nostro, meritano altre gratie che di parole. Conosco, et per 11 vostri advisi, et per le mie consideratiori, ove restava lo honore et speranza mia, se non russi su-ta resuscitata dalle opere di Sua Rev. Signoria, et quello che mi valeva e parentadi, amicitie, et fede, &c. La difEcultà di questa cosa, la diligentia, et studio di Sua Rev. Signoria fanno tanto grande il beneficio, che non solo oblig-ano me, et M. Giovanni, ma tucti quelli

che saranno mai di noi; perchè non reputo altrimenti questo beneficio, et opera di Mons. Ascanio, che se diven-tassi di morto vivo. Horamai sto in buona opinione, veduto come piglia questa cosa per me, et quello me «e han-no scripto. Sforzeromnni, se harò mai facuità, o possanza in beneficio, et hon-ore di Sua Rev. Signoria non vi mettere ne sale, ne olio; et basti, et piùtosto fare con effecto, che dire molte parole.

Oltra quello, che io scrivo al Rev. Mons. Vicecancelliere comunemente a Mons. Ascanio, desidero facciate inten-dere al prefato Mons. Vicecancelliere, che io conosco molto bene di che qual-ità è l'opera, che fa per me; et se l'honore mio non russi suto sullevato da S. Rev. Signoria restava in pessimo lu-ogo, et non so se mi fussi voluto più vi-vere. Non poteva accadere cosa, in che io conoscessi meglio l'affection, et charità di Sua Rev. Signoria verso di me, et che più me obligassi. Offeritegli liberamente non solo la persona, et tucte le cose mie, ma tucto quello, che potrà mai M. Giovanni, che sarà più suo, che mio; et so si ricorderà sempre con-seguendo quello grado riaverlo da Sua Signoria Rev. et forse acchaderà, che li potrà rendere qualche parte del merito. Prieghovi facciate efficacissimamente intendere a Sua Signoria Rev. quello, che non posso io scriverli; perchè in ef-fecto io conosco molto più questo obli-go, et molto più desidero pagarlo poten-do, che non exprimere.

Lorenzo De' Medici. Florentia;, die xxi. *Februarii,* 1488—9.

No. No VII.

(Voi. i. p. 19.) Ex orig. in Archie. Palai. Reipub. Fior. Magnifico Viro mqjori meo onorando Johanm de Lan/redinis, Oratori Fiorentino, Roma;. IO ho in-dugiato all' ultimo capitolo il facto del-la promotione; perche anchora voi volendo. VII. (ieri inflUgiate lo efFecto. Per l'ultima vostra de' dì ultimo intendo havevate gia xv. cardinali soscripti; ma che N. S. ha indugiato di prolungare, non s'intendendo altro del Fratello del Turco; io credo questa prolungatone sarà ad ogni modo, et non me ne rale-gro punto, non tanto per el pericolo, che cosi porta, che non è pocho, quanto per

vedere » ». » » » a mettere in » » » »
» ». In efiecto io ne sto di mala voglia,
et per lo exemplo mio ho gran compas-
sione di voi. Havete tempo a mandare la
forma dello adviso al publico, la quale
ha facto pressoche uno grande scanda-
lo; perchè leggendo la poliza, prima che
la lettera, et non vi essendo su copia, o
altro indino, credetti, che lo adviso fussi
vero, et manchò poco che non lo comu-
nicai. A me pare importi poco el modo dello advisare. Qui «e ne parla tanto
pubicamente, che è troppo; et però non
ci manderesti cosa nuova, et che non sia
aspectata da nessuno, salvo che da me;
che non so donde si nasca, che non mi
ci sono mai potuto appichare, pure per
non manchare di quello si può, vi mando con questa la fede del Doctorato di
M. Giovanni, et della ordinatone a Di-
acono, &c. Mandovi anchora una lettera dell' Arcivescovo a me, et benchè
sia forse passionato, pure in questi casi
d'importantia si vuole intendere ogni
huomo. Se potete strignere il papa a
trarne le mani, mi pare lo dobbiate fare.
Potresti usare a questo tucti e circun-
stanti del papa; perchè et Doris Arrivabene, et gli altri che aiutano, el Castel-
lano el Datario, Aleria, et tucti doveresti
potere muovere pure il papa a trarne
le mani. Io veggho nello indugio tanto
male, che non ardisco dirlo; se c'è modo, come dico, cavate voi e me di questa anxietà e sopratucto tenete di presso
» »

Loriszo De' Medici. *Fiorentine, die* v.
Martii, 1488—9.

No. Vili.

No-Vili.

(Voi. i. *p.* 20 J *Ex. orig. in Archiv. Palat.
Reipuh. Fior. Magnifico ac putenti viro
Laurentio de' Medicis, tanquamfratti
nostro carissimo.*

Magnifice ac potens frater noster caris-
sime, salutem.

Quod bonum, felix, et faustum sit
Reverendissimo filio vestro, Magnifi-
centiae Vestrae, et

Ci vi tati Civitati Florentine! Hac hora creatus fuit in Cardinalem, Filius
Vester Reverendissimus D. Joannes de
Mcdicis, quod nobis tantae voluptati
est, quanta: ulla res esse potuisset, &c.

Tutus vester, Romt, viiii. Martii, 1489.

Jo. Cardinalis Andecavensis.

No-IX.

(Vol. i. *p.* 20J

Ex. Carmin. Must. Poet. Ital. tom, vii.p,
182.

*Exultatio ad Joannem Medicem Jilium,
quod ad cardinalatus dignitatem as-
sumptus fuerit.* SERA quidem, fcstina
tamen gratatur honori

Littera nostra tuo; sed enim transcen-
dere dudum

Hyberna glacie obductas expalluit
Alpes.

Quod si pulchra sinu tunc me Florentia
grato

Fovisset, properata animi monumenta
benigni

. Carmina cepisses, vel quae calor ille
ministrat

Laetitia superantc furcns, nec gaudia
pectus

Attigerant nwderata meum, mihi Laurus
in ore,

Laurus in ardenti resonabat pectore,
tales

Quae nobis tulerat generoso *h* germine
fructus,

Pcrpetua quae fronde viret, semperque
virebit

Florentes totum ramos sparsura per
orbem.

Egregia de stirpe puer jam concipe dignos

His mentis animos, sensus jam sume se-
niles.

Christi sancta tuo stabunt sub cardine
signa:

Ne succumbe, oneri fac par videare fer-
endo:

Spem supera, nulli major quae contigit
umquam,

Qua tute hanc tantam meruisti scandere
sedem.

Te patriae, virtutis amor succendat,
alantque

Egregios mores laudis monumenta paternae,

Ut quandoque etiam possis majora
mereri,

Eximiumque caput sacra redimire tvara
Pontificis summi; proh gaudia quanta
parenti

Tum dabis, et quantus mihi tum spirabit
Apollo.

Jo. Francisc. Philomds.

B *(Voi.* i. *p. 20.)*

*Ex montanent. Aug. Fabronii ad vitam
Laur. Med.*

.

Ringraziato sia dio di questa buona
novella, che hiermattina a hore 9-ricevei
di Mess. Gio nostro, la quale mi pareva
tanto maggiore, quanto per la grandezza, l'aspectavo manco; parendomi cosa
molto sopra e meriti mici, et per se difficile tanto, che sapeva quasi dell' impos-
sibile. Ho cagione di ricordarmi sempre
di chi se n'è affaticato, et lasciare anchora questo ricordo a quelli che suc-
cederanno a me, perchè questa è la maggior cosa, che facessi mai casa nostra, et
a voi basta che io intendo questo, perchè
invero la reputo più che e tre quarti della diligeutia, industria et amore vostro.
Questa parte mi riserbo in altro tempo
et modo. A N. S. mi è parso scrivere
al presente una lettera di ringraziamen-
to, che sarà con questa: cosi rispondo
a Baia et Ascanio, da' quali solamente
ho per bora avuto lettere, et da voi aspet-
to più particolare adviso di più cose,
come intenderete appresso. Io non so se
sarà dispiaciuto a N. S. la dimostrazione
e festa, che qui se n' è facta univer-
salmente, che mai mi parve vedere più
vera e generale allegrezza. Sarebbesene
facti molti altri segni; ma io non ho lasciato, et questi che si sono facti, non ho
potuto impedire. Dirò questo, perchè essendo pronunziato Mess. Gio. secreto,
queste dimostrazioni pajono opposite a
questa intentione, ma voi publicasti
questa cosa costà in modo, che forse
non sarà suto carico quello che è suto
facto per lo exemplo di costà, ne io ho
potuto negare o non acceptarc la congratulatione di tucta questa città insino a
minimi; se pure è inconveniente, era im-
possibile, che non fussi, e questo harei
caro intendere, come in futuro
n'habbiamo a governare, e che vita e
modi ha a tenere Mess. Gio. et l'abito et
la famiglia, perchè non vorrei comincia-
re a pagare questo grandissimo beneficio con usarlo male e fuora dell' intentione di N. S. Intanto Mess. Gio. si sta in
casa, la quale da hieri in qua è stata con-
tinuamente piena di gente, et però ad-
visatemi quello habbiamo a fare di lui.
Cosi se accadessi che havessì a scrivere,

che soscriptione o suggello ha ad usare; et circa la Bulla sono certo harete tutti e riguardi; quando potete mandatela per consolatione degli amici. La misura della grandezza sua vi mando in questa; ma da hiermattina in quà mi pare cresciuto et mutato. Spero in Mess. Domencdio, che vi farà honore delle fatiche vostre, et N. S. ne sarà ogni di più contento. Aspecto, se vi pare, che io mando Piero secondo vi ho scripto; perchè a mio parere questo beneficio meriterebbe non che altro che io venissi in persona. Di tutto mi governerò secondo il parer vostro.

Lorenzo De' Medici.

N XI.

(Vol. i. *p.* 24 J

Ex. orig. in Arcltiv. Pa/at. Reipub. Fior. Magnifico Oratori Fiorentino maiorì meo honor andò Johanni de Lanfredinis. Roma;. IO ho avuto lettere da Monsign. d' Aleria, dal Depositario, et dal Vescovo di Cortona in congratulatione di M. Giovanni. Io non rispondo, se non ad Aleria; agi'altri fate voi No. XI. quelle parole, che vi paiono convenienti: scrivo anchora a quelli due altri congratulandomi della loro promotione, &c.

M. Agnolo da Monte Pulciano scrive una epistola a N. S. che sarà con questa, colla soprascripta di mano di Ser Piero, nella quale ringratia, *kc.* è assai lunga. Lui harebbe voluto, che si fussi data a tempo, che si fussi lecta in Consistono, non che da N. S, Io credo sia bene andare adagio nel darla alla Sta. S. non che fare quel resto; pure me ne rimetto all' Judicio vostro. Intendete che la epistola è in.nome suo.

Lorenzo De' Medici. *Florentia".* xiv. *Martti,* 1488—9.

N-XII.

(Vol. i. *p.* 25.J *Ex orig. in Archiv. Palat. Reipub. Fior. Magnifico Laurent io Medici Patrono optino.*

Magnifice Patrone mi. Voi mi havete più volte dato animo et ricordato che io stessi intento a qualche cosa honorevole, che io per me havendo horamai da vivere colla mia brigata, et non conoscendo richiedersi, nè alla qualità mia, nè a meriti, più che quello mi havete dato, non havrei havuto animo

di molestarvi uiterius; ma voi credo havete pensato quello si convengha alla grandezza dell' animo e fortuna vostra, che non suole essere contenta, ne debba dell' ordinario, &c. Intendo di buon luogho, che'l figliolo di Giovanni D'Orsino sta molto male, quello che ha la Pieve di Laterina. Se V. M. non vi facessi su disegno per altri, me gli ricordo. La Pieve è comoda, anzi vicina a Gruopina, et a me sarebbe un Vescovado, che non sarìa così a un altro. Questo solo vi ricordo, che per experientia vedrete, che li benefici mi farete non saranno mal collocati, perchè non spendo, nè la roba, nè'l tempo, se non in cose honorevole nè meno a V. M: che a me. Mandovi una Elegia di uno discendente di Dante Alighieri, che si chiama Dante quinto dal poeta, et

B 2 terzo

No XII terZ nome; el uale a rerona conobbi» et vedrete una Pistola di sua mano, dove si ricorda di me; m'e paruta una novellina di cotesto luogho e tempo.

Vorrei, che V. M. intendessi, se Maestro Pier Lione volessi durar fatica in riveder quella mia traductione di Hippocrate, e Galieno, che è quasi al fme, et così el commento, che fo sopra, dove dichiaro tutti e termini medicinali, che venghono dal Greco, et truovo come si possino chiamar Latine. Se la sua Exc. volessi durar fatica, poi al tempo la manderei fuori più arditamente-, che stimo sarà bella cosa et utile, se l'amor non me ne inganna. Mes. Hermolao, e'l Conte, mostrono pur d' haverne buona opinione.

Udii cantar improviso, hierser l'altro, Piero nostro, che mi venne assaltare a casa, con tutti questi improvisanti, satisfecemi a maraviglia, etpresertim ne' motti, et ne'l rinbeccarc, et nella facilità et pronuntia, che mi pareva tutta via veder et udir Va. Mia. Prego Iddio ce lo mantengha lungo tempo, hoc est, semper dum vivimus, et a voi dia vita lunghissima con questo godimento, et delli altri. Raccomandomi a Va. Mia.

V. M. Senmbu,

Angelus Politianus. *FloretitUt, die 5. Junii, HQO.*

No-XUl *(Voi. i.p.M.) Ex orig. in*

Archiv. Palat. Reipub. Fior. Al mio Magnifico Lorenzo de' Media.

Magnifico Lorenzo: addui vostre, una del far condurre Franciocto ad Firenze N. XIII. l'altra de haver per consiglio de' Medici proceduto al taglio, ad che non ho resposto prima, si per esser chiaro non esserli mancato nulla, che sempre ho veduto V. M. amarlo come figliolo, si anche per esser stato-el dubio de la morte de N. Sre. che bisognava pensare ad altro. Venni, e qui ad Roma, e visitai N. Sre. el quale benchè fosse senza pericolo, che havia passato un gran ponte, pur essendo stata la infermità longa, et esserli rimasta la quartana, et havendo la età che hà, non obstante non se ce veda pericolo subbito, pur ih longo viagio se trova de mal passi. Dopo visitata sua Santità, visitai alcuni Cardinali, et per lo debito mio, et perchè spero valermene, non meno che la M. V. et quod sit quies senectutis meae, li reccomandai Messer Johanni, et che volessero esserli favorevoli allo intrare in conciai. Fome resposto multo generalmente sub ista forma verborum: Domine Archiepiscope, ad tucte le rasioni de Mess. Johanni, et per respecto della casa vostra, et del Patre se li haverà riguardo de non offenderli. Strengendoli io un poco più, come la S. V. fa dubio non intre in Conclai, et che non habbia vóto; me respuse, non siamo ancora ad questo; el Papa stà bene, et quando succedesse il caso della morte, siate certo se li ha ad havere respecto, per li respecti ve ho dicti. Dolendome che Sua Santità me spacciava in sul genere, me respuse: Domine Archiepiscope, io non te posso dire altro. Con un altro cardinale d'altrafactione, o simele, o poco varia sententia ebbi. Depoi parlai col Cardinale Ursino, dal quale ho havuto quel medesimo: o che proceda da mia dapocagine, o vero da qualche particolare, in cose di simele importantia, non me hanno spacciato cosi pel generale. Non voglio non haver facto advertente V. M. et ancora che essendo io de casa Ursina de patre et de mat re; che tra el Cardinale, el Conte de Pitigliano da un canto, Virginio et li altri della casa dall' altro, sia qualche rugine, Vostra M. se chiarisca con chi sia più espediente al favore de Messer Johanni, adeiò che el Cardinale, el Conte non v'abbia ad dire, nui siamo nomini del Collegio, bisogna ne andamo con esso; e'l Sr. Virginio non ve possa dire, è stato ordinato ch'io non possa intrare in Roma. Non ho possuto più, et pero iterum replico ad una cosa, che tanto importa, voglia uscire del generale V. M. alla quale me raccomando. No-XV.

Ray. De Ursinis Archieps. Florent. *Ex Urbe, die* v. *Oitobris,* Ugo.

N»-XIV.

(Vol. i. *p.* 31.*)*

Laurentio de' Mediti. Magni/ice tir mnjor honorande, &c.

RISPONDERÒ al presente più particolarmente alla vostra de' di 15, et benchè per lamia de' 14. vi scrivessi a lungo circa le cose di M. Gio. pure vedendo quanto ne replicate di N-XIV.

nuovo, dirò quello ne intendo. Egli è vero, che io credo, che dalla parte dei cardinali non sia molta difficoltà ad consentire la pubiicatione di Mess. Gio. per li respecti che per altre vi lio scripto, anzi mi pare esser certo la debbino desiderare; ma la difficulià sarà dalle parte del Papa, il quale giudicando, che il facto di M. Gio. sia al sicuro, non credo che volentieri si disponga a pubblicarlo solo; non solo perchè facendolo offenderebbe li altri, che sono nel grado suo, et anchors e Principi, a' quali ha promesso in questa prima pubblicatione satisfargli, ma anchora perchè col tenere le cose sospese spera havere più facile el collegio alla voglia sua, disegnando volerne fare almeno uno de' sua, et quando Ascanio procurava el

Breve per assicurarsi della pubblicatione del Malleacense, più volte mi disse commendando la modestia vostra, che ad ogni modo intendeva abbreviare el tempo, et pubblicare Messer

Giovanni, imponendomi che di questo per sua parte vi scrivessi, et cosi mi pare essere certo habbi ad farlo, et però nel temptarlo hora non so in che disposinone me l'habbi ad trovare,

pure pure perchè veggo lo desiderate assai, et quando si potessi fare, sarebbe et honorevole et uno N-XIV. uscire di compromesso: quando vedrò il tempo comodo, userò ogni ingegno et diligentia,

et come gli harò parlato di simile materia, vi potrò dare migliore j lidic io di quello si possi sperare. Nè crediate, che per parlargli al presente si potessi fare alchuno frutto, che ciascuno è advertito non gli parlare se non di cose piacevoli, et sempre se gli parla col testimonio, perchè il parlare secreto, et il cerchare di parlargli solo, denoterebbe qualche cosa eVimportantia. Egli è più di uno mese, che cardinale alchuno non gli ha parlato excepto quelli di Palazzo. E ben vero che alchuni prelati piacevoli, come Messer Falcone, sono stati introdotti qualche volta al Papa, et l'Arcivescovo nostro anchora per introductione del Sig. Francesco gli ha parlato, ma di cose piacevoli, et se farà Consistono, non se gli parlerà d'altro, che di spacciare qualche Chiesa. Et però vi concludo, che il cerchare di parlargli hora, come richiederebbe la materia, non riuscirebbe, et se pure riuscisse, non so come al Papa fusse grato, trovandosi ne' termini che si trova, et dubiterei non fussi per fargli fare qualche sinistra opinione di se. A me pare che al continuo vadi migliorando, come mi parrà che il tempo lo patisca, gli parlerò, et allora vi potro dire qualche cosa con più fondamento; ma presupponete, che l'habbi'ad stare anchora parecchi giorni. Se pure ad voi paressi che habbi ad tenere altri modi, ne advisate e lo farò.

Ho visto quanto vi scrive l'Arcivescovo. A me anchora haveva decto il medesimo che scrive a voi; et perchè possiate giudicare meglio Io scrivere suo, vi nominerò quelli Cardinali, co' quali lui dice havere parlato de' facti di Mess. Gio. et che gli hanno risposto sul generale. Il primo è Vicecancelliere, S. Maria in Portico, Napoli, Siena et Orsino. Et voi sapete quello v'ho scripto del Vicecancelliere, che infra l'altre cose m'ha decto, che volendo mi farà un scripte di sua mano: S. Maria in Portico sapete quello vi ha scripto oltre quello che ha decto a me. Et del Orsino et di Napoli non vi posso dire altro se non quanto più volte vi ho scripto. Siena parla honorevolmente, et sapete quello vi mandò a dire per Messer Pandolfo, et però per lo scrivere dell' Ar-

civescovo non dovete mutare opinione. Et perchè replicate che una parte del Collegio è male disposta verso el Malleacense, non credo vi possa essere scripto con fondamento, se non il medesimo che v'ho scripto io; et il fondamento principale, che si fa per chi desiderebbe difenderlo, è che presuppongono che lui non habbi la Bolla. Et perchè v'ho per ogni mia affermato, che quando da principio gli fusse facta qualche difficoltà, in fine credo che abbi ad essere trattato nel grado di M. Giovanni, et con tutto questo vi conforto perseguitare il consiglio delli amici, che quando habbi ad venire, venga solo; pigliando quello colore che vi parrà per non generare sospeto al Sig. Lodovico, nè anchora a Ascanio, et crediatemi, che per uno Cardinale solo havete da stimare Ascanio quanto alchuno altro, perchè vi è veramente affectionato, et ha auctorità et seguito d'alcuni.:.

Romir, xix Qctobrù 1490, *hora* 5 *noctis.*

(Vol. i. *p.* 32 J

Ex orig. in Archiv. Palat. Reipub. Florent.

Magnifico Viro maiori mco honorando Johanni de Lanfredinis Oratori Florentino. Roma. NON so se havete inteso a questa hora quello, che ha risposto cl Re, circa quanta li scrips!

in favore vostro, della pensione di 200 ducati sopra el Priorato di Capua, che in effecto *Q*

mostra non ve l'avere promessa, ne havere dispositione di farlo, et in su questo me ha facta intendere la Mta. Sua, che quando io volessi acceptare il Beneficio per Julio mio Nipote,

sarì contentissima di darglielo. Intendendo io che el Beneficio e degno, et havendo facto pensicro di dare uno simile adviamento a Julio, me e" paruto d' acceptarlo. Pertanto mi pare facciate intenderlo a N. S. acciòche se ne expedisca le Bolle, et anchora che si possa fare per mezo del gran Maestro, et che el Re se sia offcrto di farmelo expedire per quella via a me pare: questa via del Papa e più breve et più certa; harete la nota della eta, et altre conditioni di Julio, et v'ingegnerete farla expedire, et facto questo, mi resta pensare a poco della famiglia mia, perche quasi tucti sono acconci. Non manchate della diligentia vostra in questa cosa, poiche se e offerta questa ventura a questo fanciullo, &c.

Lorenzo De' Medici. *Fhrentitt, die* xvii. *Augusti, hora* iii.

N XVI.

(Vol. i. *p-36.)*

Ex monument is Ang. Fabronii ad vitam Laur. Med.

Guidoni Priori Angelorum.

Persuadeo mihi non deesse isthic, qui diligent issime tibi renuncient, quae de die in diem circa nos gerantur. Ex quo enim Florentia profecti sumus, significatum fuisse quo-NO. XVI.

tidianis nunciis et cursoribus scio Magnifico Laurentio progressum itineris filii sui, unde et tu identidem certior fieri potuisti. Quamobrem factum est, ut tardius hac de re ad te scribam. Quoniam vero quae nobis grata sunt, etiam saepius repetita non displicent, et ego in perpetuo fere comitatu atque obsequio colendissimi Cardinalis ad hanc usque diem fui,

complectar summatim, quae relatu digna mihi succurrerint, ne defuisse penitus et officio meo et desidefio tuo videar. Igitur duodecima, ut nosti, Martii mensis die, hora, sicut edictum fuerat, sextadecima, conscensis jumentis egressus est Florentia Dominus Reverendissimus cum familia sua, precedentibus illum civibus spectabili pompa, qui ad duo millia

passuum

No. XVI.

passuum ipsum deduxerunt; redire in urbem jussis, post salutationem mutuam, cardinalis eo die cum majore parte familia e ad Abbatiam suam Passignani divertit. Nos vero et alii Podibontium pervenimus. Sequenti die, remorante illo animi gratia in suo monasterio, praecessimus Senas, moniti, ut ibidem prestolaremur adventum ejus. Hora circiter vigesima occurrimus ei ad secundum extra urbem lapidem. Si hic referre particulatim voluero, quo fuerit honore a Senensibus Cardinalis noster exceptusj qua totius urbis congratulatione, quibus delitiis, non sufficit dies. Occurrit extra urbem civium primariorum turba, 'occurrit et omnis populus. Et ne cuique presto esset occasio con-

tinendi se doini, publico edicto imperatum est, ut universae urbis tabernae occluderentur. Advenisse Pontificem summum credercs, ita commota est universa civitas. Haec sane Cardinali exhibila reverentia, pietas, fides adeo satis omnibus fecit, ut nemo Senis non contentus abierit. Sextadecima die inde movimus omnes, pransique ad Bonconventum, vesperi ad S. Quiricum pervenimus. Die insequenti ad Paleam accepti ad prandium sumus; et hucusquc Senensium sumptibus semper hospitati. Ad Aquam Pendentem Ecclesia e oppidum nocte requievimus. Mane profecti complures Prelati, nosque itidem Viterbium applicuimus, retento in medio itinere ab Ursinis propinquis suis Cardinali colendissimo. Invenimus Viterbii Pontificis filium, sororis cardinalis maritum, ipsius adventum praestolantem. Postera die Cardinali occurrimus, et cum eo Viterbium ingressi sumus. Inde discedentes sequenti die, vesperi Bratianum Ursinorum oppidum divertimus. Excepti ibidem sumus apparatu regio in palatium Virginii comitis, qui magna equitum turma veherat obviam nobis ad octo millia passuum. Alterum diem Bratiani percgimus, et quidem maximo omnium commodo. Tandem novissimo itineris nostri die, undecimo scilicet Kalendis Aprilis, Romam ingressi sumus, occurrentibus nunc his nunc illis in via ad deducendum Cardinalem, nulla pluviarum vi, quae magna tunc erumpebat, illos morante, quin officioso muneri satisfacerent. Ad primam urbis portam secessit Cardinalis cum paucis in monasterium S. Mariae in Populo, Mane sequentis diei convenerunt eo Cardinalcs omnes et nimboso quidem ccelo, deduxeruntque illum ad Pontificem in Consistorium publicum. Exceptus est ad osculum a Pontifice, atque ab omnibus deinceps Cardinalibus, sicuti et nos facere consuevimus, cum aliquem ad Religionem admittimus. Singuli quoque de Cardinalis familia deosculari ibidem Summi Pontificis pedes. Redeuntem domum, universa illum comitante curia, sicuti moris est, perpetua non deseruit atque ingens pluvia. Vix tnim egressi eramus palatium Pontificis, cum subito adeo largum ob-

ductae ccelo nubes excussere imbrem ut torrentis more elTusus non modo nos madefecerit, verum pene totos obruerit. Sequentibus diebus visitavit Cardinalis Pontificem; visitavit Cardinales singulos domi. Hoc peracto visitationis officio, visitatus est et ipse vicissim domi a Cardinalibus omnibus, sicuti moris est. Absoluta est heri clemum haec mutua visilatio. Ceterum ut de ipso Cardinali aliquid tibi gratius conscribam, scias eum satisfecisse omnibus prater multorum expectationem; qui se puerulum visuros putaverant, non tam presentia corporali et proceriore, quam pro etate statura, quam morum in primis gravitate, et sermone in omnibus maxime accommodato. Ceremoniis cardinalatus, quantum ego animadvertere et domi et foris potui, adeo apte et decenter utitur, ut in iis per annos multos versatum fuisse facile crederes. Humanitate quoque et affabilitate preditum, quotidie palam experimur. Verum de hoc alias. Quanti te faciat colendissimus Protector noster, et quam grate audierit secum de te loquentem, ipsiui ad te littere indicabunt; et ego coram, ubi permiserit Dominus, plenius referam.

Commendo tibi nostra isthic negotia, quae nosti. Sumus hic in obsequio Reverendissimi 0--'

Cardinalis Medicis minus certe apti et idonei, sed voluntarii, sed fideles. Ora pro felici et incolumi tum ipsius, tum nostro reditu: et nos, cum opportunum tibi fuerit, clarissimo viro Laurentio commenda. Tumultuario stilo, ac currenti calamo haec modo ad te con scripsi, quoniam re vera parum nobis ocii superest. Siquid barbare dictum invenies, excusationem admittes. Vale.

Ex Urbe. die vii. *Aprilis,* 14952.

No XVII.

(Vol. i. *p. 36.) Ex orig. in Archie. Reipub. Florent. Magnijico Viro Laurentio de Medicis Palri optima. Florentioe.*

Salvus sis. Se e non vi havessi » » *(mancante)* dare adviso di qualche cosa. Io Venerdi mattina fui ricevuto in publico, accompagnato da S. M. dal Populo insino a palazzo, e da palazzo in fino in Campo di Fiore da tucti questi Cardinali, e da quasi tucta la Corte, et da una grande piova. Fui visto da Nostro Signore molto gratiosamente; non gli parlai quasi niente; el dl sequente li Oratori visitarono Nostro Signore; hebbono gratissima audientia. El Papa mi riservò il dl sequente per udirmi, che e hoggi; sonvi ito, et la S. Sta. mi ha parlato tanto amorevolmente, quanto e possibile; hami ricordato, et confortato a fare qualche cosa in queste visitation! de' Cardinali, che le ho comincieta a fare in questi che ho visitati; che tucti che vi scriverò un' altra volta chi sono; dimostrono molto di esser volti benessimo verso voi. Delle cose passate so ne siete suta advisato. Di me non ho da dirvi altro, se non che io mi sforzerò di iarvi honore. De me proloqui ulterius, nefas. Io ho havuto molto caro l'adviso del vostro stare molto meglio; et non ho altro desiderio, se non di sentirlo spesso, et di questo per insino a hora ne ringratio Ser Piero. Io mi raccomando i voi. Non altro.

Jo. Filius. *Romte, die* xxv. *Martii.* 149?.

No. XVIII.

(Vol. i. p. 65.J

Dalt Opere volgare del Canteo.

CANZONE.

ALZA la testa al polo
Ardire; et forza prende anima lieve,
Et l' amoroso stilo nomai depone.
Un altra via si deve
Tentar; per donde io possa alzarmi a volo,
  E scriver il mio nome in Helicone.
  Rimembra dal principio la cagione,
  Perche verme in Italia dalla Iberia
  Di Goti la progenie più che humana.
  Tu Musa Antiniana,
  Comincia un suon conforme a la materia.
  Et voi O Nymphe piene
  D' Apollo, che colete l'alta Hesperia,
  Cantate hor meco; et voi dolci Sirene,
  Dite di ciò che sempre vi soviene.
  L' alma formata in cielo,
  Da l' alma Creator de la natura,
  Ogni cosa nel ciel chiaro comprende.
  Che la substantia pura,
  Separata dal nostro ombroso velo,
  Quanto si fa la sù vede et intende.
  Ma poi che per destin qua giù discende;

Et per necessità d' alcuna stella,
Se'nvolve nelle humane et gravi membra
Di nulla si rimembra.
Poi se del suo fattor non è ribella,
Ricovra la memoria
De l' alta opra del cielo ornata e bella.
Et si ricorda de l' eterna gloria;
Pur com' huom d' una udita o letta historia.
  Cosi quest' alma humile,
  Che mentre piace al ciel mi tiene in vita,
Hebbe sua parte ancor del ben celeste;
Ma poi che fu impedita
Di mille errori, et data al piacer vile,
Quell' opre di lassù le fur moleste.
  Poi dispregiando la terrena veste,
  Per ruggir di prigion si mese l' ale;
  Et tenendo per mezzo il suo camino,
  Del Palazzo divino
    Cominciò ricordarsi, et come et quale
  Era quello ch' udiva
  In quel sidereo et alto tribunale:
  Da quella voce eternamente viva
  Da cui ogni cloquentia alta deriva.
    Tra gli altri un dì per sorte,
    L' unico Padre et Dio d' huomini et divi,
Che tempra col suo grave superciglio
Foco, aria, terra, e i rivi,
Aprendosi d' Olympo l' auree porte:
Convocò gli altri Dei nel suo consiglio.
Sedendosi da la man dextra il figlio
Et volitando Amor per ogni parte,
Chiaremente li vidi insieme unire;
Come, noi posso dire,
Che non è cosa de explicare in clurte.
La mente intende il vero;
Ma la lingua mortai non ha tant' arte.
Li tre perfetti in un perfetto intero
Vidi congiunti: et rivederlo spero.
    Dunque quel Padre eterno,
  Parlando in piedi cominciò levarsi,
  Et lui dicendo, ogn un degli altri tacque.
    Vidi il vento acquetarsi,
  Tremar la terra insino al imo inferno,
  Ove Pluton pien di superbia giacque,
  Et fermarsi del mar le placide acque.
  Cittadine del cielo, Alme preclare,
  Udite attenti il suon di mie parole.
  Sotto la luna e'l sole
  Mirando quanto cinge il salso mare,

Et quanto in terra giace;
Nulla cosa più bella al mondo appare,
Ne più felice, e lieta, e più ferace,
Ch' Italia degna di perpetua pace.
  Ma parte delle genti
  Che sempre fur discordi et inquiete,
  A sua felicità contrarie trovo.
Più giù gli occhi volgete,
C 2
  In quella parte ove si stati le menti
Quete senza cercare imperio novo.
Mova vi la pietà perch' io mi movo;
Dando favore a quell' alma cittate,
Ove religion tanto si honora;
.Ove si vede ogn'hora,
Più chiaro il sol che per l'altre contrate.
Ivi temprando il raggio,
Fa assidua primavera, et dolce estate.
Ivi sempre son fior, non che nel maggio;
Ivi nasce ogni ingegno acuto e saggio.
  Una Nympha sepolta
  Si ritrovò nel placido paese,
  Ove visse, et lassò le belle spoglie.
  Et d'ella il nome prese
  La Città: nella qual cantò una volta
  Quel ch' a gli altri Latin la gloria toglie.
  Ogni vertute unita si raccoglie
  In quel luogo gentil, salubre, amico
  Di Nymphe e di Poete, e propria hospitio;
  Ne gli huomini giudicio
  Grave, e sottile; in donne il cor pudico
  Si vede, et d' honor degno.
  Togliasi dunque homai dal sceptro antico
  Ch' abhorrente di pace have l'ingegno
  Et la Gotica sterpe prenda il regno.
  A questo ultimo accento
  Le menti delli divi alte et profonde
    Restaron murmurando in vario assenso.
    Si come in mezzo l'onde
  Si suol sentire il suon del primo vento,
  Che di nocchieri il cor fa star sospenso.
  Ma chi può contradire al Padre immenso,
  Che con giusta ragion sempre si move?
  Dunque gli dei che forse eran discordi,
  Si monstraron concordi,
  Conoscendo il voler del sommo

Giove;

    Il qual nel suo conspetto
Si fe venir de l'anime più nove,
Et più tranquille, un bel numero elet-
to, Et diede un tal parlar dal sacro petto.
Ite voi felici Alme,
    Vestitevi di Regie membra humane,
Non
Non di materia di volgare schiera;
Prendete in vostre mane No. XVIII.
    Le gloriose et honorate palme;
Ite ad godere il regno che vi spera.
Et tu che prima ti dimostri altera,
Et sei per sorte prossima a la luce,
Sarai lo primo Alfonso in quella ter-
ra.
    Per te la cruda guerra j
Sarà conversa in pace, et sarai duce
Di gloria e di vertute. i
Regnarai longo tempo, essendo luce
Di ciechi, et de li languidi salute;
Facendo alto parlar le lingue mute.
Subito poi di questo
    Regnarai, tu fortissimo, animoso,
Del Aragonia gente eterno honore.
Et se' nanzi al riposo
S'apparecchia travaglio assai mo-
lesto,
Sarai pur finalmente vincitore.
Contr' al crudel barbarico furore
Tu starai salda inespugnabil torre;
Tal ch' al udir del tuo famoso nome,
Staranno hirte le chiome
Del gran nemico mio che'l cielo ab-
hor re.
    Et se prende ardir tanto
Che voglia di tua man l'imperio torre,
Io' 1 farò gir nel sempiterno pianto,
Del tribunal del Gnosio Rhadamanto.
Tu sei quel ch'ode spesso
    Parthenope, che dei scender volando
Adornato de palma, oliva, et lauro;
Tu sei quel gran Ferrando,
Da noi tante fiate a lei promesso,
Per dare al suo valor presto ristauro.
Per te dee rinovare un secol d' auro,
Qual per campi et città del regio Latio
In tempo di Saturno andar soleva.
Per te già si subleva
La vertu prisca, et fa di vitii stratio:
Jano tanto laudato
Che vide inanzi e dietro in breve spa-
tio,
Di tua prudentia vinto et superato,
Si potrà contentar sol del passato.

U Le porte del suo tempio,
NO. XVIII. Cjie sOgi;on pgr ja pace esser
serrate,
    Per tuo volere aprir non soffrirai.
Ma però ch' invidiate
Son le vertu de cui sarai 1' esemplo.
Noi potrano i vichi pater giamai.
Così strage mortai venir vedrai
De la guerra civile et intestina
Mossa di quel Soldan nocente et
vario,
    Manifesto adversario
Di gente singulare et pellegrina.
Costui con voglia accesa,
Sotto color de fare opra divina,
Contr' al imperio tuo pigliara impre-
sa; La qual con la mia man sara difesa.
Ch' alhor la providentia
    Volando al cor del principe Romano,
Chiamara per la pace un sauto et puro
Et nitido Pontano:
    Che vincera con la dolce eloquentia
Ogn'animo feroce, acerbo, et duro.
Costui ponendo lume al petto oscuro
Del promotor d horribili tumulti,
Unira insieme gli animi diversi.
Quest' è quel che con versi
    Di grandiloquo stil sonori et culti,
Et con ornate prose
Rimembrara dal cielo i varii vulti;
Poi discendendo nelle humane cose,
Dirà le tue vertu chiare et famose.
Ne mancaranno ingegni
    Imitator di questo altro Vergilio
Nel regno che t' aspetta sempre et
brama.
    Saìjnazar, Pardo, Altilio,
Summontio, di corymbo et laurea
degni,
    Faran cantando eterna la tua fama.
Tu che sai ben come la gloria s'ama,
Temprarai con amor la signoria;
Et con beneficentia et con giustitia,
Fuggendo l' amicitia
D'assentator, che vendon la bugia,
Et con atti soavi,
Al popol di ben far darai la via:
Ornando Ornando' 1 dreostumi hon-
esti et gravi,
Et con leggi emendando i modi pravi.
Con più tranquilla vista
    Mira quell' alme in muliebre gonna,
Ambedue caste et belle, ambe leggi-
adre.
Questa primiera Donna,

Benchè mostre la fronte mesta et trista,
Ti farà pur contento et lieto padre.
Questa sarà feconda altera madre
Di Re, d' Imperatori, et di Regine.
Nascer vedrai di questa alta et felice
Fruttifera radiee
    Multe piante gentili et pellegrine.
Et poi che sia arrivata,
Come nave nel porto, al suo bel fine,
Dal cieco career sciolta et liberata,
Ritornarà qua sù lieta et beata. L' al-
tra che vien dapoi
    Ch' ella havera lasciato il corpo
exangue,
    Sarà pur tua consorte amata et cara;
Di nobiltà di sangue
Et d' antiqua vertu giunta con voi.
Portarà teco il sceptro et la tiara.
Mira la vera forma ove s' impara
Come con castità beltà s' aduna,
Più eh' en donna d' honore et gloria
degna.
    Costei dolce, benegna,
Morigera, fidel, non importuna,
Ti da certa speranza
Di bella prole, et prospera fortuna.
Da costei nascerà quella sembianza
De la beltà del ciel, che l'altre avan-
za. Volgi indietro, et riguarda
    Quell' anima dignissima d' imperio
Del tuo seconda Alfonso, altro Gradi-
vo;
    Il qual nel regno Hesperio
Regnar dee nella età più saggia et tar-
da,
    Di poi che tu sarai mutato in divo.
Mirai' volto virile, audace, et vivo,
Vedi nel elmo 1' auree diademe;
Terror d' ogni barbarica phalange.
Da 1' aurora, o dal Gange
Alle Gade, del mondo parti extreme,
No. XVIII.
    Ne Ne simil ne secondo
Si vedri generar d' humano seme.
Nella pace humanissimo et giocondo,
Nela pugna superbo et iraconda.
Poi che'l misero Hydronto
    Da I' impia gente fia diretto et preso,
Et populate inerme ct d' improviso:
Questo interrito, acceso
D' un ardente vertute, et voler pronto,
Difendera 1' honor del Paradiso.
Anzi'l suo grave et animoso viso
Vedra cader la Plebe Machometa,
Et render la citta contra lor voglia.

Poi con 1 opima spoglia,

Intrando ovante nella patria lieta,

Et ringratiando i Dei,

Come pastor la gregge mansueta,

Menara presi l'inimici miei;

Carco d' honor, d'exuvie et di trophei. L' altra che segue l'orme,

Et nel solio Real si presto sicde

Ad ogni atto gentile ardita et presta,

Sara quel caro herede,

Di nome et di corraggio a te conforme,

Et de la vita Candida et modesta.

Non vedi lampeggiar sovra la testa

Un cometa ch' a voi vittoria mostra,

A la Francese indomita barbarie

Exitio et pesti varie?

D' animo più viril la casa vostra

Non fia mai che si vante.

Questo in battaglia, et in palestra, et in
giostra,

In lettere, et in opre humane et sante,

Sempre si mostrara forte et constante.

Vuò che qui si conscrbe

La gloriosa sterpe de li Goti

Con anime megliori et più perfette.

Li figli et li nepoti

Regnaran sempre, et le genti superbe

Domaran, perdonando a le soggette.

Tacque dipoi queste parole dette,

II Rettor del Olympo; alhor li Fati

Benigni, con le prospere fortune,

Fur d'un voler commune. XVIII. Al
suo parlar con volti chiari, et grati,
Ogn'un consente et fave; Si come usar
si suol ne' i gran senati, Che parlando
chi solo il poder have, Il minor volgo
applaude insieme et pave. Due porte
sono in quel celeste albergo, D'eterno
bene et di letitia pieno; L'una d'un ne-
gro et solido metallo; L'altra d' un bel
crystallo. Questa n' adduce il dì lieto
et sereno, Quella la notte ombrosa.
Dunque il Re che del mondo tene il
freno, Per la porta più chiara et lumi-
nosa Uscir fe quella schiera alta et
famosa.

N-XIX.

(*Vol.* i. *p.* 7S.)

*Tratti da Testo a penna di Fillenio Gal-
lo.*

SONETTO. *Phylenio al mandato libro.*

LIBRETTO et versi miei humili et bassi;

Rime silvestre et di dolcezza prive;

Composte al suon de le fresche acque

vive,

Fra fiere, sterpi, herbette, ucegli, et sassi;

Andate al mio Signor con prompti passi,

Che fra molti mortali, immortai vive,

Et dimonstrate come in queste rive,

Phylen, per lui servir parato stassi.

Et se tal opera ad lui fusse dischara,

Direte che ogni rivo, quasi asciutto,

Fangho produce ognihor, non acqua
chiara.

Pur una cosa mi conforta in tutto,

Che se la pianta (benche vii) fie cara,

Non debba con ragion sdegnare il frutto.

SONETTO.

*Phylento narra che Madonna gli parla
in sogno.*

Nel dolce sonno, alhor che i spirti e pol-
si

Son più leggieri, trovammi in seccho
prato,

Pensoso e mesto; ed eccho al dextro lato

Venir Madonna mia; onde io mi volsi,

E tremebundo una parola sciolsi,

"Che fai tu qui?" a che con volto irato

Nulla rispose, e'l capo havia chinato,

A guisa de hom che offende, teme, e
duolsi.

Caminava ella, ed io seguia el passo

Miser piangendo, e lei senza voltarse

Dissemi, "Indegno! ache pur prieghi un
sasso?"

Qui tacque; hor pensa s'el miser cor
arse;

Trovammi el pecto un fonte, e'l corpo
lasso:

Quando, a un tracio, e'l sonno e lei dis-
parse.

SONETTO.

*Phylenio scrive nullo accepto haver
grato senza Madonna.* QUANDO nel bel
paese ov' io son nato,

Fra parenti e amici arrivai sano;

Questo m' abbraccia, e quel toccha la
mano, Ciascun d' intorno a dir, sia'l ben
tornato;

Chi m'accarezza, e chi si mostra grato,

L' un benigno a me fassi, e 1' altro
humano;

Ayme! gli è ver, che honor e robba è
in vano; Ma contentarsi sol fa 1' hom
beato.

Guardavo spesso fra la turba intorno,

E non vedendo el bel Saphyr lucente,

Amar m'è stato ogni più lieto giorno.

Se non ch' io v' avia sculpta nella mente

Saria già morto avanti el mio ritorno,

Ne mi potea campar robba o parente.

SOVETTO. *Phylento biasma el vivcr
longamentc al Mondo.*

Lauda el vulgo insensato, e pien d' errore,

In questa vita numerar molli anni;

XIX

Ma non discerne ben quant' aspri affanni, E guai, trapassa chi in vecchiezza
more.

Felice c quel che escie del career fore

Prima che molti el pelo, e stracci e
panni;

Che chi compera ben l'acquisto a i
danni Trova corto el piacer, longho el
dolore.

Io el provo, e so che'l ciel si mi nutricha

Ch'io porto invidia a che è morto in
culla; Che stando el pesce in rete
ogn'hor più intricha.

O quanto chi più spera in van trastulla,

E cautamente el serpe in sen nutricha,

Poi nel fin Terror crcscie, e'l gaudio
h nulla.

N-XX.

. (*Vol.* i. *p.* 99.) Kestoris Dionysii No-
tariensis ordinis Minorum de observantia, ad Illustrissimttm princtpem
Lodovicum Sphortiam, in Opus ejus ex-
cellentice dieatum, versus incipit.'

Anguiger hunc princeps, tu qui auxil-
iaribus armis

Tutor ades Domino Mutinae,
Lodovice, libellum N-XX.

Accipe; quem tota tibi Nestor mente
dicavi.

Strenuus ut bellis, sic donis ipse Min-
ervae

Ingenioque valens, quando tibi quid
vacat oti,

Hunc legito, hoc curas post ardua
gesta levato.

Ardua gesta loquor, quls toto partus
in orbe

Semper honos, nomenque tuum,
laudesque manebunt.

Rebus nempe suis socium petit Itala
tellus;

Imprimis Xystus divus, summusque
sacerdos,

Te quoqne Parthenopes Rex, Hetrus-
cusque senatus,

Dux Mutinaeque socer, fluviique

Bononia Rheni.

Gaudet et ipsa tibi juncta esse Sabaudia, et urbis

D2' Inclitus Inclytus ipse novae princeps, et classe superba

Metropolis Ligurum; promptum teque excit in anna

Pro Socero, invicti magnum qui nomen adeptus

Herculis, iavisos, te preside, conteret ausus

Hostis, et Italia e dabis aurea tempora pacis.

Si quibus Ausoniis fama immortalis avorum est,

Principibus parti si sunt virtute triumph,

Ante alios leget ipsa tuos haec, posteraque aetas.

Ipse canet pugnas vates, et fortia dicet

Praelia, teque, tuasque sonabit carmine paknas.

Perge igitur; superosque habeas ad vota secundos.

Di tibi dent gazas Arabum, dent Nestoris annos,

Fortunam Augusti, et sceptra imperiosa Monarchal;

Armatasque meo hoc finnes sermone catervas.

Hectorei socii mecum durate sub armis.

Sacra etenim (si fas tamen est) per numina juro,

Stamina si geminos Lachesis mihi nerit in annos

Imperitanti, hostes cogam stricto ense subactos

Lingere humum coram, et saeva prae strage dare herbas.

Tunc omnes spoliis, tunc et fulgentibus armis,

Electis pariter et equis, opibusque superbis

Donabo; ac magno (durate age) semper honore.

Hinc bellis, picta inde jocis, fulvisque micanti

(Dona ubi pensa) tholis, mecum dignabor in aula.

Jamque vale; studioque vacet mens alta salubri;

Aspiresque tuo, Princeps clarissime, vati,

Fratrum apud Excelsum precibus servande meorum.

No-XXI.

(Vol. i.p. 102.J
Ad Galeativm Btntwolum, de imagine Codn.

DITIBUS in thalamis quos tu, clarissime Princeps, Ornasti vivis nuper imaginibus,

Me quoque jussisti sapientum vivere coetu,

Et meditabundo dicta notare statu.

Me noscunt, plauduntquc mihi quicunque tuentur,

Inventumque probant, vir memorande, tuum.

Ast ego quid contra faciam? quae dona rependam?

Quod dignum tanto munere munus erit?

Si vatum nunquam pereunt monumenta piorum, Si rapiunt Stygia, quos voluere domo,

Tu quoque de nostris semper cantabere chartis,

Deque meo semper carmine vivus eris.

Bentivolus mihi carmen eric Galeatius ille,

Cui similem non fert Ausonis ora virum.

Per mea te noscent brachati carmina Medi,

Per mea te noscet carmina foris Iber.

Et Notus et Boreas gaudebunt nomina tanti

Principis in populos missa fuisse suos.

Mille canes alii quaerunt, totidemque biformes

Mulas, tu claros quaeris habere viros: guaesitos et habes, et scis retinere paratos Muneribusque tuis, ingenioque tuo.

Ille inhiat gemmas, atque auro congerit aurum

Pauper, et assiduo.stat vigil usque metu.

Tu tua firma locas in amicis horrea fidis,

Atque tuas illos esse fateris opes:

Tu sequeris prudens hominum vestigia, at ille

Stultus de stulto carpere discit iter.

Nil igitur mirum si te fratresque paterque

Laudant, ct de te gaudia magna ferunt.

Nec mirum, si praecipue te stipat euntem,

Qui valet arte aliqua, qui valet ingenio.

Tu certe tanquam sis funis Homericus

ille,

Aureus e ccelo missus in arva nites:

Aut tanquam Photbo cum descendente, coruscum

Hesperus ardenti spargit ab ore jubar.

Obruitur Codrus tanto, clarissime Princeps,'

Splendore, &: coeco lumine tentat iter. Aut Jovis, aut Phoebi rutilantis lumen habendum est

Codiv. tui si vis ceniere facta facta Ducis: Aut alio flectenda acies, ne more volantis Pyraustae in magnam lampada forte ruas.

(Vol. i. p. 106.) Petri Criniti, de sua cegritudine et imminenti ohlu. NIL est quod ultra sit licitum mihi

Sperare tandem, nil medicze manus

Ex imminenti me miserum rogo

Referre incolumem queunt. Et jam medullis aestuat intimis

Accensa bilis, nec patitur meo

Unquam dolori finem aliquem dari,

Sed vexat magis in dies. Obducta front is lumina, per genas

Delapsa tetra cum macie cutis,

Et destitute mentis inertia, Instare exitium monent.

O quantum inanes illecebrae anxia

Passim virorum pectora distrahunt!

Quantaque rerum mole perastuat Humani generis lues!

Quam saepe dixi, Martia principum

Cantabo gesta, et saeva per Ausones

Gallorum ab altis alpibus agmina Educta in Latios duces!

At nunc parato funere frigid us

Per membra sudor labitur: et meum

Flammis cadaver rite puer sacris Jam componere destinat.

Et Cypri odores, thuraque mascula

Inferre lectis ossibus, et levi

Cum rore lymphas spargerc, quo sua Reddatur cineri quies.

Ergo sub annos pravirides mihi

Solvetur atro sanguine spiritus?

Nil est reluctandum superis: libens

Quod fata annuerint sequor. Non ille cuiquam flebilis occidit,

Quem vitae honestas, et fidei decor

Inter sacrarunt numina Caelitum, Expertem gravis ambitus.

Sed fessa tandem lumina mors tegit:

Tu me, Deorum summe Parens, velis

Vatem beatis sistere sedibus,

Ut sacros referam choros.

No XXIII.

(Vol. i.p. 117.J

Ex orig. in Archiv. Palat. Reipub. Fior.

Magnifico Viro Vetro de Medicis, fratri meo carissimo. Fiorendo;.

Magnifice frater &c. Per questa poco m' accade se non significarti, che sono sano, quale in tanto vulnere decet; paulatim tamen me ex dolore, quantum in me est, colligo. Sed N-XXIII.

haec missa, ne vulnus exacerbem. Ho alcune tua, per le quali intendo l'animo et la voglia tua. Nil eorum, quae petis, adhuc factum est; terrotti tamen avvisato del processo di tutto d' hora in hora. Così di questo, come d' ogni altra mia cosa, fa anche tu quello medesimo; che non posso havere cosa più grata, che intendere spesso di voi nuove, et come stiate tutti; sicchè non t'incresca tenermene avisato. Questo voglio aggiugnere, che intendendo, che forse s' harà a mutare el Proposto di San Giovanni, ti voglio raccomandare Ser Francesco della

Torre, quale è stato per me uno pezzo a Miramondo, et essi portato molto bene; et credo questo sarà proprio un luogo da lui, sicchè te lo raccomando. Preterea bisogna che io ti raccomandi Francesco degli Albizi, che desiderebbe che tu lo facessi sedere Gonfaloniere questo Maggio; faramene piacere facendolo, perchè ho qua uno suo figliuolo, che mi serve bene: volendolo fare, ti prego, gli facci intendere, te lo raccomandato, di che me ne ri.

metto a te. Per altra mia ti scriverò qualche cosa; per hora basti quello ti scrivono gi'

Imbasciatori, et questo. Raccomandami a te, et saluta tutta la brigata per mia parte, conteregli tutti, se non che el foglio non basterebbe. Non altro.

Tuus Io. Fr. *Jiomce diexix. Aprilis,* 1492.

io-XXIV. *(Vol.* i. *p. 118.J*

Ex Orig. in Archiv. Palat. Reipub. Florent.

Magnifico Viro Petro de Medicis, majori meo observandissimo. florent kc.

MAGNIFICO Piero mio hon. Questa mattina essendo invitati li Cardinali all' officio, et

Messa in cappella per la benedictione delle palme; congregati, che furono tutti, *ci* ante No-XXIV.

Missarum solemnia, Nostro Signore li chiamò dentro nella audientia sua secreta, et quivi presente tutto il Collegio pubblicò, et dichiarò Monsre. vostro Fratello fegato del

Patrimonio; nè vi potrei dire quanto è stata grata questa demonstratione a tutta questa

Corte, et Città. Dipoi Nostro Signore andò in Captila, et benedisse le palme, et celebrossi,

una una Messa; la quale Enita, Monsre. nostro Rmo. parti, ct fu accompagnato da tutto il ColN0' XXIV leS' 'ns'no a casa' co11 grandissimo honore, ct fu cosa bella a vedere. Giunta arrivo qui hiersera, lui ct Mariotto, et si raccomanda alia M. V. ct io insieme. Bene vale. *Roma, die* xv. *Aprilis,* 1492.

Erami scordato di dirvi, come Nostro Signore stamani era frescho e bello come una rosa, e ha dato il mal' anno a più d'uno. Non sari fuori di proposito, che voi confortiate Monsre. a curare con ogni diligentia di stare sano, e voglia al più che puo, d' accomodarsi al vivere secondo che fanno li altri Cardinali. Questodico, perche bisogna levarsi la mattina per tempo, e chi vegghia la sera, assai male lo puo fare: Saria pericolo col tempo non li facessi nocimento; questo non dico sanza cagione.,.

Serv. Stephanus De Castrocabo.

N-XXV.

(Vol. i. *p.* 141.; *Acta Eruditorum, an.* 1710. *p.* 18.

Historic de Bretagne.

Auct. Guidone Alexia Lobineau. ii. *Tomes. Par. 1707, Fo.*

Sed facere non possumus, quin ad nuptias, quas Anna Britannica, in qua linea Ducalis No. XXV. defecit, primum cum MaximilianoRomanorum, et mox, eo quidem adhuc vivo, cum Carolo Gallorum rege contraxit, paulisper subsistamus.

Sunt autem in hac historia duae quaestiones facti, a quibus totius causae justitia dependet, quarum prior est *An Maximilianus matrimonium aim Annd contractum consummaverit f* posterior *An hcec Sponsa vel Uxor Maximiliani*

a Carolo Gallorum rege (viii) *rapta fuerii?*

Quod prius concernit, Autor non negat, nuptias cum Maximiliano a. 1490. solennissime, sed per procuratores saltem, fuisse consummatas: *Legatum autem primarium, postquam nova nupta in thalamo fuisset collocata, cubiculum cum Uteris procurationis ingressum, et astantilms muUis tarn viris quam fxminis primariis, tibiam suam ad genu usque 'nudatam, inter lintea nuptialia inseruisse, ut catrimonia illa consummationi et cognitioni actuah eequipoliereputaretur.* Ipse quidem autor non affirmat, mentionem tamen, velut in transitu injicit, quod Baco de Verulamio in vita Henrici VII. singulare hoc rei gestae monumentum annotaverit: neque quicquam praterea addit, ex quo Verulamii relatio vel confirmari vel in dubium vocari queat. Ad alteram qustionem quod attinet, si bene Autorem nostrum assecuti assecuti sumus, inter coactionem physlcam et politicam distinguere videtur. Ncmpe de crassa illa violentii, qua Anna, cum iter ad Maximilianum jam esset ingressa, in finibus Hannonia e ab armata multitudine circumventa, et obtorto velut collo ad Carolum raptata, rerum Austriacarum scriptoribus quibusdam dicitur, altum in hoc opere est silentium Sed coactionem tamen subtilem intercessisse, adeo non inficiatur Lobinovius, ut etiam suspicetur, Pontificem Romanum non sine causa consensum suum in Uteris, quarum copiam facit, sub hie conditione declarasse: *dummodo illustrissima Anna propter hoc rapta nonfuerit.* No-XXVII.

Ceterum, quod tum optasse dicitur Maximilianus, *ut ex hoc monstro nuptiarum, quod ex raptH et adulterio compositum esset, nulla vnquam in Gallia regnet posteritas,* ejus voti damnatum fuisse Imperatorem, ex tabulis Genealogicis in vulgus notum est.

No XXVI.

(Vol. i. p. 152.)

DalF Opere tolgari di Cariieo.

CANZONE. FULGORE eterno, & gloria d' Aragona,

Heroe grande in fama, in arme ingente,

N-XXVI.

Fautor sol, anzi autord'ogni vertute;
Hor t' ha condotto a la real corona
La potestà de la divina mente,
Per conservarne in pace, & in salute.
Hor piace servitute
A tutti quei, ch'han libertade in pregio.
Per te, Re pio, magnanimo, & perfetto,
Et per natura, Sc per ragione eletto,
La libertade honora il nome Regio.
Che tue vertu pensando & ripensando,
Avegna che non fussi il primo figlio
Di quel divo Flu Has Do,
Saresti Re, s' al mondo e buon con-
siglio.
Lo strenuo cor, clemente, altero, k sag-
gio,
Che tl.il un sole al altro il nome spande,
In espettatione ha posto il mondo;
Tal ch'io non so, qual petto o qua! cor-
aggio
Potesse superar la speme grande,
Salvo il tuo primo a nullo altro secondo.
Tu grave, tu giocondo;
Vol i. E A cui
A cui piaccion gli affanni in opre sante,
Et nel oprar consiglio. O alma invitta,
Sola difension di gente afflitta, Nel peri-
col magior salda k constante; Nelle difficulty d' arguto ingegno, Et non di fero
cor nelle vittorie; Ma più dolce k beneg-
no; Vertuti veramente Imperatorie. Il
tuo chiaro conspetto, allegro k grave,
Che più ch' altro mortai reluce e
splende, De le vertù favor, del vitio
scorno, Atterra col suo sol le genti
prave; Si come con suoi raggi Apollo
offende Gli augei, che van fuggendo il
chiaro giorno. Hor è nel suo soggiorno
Apollo con le nove alme sorelle; Hor
quella insigne, sacra, alta dottrina, Chia-
mata humanhà, sola, divina, Ferirà con
la testa 1' auree stelle. Le selve Antini-
ane in varii canti, Risonaran la gloria de
gli Alfonsi; Et d' inelyti Ferranti; Et le
valli daran dolci responsi. Se l'un più
ch' altro human fu liberale, Et 1' altro forte, k pien di sapiehtia, Et come
Jano tien gemino viso; Hor vedemo in
un solo al sole eguale, De la vertu celeste esperientia Ch' aggualia li mortali
al paradiso.. Letitla, plauso, k riso, Si
celebre, ch'or tene il regno Ausonio Un
principe, anzi un dio, tra gli' altri humani, Ch' Italia liberò da Turchi im-
mani. Hydrunto, Europa, el mondo è

testimonio, Come costui, intrepido, animoso, Vinse del cielo gli nemici rei;
Poi venne glorioso; Carco d'honor,
d'exuvie k di trophei. Hor altrui t' ap-
parecchia un' altra gloria. Se cerca
provocar i Galli adversi A la quiete Ital-
ica imminenti; O tu riporterai lieta vit-
toria, O tu unirai in pace i cor diversi;
Come natura accorda gli elementi, Si
varii k differenti.
Chi non ritenerasi intro le porte,
Vedendo un Re degnissimo d' imperio,
Regnar nel regno Hcsperio?
Vedendo un novo Duca invitto & forte,
In forza & gagliardia altro Pelide,
In arme 8c in amor novo Gradivo
Quel mio Aragonio Alcide;
Di cui 1' inclyta fama io canto e scrivo.
Ne le sideree sedi "'i
Volando, andrai Canzon con bianche
penne
Di quella verita che ti conduce.
Vedrai vi d' Aragon la nova luce:
Ch' è ritornata in cielo ond 'ella venne.
Digli che con ragion può rallegrarsi,
D' haver sua parte nei celesti regni.
Ma più dee gloriarsi
Di veder in honor, suoi dolci pegni.
    No-XXVII.
(Voi. i. p. 156.)
Dair Opere Volgari, di Sanazzaro. p. 60.
CANZONE.
Incliti spirti, a cui fortuna arride
    Quasi benigna, e lieta,
    Per farvi al cominciar veloci, e pron-
ti;.'
    Ecco, che la fua torbida inquieta
    Rota par che vi affide;
    E vi spiani dinanzi e fossi, e monti:
    Ecco, ch' a vostre fronti
    Lusingando promette or quercia, or
lauro;
    Pur ch' al suo temerario ardir vi ac-
corde.
    Ahi menti cieche, e sorde,
    De' miseri mortali; ahi mal nut' auro;
    Qual mai degno restauro
    Esser può di quel sangue
    Del qual la terra già bagnata suda?
    E della schiera esangue,
    Ch' erra senza sepolcri afflitta, e nu-
da?
    E 2 Voi,
    Voi, che sempre fuggendo il vulgo
sciocco,

E 1 suo perverso errore,
Tutte le antiche carte avete volte;
Se racquistar cercate in vita onore,
E per coturno, o socco
Sperate d' illustrar 1' ossa sepolte;
Acciocchè il mondo ascolte
Vostri nomi, più bei dopo mill' anni,
Drizzate al ver cammin gli alti consigli;
E, come giusti figli,
Il vecchio padre, ch' or sospira i danni,
Liberate ó? affanni:
Che se mai pregio eterno
Per ben far s' acquistò con lode e gloria;
Questo (s' io ben discerno)
Farà di voi qua giù. lunga memoria.
Or, che'l vento v' aspira; e vostra nave
Ha saldi arbori e sarte,
Sarebbe il tempo da ritrarvi in porto:
Che poi, lasso, non vai 1' ingegno, o 1'
arte
Nella tempesta grave;
Quando'l miser nocchier già stanco, e
smorto,
Non trova altro conforto
Che di voltarsi a Dio con umil pianto,
Lodando 1' ozio, e la tranquilla vita.
Dunque, se'l ciel v' invita
Ad un viver sicuro, onesto, e santo,
Non v' induri il cor tanto
L' odio, lo sdegno, e 1' ira;
Ch' al ben proprio veder vi appanne gli
occhi;
Che spesso in van sospira
Chi per sua colpa avvien ch' al fin tra-
bocchi.
Rare fiate il Ciel le cagion giuste
Indifese abbandona;
Benchè forza a ragion talor contrasti.
Indi (se'l ver per fama ancor risuona)
Le sue mura combuste
Vide al fin Troja, e i tempj rotti, e
guasti,
E tanti spirti casti
    Per uno incesto a ferro, e a foco mes-
si:
Nè questa sol, ma mille altre vendette
Ch' avete udite, e lette;
Popoli alteri al fin pur tutti oppressi.
    Deh questo or fra voi stessi (Ma con
più fausto inizio)
    Signor, pensate; e se ragion vi danna,
    Non vogliate col vizio
    Andar contra vertù; che error v' in-
ganna. L' alto, e giusto Motor, che tutto
vede,

E con eterna legge
Tempra le umane, e le divine cose,
Siccome ci sol là su governa e regge,
£ solo in alto siede
Fra quelle anime elette, e luminose;
Cosi qua giù propose
Chi de' mortali avesse in mano il freno:
Che mal senza rettor si guida barca.
Però con 1' alma scu ta
Di sospetto, e di sdegni, e col cor pieno
D' un piacer dolce ameno,
Al vostro stato primo
Ritornate: e'l voler del ciel si segua:
Che, s' io non falso estimo,
Tempo non vi fia poi di pace, o tregua. Quella real, possente, intrepid' alma
Che da benigne stelle
Fu qui mandata a rilevar la gente,
Con sue vertù vi muova invitte, e belle,
Ch' ebber si chiara palma
Del barbarico popol d' Oriente,
Allor che sì repente
Col solito furor la Turca rabbia
Ne' nostri dolci liti a predar venne,
Là 've poscia sostenne
Il giusto giogo, in stretta, e chiusa gabbia.
Che se di tanta scabbia
Il nostro almo paese
Per sua presenzia sol fu scosso, e net-to;
Che fia di vostre imprese,
Se contra voi pur arma il sacro petto?
Nè vi muova, per Dio, che'l Tebro, e 1' Arno
Tra selve orrende, e dumi,
A bada il tegnan; che speranza è vana.
Ritardar noi potran monti, nè fiumi;
Che mai non spiega indarno
Quella insegna felice, e più ch' umana.
La qual così lontana
No. XXVII. (Se si confessa il ver) tim-or vi porge; £ con l'immagin sua vi tur-ba il sonno.
Onde, se i fati ponno
Quel che per veri effetti ognor si scorge;
Quanto più in alto sorge
L' error che a ciò v' induce,
Tanto fia del cader maggior la pena:

Che tal frutto produce
Ostinato voler, che non s' affrena.
Così sola, ed inerme
Come parti, Canzon, senz' altra scorta,
(Benchè ingegni vedrai superbi, e schivi)
Di '1 vero, ovunque arrivi;
Che'n cielnostra ragion non è ancor morta.
E se pur ti trasporta
Tanto innanzi la voglia;
Rimordendo lor cieco, e van desire,
Digli ch'en pianto, e doglia,
Fortuna volge ogni sfrenato ardire.
    N XXVIII.
(Voi. i. p. 159.;
Dair Opere volgari di Canteo.
CANZONE. QUAL odio, qual furor, qual ira immane,
No. XXVIII. 2uai Panete maligni,
    Han vostre voglie unite hor si divise?
Qual crudeltà vi move, o spirti insigni,
O alme Italiane,
    A dare il Latin sangue a genti invise?
    Non sian homai si fise
Le vostre menti, in voglie in foco ac-cese,
    D' esser superiori a vostri eguali.
    O cupidi mortali,
    S' ardente honor vi chiama ad alte imprese,
Ite a spogliar quel sacro almo paese
Di Christian trophei.
    Et tu, santa, immortal, Saturnia terra,
    Madre d' huomini Se dei, N-XXVIII.
    Nei barbari converti hor 1' impia guerra. O mal concordi ingegni, o da prim' anni,
    Et da le prime cune,
    Abhorrenti da dolce Se lieta pace;
    Perchè correte in un voler comune
    A li comuni danni,
    Et in comune colpa il mal vi piace?
    Perchè non vi dispiace
    Tinger nel proprio sangue hor vostre spade?
    Fu questo dato già dal fato eterno,
    Quando 1' sangue fraterno
    Tinse'l muro di quella alma cittade,
    Con quella fera invidia Se impietade?
    Et hor qual morbo insano
    Ha pollute le membra giunte in uno?
    L' una con 1' altra mano
    Pugna, senza sperar triompho alcuno.
    Se ciò che per vertu far si devria

    Si fa sol per argento,
    Et non per gloria mai guerra s' im-prende,
    Quanto mal può sperarsi ogni memento
    Da liga o compagnia
    Di cui lo proprio honor vende Se rivende.
    Io so che tal mi intende,
    Che per *V* orecchi tene un Iupp inico;
    Che'l lasciar nel tener non gli è securo.
    O petto immite Se duro,
    Contra li tuoi, di tuoi nemici amico;
    Come non ti sovien del odio antico,
    Che col primo Parente
    Nacque? perchè non aspiri ad un bel at-to?
    Che con perfida gente
    E perfidia servar promessa o patto.
    Che maladetta sia di quel Sydonio
    L' ombra perversa e sonte,
    Perfida alma crudel, superba Se dura;
    La qual de l' Alpe roppe il devio monte,
    Et nel bel piano Ausonio
    Scese per forza, Se fe si gran paura.
    Che già 1' alma natura
    Hayea munita la bella planicie
        Contra
        Contra '1 superbo Gallico furore.
XXVIII. Hor l'infinito ardore D' imperio, hor le private inimicitie,
Han la via trita in publica pernicie.
    Nulla cosa si mostra
    Difficile a mortali; il ciel teniamo
    Con la stultitia nostra;
    rulmina Giove, Se noi non paventamo.
    Non parlo per cagion del proprio affan-no;
    Ch' en questa humil fortuna
    Riposo più che gli altri in sommo impe-rio.
    Ne mi move a parlar paura alcuna
    D' alcun privato danno,
    Ma sol di pace ardente desiderio.
    Che nel bel campo Hesperio,
    Di monarchia io veggio un Duca degno,
    De la preclara sterpe d' Aragona,
    Ch aspecta aurea corona,
    Non sol del proprio suo ma d'altrui reg-no.
    Et duolmi che tal è de pena indegno
    Che havra dolor diversi.
    Che'l picciol sempre geme per discordia
    Di grandi, et non dolersi
    De mal d'altrui, mi par somma vecor-

dia.

Ben fu senza pietà qel ferreo petto,
Quel animo feroce,
   Che fu inventor del ferro horrendo &
forte.
Dallhora incominciò la pugna atroce
La venenosa Aletto;
   » Et di più breve via per l'impia
morte
Aperse le atre porte.
Ma non fu in tutto colpa di quel primo;
Che ciò che lui trovò col bel sapere
Incontro a 1' aspre fere,
Noi nelli nostri danni hor convertimo.
Questo advien (se'l falso io non estimo)
Di fame di thesoro,
Ch' ogni petto mortai tene captivo.
Che pria che fusse 1' oro,
Non era il ferro al huom tanto nocivo.
Ai pace, ai ben di buon si desiato,
Alma pace *k* tranquilla,
Per cui luce la terra, e'1 ciel profondo;
   Pace
    Pace d' ogni citade, *&l* d' ogni villa,
    D' ogni animal creato NO. XXVIII.
Letitia, & gioia del siderio mondo;
Mostra il volto giocondo,
Et con la spica e i dolci frutti in seno,
D' Italia adombra 8c 1' una *k* 1' altra ri-
va
Con la frondente oliva;
Et in questo amenissimo terreno
Di Napol, dove '1 cielo è più sereno,
Ferma i tuoi piedi gravi,
Facendone fruir quiete eterna.
Et con secure chiavi
Chiude la guerra a la pregione inferna.
Canzon, tra'l Pado *k V* Alpe
Vedrai quel disdegnoso Duca altero,
   Che di pace & di guerra in man le
habene
    Così il ciel vole) hor tene.
   Digli che voglia homai vedere il vero,
   E svegliar quel santissimo pensero
   Di publica salute;
   Che per moderne & per antique histo-
rie,
   S' acquista per vertute,
   Et non per signoria, la vera gloria.
   No XXIX.
(Voi. i. p. 6.)
Vergìcr d' honnevr. Entre autres Gorre
que faicl a racompter par excellence
pluf que chose du monde, sau s cn ce
cas me vouloir mesconter, laisser ne

veulx de dire et racompter;
Le beau maintien, la maniere faconde,
La grant beaulte, la constancc feconde,
D'une acouchee si tresbien composce,
Que brief nature sa semblable ou sec-
onde
N'a de son temps sur la terre posee,
Pour demonstrer le triumphe des dames
Au noble Roy naturel pere d'elles;
Semblablement a ses nobles gendarmes
Qui en tous lieux tant de corps comme
dames
Vol. I. F
   De
   De leur honneur soubscient lea
querelles.
Elles choisirent la plus belle d'entre
elles,
Et sur ung hourt en ung beau lict
couchee,
Soubz couvertures que point n'en est de
telles
La firent mettre ainsi q'une acouchce
Le ciel du lit fut d'ung fin drap d'or
vert,
Larges rideaulx de demas figure;
Le demeurant d'ung cramoisy couvert,
Et pouvoit on veoir tout a descouvert
Ung personnaige de grace bien heuree,
Ung doulx visaige si tresbien mesure
Que mieulx n'eust sceu, vermeil et non
paly;
Somme dedans l'on se fust bien mire
Tant estoit cler firez luysant et poly.
D'ung fin veloux cramoysy avoit
manches,
Pelissonnes de martres subelines,
Ses couleurs furent violettes et blanch-
es,
Parmy posees bagues de haultes branch-
es
Pour faire avoir les fievres jaquelines,
Gros dyamans, turquoyses, cornalines,
Perles de pris grandement estimee,
Pour decorer ses doulceurs femenines
De toutes pars elle estoit sursemee.
Aux deux costez du chevet de son lict
On avoit mis deux grans carreaux d'or
trait;
Et soubz son lict pour singulier delict
Deux d'aultrc sorte d'une figure eslit,
Qu'onque au pays de telz n'en fut retret.
Homme visaige ne vit jamais pourtrait,
De marbre blanc, d'alebastre, ou painc-
ture,

Si beau, si net, si gentement extraict,
Que lors avoit celle humble creature.
Aux quatre boutz des carreaulx et cou-
verte
Avoit boutons, monchetz, houpes es-
tranges;
Et pour mieulx voir la gorre descouverte
D'ung or de cypres avecques soye verte,
Et force perles, furent faictes les
franges.
Autour *h* dame ung tas de faces d'anges
Plus que deesses ou sibilles plaisantes,
Pour confermer toutes haultes louanges
On le tenoit trop plus que souflrisantes.
Devant le lict estoit le jeune enfant,
Beau a merveilles, sans pleur et sans
efFroy;
   D'acoustremen D'acoust remens
qu'on billebarre et fend,
   Le plus gorrier et le plus triumphant
No. XXIX.
   Qu'on vit jamais fusse le fils du roy.
   Pres de luy fut en singulier arroy
   Une tres belle gracieuse nourrice,
   Bien acoustre sans faire aulcun
destoy
   D'ung veloux vert tissu de haulte
tice.
Dames sans nombre a faces angeliques,
Bien acoustrees de drap d'or et satin;
Verges, carcans, bordures auctentiques,
Gros dyamans et saphirs magnifiques,
Pour enricher la gorge et le tetin.
La robbe longue, le gorgias patin,
Le corps trousse frisquement de
velours.
C'estoit assez, qui entend mon latin,
Pour y avoir ung tribunal d'amours.
A resjouyr l'affection humaine,
La voyoit on gorre desmesurees,
Tant en beaulte qu'en richesse
haultaine;
Oncques ne Tut si sumptueux demaine
Pour veoir autant de choses decorees.
Grans escussons a fleurs de lys dorce
Sur l'eschauffault a dextre et a senestre,
Gettans fumes de senteurs odorees,
Somme, c'estoit ung paradis terrestre.
Devant le roy ce mystere fut fait;
Tant qu'avec luy ny avoit creature
A regarder lordre de tel effect,
Qui ne fust lors royaulment et de fait
Quasi substrettes es oeuvres de nature.
Au jugement d'humaine conjecture,
Que cueur desire et l'oiel appete a voir,

Pour contenter ung homme par droicture

Possible n'est de mieulx au monde avoir.

N XXX.

(Vol. i.p. 67.) Ex. Monument. Ang. Fabronii, in vita Leon. X. Magnifici Patres honorancli.

Io non piglio altra scusa con V. M. di questa mia subita partita, perchè non credo dovere essere imputato o ripreso di quello, che secondo l'animo mio et debile judicio, mi è parso el più salutifero rimedio a conservatione della quiete della mia patria, e di manco impedimento dello universale et pericolo d'ogni altri, da me in fuori, et manco disagio a tutte le occorrentie presenti, parendomi coll' offerirmi in persona alla M. Xma. di Francia, poter meglio sedare l' ira o odio havessi conceputa contro cotesta città, o stato di quella, per le opere conservate sino a qui ad istanzia della vostra fede et oblighi verso altri. Perchè seS.M. Xina. non vuole altro che la mutazione delle operazioni vostre, Io che ne sono stato incolpato, o me ne purgherò con S. M. Xma. o ne piglierò conveniente supplicio più presto in la persona mia che in cotesta Rep. Per la quale, ancora che simile opera sia peculiare già fatta di casa mia, mi pare essere tenuto molto più ad affaticarmi che e mia predecessori, per essere io stato molto più sopra e meriti miei honorato che gli altri, che quanto mancho ne sono stato degno, più me obliga a questo che fo al presente, et a non perdonare mai a fatica, disagio o spesa fino alla morte inclusive. La quale mi reputerei a beneficio se la spendessi per ciascun di voi in particulare, e tanto più per l' universale di cotesta città, come me ingegno fare al presente, che o ne reporterò el contento et vostro et della città, o vi lascierò la vita. In tanto prego le M. V. per la fede et affectioue debbono alle ossa del vostro Lorenzo, mio padre, et lo amore havete conservato verso di me, non manco figliuolo vostro che suo in riverenza et affectione, siate contenti fare pregare Dio per me, et havere per raccomandati miei fratelli et figliuoli, de' quali se a Dio piace ch' io non torni, ne fo a tutti voi testamento, et me in-

sieme con loro vi raccomando. Io partirò di qui domattina *toc. Di V. M.Jgliuofo,*

Piero De' Medici. *In Empoli, die 2fi. Octobris,* 1494.

No-XXXI.

(Vol. i. p. 169.)

Ex. Monument. Ang. Fabronii, in vita Leon. X.

A Pietro Bibiena.

Pregovi di fare intendere al mio magnifico Mess. Marino, che poi che mio padre morì, No. XXXI b strv'lo con quella fedele affectione la M. del Sig. Re Alph. ed il suo padre, che mi è suta suta possibile, e mi sono condocto tanto in la con qnesta devotione, che ora come intenderete trahor ad immolandum, et questo e perche abbandonato da tutti cittadini Fiorentini amici et N-XXXI.

inimici miei, non mi bastando più ne la reputatione, ne li denari; ne il credito a sostenere la gucrra acccpta sponte in casa, ho preso per partito, non potendo servire colle forze (le quali jam defecerunt) alla M. del Sig. Re Alph. servirli almanco colla disperatione, la quale mi conduce a darmi in potere del Re di Francia senza condizione o speranza di bene al cuno, se non di havere mess la vita dopo le altre cose mie per quello a chi me reputavo / obbligatissimo, e mi reputerò dum vivam. Pregherete S. M. sc degni excusarmi con la

M. del Re, se prima non li ho fatto intendere questo mio concepto, che ne e suto cagione el non essere prima in necessita tale, ne mai havermi pensato per non havere mai difhdato in tanti amici, et in una tale citta come e Firenze, et me excusi S. M. che non sono el primo infermo che si conduce all' extrema untione sanza conoscersi mortale. In somma direte questo, che anche infermo conserverò la fede mia al S. Re Alph. et forse li saro più utile servitore appresso il Re di Francia, che nel primo luogo dello Stato, che e si debole a Firenze, e se ben hora io offendo in qualche parte S. M. lo To contra mia voglia, et forzato:

Prometteteli che sentira aliquando fidem immaculatam ancora in quest' alto di Piero de'

Medici: simile pregate S. M. faccia coll' Exc. del mio Duca di Calabria, e me li raccomandi humilmente.

Pisii die 27. Oct. 1494. N XXXII.

(Vol. i. p. 174.;

Ex Orig. in Archie. Reip. Flor.

Hoc est Invevtarium Librorum, *qui inventi sunt inter Libros Domini* Anceli Poli-

Tiani, *quos secernendo extraxit inde Dominus* Johannes Laschari *Graecus, ex commissione*

Dominorum; coram Domino Theodoro et coram Domino Barthohmceo de Crau; quod

inventarium confectum fuit in domo Petri de Medicis, die xxiv. *Octobris,* 14y5. *ut patet in*

originali.

Aristotelis Poetica, et quaedam alia, in Graeco. *in Papyro.*

Galeni de compositione pharmacorum. *in Papyro.* in Graco.

Petri Hispani, Dialectica et quaedam alia, in Gracum de Latino versa, *in Papyro.*

Leges quaedam, cum glossis. *In Membrana.* glossulae vero sunt in marginibus.

Omeliae Johannis Grisostomi. in Graeco.

Servius, in Virgilium. *in Membrana.* Latinus codex.

Aristotelis de Mundo, in Graeco; simul cum Polemonis meditationibus, et Aristotelis Metaphysicis. in *Papyro.*

Compendium trium Librorum Oribasii; factum per Haetium. *in Papyro.*

Instituta, in Graeco. *in Papyro.*

Xpistola: Epistolae Theodori Lascbaris. *In Papyro.* In Graeco.

N. XXXII. Actuarii opusde Medicina, de Urinis; in Graeco. *in Papyro;* et Galeni quaedam.

Galeni quaedam in Medicina, et ejusdem liber de dicto Auctore, in Graeco *in Papyro.*

Alexander Tralianus, in Medicina, in Graeco. in *Papyro.*

Liber Galeni in Medicina; cujus primum capitulum de Cardiacis. *in Papyro. In asseri bus, sine operimento.* In Graeco.

Galeni de compositione pharmacorum. *in Papyro.* Signatus NO. 225. Graeco.

Liber Galeni in Medicina; in Graeco. in *Papyro.* habens primum capitulum de Theriacis Alexipharmicis. *In asseribus, non opertus.* Signatus N-223.

Galenus de usu particularum in homine, et liber ejusdem de pulsibus. *in Papyro.* et

Graeco. Signatus NO. 215.

Priscianus quidam antiquum, in *Membrana.* Signatus No. 347. Latinus.

Priscianus iterum antiquus. *in Membrana.* No. 626. Latinus.

Demosthenis Orationes. Graecae. in *Papyro.*

Historia Zonar£. in *Papyro.* In Graeco.

Galeni de pharmacis, secundum genus. In Graeco. in *Papyro.* NO-2J8

Pedacii Dioscoride Anazarbis, in Graeco. Liber de materia, *in Papyro.* Signatus No, 230.

Compendium Philosophiae Georc.ii Protertioi. In Graeco. *in Papyro.*

Aristotelis Metaphysica parumper, et *Galeni* de Anatomia. No. 216". *(hunc Codicem D.*

Io. Lascari penes se.)

Pars Pollucis et quaedam alia, et Polienis Stratagemata. In Graeco. in *Papyro, ct antiquo codice, volumine mediocri, tecto operimento rubro.* NO, 91,

Excerpta quaedam ex diversis auctoribus, et proverbia, et quaedam alia. Sine tabulis. in *Papyro.*

Pynoari Olimpya, et pars Pythiorum, cum expositione. in *Papyro.* In Graeco. NO. 87

Xenophontis Graeciae Historia. in *Papyro.* Sine tabulis. In Graeco. No. 622.

Quaedam in Physica. Primum de Climatibus Terrae, et Expositio Tueonis in Arati phenomena, in *Papyro.* Sine Tabulis. In Graeco. No. 139.

Aristotelis Politica. In Graeco. in *Papyro. Ugata in quadam carta membranea.*

Aratus cum expositione. In Graeco. *In Mcmbranu, ligatus in quadam Carta.*

Galeni Liber antiquus. In Graeco. *In Membranis. In quadam Carta.*

Vocabula quaedam Medicinalia, ct quaedam alia, in Graeco. *In Papyro. In tabulis, sine operimento.* Vetustissima. No. 221.

Quaedam recollecta a Domino Ancelo Politiano in pueritia sua. *in Papyro.* In Latino, *et Ugata simul in quadam Carta membranea. (Vol.* i. *p.* 178.; *Vergier d'honneur.*

Comment le Roy fist son entree a Florence, en quel triumphe il y entra, Fordonance qu'il y fit,

et comment les tendes marcherent les unes après les rndtres.

En grant triumphe et en grant excellence

En bruit en los d'honneur victorieux

Le Roy des Roys entra dedans Florence, No.XXXIIJ.

Ou il conquist ung renom glorieux;

Car il portoit le glaive furieux

Pour son vouloir par tout executer;

Et pour la guerre ou la paix discuter

Par haulx exploits d'emprise vertueuse.

Dont pour au vray du droit en disputer,

Dechirer veulx la façon merveilleuse.

Quant les seigneurs du Roy furent venus,

Ils luy baillerent les grans clefs de la porte,

Et luy priant qu'ils feussent sousteuus,

Et maintenu! soubz Sa haulte puissance;

Et desormes en son obeyssance

Tres humblement tous ils se maintiendroient,

Son nom gardroient, ses armes deffendroient;

Et outre plus pour leur erreur distraire,

A telle loy quil vouldroit se joindroient

Sans jamais jour eulx ayder du contraire.

Quant leur vouloir par leur parler conceupt,

Sur leur requeste, a bien peu de langaige,

Benignement le bon Roy les receupt,

Sans leur vouloir faire mal ne dommaige,

Et des plus grans receupt foy et hommaige

Incontinent par grant solempnite,

En rabaissant leur temerairete,

Et leur vouloir de soubdaine chaleur

Dont ils s'estoient contre luy despite,

Bien leur monstra qu'il estoit leur seigneur.

Processions comme j'ay devant dit,

Dignes corps sainetz, precieuses reliques,

Sortirent hors sans aucun contredit,

Croix, confanons, banieres autenticks,

Cures vestus de chappes magnifiques,

Abbes, doyens, chantres, archediacres,

Prestres Prestres chantaiu, chanoynes, soudiacres,

No. XXXIII. Portans joyaulx de saincts, de vierges, d'anges,

Et beaulx vaisseaulx de precieulx lavacres

Vindrent vers luy pour luy rendre louenges.

Tous les estats du grant jusques au moindre,

Tant fussent ils de noblesse ou clergie,

' Bourgois, marchans, furent contraints d'eulx joingdre,

A ceste loy pour le plus abrege;

Et de venir dessoubs ung train renge

Bien acoustres devers ledit seigneur;

Portans joyaulx, bagues de grant valeur,

Et beaulx habits de sumptueux arroy,

En luy faisant reverence et honneur,

Ne plus ne moins que leur souverain Roy.

Que diray je pour parler court et brief;

Quant si pres d'eulx le bon seigneur sentirent,

Quoy qu'a aulcuns le cas fust ung peu grief,

Ce neantmoins grans et petis sortirent,

Et toutes bonnes obeyssance firent

Faveur, support, subjection, souffrance,

Ce que devant en effect et substance

Ne pensoient pas Tuscains parolle tonde.

Qu'a ceste loy la ville de Florence

Eussent peu mettre tous les princes du monde.

Les Florentins a face angeliques,

Sur eschauffaulx, fenestres, et tauldis,

Venysiennes, Rommaines autenticques,

Vindrent illec veoir le Roy des hardis;

Et leur sembloit estre a ung paradis

De veoir Francoys en leurs terres marcher,

Car bien scavent que pour enharnacher

La nef Venus d'amoureux ad virons;

Et pour apoint ung connin embrocher

Qu'ils ny vont pas ainsi que bougerons.

Apres recueil los, honneur, reverence,

Faicte au bon Roy sans vouloir denigre,

L'on commenca de marcher vers

Florence
En ordonnance de degree en degre.
Et si fut tel du bon seigneur le gre,
Que Florentins tous les premiers mar-
chassent,
Affin que nuls les Francoys
n'empeschassent;
Mais fust a tous ceste entree famee.
Tendant a fin que Florentins goutassent
L'excellence de sa pompeuse armee.
*S'ensuyt comment apres que les
Seigneurs tant dc l'Eg/ise que dc la
Ville, marchans, bourgoys et aultres
mecaniquts, furcnt entres, Les bendcs
du Roy commencerent a marcher, qui
Jut la chose la plus singuliere quon veit
jamais pour entree de ville.* ET PRE-
MIEREMENT LES COULEUVRINIERS.
QUANT Florcntins avec leurs instru-
mens,
Furent entres vestus d'habits propices,
No. XXXIII.
  Premierement vindrent les Allemans,
  Lancequenets, foussignerans,
souysses,
  Portans plastrons, bracelets, es-
crevices,
  Et mesmement tous les couleivriniers;
  Plus barboilles que puures charbon-
niers,
  De manier leur salpestrc et pouldre.
  Et quant il fault ruer sur les paniers,
  A doubter sont plus que tonnoirre ou
fouldre.
LA BENOE OES PICQUIERS. Apres
marcherent les bende des grans picques,
Moult frisques a grans pas furieux;
Saichans des ars marciens les pratiques,
Plus qu'autres nez a cella curieux.
Car gens y a de nom victorieux,
Dignes d'avoir par leurs beaulx faits
maints don.
Et parmy eulx avoit fleustes, bedons,
De leurs explets sonnans les extremets;
Sans oublier estandars ne guydons,
Le mieulx en point que Ton les veit ja-
mais.
LA BENDE DES ARBALESTRIERS.
Apres marcha la bende aux arbalestri-
ers,
Entremesles de grans joueurs d'espees;
Gens acharnez au sang comme loudiers,
Par lesquels sont maintes gorges
coppees.
Et pour donner bauffree et lippees,

Autant expres que Ton ne saiche point;
Tous acoustres en chausse et en pour-
point,
D'uhe parure et des couleurs royalles.
Lesquelles bendes, pour en parler
apoint,
Ont vers le Roy tousjours este loyalles.
A son coste chascun la courte dague
De fin drap d'or, chaulses, escartelees;
La chayne au col, et au bonnet la bague;
Les grans perruques jusqu'au dos
avallees;
Neyves plumes de paillettes fueillees-
  Vol. 1. G Et Et sur leurs bras grans
devisses de perles,
No. XXXIII. A beaulx oyseaulx comme
pigeons et merles
  D'orphaverie a roleaux enlacez;
Et aultres choses singulieres et belles
Sur leurs personnes ils portoient assez.
LES CAPITAINES.
En tel estat passerent bien six mille,
Tous deux a deux, et a grans pas divers;
Desquels fut chief comme le plus ha-
bille
Monsieur de Cleves et Conte de Nevers;
Escartele de tort et de travers
De fin drap d'or seme de pierreries,
A grosses houppes de fine orphaverie;
Marchant a pied aussi droit comme ung
jon.
Avecques luy l'escuyer d'escuyrie;
Lornay aussi, le bailly de Dyjon
LES ARCHIERS O'ORDONNANCES. Apres
ceulx cy les archiers d'ordonnances
Vindrent soudain a tout leurs arcs ben-
des;
La belle trousse a flesches de deffenees;
Hommes bien pris, bien formes, et
fondes,
Tous deux a deux en belle ordre guydes.
A leurs costes le espees moult fines,
Beaulx gorgerins, dorees brigandines,
A soustenir ou escousse ou desserre.
A mon advis bien suffisant et dignes
Pour estre gens vertueulx a la guerre.
LES HOMMES B AUMES. Incontinent vin-
drent les hommes d'armes
Sur grans coursiers, sur genets et destri-
ers,
Comme beaulx dieux reluysans en leurs
armes;
La bride au poing et le pied aux estriers,
Tous habilles non pas comme peaultri-
ers,

Mais comme roys, princes, ou em-
pereurs,
Et pour monstrer qu'ils estoient em-
pareurs
D'honneur mondain a grans saulx et ru-
ades,
Sur le pave sans estre en rien paoureux
Devant les dames firent mille pennades.
Sur leurs chevaulx d'or et d'argent son-
nettes,
Orphaveries par despit mesurees,
Chanfrains dores, plumes a grans bro-
chettes,
De pailles d'or assez desmesurees,
D'azur dacre grans bardes asurees
Estincelantes
  Estincelantes au soleil radieux;
Et parmy eulx clairons melodieux
Trompes, cornets, et tabourins de
guerre.
Brief il sembloit que deesses ou dieux
Fussent des cieulx descendus sur la
terre.
LE NOMBRES DES HOMMES O'armes.
  Ils cstoient bien en nombre huyt cens
lances,
  Montez, bardez ainsi comme dit est,
  Tous gentils hommes dignes de grans
vaillances
  Pour tost avoir d'ung pays le con-
quest;
  Sans regarder au gaing ne a l'aquest,
  Mais aux honneurs et aux louenges
famees,
  Ainsi que gens de maisons renom-
mees,
  Progenies plains de noble vouloir,
  Qui ont toujours les provinces
aymees
  Ou guerre gist pour eulx faire valoir.
LA BENDE DES DEUX CENS AR-
BALESTR1ERS. Ces huyt cens lances en
tel estat passees,
Trop mieulxen point que je ne dis le
tiers,
Des ordonnances frisquement com-
passees,
Vindrent apres deux cens arbalestriers,
Hardis, vaillans, couraigeux, et entiers,
Dessus le col l'arbalestre bendee
Qui n'estoit pas de foiblesse fardee,
Mais par raison, grosse, puissante et
forte;
Et le garrot ou la vire fondee
Pour trespercer ung demy pied de porte.

A leur coste l'espee longue et large,
La courte dague pour son homme abor-
der,
Le grant bauldrier avecques le
guindage,
Pour a deux coups l'arbalestre bender,
Et pour a point plusieurs coups desben-
der
La grosse trousse de garrots et de vires
Pareils a ceuix qu'on voit en les navires,
Le plus souvent user a volunte,
Il nen est point en ce monde de pires,
Pour en narrer la pure verite.
Petis chappeaulx, deschiquetes, coppes,
Trouez, percez, fretaillez, entrouvers,
Par aucuns lieux de soye enveloppes.
Et de ruben, rouges, blancs, noirs, et
vers,
Grosses taillades de tort et de travers,
Petis plumars de faisans et d'ayrons,
G2
Bien enrichis par tout les environs,
No. XXXIII. De perleries et de belles
paillettes;
Et si estoient leurs pourpoints et sayons
Tous atachez a fer d'or d'esguillettes.

LA BENDE DES ARCHIERS DE LA GARDE
DU ROT.

Apres vindrent les archiers de la garde,
Grans et puissans, bien croises, bien
fendus,
Qui ne portoient picque ne halebarde,
Fors que leurs arcs gorrierement tendus;
Leur bracelets aux pongnets estendus
Bien ataches a grans chaynes d'argent;
Autour du col le gorgerin bien gent,
De cramoisy le plantureux pourpoint
Assez propre fusse pour ung regent,
Ou grant duc acoustre bien apoint;
Dessus le chief la bien clere sallade,
A cloux dores fournis de pierrerie;
Dessus le dos le hocqueton fort sade,
Tout surseme de fine orphaverie;
La courte dague, l'espee bien fourbie,
La gaye trousse a custode vermeille,
Le pied en lair aux escoutes loreille.
Brief on disoit tout veu et regarde,
*Quoeste my pare ou ne grande mer-
veille,*
Et sou mirato, par le sang que de de.
Quant les archiers en leurs pompes
haultaines
Furent passes, trois a trois, quatre a qua-
tre,
Pied a pied vindrent leurs nobles capi-
taines,
Qui.ne sont pas gens pour cropir en las-
tre.
Comme Cresol, et Claude de la chastre,
Avec son fils dit monsieur Quoque-
bourne;
En ordonnance chevaleureuse et bonne;
Par excellence habilles richement.
Brief pour planter des grans gorres la
bonne
C'estoit je croy suffisant parement.

LA RENDE DES CENT GENTILSHOMMES
DU ROY.

Ces gens passez en si pompeux arroy,
Incontinent sans servir d'aultre mets,
Vindrent les cent gentilshommes du
Roy,
Les mieulx enpoint que l'on les vit ja-
mais,
Ayans habits de divers entremets,
Tant de drap d'or comme de cramoisy
Le plus exquis qui fut oncques choisy;
Satin de pris grant, damas figure,
En son endroit chascun l'avoit saisy,
Pour estre mieulx des dames honnoure.
Larges sayons, decoppes, taillades,
Deca, dela, de tort, et de travers,
De pierreries farcis entrelardes,
Et de perles saulgrenes et couvers,
Par plusieurs lieux mistement entrou-
vers
Pour veoir dessoubz les enrichemens
De leurs harnoys, plus clers que dya-
mans;
En tous endroits trop mieulx fails que
cire.
Conclusion de leurs assualcemens
Possible n'est de la disme estimer.
Genets, coursiers, riches bardes, hous-
surcs,
Plumars remplis d'orphaveries fines,
Chan Trains dores a grans entrelassures,
Armets luysans, bicquoquets, capelines,
Bucques de pris, tres riches mantelines,
Venanssans plusjusqu'au dessus des
fauldes,
A gros rubis, tutquoyses, emerauldes;
Et pour attaindre aux belliques accors,
lis monstroient bien par leurs ruades
bauldes
Qu'en France y a gens qui ont cueur et
corps.

PAIGES D'HONNEUR ET LAQUAIS.

Sur grans chevaulx leurs pages les
suyvoient,
Et a beau pied laquais de point en point,
Qui de drap d'or et de velours avoient
Le grant sayon, ou du moins le pour-
point.
Possibile n'est de veoir gens mieulx en
point.
Le petit dard, le poignart, la rapiere,
Chausses tirantes, perruque singuliere,
De beau drap d'or la gorriere barrette,
Ou de velours, puislabague treschiere,
Et leplumart de faisant ou d'aigrette.

DU ROY.

En bruyt, en los, et en magnificence,
En grant triumphe de pondereux arroy,
En tout estat de pompeuse excellence,
Entra dedans le treschrestien Roy.
Laquais, archiers, avoit pour le desroy,
Autour le luy, luy preparant sa voye,
   No. XXXIII.
   Monte Monte dessus son courtier dit
Savoye,
NO. XXXIII. Le mieulx en point
d'omemens de valeurs
   Qu'on vit jamais, ne possibile est
qu'on voye,
Fust pour cent roys ou autant
d'empereurs.
Le bon seigneur vertueux et plaisant,
Plus qu'autre ne des humains honnore,
Armeestoit d'ung harnoysplus luysant
Q'ung dyamont, en plusieurs lieux dore
De grosses perles et pierres precieuses,
Tout son chief fut acoustre, decore,
.   Comme rubis, turquoyses
sumptueuses;
En sa couronne une grosse eschar-
boucle,
Et au surplus, en ses armes joyeuses
Ne Iuy failloit ne hardillon ne boucle.
Ses bardes furent d'ung drap d'or de-
copees,
Toutes chargees de riche orphaverie,
A rubens d'or frisquement agrappees,
Et grosses houppes toutes de perlerie.
Sa manteline estoit a pierrerie
Et broderie qui avoit moult couste.
Le bel estoc autour de son coste;
Et en son col l'ordre des preux estoit.
Brief ie n'auroys en quinze jours
compte
La grant richesse que dessus luy portoit.
Ung riche poille hault et droit sur la
teste,
De drap d'or traict a la mode de France;
Le tout en signe de victoire et con-

queste,
De tout triumphe et de toute excellence.
Quatre seigneurs des plus grans de
Florence
Luy comportoient tresmagnifiquement,
Vestuz d'abis moult sumptueusement,
Tresbien fourrez de martres subelines;
Et si avoient dessus leurs capelines,
Rubiz, saphirs, fins balais de bigorre,
Orientalles, perles et cornalines.
Brief vivant n'est qui vit one si grant
gorre.

No XXXIV.

(Vol. i. *p. ISS.J Raccolta d' Opuscoli di Calogefà, vol.* xviii. *p.* 38.
Capitolo D' Incerto *al Serenissimo Agostino Barbarigo Doge di Venezia, in occasione che Carlo Vìli, si portava ad occupare il Regno di Napoli.*

Giovambattista Parisotti A' Lettori.

Io mi stimo colui, al quale essendo la fortuna di tanto stata cortese, che gli fece venire alle mani Opere di chiari, e valorosi uomini, che già da molto tempo si stavano nell' obblio No.XXXIV. sepolte, essere da non picciolo obbligo astretto di mandarle quanto prima alla pubblica luce, ed in tal guisa, più non essendogli permesso, far corre in alcun modo il frutto delle fatiche loro a que' valentuomini, i quali, o per impotenza, o per non curanza, o dall' avara morte prevenuti, defrauditi furono di mandare ad effetto quanto per il bene pubblico, e per la propria gloria avevano egregiamente operato. Credei in tanto me essere uno di coloro, in cui un si fatto obbligo si ritrovava; poiché per buona sorte in poter mio pervenne un rarissimo Mss. di Poesie tutte in terza rima d'Autori del secolo xv. in cui tra le altre si leggono molte terze rime d' Antonio Tibaldèo, le quali non furono mai stampate, siccome ho scorto dal rincontro ch' io feci a questo fme dell'ultima, per quanto stimo, edizione fatta in Venezia per Bartolomeo detto l'Imperator, e Francesco Veneziano l'anno 1554. in 8. e sono delle più belle composizioni, che il Tibaldèo, seguendo il suo stile, abbia lasciato uscire dalla sua penna. Si leggono oltre a ciò molte rimedi Francesco Nursio Veronese, di Girolamo Berardo, di Lodovico Mili.mi. e di molt' altri, i di cui nomi, per diligenza usata non si

possono rilevare. Poiché per fatalità il Mss. capitò in mano o di ragazzi, o di gente cosi ignorante, che si presero piacere di cassare tutti i nomi degli Autori delle composizioni, fuorché quello del 'l ibai dèo, e degli altri soprannomati, li quali però, non essendo all'atto annullati, a gran fatica si sono potuti intendere. Ma quello che molto più mi spiace si è, che non fu possibile di capir mai nè il nome, nè il cognome dell'Autore della composizione, le quale è il soggetto del mio discorso, poiche non solo fu cassato con la penna, ma raso col coltello, talchè ha tolto ogni speranza di saper mai l'Autore della medesima.' Io perciò, vedendomi, come dissi in possesso del suddetto Mss. pensai da molto tempo di farne partecipe il pubblico, ristampando le pocsic del Tibaldèo, ormai divenute si rare, che con gran difficoltà si possono, da chi le brama, rinvenire, aggiungendovi ancora que' Capitoli del medesimo ehe sono inediti appresso il Mss. ed oltre a ciò il Capitolo, di cui si parlerà appresso, col fare alfine una scelta de' belli componimenti degli altri Autori, di cui parte ci sono rimasti i nomi, e parte per il suddetto accidente ci sono, come dissi, rimasi ignoti. A questo mio onesto desiderio vi.si opposero di molte cose si per la stampa, e si per essere io talvolta impedito per" poter eseguire l'intento mio. Sicchè io pensai, che se al presente non mi è permesso di mandare pienamente ad effetto quant' io bramo, contentarmi di vederne effettuata qualche parte, pubblicando una composizione in terza rima, la quale, s' io non m' inganna, e per la bellezza del soggetto sopra cui è scritta, e per il pregio della poesia supera tutte quelle del Mss. e può può andar del pari con qualunque altra; sicchè ella ben merita che tosto tosto sia tolta dalle NO. XXXIV. tenebre, e che ne siano fatti partecipi tutti coloro, che godono di vedere conservate le fatiche de' chiari uomini, vale a dire tutti quegli, che sono o punto, o troppo delle belle, e buone lettere amanti. Il Capitolo intanto è scritto, come si ricava dalla lettura del medesimo, ad Agostino Barbadico Doge di Venezia nell' occasione della famosa venuta di Carlo Vili. Re di Fran-

cia in Italia per prendere il Regno di Napoli, che fù l'anno 1494. anzi, per parlare con più verità, egli è scritto quando già il Re aveva occupato il Regno, mentre il Poeta, esortando all' impresa il suddetto Doge, tra le altre cose dice, che egli non tema, poiché con lui se ne viene il gran Francesco Gonzaga, il quale, come si sa dalle Storie, fu da Veneziani fatto Capo della Lega conchiusa per impedire il vittorioso ritorno del Re in Francia; perchè poi nell' esprimer che fa il Poeta i lamenti delle principali Città d' Italia sbigottite per il timore dell' imminente loro ruina, e nel toccare alcune altre particolarità, egli si serve d espressioni, che 'racchiudono in sè l' erudizione di que' tempi, ho stimato bene, per maggior facilità, e chiarezza di chi legge, illustrar con qualche annotazione que' luoghi, che patir potessero alcuna oscurità.

Passando ora a discorrere qualche cosa della persona del nostro Poeta, io dico che dalla composizione stessa si ricava, ch' egli era Soldato, e Soldato di non poco riguardo, perchè nella fine egli prega il Doge, che 1' accetti nel numero de' suoi Condottieri, e gli rammenta, perchè non gli neghi la grazia, come nella passata guerra fu per lui prigione a Milano e come non fu possibile nè per oro, nè per argento farlo dal medesimo ribellare. Ognuno pertanto vede quanto ragguardevole officio nella Milizia sia quello di Condottiero, e come un' ordinario Soldato non si tenta a costo d'oro staccarlo dal suo Sovrano, facendosi sì fatti tentativi solo con Soldati di considerazione, e che possono molto cooperare per la vittoria. Dico ancora, che da questo fatto a mio giudicio si ricava, ch' egli non era Suddito della Repubblica, poiché uno ch' è tale, non può rammemorare al suo Principe per punto di merito, non essergli nell' occasione stato ribello, anzi facendolo non poco 1' offenderebbe, poiché è stretto debito di un Suddito 1' essere fedele al suo Principe; oltre di che ordinariamente a un personaggio di riguardo non verrebbe molto a conto a tradire il suo Sovrano, poiché al certo perderebbe ogni avere ch' egli possedesse nello Stato del suo Principe; sicchè per tutte queste riflessioni panni al certo potere ragionevolmente concludere, che il nostro Poeta non era Suddito della Repubblica di Venezia. Chi poi egli si fosse non ho mai potuto per diligenza usata in coloro, che scrivono le vite de' Poeti, rinvenire, e nel Mss. il nome dell' Autore è come dissi talmente raso, che non è possibile il poterlo capire: solo pare che il suo cognome, guardandolo col Microscopio, finisca in NORI. Se da tutte queste circostanze, che ho narrate, alcuno potesse scoprire in qualche guisa chi si fosse l' Autore, o pure, se si ritrovasse appresso di se la medesima composizione, che non avesse patita la disgrazia d' essere stato cancellato il nome di quello, farebbe alcerto di molto utile 1 pubblico, se lo palesasse: poichè da questo Capitolo si scorge che il nostro Autore è grande, e felice nelle su idèe, magnifico, e naturale insieme nell' espressioni, forte, e vivo ne' colori, e nelle figure, talchè pare, ch' egli sia un vero ritratto di Dante. Se queste prerogative in ogni Poeta sono rare, ed ammirabili, molto più lo deono essere nel nostro, poichè egli si vivea nel Secolo XV. vale a dire in un tempo dove la Scuola di Dante, e del Petrarca, era affatto abbandonata, la coltura della Lingua perduta, duta, sicchè a gran fatica si può trovare alcuno, che in quel Secolo sodamente, e purgatamente componga. Pertanto, se il nostro Poeta per una particolar felicità, ed elevatezza d' N. XXXIV. ingegno si è in tutte queste cose distinto dagli altri del suo tempo, egli ben merita, che ognuno adopri ogni diligenza per iscoprire chi egli si sia; mentre, fatto che fosse questo, potrebbe succedere, che con non molta difficoltà si rinvenissero altre composizioni dello stesso ugualmente belle, e più. Poichè dal Capitolo si ritrae, che quando egli lo scrisse era vecchio di molto: e perciò, se in una età, in cui il fervore della fantasia, producitrice delle, sublimi, e pellegrine idèe poetiche, era presso che raffreddato, sì fattamente componeva, che dobbiamo noi sperare ch' esser possano que' Componimenti da lui prodotti in un tempo che la mente era nel maggior colmo del suo vigore? Al certo maravigliosi, e rari dovranno essere; sicchè

ciascheduno, come ho detto, impieghi ogni diligenza per ritracciare chi si sia questo valente Poeta, poichè sicuramente di molta gloria gliene verrà, e maggiore ancora se avesse la sorte di cavar dalle tenebre altre Opere dello stesso, le quali ben mostrano, da ciò che s' è detto, dovere esser degne d' arrichire la Volgar Poesia.

Di Rama, li 27. *Aprii* 1737 AD SERENIS3IMI M PRINCIPE! VENETUM.

Signor, sentendo che Bellona in campo
 Quassa l'orrendo, e marzial flagello,
Spargendo, come Drago, ardente vampo;
E per troppo levar il gran martello,
 Sterope suda, sospira Vulcano, Rimbomba lo fornace in Mongibello;
E vedendo la spada a Marte in mano,
 Che fulminando va con gran tempesta Verso 1' antiquo suo Seggio Romano;
E con 1' ira al mal far crudele, e presta,
 Con più di mille Navi, il Mar Tirreno,
(1) E 1' Elesponto acerbamente infesta;
E per sparger ben tutto il suo veleno
 Vol. t. H Lo (1) li Mar *Tiretto*. Qui il Poeta, per ben mostrare la futura ruina d' Italia, comincia a dire come il Turco con 1' Armata Navale danneggiava i paesi de' Christian!; lo che si comprende nominando il Poeta 1' Elesponto, leggendosi oltre a ciò, per maggior confermazione, le seguenti parole nella settima, d ultima parte delle Storie Milanesi del Cono. *I Veneziani ti icusano di dar ojuto a Cario Vili, perchè erano sforzati con quanta forza avevano, a re-*sistere *al Turco ne' confini di Cipro*.

Lo squamoso (2) Biscion fatto ha il (3) Tesino N. XXXIV. Mutar il corso, e giungersi col Reno;
 E già (4) Marzocco sta col capo chino,
 Come fa il can battuto nella paglia, E la Lupa (5) ha pigliato altro cammino;
Temo, che la rnina di Tessaglia,
 Di Canne, e Trassimeno, Italia afflitta, Non senta, che 1' invidia ogni ben taglia.
Italia tanto celebrata, e scritta,
 Italia già sì trionfante, e degna, Or dolorosa appena si tien dritta.
Movi, Signor, la gloriosa insegna,
Che mossa a tutto il Mondo fa paura,

 Soccorri lei, che di miseria è pregna;
Slega il Leon, che tanto è di natura
 Orrendo, e forte, ch' ogni altro animale A lui, come la cera al foco, dura.
Ha il dente acuto, e ben pennate 1' ale,
 Nervosa seta, ed unghiuta la branca;
 Non potrà contra lui forza mortale.

(6) Ercol (2) *Burìm*. Gli Sforzeschi, che successero a' Visconti nel Dominio di Milano, ritennero la stessa Arme che quelli portavano, eh' era una Serpe, e perciò il Poeta nominando il Biscione, significa sempre in questo componimento Lodovico Sforza detto il Moro, ad istigazione del quale si mosse Carlo Vili, a prendere il Regno di Napoli. Ciò fece Lodovico, perchè, ritenendo egli ingiustamente il Dominio di Milano dovuto a Giovanni Galeazzo suo Nipote, Alfonso Re di Napoli, a cui aveva data in moglie Isabella sua Figlia, aveva già mossa a Lodovico la guerra, perchè a ni&sun modo voleva egli rinunziare il governo al detto Galeazzo suo Nipote. (3) *Il Tesino*. Qui dicendosi, che Lodovico fece unir il Tesino col Reno, non può significar altro, che Giovanni Benti voglio Signor di Bologna s' era unito con lui, e lo confermano queste parole del Corio nel sopraddetto luogo. Ercole *Estense Marchete di* Feretro, e Giovanni *Bentivoglio, che di Bologna teneva il Principato, j' offersero in tutti i mandati a Carlo*. (4) *Marzocco*. Marzocco vuol dire propriamente Leone dipinto, o scolpito, perciò, il Poeta con questa parola dinota Firenze, nell' antica Arme della quale, eh' era una Croce, i Guelfi v' aggiunsero il Leone. Non può significare al certo Venezia, poichè alquanto dopo si vede eh' egli dipinge il Leone de' Veneziani terribile, e feroce siccome quello, che solo doveva liberar 1' Italia oppressa. Nominando il Poeta subito Siena vicina a Firenze conferma maggiormente il detto mio. (5) £ *la Lupa*. La Lupa mostra Siena, portando essa quell' animale per Arme, a tenore di cui disse il Petrarca nella Canzone XI.
Orsi, Lupi, Leoni, Aquile, e Serpi
Ad una gran marmorea Colonna
Fanno noja sovente, ed a se danno.

Ecco poi come qui Leoni significano Firenze, che il nostro Poeta ha espresso con la parola Marzocco.

(6) Ercolnon vedi tu, che batte l' anci,
Per far al tuo Leon, come al Nemèo,
(7) Benchè la forza spesso al voler man-
ca.
Serse, Alessandro, Dario, e Tolomeo
Han fatto lega, e già son sopra l' Arno,
E van per rumar il Colisèo.
 Grida (8) Bren furioso, s' io non
scarno
Questo mio corpo anzi il finir dell' an-
no,
Dimostrerò, che non combatto indarno.
 Chi usa la forza, chi adopra l' ingan-
no;
Non tardar più, che spesso il tardar
noce;
Mal si provedde, quando è giunto il
danno.
 L'amaro pianto, e la dolente voce,
 Che fa Romagna, fin al Ciel rimbom-
ba,
Lacerata dal vulgo aspro, e feroce."
 Senza colpo di spada, (9) o suon di
tromba,
Fa della gente nostra il popol crudo,
Come il Falcon suol far della Colomba.
 Ogni cor di valor è casso, e nudo,
Tutta la terra di Saturno trema,
Che fu già di Bellona il primo scudo.
 Non è spirto sì fier, ch' ora non tema,
Nessun aspetta un sol colpo di lancia,
Par che sia giunto Italia all' ora estrema.
 Posto è di Roma il Seggio alla bilan-
cia,
Che trionfava in tanto onor, e fama,
£ domata ha più volte e Spagna, e Francia.
H2
(6) Erro/. Vuol dire Ercole primo Duca
di Ferrara nemico de' Veneziani sino
dall' anno 1482. nel qua tempo essi ten-
tarono di torgli Ferrara con una lunga
guerra di due anni.
(7) Benchè. Significa il picciolo Stato,
e perciò le picciole forze di quel Duca
a rispetto de' Ve nciziani molto potenti.
(8) Bren. Col nome di Brenno Capitano
de' Galli, che presero Roma fuorchè il
Campidoglio, vuol dinotar Carlo Vili, a
cui ben conveniva il titolo di *Furioso*
a riguardo della prestezza, della difficoltà, e de' perigli di lla sua impresa,
che con tanto coraggio volle eseguire.
Si avverta ancora, che il Poeta fa dire
queste due parole a Brenno con uno

espressione, e con un suono molto aspro, come appunto era conveniente ad
un Barbaro qual era Brenno. (9) *Sensa
colpo di Spada.* Con queste parole il
Poeta vuol dinotare le continue sedi-
zioni, e tumulti, ond' era oppressa la
Romagna tutta in quel secolo, che obbe-
diva a molti piccioli Signori, li quali per
lo più la governavano da Tiranni, come
si ha dalle Storie.
No. XXXIV.
 Giunge Giunge Fiorenza dolorosa, e
grama,
NO. XXXIV. Chiamando l' ombra afflitta
di Lorenzio, (10)
Che così morto estolle, onora, ed ama;
Afflitta perchè vede il fier Mezenzio,
E Turno andar contra il pietoso Enea,
Spargendo amaro più che nell' assenzio.
E come in sorte acerba, iniqua, e rea,
Il superbo Ilione fu combusto,
Opra del crudo strai di Citerèa,
Al fin sotto l' Imperio iniquo, e ingius-
to
Teme star serva della turba fera,
Che perso ha di pietate il dolce gusto.
Il tuo soccorso chiama la Pantera,
(11) La Pantera, che Lucca abbraccia, e
onora,
Perchè in te sol, come in suo porto,
spera.
Ahimè, che piaga è questa, che m' acco-
ra,
Ove va lo mio regno, e lo mio scetro,
Qual fato contra me crudel lavora?
O gloria umana, come sei sul vetro
Fondata, e come presto il tempo chiaro
Diventa nubiloso, oscuro, e tetro!
Debbo ber un velen sì forte, amaro,
Debbo servir a sì spietata plebe,
A un popol del mie sangue fatto avaro'
Chi goderà le mie fiorite glebe?
Gente senza clemenza, e senza legge,
Che una Cucina fu di Atene, e Tebe;
Indomito, superbo, e pazzo gregge,
Che adora per suoi Dei Venere, e Bac-
co,
E sotto al suo trionfo se corregge.
Menerà con gran furia a foco, e sacco
Il grato ospilio, il dolce seggio, e nido,
Ove riposo il corpo afflitto, e stracco;
Più di me stessa, trista, non mi fido,
Poichè San Marco tanto mal comporta,
E non ascolta il mio lamento, e grido.
 Pallida (10) *Lorenzio.* Lorenzo de'

Medici, cbe fu Padre di Papa Leone X.
morto due anni avanti, cioè l' anno
1493. essendo slata la venuta di Carlo
VIII. in Italia l' anno 1494. come si è
detto di sopra. Il Poeta poi dice Firenza
afflitta per la morte di Lorenzo, poichè
quegli, sino che visse, con la sua pru-
denza tenne ottimamente bilanciate le
cose d' Italia; e morto lui, ne insorsero
quelle rovine, che danneggiarono la sua
Patria non meno, che l' Italia tutta;
come dicono particolarmente gli Storici
Fiorentini.
(11) *La Pantera.* Arme della Republi-
ca di Lucca.
Pallida in vista, lagrimosa e smorta,
 D' affanno, di tormento, e doglia
piena, No. XXXIV.
Or son, vivendo, assai peggio che mor-
ta.
Grida con voce sì misera Siena,
Che farebbe spezzar un cor di sasso, E
pianger seco un Aspe la sua pena.
Dicendo or sei pur giunta a quel dur
passo, (12)
 Che temuto hai più volte, o
meschinella!
Ogni tua gloria è rninata al basso.
Sarai tra Lupi una vii pecorella,
Che quando t' a ran tutto toso il pelo, Ti
straccieran con voglia irata, e fella.
Leva dagli occhi miei, leva quel velo,
 Che mi turba la vista, o Leon Santo,
Torna la Primavera incontra il gelo;
Tu solo mutar puoi l' angoscia, e il
pianto
 In pace, in allegrezza, in festa, in gio-
ja, A te di questa impresa è dato il van-
to;
Non comportar, che pianga come Troja,
 Misera, ed infelice, ch' al fin creggio,
Che tu ne patiresti affanno, e noja.
E Pisa dolorosa, al tutto veggio
 Voltarsi contra me l' aspra fortuna,
Per minar il mio felice seggio.
Son stato un tempo d' ogni ben digiuna,
 Or ch' io credeva star contenta, e li-
eta, Vedomi apparecchiar la vesta
bruna.
Irato è il Cielo, e ciascun suo Pianeta
 Tanto verso di me, che più non posso
Toccar la prima mia trionfai meta;
Stracciata m' ha la carne, e rotto l' osso
 Una bestia crudel; or fiera gente L'
ultimo carco mi vuol porre addosso.

Con furia è mosso tutto l' Occidente,

Guasconi, Inglesi, Piccardi, Alemani
Disposti a morte con tutta la mente;

Galli (lì) *Dur passa.* La parola *dura* regolarmente non s' accorcia, ma qui il Poets l' accorciò, per esprimere con la parola l' aspro, e duro stato in cui si ritrovava *V* Italia: la qual cosa si vede fatta da' più valorosi Poeti, cioè d' accomodare il suono delle parole al significato delle medesime.

Galli spigati, e feroci Germani,
N-XXXIV. (13) Lingoni orrendi, e di lunghe aste armati,
e Nervi barbari inumani,
Come indomite Tigri, ed Orsi irati,

Onde mugghia Garonna, e stride Ibero, E tutti gli altri fiumi son turbati;
Poichè San Marco non move il suo Impero,

So che a ogni modo porterò la soma,
Nè in tempo alcuno aver mai più ben spero.

Con vesta oscura, e con incolta coma,

Afflitta, lassa, trista, e sconsolata Miseramente si lamenta Roma;
Ahimè, dicendo, ov' è la gloria andata

De' miei trionfi, ov' è quella eccellenza, Che mi fece Regina incoronata!

Solca portarmi onor, e riverenza

Ogni Stato, Dominio, Imperio, e Regno, Mossi da mia real magnificenza.

E per mostrar di vera fede il segno,

Mi davan con amor tributo, e omaggio, Seguendo ogni mia voglia, ogni disegno.

Splendeva il lume del mio chiaro raggio,

Da Scitia inculta alla felice Arabbia,
Dall' Oriente fin dove il viaggio Finisce il Sol, e come fa la sabbia

Girar or alto, or basso, quando spira Il vento irato, con gran furia, e rabbia,

Quando-di fuoco il cor mi facea l' ira,

Tremava intorno a me tutta la terra,
Stupida, come l' occhio, che il Sol mira.

Vinsi Sanniti, e Fidenati in guerra,

Toscani, Volsci, Campani, e Sabini,
E ciò, ch' Abruzzo, e la Calabria serra-f
E coronai allor gli aurati crini,

Portando ancor di Romolo la gonna,
E chiusa essendo tra stretti confini;

Quattro (13) *lingoni,* e Nere;'. Popoli della Gallia Belgica espressi dal Poeta co' nomi antichi, i primi de' quali oggi sono chiamati *Langra,* ed i secondi *Bavay.* Nel Afjs. poi non si può leggere il principio del tento verso perchè è roso dal tempo, ma da quello, che si può da' vestigi rimasi comprendere, e dall' ordine dell discorso ancora, si nominavi un' altro di que' popoli circonvicini.

Quattro altri Regi poi mi fecer Donna (14)

Di grand' Imperio, e giunsero al mio fianco, N-XXXIV.

Per sostentarmi, una salda Colonna.

Era quel popol sì gagliardo, e franco,
Che non durava alcun sotto sua forza,
Nèmai fu visto per battaglia stanco.

Ma ben conosco che presto s'ammorza

Ogni fama mortai, et ogni gloria Al fin si trova aver secca la scorza.

Colui, che celebrato in ogni Istoria

Più non è meco, (Jesar glorioso, Che acquisterà, come solca, vittoria.

O Scipion magnanimo, e famoso,

Se tu vedesti Roma tua meschina, Tu piangeresti il caso doloroso!

A terra cade con furia, e ruina.

Ogni Tempio sacrato, ogni edilizio;
La Starna è data al Falcon in rapina;
O severo Catone, o buon Fabrizio,

La Patria tua dolente, stanca, e lassa
Non trova un sol del ver sangue Patrizio.

Un crudel Annibal, Fabio, conquassa

Il seggio de' tuoi lieti, e antiqui Patri,
E non èchi per lui la lancia abbassa.
Portici, Curie, Pretorii, e Teatri

Torri, Rocche, Colossi, aurati Tetti
Lochi presto saranno inculti, et atri;
Feste, canti, piacer, giochi, e diletti,

Ogni solazzo, ogni piacevolezza,
Muteransi in affanni, ire, e dispetti.
Lassa, Signor, omai questa durezza,

Conforta la tua Eccelsa Signorìa, Che fuor mi cavi di tanta tristezza:
Non comportar, che il Figliuol di Maria

Veda il Vicario suo con tanta furia
Cacciar da gente truculenta, e ria.

Abbraccia (14) *Donna. H* Poeta si serve del numero definito di quattro Re per esprimere tutti gli altri Re, che in breve tempo Roma domò, soggiogata eh' ebbe l' Italia con difficili, e lunghe guerre.

Abbraccia (15) Alfonso tuo, che la mia curio

Si sforza d' esaltar, come ognun vede,
E vendecarmi di sì grave ingiuria.
Non ti fidar, che non si trova fede

In barbarico cor senza pietate,
Nato a sangue, tumulto, incendio, e prede.

Difendi la tua dolce libertate

Non patir mai, che il fier Biscion si alloggia,
E il Gallo appresso della tua Cittate;
Che il mondo andar vedresti a un' altra foggia.

Sai, che la Serpe per natura tiene

Da velenar ciascuno in cui s' appoggia.
Non temar poi, che teco armato viene
(16) Francesco illustre di Casa Gonzaga,

Che collocato ha in te tutta sua spene.
Credi alla mente mia di ben presaga,

Che questo a noi sarà come Camillo,
Un' altra volta a me di pianger vaga.
Movi il vittorioso, e bel vesillo,

Augustin, anzi augusto, inclito, e sacro,
E farai il mar a tua posta tranquillo;
Non si può, senza il tuo chiaro lavacro,

Questa macchia purgar, e levar alto
Il mondo, or di valor sì nudo, e macro;
Rompi Venezia ormai lo duro smalto,

Che come Brescia, Padoa, e Verona
Pigliasti già con glorioso assalto,
Ancora in capo porterai corona

Di tutta Italia, e di Francia, e di Spagna,
Ch' alla giustizia il Ciel ogni ben dona;
Io sempre a te sarò folel compagna,

Finchè l'Imperio mio durerà in vita:
Chi acquista vera fede assai guadagna.
Vieni a sanarmi la crudel ferita;

Viridomauro, e Bren caccia in esilio,
Chem' ha contra ragion tanto smarrita.

Facendo (15) *Alfonso tuo.* Alfonso Re di Napoli, il quale era successo nel Regno poco tempo prima a Ferdinando suo Padre morto di dolore, vedendo, che già Carlo Vili, contro di lui ce ne veniva.

(16) *FrancetCQ.* Vuol dire, che Francesco Gonzago Signor di Mantova aveva posta la speranza della sicurezza del suo Stato ncll' armi de' Veneziani, che l' avrebbero difeso dal comun nemico. Notisi poi come il detto Gonzago fu latto da' Veneziani Capo della Lega conclùsata contra Carlo Vili.

Facendo adunque ogni Città concilio Per domandar a te, Signor, soccorso,

Mi rendo certo, che, còl tuo Consilio,
  Hai destinato di frenar il corso
Alla turba, che va senza ragione,
E porre a tal, che non si pensa, il morso
j
  Ond' io che son divoto al tuo Leone,
Vorrei seguirlo, e sotto al tuo Stendardo
Star, fin ch' io fossi in vita, al paragone.
  Che benchè ognun di me sia più gagliardo,
Io so che almanco son servo fedele;
Non lassa esser la fede al vecchio tardo.
  Ricordati, Signor, quanto amar fele
Gustai, per star a te servir intento,
E non voler mutar le prime vele,
  E movermi per oro, e per argento,
In prigion a Milan con tanto strazio,
Che fino al giorno d' oggi ancor ne sento;
  Ma per questo non son di scrvir sazio
A te, Signor, anzi non sarò mai
Finchè avrò della vita qualche spazio.
  Io son stato senz' arme intorno assai;
Quando era l' ozio al tempo della pace
Portato ho con silenzio li miei guai,
  Per dimostrar, che non era rapace
Del suo stipendio, e dedito al tesoro.
Or che s' accende il foco, e la fornace,
  Ti prego, che nel forte e fedel coro
De' Condottieri eccelsi, e degni Eroi
M' accetti, e arrendi il trionfai alloro;
  Che facilmente lo puoi far se vuoi:
E dei voler, perchè mia fede il vole,
E l' ordin degli antiqui, e forti Eroi.-
  Colui cerca far fatti, e non parole,
Che vedendo in battaglia Marte andare
Voi seguir lui, come Aquila fa il sole.
  Desidero vederti trionfare
In pompa, in gloria, e tanto ho acceso il core,
Che per te voglio la morte abbracciare;
  Ghe morte non estima un vero Amore.
  I
  No XXXV.

(Vol. i. p. 197.J Diary of BurcAard, from Gordon's Hist. of Alexander VI. in App. CapUula Conventionis Papa et Regis Frond, fyc.

Dominica XI. mens Is Januarii conclusion But et deliberatum inter S. D. N. et Illui XXXV. triss. D. Philippum de Bressa avunculum Regis Franciae locum tenentem ejusdem Regis, quod S. D. N.

assignare debet, Gem Sultan, fratrem magni Turcae ad sex Menses Regi Franciae, qui ex nunc solvere deberet Papae xx. millia ducatorum, et *dart Cautionem Mercatorum Florentinorutn et Venetorum,* de restituendo ipsumGem Sultan, ipsi Papae, elapsis sex Mensibus, sine mori. Item *coronare Regem Francue Regem NeapoUtanum sine prttjudicio,* et been securos, Cardinales S. Petri ad Vincula, Gurcensem, Sabellum, et Columnam de non ofiendendo eos: pro quorum securitatis declaratione deberent convenire in sero illius diei coram Reverendo D. Cardinale Alexandrino, Rever. in Christo Patres D. D. Bartholomaeus Nepesinus et Sutrinus Secretarius, etjo. Perusinus Episcopus Datarius, nomine Papae; et D. de Bressa et de Montpcnsicr ct D. Johannes de Gannay primus Praesidens Parliament! Parisiensis. Sed Cardinalis Sancti Petri ad Vincula, et Gurcensis, intellecta conclusione sine eis quaesta et facta, conquesti sunt Regi de pactis ipsis per eum non servatis, cum ipsis promisisset per coronam regiam, sine eorum scitu et voluntate cum Pontifice non velle concordare vel aliquid concludere. Et hoc modo conclusionem hujusmodi, et ne illi ad Rev. Cardiualem Alexandrinum venirent, impediverunt.

Feril secundi, duodecima Januarii, Rex Francia e equitavit per urbem solus, et illam videndi causa, quem associavit Rev. Cardinalis S. Dionysii longe post Regem, cum aliis nobilibus equitans: inter ipsum et Regem equitabat quidam Capitaneus peditum custodiae Regis circa ipsum incedentium, curam habens quod pedites sequerentur: Sequebatur Cardinalis cum nobilibus aliis. Sequenti die, 18 Januarii, Rex equitavit ad Sanctum Sebastianum ab istis etiam associatus. Aliis sequentibus diebus alibi pro libito suae voluntatis. FeriS sextS, octava decima dicti mensis Januarii, bono mane recesserunt ex urbe Rev. Ascanius Vicecancellarius, et de Lunate, Cardinales, Mediolanum ituri, ut a nonnullis asserebatur. Eodem die in mane, Rex Franciae equitavit ad Basilicam S. Petri, ubi audita missa in capella Sanctae Petronillae per unum ex capellanis suis, si recti memini sine cantu, missa cele-

brati, ascend it ad Palatium Papae, ad cameras novas pro eo paratas, ubi fecit prandium; deinde circa horam vigesimam Papa portatus fuit per deambulatorium discoopertum in rocclioso et capucino, Cruce praecedente, quam portavit Dominus Raphael Diaconus Capellae, cum nullus adesset Subdiaconus Apostolicus, de Castro ad Palatium praefatum. Rex adventum Papae intelligens occurrit ei usque circa finem secundi horti secreti, de quo ad dictum deambulatorium ascendit, deinde Cardinales secuti sunt Regem, qui tunc cum eo praesentes erant, et ipsi Papain expectantes; Papa cum esset in piano horti praedicti praecesserunt Cardinales Regem usque ad Pontificem. Rex viso Pontifice ad spatium duarum cannarum genu flexit bis successive, competenti distantia, quod Papa finxit se non videre; sed cum Rex pro tertij genuflexione facienda appropinquaret, Papa deposuit biretum suum, et occurrit Regi ad tertiam genuflexi venienti, ae eum tenuit ne jrenuflecteretur, et deosculatus est eum. Ambo detectis

No XXXV ; erant, *sicque Rex, nec Pedem nec Manum Papce deosculatus est,* Papa noluit reponere biretum suum, nisi prius se tegeret Rex; tandem simul capita cooperuerunt, Pontifice manum bireto Regis ut cooperirctur apponente. Rex quam primum a Pontifice, ut praemittitur, receptus fuit, rogavit Papain, velle pronunciare Cardinalem, Episcopum Macloviensem Consiliarium suum, quod Papa dixit se facturum, mandans mihi, quod ad eftectum hujusmodi cappam unam cardinalem, et capellum reperirent; cappam mutavit Cardinalis Sanctae Anastasiae. Rex exist imans ibidem id statim fieri debere, interrogavit me ubinam et quando Papa esset expediturus, respondi, in camera Papagalli, ad quam continuo ibant.

Papa sinistra manu Regis dextram accipiens, eum duxit usque ad dictam cameram Papagalli; ubi antequam intraret, finxit se Pontifex SyncopS turbari, intus autem pervento Papa sedit super sedem bassam ante fenestras ibi apportatam, et Rex juxta eum supra scabellum; pro quo continuo sedem Suae Sanctitatis similem fecit apportare, me autem instante, repugnance, et sessionem hujusmodi nequaqaum convenire asserente; Papa ascendit ad sedem eminentem Consistorialem, et ibi, ordinante me, positam dimissis prius bireto et capucino rubro, et acceptis bireto et capucino albo, et stola pnetiosa, posita fuit sedes Papae cameralis ante dextram suam in qui sedit Rex, retro sedem Regis et ante in modum coronae posita scabella pro Cardinalibus, in quibus sederunt Cardinales. Papa noluit sedcre, nisi prius Rex sederet, quem manu coegit prius sedere. Deinde sedit Rev. D. Cardinalis Neapolitans, et sedit ad dextram Papae juxta murum in scabello, prout sedere solet Diaconus Cardinalis a dextris in Capella Papae existens; alii Cardinales ordine Consistoriali post eum seu prius ad ante eum, sicque *Rex, non sedit redd lined inter Cardinales, sed ante eos, seu in medio eorum.* Omnibus sic sedentibus, Papa dixit, nuper se vota omnium Cardinalium habuisse pro creatione Rev. D. Episcopi Macloviensis in sanctae Romana e Ecclesiae Cardinalem, quem Majestas Regis ibidem praesens instanter fieri supplicaverat, et ipse facere paratus erat ipsis Cardinalibus complacentibus. Respondit Rev. D. Cardinalis Neapolitans, et post eum alii, in eandem sententiam, quod non solum id ipsis placeret, sed fieri supplicarent pro Regis honore et voluntate. Tunc vocatus per me praefatus Dominus Macloviensis Cardinalis Gulielmus Brigonnetus, depositis ibi mantelloet capucino de ciambelotto nigro et bireto nigro, induit ipsum Cappa Cardinalis Valentiniensis, in qua coram Papa genu flexit, qui detecto capiteex ceremoniali, pronunciavit ipsum Cardinalem per verba, auctoritate Omnipotentis Dei, *SfC.* et Ecclesiam Macloviensem, et singula ac omnia monasteria et beneficia Ecclesiastica, quae prius in titulum et commendam obtinebat, sibi commendavit; Macloviensis osculatus est pedem et manum'Papae, et a Pontifice elevatus, ad oris osculum est receptus, tunc iterum genuflexit, et Papa imposuit capiti suo Capellum rubrum verbis in Ceremoniali positis. Quo facto Macloviensis egit gratias Pontifici, qui dix-

it Regi agendas esse, coram quo Rege ipse Macloviensis genuflexus, immemor novae dignitatis adeptae, et Episcopalis, egit ei gratias: sic flexus surrexit, et a singulis Cardinalibus ad oris osculum receptus est, mantellum praefato Domino Macloviensi exutum receperunt sui, nec me advertente, Dominus Jacobus de Casanova et Franciscus Alabagnes, secreti cubicularii, et sibi indebite usurparunt et retinuerunt. Capucinum autem et bi retum ego retinui. Interim surrexit Pontifex, et dixit se velle Regem usque ad regias Cameras associare; sed Rex id fieri omnino recusans, fuit ab omnibus Cardinalibus associates ad hujusmodi cameram, iter faciens per cameras paramcnti et om

I % nes nes Aulas et deambulatorium Rev. Domini Cardinalis Sanctae Anastasiae, et Aulam et Came XXXV. ras novas aj qUag ipjg erat inhabitaturus. Ibat autem Rex medius inter Neapolitanum a dextris, et Sancti Clementis Cardinales a sinistris, Cardinalibns omnibus binis et suo online sequentibus.

Pervento ad *quart am* praedictam, Rex egit gratias Cardinalibus, qui ab eo recesserunt omnes, dempto S. Dionysii et Macloviensi, usque ad Cameram sibi deputatam, quae fuit olim D. Falconis, quam cum non possent intrare defectu servitorum claves habendum, iverunt ad Cameram Episcopi Concordiensis, ubi aliquandiu manserunt, tum venerunt ad cameram Domini Macloviensis praedictam, ubi ante ostium Cardinalis Sancti Dionysii ab eo licentiatus discessit. Porta prima Palatii et omnia alia aditum ad Rcgem prabentia data fuerunt Scotis pro custodia Regis deputatis, qui non permittebant nisi suos aut paucissimos ex nostris intrare: interfuerunt praemissis 14. Cardinales,'videlicet Rev. Dominus Neapolitanus Episcopus; S. Clementis, Parmensis, S. Anastasiae, Montis Regalis, Ursinus, S. Dionysii, Alexandrinus, Carthaginensis, Presbyteri; Sancti Georgii, S. Severini, Valentinus, Caesarinus et Cermanus, Diaconi. Dedi e &dem die Rev. Domino Macloviensi Information cm competentem de strenis consuetis persolvendis, per schedulam hujusmodi tenoris:

Cubiculariis secretis S. D. N. duca-

torem centum--rf. 100

 Scutifero Capelli-----------rf. 100

Magistris Caeremoniarum, d voluntatem suam---/.

 Servientibus Armorum----------rf. 15

 Magistris OfEciariis-----------rf. 15

 Portae ferreae custodibus---------rf. 6

 Custodibus Portae prima:---------rf. 3

 Custodibus horti secret!--------rf. 3

Custodibus S. D. N. Pap rf. 10

Sum ma ducat. 252

Dominica, 18januarii, le Pape dit aut Maistre des Ceremonies qu'il tiendroit consistoire pour la reception du Roy de France, et comme il la falloit faire. Comme le Pape parloit de cela, le Roy survint, le Pape le fust recevoir et la parlerent de la restitution du Turc. L'article portoit que le Roy donneroit fidejussores nobiles Barones et Prelatos Regni ad voluntatem Pontificis; le premier President de Gannay vouloit restraindre a dix personnes, le Pape en vouloit trente ou 40. lis contesterent sur cela 3. heures. Sur cela le Pape entra en une sale, Oh il avoit de chaires, il fist seoir le Roy dans l' une, et luy dans l' autre, la le traicte' fust leu, et de la part du Pape il y avoit les Cardinaux de S. Anastase et Alexandrin, et pour le Roy les Cardinaux S. Dennis et S. Malo; les deux Secretaires du Pape, et le Dataire et peu d' autres; et furent leu les articles du Traicte; le Notaire pour le Pape nomme Stephanus de Narnia. et celui pour le Roy Oliverius Yvon Clericus Caenomanensis. II fust faict deux Copies du Traicte, en Francois pour le Roy, et en Latin pour le Pape.

If) Janvier. 1495. Destine pour la reception du Roy et l' obedience. Le Maistre des

Ceremonies

Geremonies envoye au Roy luy dire ce qu'il avoit a faire, circa osculatidnem pedis Papa: et obedientiam praestandam, de loco inter Cardinales seu post primum Cardinalem. Rex ip-n' se cum suis decrevit ibi non sedere, sed apud Pontificem in solio stans, aliqua pauca verba. praestationis obediential proferre. Le Roy dit qu'il vouloit ouir la Messe a S. Pierre, puis disner, et de la aller veoir le Pape, et on ne peut rien obtenir de plus sur cela. Le Pape tint conseil; de la vint in cameram Papagalli fort prepare, puis en la salle du consistoire public. Les Cardinaux Alexandrin et de Carthage eurent ordre d'aller au devant du Roy. Le Pape ne voulut pas que celuy de S. Malo le dernier des Cardinaux en fust, quoy que ce fust l'ordre, mais parce qu'il estoit creature du Roy, il crut luy faire plus d'honneur. Le Pape envoya donc ces Cardinaux avertir le Roy, qui le trouverent disnant. Le Roy adverty que Ton l'attendoit, interrogea le Maistre des Ceremonies de ce qu'il falloit faire, et l'ayant escoutè, il alla dans une autre chambrc, ou il tint conseil une demie heure, fit appeller le dit Maistres des Ceremonies, et lui demanda encore une fois ce qu'l falloit faire, qui luy repeta; et de la alla trouver les deux Cardinaux et Evesque qui l'attendoient. Le Roy donc fust au consistoire avec ces Cardinaux, et medius inter eos, suivy des Princes et Grands Francois, Philippus Dom. de Bressa, Dom. de Montpensier, Dom. de Foix, Dux Cliviae, Dux Ferrariae, et alii plures. Rege veniente, Papa assumpsit pretiosam mitram, Rex fecit debitas reverentias in terram, primam in introitu Consistorii, secundam in piano ante solium Papae, tertiam in solio ante Papam, ubi genuflexus pedem, dein Papae manum-osculatus, quem Papa elevans, ad oris osculum recepit. Rex stans ad sinistram Papae, tunc Dominus Johannes de Gannay Praeses Parliamenti Parisiensis coram Pontifice venit, et genuflexus exposuit Regem ad praestandam obedientiam Sanctitati suae personaliter advenisse; velle tamen prius tres gratias a sua Sanctitate petere, esse consuetum vassallos ante eorum praestationem sive homagium investire; petebat propterea 1. omnia privilegia Christianissimo Regi, ejus conjugi et primogenito concessa, et omnia in quodam libro cujus titulum specificabat contenta confirmari; 2. ipsum Regem de Regno Neapolitano investiri; S''. de dando fidejussores de restituendo fratre magni Turci inter alia heri stipulatum cassari et aboleri. Pontifex ad haec respondit se confirmare hujusmodi primo petita, quatenus essent in usu. Ad 2. quod agitur de praejudicio tertii, propterea

oportere, cum concilio Gardinalium super hoc maturius deliberare, et in eo velle, pro posse suo, Regi complacere. Ad 3. velle esse cum ipso rege et Sacro Cardinalium Collegio, non dubitans concordes futuras. Qua responsione facta, Rex stans ad sinistram Papae protulit haec verba: Sainct Pere; Je suis venu pour faire obedience et reverence a vostre Sainctete comme ont accustume de faire mes predecesseurs, Roys de France. Quibus dictis, dictus Praeses adhuc genuflexus surrexit, et stans coram Pontifice verba Regis Latine extendit, his verbis.

Beatissime Pater; consueveruntPrincipes, et praesertim Francorum Reges Christianissimi, per suos Oratores Apostolicam sedem, et in ea pro tempore sedentem, venerari. Christianissimus vero Rex, Apostolorum Limina visitaturus, id non per Oratores et Legates suos facere, sed in propria persona voluntatem suam ostendere volens, statuit observare. Vos igitur, Pater Beatissime, Christianorum summum Pontificem, verum Christi Vicarium, Apostolorum, *Petri et Pauli successorem,* fatetur, et debitam reverentiam et obedientiam, quam Praedecessores sui, Francorum Reges, summis Pontificibus facere consueverunt, vobis p nest at, seque et omnia sua Sanctitati vestrae et huic Sanctae sedi oHert.

Papa

Papa salens, el sinistra manu sua Regis dextram tenens, respondit brevissime et conveN. XXXV. iiiente,-propositis, Regem ipsum in suo responsorio hujusmodi primogenitum filium suum appellans. Interim dum praemissa fierent, accesserunt ad solium Pontificis omnes Cardinales cum confusione propter Gallorum impetum et insolentiam. Completa Pontificis rejponsione, surrexit Papa, et sinistra manu sua Regem apprehendens, ad Cameram Papagalli reversus est, ubi depositis sacris vestibus, fingit Regem ipsum velle associare. Rex illi gratias agens ad cameram suam rediit, a nullo Cardinalium associatus. Interfuerunt omnibus prsemissis 20 Cardinales.

Le 20 Janvier, le jour de S. Sebastien, le Pape voulut celebrer Pontificalement

la Messe en faveur du Roy, le Roy avant que d'y aller voulut disner, et le Pape l'attendit un quart d'heure, et vint enfin assiste de sa noblesse sans amies: ses gardes demeurerent hors la chapelle. Rex ex commissione Papae sedit in sede nuda cum cussino de brocato tantum. Ordinatis pro ministranda aqua manibus Episcopi, de Pontificis voluntate Regem D. D. de Foix, Bresse et Montpensier, tamen quia eorum praecedentia mihi ignota erat, communicavi id Regi, quem interrogavi si ipse dare aquam vellet, respondit id libentur facturum, si Regibus conveniret; de aliis tribus quod digniorem locum D. de Bresse, 2. D. de Foix; primo igitur dedit aquam D. de Foix, 2 D. de Montpensier, 3. Domino de Bresse, Rex cui portari feci *bachilia et credentia Papce* per Dominum de Ligni camerarium suum secretum, qui singulis noctibus cum Rege solet dorm ire; et ego portavi *lobaliam pro collo* usque ad gradus solii Papae, ubi Regi ipsam imposui; et acceptis per Regem bacilibus, ascendit ad Papain, et dedit stans aquam manibus Papae; qui voluit quod ipse Rex de aqna credentiam faceret. Papa aquam post communionem accepit de manibus Regis Francprum. De multis interrogavit me Rex quid hoc esset, declaravi singula ut potui, replicavit Rex ut clarius exponerem-, nihilominus non cessavit repetere, et non potui illi semper satisfacere.

22 Janvier, le Cardinal de Gurce reconcile avec le Pape en receut la Benediction, et culpam suam Pontifici agnovit; sed in praesentia Cardinalium de Ursinis, et Sancti Georgii crimina Pontifici objecit; Simoniam, peccatum carnis, informationem Magno Turco missam et mutuam intelligentiam; asserens ipsum Pontificem magnum simulatorem et veram deceptorem esse, si sui veram mihi rctulerunt. 28 Janvier, post prandium le Pape monta a Cheval et le conduit aussy, et furent a la place de Saincte Pierre, le Roy de France s' y trouva-, qui cum Papa biretum deposuisset ' amovit etiam Papa capellum et biretum, nec voluit Papa illa prius reponere, quam Rex caput suum cooperuisset; tenuit Papa continuo Regem a sinistris; Dom. de Bressa continuo equitavit ad

sinistram Regis; sicquc Regem medium posuit inter se et Papain: Omnes alii Principes et Nobiles equitarunt immediate post Regem, et post eos gentes sui armorum. 28 Janvier, Gem Sultan Frater Magni Turcae, equester de Castro Sancti Angeli associatus fuit usque ad Palatium S. Marci, et ibidem Regi Francorum assignatus. Erecta iuerunt per urbem duo patibula, unum in Campo Florae, alterum in platea Judaeorum per officiales Regis Franciae, et per eos ministrabatur justitia, non per officiales Papae, et mandata publica sivc banni per urbem fiebant sub nomine dicti Regis, et non sub nomine Papae. Rex finxit se velle pedes Papae deosculari, Papa autem non voluit. Cardinalis Valen tinus

W XXXVf PPUloS misero diutuma: servitutis jugo vindicare, et pristinae libertati restituere posse; hac spe elatus, secum animo cogitans, quod a se tanto principe dignum, in tanta ac tam fcelici expeditione prcestari posset, vel quod suae Celsitudini placeret, vel quod ad rem fcelkiter gerendam, hostesque ipsos Turcos facilius debellandos conduceret, et summae ipsius gloria; ac supremis honoribus accederet; tametsi quod se Imperium ipsum Constantinopolitanum pro derelicto quodammodo haberetur, cum tamen pro deperdito numquam habitum fuisset, tantoque Imperio ipsum invictum Francorum Regem omnibus aliis praeferundum esse dijudicans; Deo Optimo, bonorum operum Fautore, sic in ejus aspirante, in animo suo, nullo alio promovente, *constituit ac decrevit jus otnne ad dictum Constantinopolitanum Imperium, in ipsum Serenissimum, ac Christianissimum Regem Uberaliter transferre, et cedere.* Quocirca idem illustris D. Andreas Paleologus Dispotus constitutus ut supra, nullo juris aut fecti errore ductus, ex suit mera libera et spontanea voluntate, gratuitaque liberalitate, ex certS animi sui scientia, deliberatoque proposito, et causis et rationibus supra expressis, *irrevocandd donalione, qua dicitur inter vi vos iargiendo donacit, et titulo donationis transtulit, cessit, concessit ac mandavit Serenistimo, ac Christianissimo Carolo, Dei gratid Francorum Regi,*

absenti, et nobis notariis et publicis personis, praesentibus recipientibus ac legitime stipulantibus pro ipso Serenistmo ac Christiantssimo Rege, et suis in regno legitimis successoribus, omnia et singula jura, quae habuit et habet in supradicto Imperio Constantinopolitano, ac Trapeguntino, et Oispotatu Cerviano, cum omni plenitudine quarumcunque potestatum, et jurisdictibnum, tam dicta; Regies Civitatis Constantinopolitanx, quam aliarum quarumcunque Civitatum, et cum omnibus potentatibus, Dispotatibus, Ducatibus, Comitatibus, praeminentiis, insignibus, privilegiis, preerogativis, et cum omnibus adhaerentiis, pertinentiis, usibus, utilitatibus, commoditatibus, membris et adjentiatiis quibuscunque, ad dictum Imperium et Dispotatus, Civitates et Potentatus, Ducatus et Comitatus spectantibus et pertinentibus, tam de jure quam de consuetudine, et per alios suos auctores et superiores Impcratores Ghristianos possideri solitas et consuetas, et cum omnibus fetidis et locis feudalibus et superioritatibus et immutatibus, necnon actionibus realibus et personalibus, utilibus et directis, civilibus et praetoris, hypothecariis seu mixtis et in rem scriptis; reservato sibi tamen jure Dispotatus Moreae, seu Peloponnensis Provincial, cum omnibus juribus et prasheminentiis ipsius Dispotatus, nullo alio jure, nullaque alia actione sibi aut suis successoribus in hiis quomodolibet reservatis; Constituens ipsum Serenissimum et Christianissimum Regem in locum jus et privilegium ipsius Donatoris, ac etiam constituens eumdem procuratorem, ut in rem suam propriam; ita quod pro dictis juribus agat, excipiat, utatur, experiatur utilibus et directis actionibus, et quantum in ipso Donatore facultas existat et extendatur dedit idem Serenissimo Regi potestatem ac facultatem intrandi, capiendi, retinendi possessionem dicti totius Imperii, Dispotatuum et potentatuum et Civitatum, propria ipsius Serenissimi et Christianissimi Regis et suorum legitimorum successorum auctoritate, et absque alicujus alterius jurisdictionem habentis licentia. Quam quidem possessionem donee corporaliter et naturaliter nactus

fucrit et apprehenderit, constituit idem Donator se tenere et possidere nomine ipsius Serenissimi et Christianissimi Regis et suorum legitimorum successorum pradictorum; nobis Notariis praesentibus recipientibus et legitime stipulantibus, ut supra; asscrens idem Illustris Doiu. Dispotus Donator dicta jura donata ad eum spectasse ac spectare spectare, ct nulli alteri donata, cessa, concessa, seu aliter alienata extitisse in totum, vel pro parte. Promittens etiam hujusmodi, et omnia et singula contenta in ea, ratam et ra-N0,XXXVi. ta, grata et firma habere, et perpetuo tenere, et ipsam non revocare ex aliqua causa, et maxime supervenientia liberorum, nec aliter contra facere, dicere, vel venire, sub poena perjurii; et renuntiavit expresse, etiam sub religione et vinculo juramenti, solemn iter tactig corporaliter sacris scripturis in manibus nostrorum Notariorum, solemnitali a jure introductae insinuationis de donatione hujusmodi fiendae, quatenus ipsam insinuare opporteat. Et nihilominus ad majorem abbundantioremque cautelam Procuratorem constituit eumdem Revm. Dom. Raymundem Cardinalem *Gorccns.* ad comparandum ipsius constituentis nomine coram quocunque ordinario judice Ecclesiastico vel Seculari cujuscunque fori, quem ipse elegerit, cui plenam facultatem dedit eligendi qucmcunque sibi placuerit judicem, in quem ex nunc expresse consensit ac consentiit, quoad hunc voluntatia e jurisdictionis insinuationis fiendae, suo et dicto nomine dictam insinuationem solemniter faciendum cum expressa ratificatione, nec non ad petendum hujusmodi donationem in actis publicis redigi, mandari, et solemne decretum interponendi, ita quod perpetual vires habeat et inviolabilis roboris firmitatem obtineat, et nullo unquam tempore infringi possit, aut valeat, tam ex defectu insinuationis praedictae quam ex alia causa, seu titulo, vel ex alio quocunque quaesito colore; Renuntians etiam omnibus aliis et singulis solemnitatibus, exceptionis juris vel facti, defensionibus quibus contra facere vel venire posset. Nobis Notariis praesentibus, recipientibus et legitime stipulantibus ut supra in omnibus et singulis capitulis praesentis contractus, pro dicto Serenissimo ac Christianissimo Rege et suis legitimis successoribus; de quibus omnibus et singulis rogati fuimus, ut publicum conficeremus instrumentum unum vel plura, et toties quoties opus fuerit.

Actum Romae in Ecclesia S. Petri in Montorio post celebratam Missam Spiriuls Sancti per praefatum Revm. Dom. Cardinalem, ipiis Dmo. Cardinali, et Dmo. Dispoto existentibus inter duas sacratissimas Columnas, in quo loco Beatus Petrus Apostolorum princeps Sacri Martyrii coronam suscepit; praesentibus, audientibus, et intelligentibus videlicet; Venerab. viris Dom. Petro de Militibus, Domino Dominico de Rubaeis, Canonico Basilicae Principis Apostolorum, Nobilibus Civibus Romanis ac Dmo. Fratre Joanne Augustino Vercellens. Praeposito Ecclesiae S. Mariae de pace, et Dom. Fratre Jacobo Cremonens. ejusdem Ecclesiae Vicario, Ordinis Canonicorum Regularium Congregationis Lateranens. ac Fratre Francisco de Mediolano, Ordinis Minorum S. Francisci, residenti in dicta Ecclesia S. Petri, Testibus ad praemissa habitis et rogatis.

Et quia Ego Franciscus de Schracten de Florentia, Civis Romanus, Pontificali et etiam Imperiali auctoritatibus Notarius Publicus, de omnibus et singulis praemissis rogatus fui, uno cum praeclaro U. J. Doctore Dom. Camillo de *Bene in Bene*, Civi et Notario Romano, hanc *Not am* manu mei propria scriptam et subscriptam per eumdem dictum Camillum tenendam feci, et subscripsi in fidem, robur, et testimonium Veritatis.

N XXXVII.

(*Vol.* i. *p.* 201.; *Opere Volgari di Sanazzaro*, SON ETTO.

O di rara vertù gran tempo albergo,
Alma stimata, e posta fra gli dei;
Or cieco abisso di vizj empj, e rei,
Ove pensando sol, m' adombro, e mergo:
Il nome tuo da quante carte vergo
Sbandito fia; che più ch' i' non vorrei,
E' per me noto; ond' or da' versi miei
Le macchie lavo, e'l dir pulisco, e ter-

go.
Di tuoi chiari trionfi altro volume
Ordir credea; ma per tua colpa or manca;
Ch' augel notturno sempre abborre il lume.
Dunque n' andrai tutta assetata, e stanca,
A ber l' obblìo dell' infelice fiume;
E rimarrà la carta illesa, e bianca.

SONETTO.

SCRIVA di te chi far gigli, e viole,
Del seme spera di pungtnti urtiche,
Le stelle al ciel veder tutte nemiche,
E con T Aurora in occidente il Sole.
Scriva chi fama al mondo aver non vuole;
A cui non fur giammai le Muse amiche:
Scriva chi perder vuole le sue fatiche,
Lo stil, l'ingegno, il tempo, e le parole.
Scriva chi bacca in lauro mai non colse:
Chi mai non giunse a quella rupe estrema,
Nè verde fronda alle sue tempie avvolse.
Scriva in vento, ed in acqua il suo poema
La man che mai per te la penna tolse;
E caggia il nome, e poca terra il prema.

No. XXXVII.

N XXXVIII.

(*Vol.* i. *p.* 202J

Opere di Antonio Tibaldeo. Ed. Fen. 1534.

SONETTO.

Se gran thesor, se inespugnabil mura,
Se squadre, e un capitan de astuto ingegno,
Havesser forza a mantenire un regno,
De Napoli havria Alphonso anchor la cura.
Qualunque regnar vuol senza paura,
Cerchi l' amor de i populi, e no il sdegno
Che chi se fonda sopra altro sostegno
Per qualche tempo, ma non molto dura.
Scorno eterno a l' Italico paese,
Quando fia letto, che un regno si forte
Contra Francesi non si tenne un mese!
Sagunto che Annibale havea a le porte,
Per Roma, fin che puote si diffese,
Che per Principe buon dolce par morte.

N XXXIX.

(*Voi.* i. *p.* 202J

MaruUi Op. Ed. Paris. 1561.

Ad Caroi.um Recem Francia. INVICTE
magni Rex Caroli genus,
Quem tot virorum tot superum piae
Sortes jacenfes vindicemque
Justitiae, fideique poscunt:
Quem mcèsta tellus Ausonis hinc vocat,
Illinc solutis Grecia crinibus,
Et quicquid immanis profanat
Turca Asiae, Syriaeque pinguis;
Olim virorum patria et artium,
Sedesque vera ac religio Deum,
Nunc Christianae servitutis
K2
Nomina per populos itura;
At supplicantum tot misere exulum,
Sordesque tangant, et lacrymae piae:
At Christianonun relicta
Ossa tot, heu, canibus lupisque:
Fcedisque tangat, relligio modis
Spurcata Christi, sospite Galliae
Rectore te nobis potentis;
Cujus avum proavumque clara
Virtus, furentem Barbariem unice
Et Sarracenos contudit impetus,
Cum satva tempestas repente
Missa quasi, illuviesque campis.
Non occupatx finibus African
Contenti Hiberi, non opibus soli,
Sperare jam Gallos, et ipsum
Ausi animis Rhodanum superbis.
Sed nec bonorum tunc Superum favor
Desideratus, nec tibi tam pia
In bella eunti defuturus,
Carle, moras modo mitte inertes.
Occasionem et quam tribuunt cape:
JEque nocentes dissimiles licet
Gnarus, patrantem, quique possit
Cum, scelus haud prohibet patrari.

(*Vol.* i. *p.* 203.; *Petri Criniti Op. p.* 538.

Ad Faustum, Dk Carolo, Rege Francorum, Cum Ab Urbem Tenderet Cum ExERcmr.

QUID occupatum litteris urges tuis, Frustraque toties flagitas,
Ut impotentis Galliae fastum gravem,
Regemque dicam Carolum?
Satis superque, Fauste, dedimus lacrymic,
Claderaquc nostram luximus.
Et ccce rursus additur malis scelus,
Fovemus ipsi Galliara:

Ac studio inerti opes et omnem militem
Jungimus ad hostilem manum.

Irrepsit altum virus animis Italum,
Ac pervagatur latins.

Vides nefandis ut trahuntur odiis
Plerique Thuscorum duces.

Et dum vicissim fluctuantes dimicant,
Bacchantur in caedem suam.

Sed interim Carolus ad urbis moenia
Cum copiis victor agitur:

Audaxque monstrat militi Romam suo
Et conuninatur patribus.

Intorquet hastam miles in Humeri
sacrum,

Patremque Tybrim despicit.

O prisca uirtus, o senatusRomuli,
An haec videtis Caesares?

Vidi moventem Martios fasces Jovem,
Et annuentem Barbaris.

Quantum hinc maioruih, quantum adest
incendii,

Quantum cruoris effluct?

Poenam rependet innocens Neapolis
Virtutis immemor suas:

Et occidet Aragoniae clarum decus
Sic Mars cruentus imperat:

Qui nunc feroces Galliae turmas fovet,
Ridens inertes Italos.

Grave est videre, Fauste, quae fata imperant.

Vas! tibi,' cave Neapolis.
No-XLI.
(Vol. i. *p.* 5205.; *Diary of Burchard,
from Gordon's Hist. of Alex. VI. in App.
(see also the Lettere di Principi, vol. i.
p. 5.) Instructions donntes par le Pape
Alexandre au Nonce par luy emoye* J
*Sultan Bajazet Emperevr des Turcs.
Item Itttrcs du dit Sultan au dit Alexandre VI.*

N-XLI. SUPERIORIBUS diebus, Cardinale
Gurcense referente, Dominus Georgius
Bosardus literarum Apostolicarum
Scriptor per S. D. N. Papam ad magnum
Turcam Nuncius Oratorque missus, ut
ipse Cardinalis dicebat, per Illust. D.
Joannem de Rovere Abuae Urbis prafectum, Illustrissimi D. Cardinalis S.
Petri ad Vincula fratrem Germanum,
captus fuit, et apud Senogalliam detentus, apud quem idem Cardinalis
Gurcensis compertas fuisse dixit informationes per eundemSanctum D. N.
sibi datas, super iis quae apud magnum
Turcam agere deberet, quae'dictus Cardinalis Gurcensis Sanct. D. N, ad infamiam improbrabat, quarum informationum Nuntii et Oratoris ad magnum
Turcam tenor.

Alexander Papa Sextus. INSTRUCTIONES
tibi Georgio Bosardo Nuntio et familiari
nostro: postquam hinc recesseris, directe et quando citius poteris, ibis ad
potentissimum magnum Turcam Sultan
Bajazet ubicunque fuerit, quem
postquam debitc salutaveris, et ad Divini Numinis timorem et amorem excitaris, sibi significabis nomine nostro,
qualiter Rex Franciae properat cum
maxima potentia terrestri et maritima
cum auxilio status Mediolanensium,
Britonum, Burdegalensium, Normandorum et cum aliis gentibus hue Romam
veniens eripere *k* manibus nostris Gem
Sultan, fratrem Celsitudinis suae, et acquirere regnum Neapolitanum, et
ejicere Regem Alphonsum cum quo
sumus in strictissimo sanguinis gradu et
amicitia conjuncti, et tenemur eum defendere, cum sit feudatarius noster et
annuatim sol vat nobis censum; et sunt
anni sexaginta tres, et ultra quod fuit
investitus Rex Alphonsus' avus ejus,
deinde Ferdinandus Pater, cui successit
Rex, qui per praedecessores nostros et
per nos fucrunt investiti et incoronati
de dicto regno. Ideo hac de causa praedictus Rex Franciae effeclus inimicus
noster, qui non solum properabit ut dictum Gem Sultan capiat et ipsum regnum
acquirat, sed etiam in Graeciam transfrctare et patrias Celsitudinis suae debellare qucat, prout suae M. innotescere
debet: et dicuut quod mittant dictum
Gem Sultan cum classe in Turchiam. Et
cum nobis opus sit resistere et nos defendere a tanta Regis Franciae Potentia, oinnes conatus nostras exponere
oportet, ct se bene praeparare; quod
cum jam fecerimus, opusque sit facere
maxim as impensas, cogimur ad subsidium praefati Sultan Bajazet recurrere,
spcrantes in amicitia bona quam ad invicem habemus, quod in tali necessitate
juvabit nos: quem rogabis et nomine
nostro exhortaberis, ac ex te persuadebis, cum omni instantia; ut placeat quam
citius mittere nobis ducatos quadraginta
millia in auro Venetos pro *annata* annir
praesentis, quae finiet ultimo Novembris venturi, ut cum tern-1.. pore possimus nobis subvenire, in quo Majestas
sua faciet nobis rem gratissimam: cui in
praesentiarum nolumus imponere aliud
gravamen et exponendo vires et conatus
nostras in resistentia facienda ne dictus
Rex Franciae aliquam victoriam contra
nos potiatur et contra fratrem S. Majestatis. Cum autem ipse Rex Franciae terra marique sit longe potentior nobis, indigeremus auxilio Venetorum, qui sistunt, nec volunt nobis esse auxilio, imo
habent arctissimum commercium cum
inimicis nostris, et dubitamus quod sint
nobis contrarii, quod esset nobis magnum argumentum offensionis, et non
reperimus aliam viam convertendi ad
partes nostras tractandas, quam per viam ipsius Turcae, cui denotabis ut
supra, et quod si Franci victores forent,
sua Majestas pateretur magnum interesse; tum propter ereptronem Gem Sultan fratris sui, tum etiam quia prosequereatur expeditionem et longè cum
majori conatu contra *Altitudinem suam,*
et in tali causa habebunt auxilium ab
Hispanis, Anglicis, Maximiliano et
Hungaris, Polonis et Bohemis, qui
omnes sunt potentissimi Principes. Persuadebis et exhortaberis Majestatem
suam, quam tenemur certiorem reddere
ob veram et bonam amicitiam quam
habemus ad invicem, ne patiatur
aliquod interesse; ut statim mittat unum
Oratorem ad dominium Venetorum, significando qualiter certo intellexit
Regem Francia e movere se ad veniendum Romam ad capiendum Gem Sultan
fratrem, inde regnum Neapolitanum,
demum terraque et mari contra se
praeparare, quod velit facere omnem resistentiam et se defe.ndere contra ipsum, et devitare, ne Crater suus capiatur
cx manibus nostris, quos exhortetur et
adstringat pro quanto correspondet pendant cari perdant amicitiam suam, debeant esse adjumento et defensioni nostrae et Regis Alphonsi terra marique,
et quod omnes amicos nostros et pnememoratum Regem habebit pro bonis
amicis suis, et nostras inimicos pro inimicis; ct si dominium pollicebitur consentire tali petitioni suae, Orator habeat
mandatum de non recedendo Venetiis
quousque viderit effectum, et quod dicti

Veneti declarent fecisse amicos et adjumento nobis, et Regi Alphonso, et esse contra amicos Francorum et aliorum adhaerentium Regi Franciae: et si contradixerint, Orator significet, quod non habebit eos amicos, et postea rccedat ab eis indignatus; quamquam credimus, quod si sua Majestas ardenter adstringet eos, modo couvenienti, condescendent ad faciendam voluntatem Majestatis suae. Et sic persuadeas ei multum, ut facere hoc velit, quia istud est majus adjuvamen quod habere possumus impetret, resistet injuriis nostris et sollicitabis quanto citius talem Oratorem, ut recedat ante, nam multum importat acceleratio tua.

Denotabis pariter magno Turcae, adventum Oratoris magni Soldani ad nos cum litteris et muneribus quae transmisit nobis quando Gem Sultan, fratrem suum ac magnas pblationes et promissiones quas nobis fecit de magno thesauro ac de multis alijs rebus, et bene scis quandoquidem tuo medio omnia sunt praticata, et sicut continetur in capitulis quae dictus orator fecit et dedit; signifieabis Majestati suae intentionem nostram in quantum sibi promisimus firmiter tenebimus, et nunquam contraveniemus in aliqua re. Imo nostra; intentionis est accrescere et meliorare nostram bonam amicitiam. Bene gratum nobis esset, et de hoc multum precamnr et hortamur D. S. quod pro aliquo tempore non impediat Hungarum neque in aliqua parte Christianitatis, et maxime in Croatia et Civitatibus Ragusiae et Leguiae; quod faciendo et observando nos faciemus quod Hungarus non inferat ei aliquid illiquid damnum, ct in hoc Majesias sua habebit compassionem complacendi nobis, attento maxime motu Francorum et aliorum Principum. Quod si in bellando perseveraret, habeat pro comperto sua Magnitude, quod in ejus auxilio essent quamplures Principes Christiani et doleret Majestatem suam non fecisse, in ejus auxilio, secundum auxilium quod damus sibi, primo, ex officio quando sumus Pater et Dominus omnium Christianorum. Postea desideramus quietem Majestatis suae ad bonam et mutuant amicitiam: quoniam si Majestas sua aliter statueret prosequi et molestare

Christianos, cogeremur rebus consulere, cum aliter non possemus obviare maximis apparatibus qui fiunt contra Majestatem suam. Dedimus tibi duo brevia, quae exhibebis Turcae, in uno continetur *quod Jaciat,* tibi dare et consfgnare 40000 ducatos pro *Amtataproesenti:* aliud est Credentiae ut praestet tibi fidem, in omnibus quacunque nomine nostro sibi expomeris. Habitis 40000 ducatis, in loco consueto, facies quietantiam secundum consuetudinem, et venies recto tramite cum navi tuta, et cum illuc applicaveris certiores nos reddes et expectabis responsum nostrum: Presens tua intimatio consistit in acceleratione, facies ergo diligentiam hie in eundo ad Turcam in expeditione et in redeundo similiter.

Ego Georgius Bosardus, Nuntius et familiaris praefatae Sanctitatis, per praesens scriptum et subscriptum manu mea propria, fidem facio et confiteor supradicta habuisse in commissis abore praefata e Sanctitatis, Romae de mense Junii M.cccc.lxxxxiiii, et executum fuisse apud magnum Turcam in quantum fuit mihi ordinatum, ut supra: et quantum ad Oratorem quem requisivit Sanctitas sua a Turca mittendum Venetias est obtentum, qui e vestigio debebat recedere Constantinopoli de mense Septembris post me, ad exequendum in quantum erat voluntas praefatae Sanctitatis cum illustrissimo Domino Venetorum; idem Georgius Bosardus manu propria scripsi et subscripsi. Etego Philippusde Patriarchis Clericus Foroloviensis, Apostolica et Imperiali Autoritate Notarius Publicus, suprascriptum inscriptionem et instructionem ex Originali de Senogallia transmisso, de verbo ad verbum transumpsi, et scripsi, nihil mutando aut addendo, et hoc ipsum transumptum prout jacebat ad literam feci requisitus et rogatus: In cujus testimonium nic me subscripsi et signum meum apposui consuetum. Florentine die 25. Novembris, anno 1494.

I.

SULTAN Bajazet Chan, Dei Gratia Rex Maximus et Imperator utriusque Continentis Asiaeque et Europae, Christianorum excellenti Patri et D. D. Alexandro

divina Providentia Romana e Ecclesia Pontifici dignissimo, Reverentiam debitam et benevolam cum sincera dispositione. Post convenientem et justam salutationem significamus tuo supremo Pontificio quemadmodum in praesenti misistis vestrum hominem et legatum Georgium Bosardum cum literis quae continebant de vestra salute et amore et amicitia: venh et pervenit in optimo tempore ad meam altissimam portam, et didicimus qua; per literas significabantur: et quae commisistis ipsi dicere ex ore, retulit etiam coram magnitudine mea Integra quemadmodem tua Gloriositas ipsi mandavit. Cum didicerimus primum nos de salute et bona habitudine tua; Dominationis delectati sumus maxime, et exultavit spiritus meus propterea, et illis quae per ipsum significastis assensi sumus etiam, et fecimus ipsa, et misimus etiam ad loca quae significastis, ut mitteremus sicut volebat Magnitudo vestra. Ulterius et id quod conventum est, *quamvis ad nostrum terminvm satis tempo ris re/iquum sit,* taihen de quo scripsistis et petiistis ipsum cuiu festinatione datum est. Praedictus Legatus Georgius jam perfecit omnia bene, quaecunque requirit oficium Legati, imde et honoratus est digne a mea altitudine, ut ipsum dccet: misimus etiam una cum ipso a nostra altissima porta fidelem nostrum hominem Cassimen, et data est sibi licentia, ut rursusad tuum Pontificium redeat: nostra enim amicitia Dei voluntate in dies augebitur_ Nuntiis autem vestrae salutis nunquam nos privetis, ut audientes magis delectemur. Datum in Aula Nostrae Sultanicae Autoritatis in Constantinopoli 1494. anno a Jesu Prophetae Nativitate, SULTAN Bajazet Chan, Dei Gratia, Rex Maximus, et Impcralor utriusque continentis Asiaeque et Europae, Christianorum omnium Excellenti Patri et Domino Alexandro divina Providentia summo Pontifici dignissimo, reverentiam debitam ct benevolentiam cum sincera dispositione: dignum et fidelem vestrum hominem et legatum Georgium Bosardum in Altissimam portam misistis: venit et attulit nuntios de vestra salute et bona habitudine et delectavit nos mirifice; attulit ctiam et verba quae mandastis ipsi privatim et etiam misistis integrè: et didicimus, et bene commisimus et nos ipsi sermones, ut nuntiet ipsos coram tuo Pontificio, et detur sibi fides in his: quaecunque enim dixerit, sunt verba nostra indubitata: etiam praefatus Georgius perfecit omnia bene quaecunque requirit Oficium Legati,unde et honoratus est digne a mea Altitudine secundum ipsius decentiam, et data est sibi licentia, ut redeat rursus in Aulam tuae Magnitudinis et manifestet illi illa quae nos ipsi commisimus. Datum in Aula nostrae Sultanicae Autoritatis in Constantinopoli 1494, anno a Jesu Prophetae nativitate, 18. Septembris. III. SULTAN Bajazet Chan, Dei Gratia &c. Alexandro Divini Providentia Romanae Ecclesiae supremo Pontifici dignissimo, &c. post convenientem et justam salutationem significamus tuae Dominationi quemadmodum in praesenti fidelem nostrum Cassimen servum cum nostris literis misimus ad summum tuum Pontificium, ut ferat ad nos de vestra salute et bona habitudine quod nos cupimus quotidie audire et delectari; similiter significet etiam et vobis de nostra felici sanitate et amore, ut et vos quae dc nobis sunt ab ipso dicenda audientes delectemini sicut et nos delectamur: jussimus etiam, et est datum id quod est conventum praedicto servo meo Cassimi, ut perferat ipsum ad tuam gloriositatem; et cum auxilio Dei reversus fuerit rursus ad meum Altitudinem, significet nobis vestram salutein et amicitiam, ut inde cum audiverimus magis etiam delectemur, et quae ipsi mandavimus nota faciei tuae magnitudini. Dajtae autem ipsi fidem in his quaecunque dixerit: datum in Aula nostrae Sultanicae Auctoritatis in Constantinopoli, 1494. anno a Jesu Prophetae nativitate, 18. Septembris. IV. SULTAN Bajazet Chan, SLc. Alexandro, &c. post convenientem et justam salutationem notum sit tuo supremo Pontificio, quemadmodum Reverend, D. Nicolaus Libo Archiepiscopus Arelatensis est dignus et fidelis homo ipsius, et a tempore praecedentis Papae su L premi premi Pontificis Domini Innocentii usque in hodiernum diem in tempus suae magnitudinis continue ad

pacem et amicitiam festinat, semperque anima et corpore in fidelissima fide duabus partibus servivit, et adhuc servit; hujus igitur rei causa justum est a vobis decerni majori in ordine ipsum esse debere, unde et *rogaoimus supremum Pontificem, ut faceret ilium Cardinalem, et assensus est nostra: petitioni,* adeo ut Uteris et nobis significaverit quod petitum est datum fuisse ipsi, verum, quia non erat tempus id Septembris Mensis, non sedet in ordine suo et ut requirit consuetudo. Interea vero jussu Dei dedit Pontifex commune debitum, et sic ipse remansit. E£ igitur de causa scribimus et rogamus tuam magnitudinem propter amicitiam et pacem quam inter nos habuimus, et propter meum cor, ut adimpleat ipsi tuum Pontificium, videlicet, ut faciat ipsum perfecturu Cardinalem: habebimus et nos id in Magna Gratia. Datum, fcc. ut supra.

Supra scriptae quaternae literae erant scriptae sermone in carta authentica more Turcarum cum quodam signo aureo in capite, quas literas transtulit in Latinum de verbo ad verbum me excipiente et notante auditus vir Lascaris natione Graecus; assistente illi et adjuvante interpretationem Rever: D. Aloysio Cyprio Episcopo Famagustano Illustriss: Principis Salernitani Secretario. In cujus rei fidem et testimonium ego Philippus de Patriarchis Clericus Foroliviensis Apostolica et Imperiali Autoritate Notarius Publicus omnia supradicta manu mea propria scripsi et subscripsi, et meum signum apposui rogatus et requisitus.

V.

SULTAN Bajazet Chan, Filius Soldani Mahumeti, Dei Gratia Imperator Asiae, Europae et oris maritimae, Patri et Domino omnium Christianorum Divina Providentia Papae Alexandro sexto Romanae Ecclesiae digno Pontifici, post debitam et meritoriam salutationem ex bono animo et puro corde significamus vestrae Magnitudini per Georgium Bosardum servitorem et nuntium vestrae Potentiae. Intelleximus bonam convalescentiam suam, et etiam quae retulit pro parte ejusdem vestrae magnitudinis, ex quibus laetati sumus magnamque

consolationem cepimus: inter alia mihi retulit quomodo Rex Franciae animatus est habere Gem frarrem nostrum, qui est in manibus vestrae Potentiae, quod esset multum contra voluntatem nostramj et vestrae Magnitudinis sequeretur maximum damnum, et omnes Christiani paterentur detrimentum. Idcirco una cum praefato Georgio cogitare ccepimus pro quiete, utilitate, et honore vestrae potentiae, et adhuc pro mea satisfactione, bonum esset quod dictum Gem, meum fratrem, qui subjectus est morti et detentus in manibus vestrae Magnitudinis, omnino mori faceretis, quod sibi vita esset, et potentiae vestrae utile, et quieti commodissimum, mihiq; gratissimum; et si in hoc Magnitudo vestra contenta sit complacere nobis, prout in sua prudentia confidimus facere velle, debet pro meliori suae potentiae et pro majori nostra satisfactione quanto citius poterit cum illo meliori modo quo placebit vestrae Magnitudini, dictum Gem levare facere ex angustiis istius mundi, et transferri ejus an imam in alterum saeculum, ubi meliorem habebit quietem; et si hoc adimplerc faciet vestra potentia et mandabit nobis corpus suum in qualicunque loco citra mare, promittimus Nos Sultan Bajazet supradictus, in quocuuque loco placuerit vestrae Magnitudini ducatorum dueatorum 300,000. ad emenda filii's suls aliqua Dominia, qua ducatorum 300,000. consignare faciemus illi cui ordinabit vestra Magnitudo antequam sit nobis dictum corpus datum et per vestros meis consignatum. Adhuc promitto vestrae potentiae pro meliori sua satisfactione, quod neque per me, aut per meos servos, neq; etiam per aliquem ex patriis meis erit datum aliquod impedimentum aut damnum dominio Christianorum cujuscunquc qualitatis aut conditionis fuerit, sive in terra sive in mari, nisi issent aliqui qui nobis aut subditis nostris facerent damnum. Et pro majori adhuc satisfactione vestrae MagnitudiniS, ut sit secura sine aliqua dubitatione de omnibus his quae supra, promitto, juravi et affirmavi omnia in praesentii prafati Georgii per verum Deum quem adoramus, et per Evangelia nostra observare vestrae potentiae omnia usque ad complementum, nee aliqui re dencere sine defectu aut aliqui defectione. Et adhuc pro majori securitate vestrae Magnitudinis, ne ejus animus in aliqui dubitatione remaneat, imo sit certissimus de novo, ego supra dictus Sultan Bajazet Chan juro per Deum verum, qui creavit ccelum et terram, et omnia quae in iis sunt, et in quem credimus et adoramus, quod faciendo adimplere ea quae supra eidem requiro, Promitto per dictum juramentum servare omnia quae supra continentur et in aliqua re nunquam contra facere neque contravenire vestrae Magnitudini. Scriptum Constantinopoli in Palatio nostro secundum adventum Christi, Die 12. Septembris, 1494.

Ego Philippus de Patriarchis Clericus Foroliviensis Apostolica et Imperial; Authoritate Notarius publicus infra scriptus, literas ex Originali quod erat scriptum Uteris Latinis, in sermone Italico in carta oblonga Turcarum, quae habebat in Capite Signum Magni Turcae aureum in calce nigrum, transumsi fideliter de verbo ad verbum, et manu propria rogatus et requisitus scripsi et subscripsi, signumque men in in (idem et testimonium consuetum apposui Florentiae die vigesimi quinti Novembris, 1494. in Conventu Crncis Ordinis minorum.

N«. XLII.
(Vol. i.p. 211J
Opere di Tebaldeo. Ven. 1534.

SONETTO. NE i tuoi campi non pose il pie si presto
Annibal, che combatter li convenne, N. XLII.

Ne mai si alflitta il Barbaro ti tenne,
Cheal di fender non fusse il tuo cor desto;
Et hor, Italia, onde precede questo,
Che un picciol Gallo che l'altri hier qui venne
Per ogni nido tuo batta le penne
Senza mai ritrovarse alcuno infesto?
L2 Ma
Ma giusto esser mi par ch'el ciel te abassi,
Che più non fai Camilli, o Scipioni,
Ma sol Sardanapali, e Midi, e Crassi;
Gia una Occa tua (se guardi a i tempi buoni)

Scacciar Io puote de li Tarpei sassi,
Hor Aquile non pon, Serpi, e Leoni.
Poesie Toscane di Vincenzio da Filicaia. SONETTO.

Italia, Italia, O tu, cut feo la sorte
Dono infelice di bellezza, onde hai
Funesta dote d' infiniti guai,
Che in fronte scritti per gran doglia porte;
Deh, fossi tu men bella, o almen più forte,
Onde assai più ti paventasse, o assai
T'amasse men, chi del tuo bello a i rai
Par che si strugga, e pur ti sfida a morte!
Che or giù dall' Alpi non vedrei torrenti
Scender d' armati, nè di sangue tinta
Bever l'onda del Po Gallici armenti;
Nè te vedrei del non tuo ferro cinta
Pugnar col braccio di Straniere genti,
Per servir sempre, o vincitrice, o vinta.

N. XLIII.
(Voi. i.p. 213 J
Vergier d'Honneur.
Le samedy son armee diverse
No..XLIII, Assez matin se partit du dict Verce,
Et tost apres il monta a cheval
Pour aller boire dedans *Pouge Real;*
Qui est ung lieu de plaisance confit,
Aussi Alphons pour son plaisir le fit,
Aupres de Napples ou en toutes manieres,
Y a des choses toutes singulieres;
Camme Cennme maisons, ami goons, fenest rages,
Grans galeries, longues, amples et larges;
Jardins plaisans, fleurs de doulceurs remplies,
Et de beaulte sur toutes acomplies,
Petis preaulx, passaiges et barrieres
Costes, fontaines et petites rivieres,
Pour sesjouyr et a fois sesbatre;
Ou sont ymaiges antiques d' alabastre,
De marbre Wane, et de porphire aussi,
Empres le vif ou ne fault ca ne si;
Ung pare tout clos ou sont maints herbes saines
Beaucoup plus grans que le bois de Vicennes;
Plains d'oliviers, orangiers, grenadiers

Figuiers, datiers, poiriers, allemandiers,
Pommiers, lauriers, rosmarins, mariolaines,
Et girofflees sur toutes souveraines;
Nobles heueillets, plaisantes armeries,
Qui en tous temps sont la dedans dories;
Et de rosiers assez bien dire j'ose
Pour en tirer neuf ou dix muyts d' une rose;
D'aultres costes sont fosses et herbaiges
La ou que sont le grans bestes saulvaiges;
Comme chevreulx a la course soubdains,
Cerfs haulx branchez, grosses biches et dains;
Aussi y sont sans cordes ne ataches
Aux pastouraiges grans beufs et grasses vaches;
Chevaulx, mulets et jumens par monceaulx
Asnes, cochons, truyes et gras pourceaulx;
Et puis au bout de toutes ses praeries
Sont situes les grandes metairies,
La ou que sont avec chappons, poullailles,
Toutes manieres et sortes de voulailles
Cailles, perdris, pans, signes et faisans
Et maints oyseaulx des yndes moult plaisans
Aussi a ung four a oeufs couver,
Dont Ton pourroit sans geline eslever;
Mille poussins qui en auroit affaire,
Voire dix mille qui en vouldroit tant faire.
De ce dit pare sort une grant fontaine
Qui de vive eaue est si trescomble et plaine,
Que toute Napples peult fournir et laver.
Et toutes bestes grandement abeuvrer.
Aussi y a vignoble d' excellence,
Dont il en sort si tresgrant habondance
De vins clairets, de vin rouge et vin blanc.
Grec et latin que pour en parlor franc

Sans les exquis muscadets et vins cuyts
Q'on y queult bien tous les ans milk muyts;
Voire encore plus quant le bon heur re-vient.
Et tout cela au proufiit du roy vient.
Et an regard des caves qui y sont
En lieu certain approprie parfont,
Si grandes sont, si longues et si larges,
Et composees de si subtils ouvraiges
Tant en piliers comme voulsture ronde
Qui n' en est point de pareilles au monde.

N. XLIV.

'*(Vol.* i. *p.* 220.)

Petri Criniti Opera, p. 548.

AD DER. CAKAPHAM, DE MAI.IS ATQUE CA1.AMITATE NEAPOLU.

MIttantur veteres tot querimoniae,
  Carapha, et lacrymis pone modum tu-is;
  Indulsti patriae, dum licuit, satis; Sed frustra superos vocas.
Nam fatis trahimur, fata Neapolim
  Vexari miseris cladibus imperant,
  Et duro pariter servitio premi, Donee, non alium, queat
Regem Parthenope cernere maximum,
  Qui clarum propriis nomen honoribus
  Sublimis liquidum tollat in aethera,
Et firmum reparet decus.
Id quando acciderit, non satis audeo
  Effari; si quidem non Clarius mihi
  Per sacros tripodes certa refert Deus,
Nec servat penitus fidem.
Quod si quid liceat credere adhuc tamen,
  Nam laevum tonuit, non fuerit procul
  Quaerendus celeri qui properet gradu,
  Et Gallum reprimat ferox.

N». XLV.

(Vol. i. *p.* 224.;

Vergier d'.Honneur.

Comment le Roy fist son entree dedans Nappies, et quel honneur on luy fist, et comment il disposa de ses affaires.

Mardy xii jour de May le roy en Nap-ples ouyt la messe a la nunciade, et apres disner il s'en alla en Pouge Real, et la se assemblerent les princes et seigneurs tant de France, de N. XLV. Napples que des Ytalles pour accompa-igner le Roy a faire son entree dedans Napples comme Roy de France, de Ce-cille et de Jhcrusalem, ce qu'il fist a grant triumphe et excellence en habille-ment imperial nomme et appelle Au-guste, et tenoit la pomme d'or ronde en sa main dextre, et a l'autre main son ceptre, habille d'ung grant manteau de fine escarlate fourre et mouchete d'ermines a grant collet renverse aussi fourre d'ermines, la belle couronne sur la teste, bien et richement monte et housse comme a luy affiert et appar-tient. Le poille sur luy porte par les plus grans de la seigneurie de Napples, acompaigne a l'entour de luy de ses laquais tous habilles richement de drap d'or. Le prevost de son hostel luy aussi acompaigne de ses archiers tous a pied. Monsieur le seneschal de Beaucaire representant le Connestable de Napples, t devant luy estoit Monsieur de Mont-pencier comme vis roy et lieutenant general. Monsieur le prince de Salerne avec d'aultres grans seigneurs de France, chevaliers de l'ordre et parens du Roy, comme Monsieur de Bresse, Monsieur de Foues, Monsieur de Lucembourg, Loys Monsieur de Ven-dosme, et sans nombre d'aultres seigneurs: lesquels seigneurs dessus nommes estoient habilles en manteaulx comme le Roy. Monsieur de Piennes avec le maistre de la monnoye dudit Napples eurent la charge d'aller par toutes les rues de la dicte ville de Nap-ples pour faire nos gens, tant de guerre que aultres,afhn de laisser approucher ceulx de Napples, en especial es cinq lieux et places ou se vont jouer et solaci-er les seigneurs et dames dudict Napples a toutes heures que bon leur semble. En cesdicts lieux estoient les nobles de Napples, leurs femmes et aussi pareille-ment leurs enfans, et la plusieurs des-dicts seigneurs en grant nombre presen-toient au roy leurs enfans de. viii. x. xii. xv. et xvi. ans, requerans que il leur donnast chevallerie, et les fist chevaliers a son entree de sa propre main, ce qu'il fist; que fut belle chose a veoir et moult noble et leur venoit de grant vouloir et amour. Comme dit est, ledit seigneur de Piennes et maistre de la monnoye avoit esdicts lieux cy devant nommes pour faire lieu ausdicts seigneurs de Napples. Au regard de la compaignie que le Roy avoit avec luy, c'estoit la plus gorgiase chose et la plus triumphante qu'on vit jamais, car il avoit avec luy grans seigneurs, chamberlans, maistresd'hostels, pensionnaires, et gentils hommes sans quatre cens archiers de sa garde, deux cens ar-balestriers tous a pied armes de leurs habillemens acoustumes. Jehan Daunoy estoit arme de toutes pieces, avec ce avoit ung sayon de cramoisy decoupe bien menu sur son dit harnoys, monte sur ung grant courcier de peuille bien barde de riches bardes et disoient ceulx de Napples que jamais n'avoient veu si belle homme d'armes. Apres que le Roy eust este en ces cinq lieux cy devant nomme ou il y avoit plusieurs enfans des seigneurs de Napples et d'autres seigneurs circonvoysins que estoient venus en ladicte entree du Roy pour pour estre faicts chevaliers de sa main, il fut mene en la grande et maistresse eglise de Napples au maistre autel. Et sur l'autel de ladicte eglise estoit le chief de monsieur Sainct Cenny et son precieulx sang de miracle, qui avoit este autrefois monstre au Roy, comme cy devant a este declaire assez au long. Et en icelle eglise devant ledit autel le Roy fist le serment a cieulx de Napples, c'est assavoir de les gouverner et entretenir en les droicts. Et sur toutes choses ils luy prierent et requirent franchise et lib-erte ce qu'il leur octroys et donna, dont lesdicts seigneurs se contenterent a mer-veilles et firent de grans solenites tant pour sa venue que pour le bien qu'il le faisoit. En ladicte eglise fut assez bonne piece, car les seigneurs de l'eglise y es-toient aussi tous acoustres de leurs rich-es ornemens, lesquels semblablement firent leurs requestes et demandes au Roy touchant leurs cas particuliers. Ausquels ledit seigneur, comme debon-naire et humain, le fist et donna re-sponce tout en facon telle qu'ils se tin-drent pour contens. Puis tout ce faict et ordonne en la facon et maniere que dit est, et de la se partit et s'en alla le Roy, et alla souper et coucher a son logis.

N. XLVI.

(Vol. i. *p.* 242.;

Petri Criniti Opera, p. 541.

DE LAUDE FR. OOZAGAG.f. PRINCIPIS 1LLUSTKISSIMI MANTUANI, CUM AD

TAB RUM CONTRA GALLOS DIMICAVIT.

O QUIS beato carmine tam potens,
   Tantumque clara nobilis indole,
   Aut dote rara polleat ingeni,
   Ut hoc egregium decus Cantare Ital-
idum queat?
Qui nuper audax vindice dextera
   Horrenda victos repulit agmina
   Gallorum; et idem reddidit I talis
   Antiquum imperium, atque opes;
Salve ò presidium et salus.
Tu solus autor Barbaricam lucm
   Visendus acri ferreus agmine
   Represti: et inter mille cadentium
   Caedes horrificas virum, Virtutis
retines decus.
Tu praepotentis gloria Mantuae
   Tarrum cruentas casde potentior
   Ferrata saevae robora Galliae
   Perrumpens, simul impetu
   Obtruncans aciem hostium.
   Nod Non aliter atrox diruit in Gethas
,. No. XLVI.
   Gradivus olim; cum clypeo gravi,
   Oppressa Thracum fortia pectora,
   Contrivit miseris modis, Sese con-
stituens Deum.
Sic tu receptis arduus Italis,
   Vindex nefandi vincula servitt
   Injecta rumpis; nec pateris tuos,
   Fidentes male Barbaris, Servire im-
perio truci.
Hinc promerenti populifer Padus
   Illapsus undis suave virentibus,
   Gestit perennes reddere gratias;
   Et gramen tenerum ferens, Acclinat
capiti sacro.
Porgunt et Alpes Candida brachia,
   Possint ut alto vertice clarius,
   Summum tueri presidium Ausonum,
   Quo stat militiae gradus, Et firmum
columen suis.
Laetare tanto Mantua principe.
   Et die, quiescam sub clypeo Jovis,
   Donee Iicebit cernere sospitem,
   Qui signa et veteres opes
Devictae Italiae refert.
   N. XLVII.
(Vol. i. *p. 242J*
Carm. illust. Poet. Ital. tom. iii. *p.* 183.
LELII CAPILUPI. *In Effigiem Trancisct
Gonzaga Marchionk Mantuce IV.*
O Decus Italiae, quondam dum vita
manebat, . N. XLVII.
   Sceptra tenens, tardis ingens ubi flex-

ibus errat
   Mincius, et tenera praetexit arundine
ripas,
   Semper honore meo, semper cele-
brabere donis,
   Dum memor ipse mei, dum spiritus
hos regetartus!
   Salve vera Jovis proles, Tu maximus
ille es,
   Unus qui nobis, magno turbante tu-
multu,
   Ante annos animumque gerens, cu-
ramque virilem,
   M Ultro Ultro animos tollis dictis; et
pectore firms,
   Arduus arma tenens, fulgentes aere
catervas
More furens torrentis aquae, Gallumque
rebellem,
   Sternis humi, campique ingentes ossi-
bus albent.
Parthenope, meriti tanti non immemor
umquam,
   Dextera caussa tua est, solio consedit
avito.
Quid memorem spolia illa tuis penden-
tia tectis
Jam vulgata? quibus ccelo te laudibus
aequem,
Flos veterum virtusque virum? cui cura
nitentes
Pascere equos, merita e expectant qui
praemia palmae,
Europa, atque Asia, tantae est victoria
curae;
Tu decus omne tuis, tu servantissimus
aequi
Omnibus exhaustos jam casibus, omni-
um egenos
Urbe, domo, socias. Tua terris didita
fama;
Munera praeterea ex auro, solidoque
elephanta
Conjunxere tibi (cuncti se scire faten-
tur)
Regnatorem Asiae, genus insuperabile
bello,
Et penitus toto divisos orbe Britannos:
Salve sancte parens, Italum fortissime
ductor,
Felix prole virum, si quid mea carmina
possunt,
Semper honos, nomenque tuum,
laudesque manebunt.
   N XLVIII.

(Vol. i. *p. 268.) Burchard. Diar. from
Gordon's Life of Alex. VI. App.
De ccede Ducts Gandia.*
Feria quarta, octava Junii Rever. D.
Cardinalis Valentinus et Illustrissimus
Johannes N. XL VIII. Borgia de Arragonia Gandiae Dux, Princeps, S. R. E.
gentium Armorum videlicet Capitaneus
generalis, S. D. N. Papae Elii carissimi,
fecerunt ccenam D. Vanotiae, matri eorum, positae prope Ecclesiam Sancti
Petri ad Vincula, cum ipsa eorum matre
et aliis; ccena facta, nocte cursum
agente, et Reverendissimo Domino Cardinali Valentino reditum eorum ad
Palatium Apostolicum sollicitante, apud
Ducem tt Capitaneum fratrem suum
praedictum, ascenderunt equos sive mulas ambo ipsi cum paucis ex suis, quoniam paucissimos servitores secum
habebant; et simul ambo equitarunt
usque non longe a palatio R. D. Ascanii
Vice-Cancellarii quod olim S. D. N.
tunc Vice-cancellarius inhabitare consueverat et constfuxerat; ubi D. Dux asserens se priusquam ad Palatium rever-
eretur, alio solatii causa iturum, accepta
a pradicto Cardinali fratre venia retro-
cessirj remissis omnibus illis paucis
servitoribus quos secum habebat, rcten-
to solum Stafiero, et quodam qui *facie
vclata* ad ccenam ad eum venerat, et per
mensem vel circa prius singulis vel quasi diebus eum in
   I in Palatio Apostolico visitaverat, in
mula quam ipse Dux equitabat retro se
accepto, equitavit ad plateam Judaeorum, ubi praedictum Stafierum licenti-
avit et a se versus Palatium remisit, tantum cowmittens quod ad horam vigesimam tertiam in dicta platea expectaret»
infra quam si ad eum noo revcrteretur,
ad dictum palatium rediret; et his dictis
praefatus Dux cum velato in groppa
suae mulae considente a Stafiero recessit, ex quo equitavit nescio, ubi, inter-
fectus et necatus est, et in flumen prope'
eum locum juxta seu prope hospitale
Sancti Hieronymi Sclavorum nuncupa-
tum in via qua de ponte Sancti Angeli
recta via itur ad Ecclesiam *btutx* Mariae
de populo juxta fontem ex terra conduc-
tum situm, per quem fi. nous super car-
rucis seu carretis ad ipsum flumen projici consuevit, et projectus est. Stafierus

autem praedictus in plateam Judaeorum dimissus graviter vulneratus et usque ad mortem mutilatus est, et a quodam misericorditer exceptus et cura et impensa, qui sic perturbatus, nequicquam quid de Domini sui commissione et successu significavit. Mane autem facto Jovis quindecima, Junii, Duce praedicto ad Palatium Apostolicum non redeunte, servitores sui secreto conturbantur, et unus eorum Ducis praedicti et Cardinalis Valentini serotinum recessum et expectatum ejus reditum mane Pontifici iudicat.. Perturbatus exinde Pontifex et tamen ipsum Ducem alicubi cum puella intendere luxui sibi persuadens et ob eam causam e puellae domo exire illa die ipsi Duci non licere, sperabat eum in sero illius diei Jovis omnino rediturum, quo deficiente, Pontifex animo contristatus, ac totis visceribus commotus incepit omnibus conatibus causam inquirere apud quoscunque per plures ex suis ad hoc appellatos. Inter inquisitos quidam Georgius Sclavus, qui ligna habebat supra fontem prope designatum, in Tyberis littore ex nave exonerata, et ut illam custodiret, ne sibi in nocte a quoquam furarentur, in naviculam ibidem in Tyberi natantem se quieti dederat, interrogatus si quidquam vidisset in nocte Mercurii tunc proxime praeteriti in flumen projici, interrogantibus fertur tale responsum dedisse: Quod nocte illa ligna sua ipso custodiente et in dicta navicula quiescente, venerunt duo pedites per viculum sinistrum dicti hospitalis Sclavorum et Sancti Hieronymi contiguum circa horam quintam super viam publicam dicto flumini contiguam, et hinc inde, ne quisquam foreitan esset transiturus, diligenter perspexerunt; ac nemine viso, retrocesserunt per eumdem viculum: intermisso modico temporis intervallo duo alii eumdem viculum exiverunt et fecerunt idem quod primi fecerant, et nemine comperto, dato signo sociis, venit unus equestris in equo albo retro se habens cadaver hominis defuncti, cujus caput et brachia ab una et pedes ab alia parte dependebant, penes quod cadaver duo pedites primi praedicti ambulabant, hinc inde cadaver ipsum ne de equo caderet sustinentes; recesseruntque ac equitarunt supra

locum per quem flmus ad flumen projicitur superius specificatum, ac circa finem ejusdem loci constituerunt equum verterunt, ut caudam verteret flumini, et duo alii pedites praedicti cadaver observantes alter per manus et brachia, alter vero per pedes et crura cadaver ipsum ex equo detraxerunt et ad partem sustulerunt brachiis, et ad flumen ipsum cum omni vi et potentia projecerunt.

Interrogavit eos astans insidens equo, si dejecissent; illi autem responderunt, *Signor si;* respexit tunc insidens in equo in flumen, et mantellum introjecti vidit natantem supra flumen, et interrogavit pedites quid esset nigrum illud natans quod videtur; illi respondemantellum; ad quod alter lapides projecit ut mergeret in profundum, quo facto man

M 2 telle NT XI VIII te" merSo recesserunt omnes quinque, nam pedites alii duo qui secimdo stratellam praedictam exiverant prospicientes si quis pertransiret, se equiti pradicto et aliis duobus associaverunt, eosque comitati sunt, et per alium vicukun qui ad hospitale Sancu" Jacobi dat aditum, iter arripuerunt et ultra non comparuerunt. Interrogaverunt Pontificis servitores, cur ipse Georgius tantum crimen non revelasset gubernatori urbis, respondit se vidisse suis diebus centum varie occisos in flumen projici per locum praedictum et nunquaxn aliqua eorum ratio habita fuit, propterea de causa hujusmodi aestimationem aliquam non fecisse. His intellectis vocati sunt piscatores et nautae per urbem et eis ejus hominis piscatio commissa: convenerunt piscatores et nautae, ut intellexi, tres vel circa, qui omnes suis instrumentis per fluminis alveum projectis circa horam vesperarum reperierunt ducem cum omni adhuc habitu suo, videlicet calceis, caligis, diploide, vestello, mantello vestitutum, sub cingulo habens chirotecas suas cum Ducatis triginta, vulneratus novem vulneribus, quorum unum erat in collo per guttur, alia octo in capite, corpore, et cruribus: compertus Dux naviculae impositus est et ad castrum Sancti Angeli ductus in quo exutus, lotum est ejus cadaver et pannis militaribus indutum, *Socio meo Bernardino Gutter Clerico ceremoniarum* omnia ordinante. In sero il-

lius diei, circa horam vigesimam quartam, cadaver portatum est per familiares nobiles suos, si recte memini, ex dicto castro ad Ecclesiam beatae Maria de populo praecedentibus intorcitiis circiter centum et viginti, et omnibns praelatis palatii, cubiculariis et scutiferis Papae ipsum comitantibus cum magno fletu et ululatu sine ordine incedentibus, publice portabatur cadaver *in Cataletto* honorifice, et videbatur non mortuus sed dormiens. In Ecclesia praedicta factum est ei depositum, et in eo reconditum ubi manet usque ad hodiernum diem. Pontifex ut intellexit Ducem interfectum et in flumen, ut stercus projectum compertum esse; commota sibi fuerunt omnia viscera, et prae dolore et cordis amaritudine reclusit se in quadam camera, et flevit amarissime; Reverendisshnus Dominus Cardinalis Segobiensis cum certis aliis servitoribus Sanctitatis suae adierunt ostium camerae, et tot exortantibus et rogantibus supplicaverunt et persuaserunt Pontificem, ut tandem plures post horas aperto ostio eos intromitteret: non comedit nec bibit Pontifex ex sero die Mercurii quatuordecima, usque ad praedictum Sabbatum sequens, nec a mane Jovis usque ad diem sequentem ad punctum quidem horae quievit; persuasu tandem multiplici et continuo praefatoruiu victus postremo inccepit pro *posse* luctui finem imponere, majus damnum et periculum quod personae suae evenire exinde posset considerans.

No. XLIX.

(Vol. i. *p. 2990 Burchard. Diar. from Gordon's Life of Alex.* VI. *in App.*
Ingressus Borgice Romam.
FERIA quarta, vigesima sexta dicti mensis Februarii, intimatum est de mandato SanctisN XLIX. simi Domini nostri omnibus Cardinalibus, quod dicta die hora nona decima mitterent fa"milias suas extra portam beatae Mariae de populo obviam Duci Valentino venienti: et omnibus bus Oratoribus conservatoribus et officialibus urbis et Romans Curiae Abbreviatoribus, Scriptoribus, quod personaliter irent obviam eidem. Die Veneris proxime praeterita, vigesima prima hujus, Cardinalis Ursinus venit obviam Duci praedicto usque ad Civi-

tatem Castellanam, et die Sabbati vigesima secunda Cardinalis de Farnesio ivit obviam eidem usque ad eumdem locum, omnes urbis Ordines extra pontem Milvium, ad tria vel quatuor milliaria equitarunt usque ad prata, ibidem Ducem expectantes; pulsata hora nona decima Cardinalis Sanctae Praxedis recessit de palatio et equitavit ante Domum Cardinalis Ursini, qui ibidem in mula eum expectavit in via; equitarunt simul ad Ecclesiam beata e Mariae de Populo, ubi expectarunt Ducem, qui intravit portam inter vigesimam secundam et vigesimam tertiam horam, et receptus fuit ab omnibus familiis, oratoribus et officialibus Cardinales prasdicti intelligentes Ducem appropinquare portae, ascenderunt mulas, et expectaverunt eum ante portam in loco consueto, ubi detectis capitibus receperunt Ducem, detecto capite eis gratias agentem, qui equitavit medius inter dittos Cardinales usque ad palatium, via recta ad Ecclesiam Beatae Mariae in via lata, Minervam, domum de maximis, campum Florae, hide recta via ad palatium. Ego non potui ordinare familiares, quia errant pedites Ducis circiter mille, quini et quini incedentes suo ordine, *Suicenses et Gnascones* sub quinque vexillis armorum Ducis, qui non curarunt ordinem nostrum. Dux habuit circa se centum stafieros singuli singulos Roncones deferentes. Indutus erat veste velluti nigri usque ad genua collanam habens satis simplicem; habuit multos tibicines omnes cum armis suis et duos araldos suos et umun Regis Franciae, qui volebat omnino ire post servientes armorum; conquestus fuit Duci, qui mandavit ei quod iret ante eos, quod fecit male libenter. Post nos equitarunt Dux Bisiliariim a dextris, et Princeps Squillaci filius Papae a sinistris, quos secutus est Dux medius inter Cardinales pradictos: post eos Archiepiscopus Ragusinus a dextris, et Episcopus Sygoviensis *Orator Romanorum Regis* a sinistris. Archiepiscopus Cusentinus a dextris, Episcopus Trecorensis Orator *Regis Francia;* a sinistris, Episcopus Zamorensis a dextris, et Orator *Regis Hispaniee* a sinistris successive, et alii eodem ordine. Duo Oratores Regis *Navarroe* contendenmt cum Oratore Regis *Neapolitani* et *Anglice* qui se ill is animose opposuerunt; victi tamen illi duo Regis Navarrae cesserunt et recesserunt. Papa stetit supra lodiam in camera supra portam palatii et cum eo Cardinales Montis Regalis, Alexandrinus, Capuanus, Cesarinus, et Farnesius, postquam Dux venit ad cameram paramenti, Papa accessit ad cameram Papagalli, apportari fecit quinque cussinos de broccato auri, unum poni ad sedem eminentem in qua sedit, unum sub pedibus suis et tria alia in terram per Ordinem in transvcrsum ante scabellum pedum suorum; aperto ostio intraverunt omnes nobiles Ducis et post eos inter Cardinales Dux qui genuflexus ante Pontificem fecit brevem Orationem ad ipsum in vulgari *Hispanico,* agcns sibi gratiam quod sibi absenti dignatus est facere tantam gratiam ncscio quam, Papa respondit et in eodem vulgari, cum dux osculatus est pedes ambos Papae et manum dextram, receptus a Pontifice ad osculum oris et post ducem nobiles qui volebaot osculati sunt pedem. N-L.No LI. *(Vol.* i. p. 300J PerW *Criniti Opera, p.* 546.
De Ludovico Sfortia Principe Clarissimo Qui Proditus Est Per Helvetios.
OLIM vigebat Sfortiadum genus, N0, 1-
Et prapotenti milite nobilis

Princeps et astu, et consilio fuit: Qui nunc Helvetium dolis
Vinctus nefanda compede, proh pudor,
Nequicquam inertes advocat Insubres;
Ut impudenter perfidus Allobrox Stringendum dedit hostibus.
An haec sac ratae fcedera dexterae?
Quid jura belli sancta refringitis?
O non ferendum flagitium insolens; Quid culpam sceleri additis?
Non hoc decebat Martia pectora.
Sed tuta nusquam est heu miseris fides.
Fortuna, certis nescia viribus Tutari veterem gradum,
Cur tam procaci lubrica gaudio
Gestis potentum vota repellere,
Et celsa diro concutis impetu?
Ne virtus nimium sibi
Coufidat, aut jactet proprium bonum, Si quando summis pollet honoribus?
Tu nunc catenas, Sfortia, priucipum

Immortale decus, teris.
Circunligarunt undique barbara
Nodis revinctum vincla tenacibus,
Ne possit ullo tempore liberum
Monstrare Italiae caput.
(Vol. i. *p.* 300./ *Cartn. Ulttftr. Poet. Ital. tom.* i. *p.* 358..
Ludovici Areosti,
Ad Hercultm Strozzam.
Audivi, et timeo, ne veri nuncia fama
Sit, quae multorum pervolat ora frequens. Scin verum quaeso? scin tu Strozza? eja age fare, Major quam populi, Strozza, fides tua sit.
Ao noster fluvio misere? heu timeo omnia: at illa
Dii prohibete, et eant irrita verba mea.
Et redeat sociis hilari ore, suasque Marullus
Ante obitum ridens audiat inferias.
Fama, tamen vatem sinuoso vortice raptum
Dulciloquam fluvio flasse, refert, animam, Scin verum quaeso? scin tu Strozza? eja age fare
Major quam populi, Strozza, fides tua sit. Ut timeo! nam vana solet plerumque referre
Fama bonum, at nisi non vera referre malum. Quamque magis referat saevum, crudele, nefandum,
Proh superi, est illi tam mage habenda fides; Quod potuit gravius deferri'hoc tempore nobis,
Qui sum us in Phoebi, Pieridumque fide, Quam mors divini (si vera est fama) Marulli?
Juppiter, ut populi murmura vana fluant! Scin verum quaeso? scin tu Strozza? eja age fare,
Major quam populi, Strozza, fides tua sit. Nam foret haec gravior jactura mihique, tibique,
Et quemcumque sacrae Phocidos antra juvent, Quam vidisse mala tempestate (improba saecli Conditio) clades, et Latii iuteritum,
Nuper ab occiduis illatum gentibus, olkn
Pressa quibus nostro colla fuere jugo.
Quid nostra? an Gallo Regi? an servire Latino?
Si sit idem, hinc atque hinc, non leve servitium. Barbaricone esse est pejus sub nomine, quam sub

Moribus? at ducibus Dii date digna malis; Quorum quam imperium gliscente Tyrannide, tellus

Saturni Gallos pertulit ante truces,

Et sen-ate din doctumque, piumque Marullum;

Redditeque actutum sospitem eum sociis; Qui potent dulci eloquio, monitisque severis,

Quos musarum haustu plurimo ab amne tulit, Liberam, et immunem (vincto et si corpore) mentem

Reddere, et omne animo tollere servitium. Sit satis abreptum nuper flevisse parentem; Ah grave tot me uno tempore damna pati!

Tarchoniota aura aetheria vescatur, et inde

Cetera sint animo damna ferenda bono.

Scin verum quaeso? scin tu Strozza? eja age fare,

Major quam populi, Strozza, fides tua sit.

At juvat hoc potius sperare, quod opto, Marullum

Jam videor beta fronte videre meum.

An quid obest sperare homini dum grata sinit res?

Heu lacrimis semper sat mora longa datur.

CPSIA information can be obtained at www.ICGtesting.com
Printed in the USA
BVOW06s1423111113

336012BV00013B/615/P

9 781236 575289